The Legacy of Nazi Occupation

Patriotic Memory and National Recovery in Western Europe, 1945–1965

This latest volume in **Studies in the Social and Cultural History of Modern Warfare** examines how France, Belgium and the Netherlands emerged from the military collapse and humiliating Nazi occupation they suffered during the Second World War. Rather than traditional armed conflict, the human consequences of Nazi politics were resistance, genocide and labour migration to Germany. Pieter Lagrou offers a genuinely comparative approach to these issues, based on extensive archival research; he underlines the divergence between ambiguous experiences of occupation and the univocal post-war patriotic narratives which followed. His book reveals striking differences in political cultures as well as close convergence in the creation of a common Western European discourse, and uncovers disturbing aspects of the aftermath of the war, including post-war antisemitism and the marginalisation of resistance veterans. Brilliantly researched and fluently written, this book will be of central interest to all scholars and students of twentieth-century European history.

PIETER LAGROU is a researcher at the Institut d'Histoire du Temps Présent, Centre National de la Recherche Scientifique, Paris. He has published in several languages on the Second World War and comparative history.

Studies in the Social and Cultural History of Modern Warfare

General Editor
Jay Winter *Pembroke College, Cambridge*

Advisory Editors
Paul Kennedy *Yale University*
Antoine Prost *Université de Paris–Sorbonne*
Emmanuel Sivan *The Hebrew University of Jerusalem*

In recent years the field of modern history has been enriched by the exploration of two parallel histories. These are the social and cultural history of armed conflict, and the impact of military events on social and cultural history.

Studies in the Social and Cultural History of Modern Warfare presents the fruits of this growing area of research, reflecting both the colonisation of military history by cultural historians and the reciprocal interest of military historians in social and cultural history, to the benefit of both. The series offers the latest scholarship in European and non-European events from the 1850s to the present day.

For a list of titles in the series, please see end of book.

The Legacy of Nazi Occupation

Patriotic Memory and National Recovery in Western Europe, 1945–1965

Pieter Lagrou

CAMBRIDGE
UNIVERSITY PRESS

PUBLISHED BY THE PRESS SYNDICATE OF THE UNIVERSITY OF CAMBRIDGE
The Pitt Building, Trumpington Street, Cambridge, United Kingdom

CAMBRIDGE UNIVERSITY PRESS
The Edinburgh Building, Cambridge CB2 2RU, UK
http://www.cup.cam.ac.uk
40 West 20th Street, New York NY 10011–4211, USA   http://www.cup.org
10 Stamford Road, Oakleigh, Melbourne 3166, Australia

First published 2000

Typeset in 10/12pt Plantin   [CE]

A catalogue record for this book is available from the British Library

Library of Congress cataloguing in publication data

Lagrou, Pieter.
The legacy of Nazi occupation: patriotic memory and national recovery
in Western Europe, 1945–1965 / Pieter Lagrou.
    p.   cm. – (Studies in the social and cultural history of modern warfare)
Includes bibliographical references and index.
ISBN 0 521 65180 8 (hardback)
1. Reconstruction (1939–1951) – Europe.
2. Europe–History–1945-   3. Memory.
I. Title.   II. Series.
D809.E8L44 1999   940.55–dc21   99–24431   CIP

ISBN 0 521 65180 8 hardback

Transferred to digital printing 2003

Contents

Illustrations

Acknowledgements

The research for this book has been possible through the exceptional generosity of the Belgian state over six long years. I am indebted to the Nationaal Fonds voor Wetenschappelijk Onderzoek and the University of Leuven for their support in obtaining this funding. Research abroad was sponsored by the Belgian–American Educational Foundation, the European University Institute in Florence, the Vlaamse Leergangen Foundation and the Biermans–Lapôtre Foundation.

Monographs are monologues, but this book was born out of the continuing dialogue I have had with teachers and colleagues. I am indebted to Manu Gerard, Richard Griffiths, Gerhard Haupt, Louis Vos and Stuart Woolf at the European University Institute in Florence and the University of Leuven. My work has benefited from the critical response received during seminars and conferences or on partial publication of my results. I am particularly grateful for the stimulating exchanges in Halle–Wittenberg in October 1993; in Geneva in February 1992 and May 1993; and in Arezzo in June 1994. Jean-Michel Chaumont, Elaine Chalus, Harry Lubasz, Gie Van den Berghe and Chris Wickham have, at various stages, read and commented on my work on Nazi persecution; Bruno De Wever, Kris Hoflack and Luc Huyse have done the same on Belgian post-war politics.

The CEGES/SOMA in Brussels can rightly consider this book as partly a product of its activities. José Gotovitch and Rudi Van Doorslaer accompanied me on my first and later ventures in post-war history with enthusiasm, erudition and friendship. In Amsterdam, the RIOD has facilitated by all possible means the discovery of the history, the historiography and the archives of the Netherlands. I am indebted to Dick Van Galen Last and to Peter Romijn, who has been my mentor for the Dutch part of this project. During my research in Paris, the Institut d'Histoire du Temps Présent has been a stimulating host, thanks to its seminars and library collection. Henry Rousso has guided me in the formulation of my project. Robert Frank has kindly provided me with the necessary entries into libraries and archives. Serge Barcellini and

Christina Jacobs at the Ministère des Anciens Combattants et Victimes de Guerre have been enthusiastic supporters and goldmines of information.

My appreciation for Dutch archivists is expressed further in these pages, but I want to thank personally Mr Plantinga, Mrs Poldervaart, Jaap Van Doorn, E. Starmans and Fred Van den Kieboom. I also thank Chantal Bonazzi at the Archives Nationales in Paris and the personnel of the National Archives in Paris for their outstanding efficiency. The CNPPA in Brussels and the FNDIRP in Paris have given me unlimited and unconditional access to their archives. I hope my work does not disappoint their courageous openness. The secretaries of both organisations have helped me to find boxes shelved in basements or on top of overburdened bookshelves; they have kindly shared their limited office space and coffee over many weeks.

Comparative history is a continuous journey that was turned into an agreeable discovery thanks to the hospitality of the friends who hosted me. Ynse Alkema, Rolande Cousin, Gene Foley, Bernard Laffont, Sylvie Rab, Claude Scheldeman, Pascal Sebbag, Thomas Tavernier and Jean-Paul Zuniga have been irreplaceable guides and friends.

Jay Winter has been the motor behind the transformation of this research project into a book. Faced with a manuscript sent to him by an unknown, he invested it with enthusiasm, empathy, erudition and rigour. Both as an exceptional host in Cambridge and through an intense correspondence, he has challenged my approach and dramatically improved the presentation. Helen McPhail rewrote my broken English into true English. The readers of these pages will never know how grateful they should be for the elegance and intuition with which she accomplished this. Karen Anderson Howes at Cambridge University Press edited my text with astounding accuracy and deservedly forced me to check references, quotes, numbers and abbreviations.

Sophie, Jules and Elvira have been the heroes and victims of the writing of this book. Jules and Elvira have been too consistently cheerful to have any clue to its content, which has been invaluable. Sophie has heroically borne with deportation statistics, resistance medals and repatriation reports for many years. Whether they have been martyrs, suffering for a noble cause – that only the readers of these pages can decide.

Abbreviations

AAsN	Archives de l'Assemblée Nationale, Paris
ACPM	Archief van het kabinet van de Minister-President, Ministerie van Algemene Zaken (The Hague)
ADIR	Association Nationale des Anciennes Déportées et Internées de la Résistance
AN	Archives Nationales (Paris)
ANACR	Association Nationale des Anciens Combattants Résistants
ANCVR	Association Nationale des Combattants Volontaires de la Résistance
AO	Archief Oorlogsslachtoffers (Brussels)
ARA	Algemeen Rijksarchief (The Hague)
ARP	Anti-Revolutionaire Partij
CEGES/SOMA	Centre d'Etudes et de Documentation Guerre et Sociétés Contemporaines/Studie- en Documentatie-centrum Oorlog en Hedendaagse Maatschappij (Brussels)
CFLN	Comité Français de Libération Nationale
CNCVR	Confédération Nationale des Combattants Volontaires de la Résistance
CNPPA	Confédération Nationale des Prisonniers Politiques et Ayants-Droits
CNR	Conseil National de la Résistance
Commission Pensions	Commission des pensions civiles et militaires et des victimes de la guerre et de la répression of the Assemblée Nationale
COSOR	Comité des Oeuvres Sociales de la Résistance
CPN	Communist Party, Netherlands
CVP/PSC	Christelijke Volkspartij/Parti Social Chrétien
Documents AsN	*Documents Assemblée Nationale*
DP	displaced person
EEC	European Economic Community

ExPoGe	Nationale Vereniging der Ex-Politieke Gevangenen (also known as NVEPG)
FFC	Forces Françaises Combattantes
FFI	Forces Françaises de l'Intérieur
FFL	Forces Françaises Libres
FI	Front de l'Indépendance/Onafhankelijkheidsfront
FIAPP	Fédération Internationale des Anciens Prisonniers Politiques
FILDIR	Fédération Internationale Libre des Déportés et Internés de la Résistance
FIR	Fédération Internationale des Résistants
FNDIR	Fédération Nationale des Déportés et Internés de la Résistance
FNDIRP	Fédération Nationale des Déportés et Internés Résistants et Patriotes
FNDT	Fédération Nationale des Déportés du Travail (Paris)
FNTDR	Fédération Nationale des Travailleurs Déportés et Réfractaires/Nationaal Verbond van Weggevoerden en Werkweigeraars (Brussels)
FRG	Federal Republic of Germany
FTP	Franc-Tireurs et Partisans
GAC	Grote Adviescommissie der Illegaliteit
GDR	German Democratic Republic
GOIWN	Gemeenschap Oud-Illegale Werkers Nederland
JOC	Jeunesse Ouvrière Chrétienne
KZ	Konzentrationslager
Le DT	*Le Deporté du Travail*
LKP	Landelijke Knokploegen
LO	Landelijke Organisatie
MNB	Mouvement National Belge/Belgische Nationale Beweging
MRP	Mouvement Républicain Populaire
NATO	North Atlantic Treaty Organization
NCPGR	Nationale Confederatie van Politieke Gevangenen en hun Rechthebbenden
NSB	Nationaal Socialistische Beweging
OD	Ordedienst
PCF	Parti Communiste Français
PoW	prisoner of war
RIOD	Rijksinstituut voor Oorlogsdocumentatie, Amsterdam
Serdoc FNDIRP	archives, Fédération Nationale des Déportés et Internés Résistants et Patriotes

SFIO	Section Française de l'Internationale Ouvrière
SHAEF	Supreme Headquarters of the Allied Expeditionary Forces
SS	Schutzstaffeln
STO	Service du Travail Obligatoire
UDB	Union Démocratique Belge
UFAC	Union Française des Anciens Combattants
UIRD	Union Internationale de la Résistance et de la Déportation
UNADIF	Union Nationale des Associations des Déportés et Internés et Familles des Disparus
UNRRA	United Nations Relief and Rehabilitation Administration
URPE	Union de la Résistance pour une Europe Unie

Introduction

Did the Second World War fundamentally affect the history of Belgium, France and the Netherlands? Was it a turning point, an experience that created something substantially new? Seen from a continental perspective, this seems doubtful. The war did not redraft the frontiers of these countries. Most of their displaced populations returned to the places from which they came. There were casualties, but their numbers did not exceed 2 per cent of the population. Some groups were hit harder than others, particularly the Jewish community, but they did not constitute numerically large segments of pre-war society. Material damage was repaired quickly in Belgium, more slowly in France and slower still in the Netherlands, but these countries did not lie entirely in ruins. The power balance between political parties changed little, tilted perhaps slightly to the left, but no substantially new political forces emerged, and – apart from the fascists – no substantial old political forces disappeared. The constitution was unchanged in Belgium and the Netherlands. In France, at least in the eyes of many contemporaries, and certainly in the eyes of those who voted for its thorough reform in 1958, the Fourth Republic differed only slightly from its predecessor.

The same question applied to the countries of Eastern Europe elicits a different answer. Frontiers *were* redrafted. Death rates reached double figures, with peaks in Poland and the Soviet Union. Population displacement to different countries was permanent. The genocide of the Jews implied the destruction of a centuries-old culture of *Yiddishland*, representing entire social strata of urban culture, and locally affecting 40–60 per cent of the population. Jews continued to flee Eastern Europe after the war. So did eight million ethnic Germans and hundreds of thousands of political refugees, leaving the eastern part of Europe demographically transformed and in a state of complete social and political turmoil. Democracy and industrialisation had never really taken root, and modernisation of the eastern half of the continent was left to new communist regimes.

Observers who propose that the Second World War changed the

occupied societies of Western Europe have to cite specific subtler criteria such as modified labour relations or altered cultural patterns. Most significantly, historical research tackling the legacy of the Second World War during the last decade has framed its questioning in terms of the 'memory' of the event, or post-war society's representations of the Second World War, rather than war's general effects on post-war society.

This book regards this inversion of the questioning as a methodological necessity. Awareness of and explicit research into representations of a historical event immediately afterwards generally help the historian to avoid the bias implicit in many of his or her sources, and to avoid the pitfalls of partisan accounts or carefully constructed self-serving narratives that might otherwise impose themselves as ready-made interpretations. This methodological precaution is particularly indispensable when studying the consequences of the Second World War, because of the nature of the war experience and the overwhelming post-war requirement for retrospective glorification.

The first assumption of this research is located in the specificity of the war experience in Belgium, France and the Netherlands. The national collapse in 1940 was unambiguous, but more imagination was needed to turn the victory of 1945 into a national victory, and what lay between those dates had been deeply traumatic. Unprecedented military defeat, humiliating occupation and liberation by foreign armies – albeit friendly and Allied – had been a triple demonstration of national impotence. The nation-state, carefully constructed since the nineteenth century, was supposed to guarantee its civilians protection, the rule of law, national loyalty, international prestige. Defeat, collaboration, economic plunder, deportation of the work force and unprecedented persecution threw it into a deep crisis of confidence. Active resistance had been the radical choice of a determined and, in many cases, politically marginal minority. The dominating collective experience was not heroism: it was, rather, economic hardship, individual suffering, humiliation and arbitrary persecution. The liberated societies of Europe were traumatised, and their now fragile national consciousness was in urgent need of the kind of patriotic epic that only the resistance could deliver. In this context persecution as a more fundamental experience was unacceptable, something not to be spoken of. Mourning without triumphalism would undermine post-war national recovery. The threatening memory of, at best, impotence, humiliation and loss of meaning and, at worst, complicity could be dealt with only through the prism of resistance and patriotism. Any study of the consequences of the occupation must take into account the tremendous effort to reconstruct the nation's self-esteem. The social consequences of war and occupation cannot be deduced mechanically, since they are refracted and recast through this prism of ideological and political context. I will illustrate in detail how the post-war collective memories of resistance, forced labour migration and persecution were all shaped by the straitjacket of post-war patriotism. This systematic research into the commemorators' transformation of the commemorated inevitably leads us away from the history of the Second World War to the history of the post-war period. The interpretational framework elaborated after the events is indeed more revealing about the subjects than the objects of these memories. This book is therefore first and foremost about post-war history.

It is not my intention to make the history of collective memories the sole subject of this research, as if the events with which it is concerned never happened. History is not only about representations. This study is also an attempt to begin constructing a social history of the consequences of the Second World War.

As social history, it proceeds from a second assumption about the nature of the war experience in Belgium, France and the Netherlands. Despite commemorative efforts at a patriotic amalgamation of the two wars, the Second World War could not be assimilated into the first. For these three nations the military phase of the war was very limited: the armed confrontation during invasion and liberation lasted only a few weeks; and for Belgium, France and the Netherlands, the Second World War was essentially a passive experience of occupation. The classic distinction between soldiers and civilians lost its relevance. The occupation, through both the contingencies of total war and the ideological designs of the Nazi occupier, affected the population in discriminatory ways: deportation of the work force, political and racial persecution, repression of resistance – each targeted specific social groups. The social consequences of the Second World War were inevitably multiple: more diverse, more particular and more contradictory than those of previous wars. This multiform social experience of the war became the central challenge for commemorators, and the patriotic interpretation of the occupation had to come to terms with disruptive issues. There was no homogeneous and properly national *milieu de mémoire* such as the veterans of the First World War had created, as conscripts of a national army. The soldier-hero was replaced by much more controversial herotypes: terrorist guerrillas, often primarily engaged in an ideological battle. Many were foreigners, and even more numerous were the communists who fought for an ideal seen as anti-national by traditional patriots. Could they be national heroes? The problem of interpretation was greater still for the martyrs: no fallen soldiers, but tens of thousands of civilian victims of ideological persecution and genocide. Could they become national martyrs? And what was the legacy of the labour conscripts, taken to Germany against their will, but working for the Nazi war economy? Contrary to the homogenising effects of the First World War, the consequences of the Second World War need to be studied in specific groups, identified according to their specific war experience, and not according to pre-established categories of analysis.

Much of the literature on the subject labours to interpret the social consequences of war by applying categories of religion, social class, region or gender. First, many publications use religion as the ultimate category of distinction. Where Christianity is concerned, this conceptualisation is unconvincing. Much has been written about the resistance by and persecution of the churches in Belgium, France and the Netherlands. These issues are considered in this book, but nowhere does religious affiliation appear to be central to the experience of the individuals concerned. The only group that truly experienced an entirely different war was the Jews, but their religion did not matter to their persecutors, since they defined them in terms of race and not religion. Indeed, in many cases it was not even the way in which the persecuted identified themselves. I will deal with the debate on 'assimilationism', 'universalism' and Jewish distinctiveness in chapter 13.

Secondly, distinctions of class, region or sex do of course matter in time of war, as in any historical circumstance, and at times they may even be accentuated. Farmers and employers, rural populations and city dwellers experienced the war in different ways; yet when investigating the specific impact of war, more precise categories are also more rewarding. When dealing with forced economic migration, for example, working-class solidarity evaporated. The gender perspective is an indispensable tool, particularly where women's being female affected their fate, but it is unconvincing at least to argue that gender was the fundamental distinction in the trajectory of the social effects of the Second World War.

Taking three particular groups – resistance veterans, labour conscripts and victims of persecution – this study attempts to offer a reinterpretation of the consequences of war in terms of the concrete wartime experiences of distinct groups. The choice of these three groups, rather than any other particularly affected by war, serves to underscore the specificity of the Second World War. Most notably, this research into the social consequences of war does not involve soldiers, legitimately the traditional focus of the history of war. The marginality of the role of soldiers of the regular national army in their nation's destiny during the Second World War in the three countries studied here constitutes their most obvious characteristic. The soldiers who took part in the battles of

1944 and 1945 in traditional military formations were a tiny minority, many of whom had spent the war in exile. Their war experience is characterised by the fact that they did not live through the occupation, the focus of this study. The soldiers of the battles of 1940 – the armies of the defeat – were either liberated and, reintegrated into the occupied societies, disappeared as a distinct group, with some eventually reappearing as resistance fighters, victims of persecution or labour conscripts, or they were captured and held in captivity as prisoners of war (PoWs). The experience of the latter group cannot easily be integrated into this comparative project: first, because as a group they barely existed in the Netherlands, predominated in France, and in Belgium were divided between the Flemish part, whose captive soldiers were liberated during the summer of 1940 at the same time as their Dutch counterparts, and the Walloon part, most of whose soldiers shared five long years of captivity with their French counterparts. Secondly, theirs was a traditional military experience and distinct from the main object of this study of a war that first and foremost had repercussions for the civilian populations. Thirdly, a substantial proportion of PoWs were *de facto* employed as workers in Germany, and as such are part of this study.

Collaborators form a second group with a particular war experience that lies outside this study. They formed a large group, and were undoubtedly one of the distinctive features of the Second World War – one that has, moreover, received scholarly attention.[1] In tracing the legacy of the war in post-war society, collaborationists represent what one might term a dead-end street. Once the tide of war had turned, collaborationists as a group were irredeemably alienated from the rest of the population. Their national treason was condemned and their ideology seen as a venture that was now terminated, excluded from the national collective memories. Even when its legacy resurfaced once the first post-war ostracism faded, it did so only after a transformation, at least in appearance. It was not integrated into a post-war national epic, and it did not contribute to any post-war ideology or identity. On the contrary: this ideology and this identity were to a large extent constructed in opposition to their legacy, out of the experiences of resistance and persecution, which were described and partially internalised as formative experiences for a new post-war order – on the levels of nation, moral philosophy and internationalism.

---

[1] See Henry Rousso, *Le Syndrome de Vichy* (Paris, 1987 [new edn., 1990]). Focusing on the legal and political aspects of the purge are Peter Romijn's study for the Netherlands, *Snel, Streng en Rechtvaardig. Politiek beleid inzake de bestraffing en reclassering van 'foute' Nederlanders* (Amsterdam, 1989), and Luc Huyse and Steven Dhont, *Onverwerkt verleden. Collaboratie en repressie in België, 1942–1952* (Leuven, 1991).

It could be objected, finally, that by focusing on the particular this project loses sight of the general picture. Was the lasting social impact of the war not determined by the most numerous group, the amorphous mass, the grey zone (between the black past of the collaboration and the candidly white past of the resistance), which lay outside the extremes of heroism, martyrdom and victimisation? This 'silent majority' identified itself retrospectively with particular groups, turning them into *milieux de mémoire*, thereby denaturing what had been their true experience. It is in fact only in the Netherlands that collective victimisation has become an object of commemoration. How could this 'grey mass' be conceptualised for the purpose of historical research? To the extent that the absence of particular characteristics constitutes its only definition, it is the product of an abstract reasoning. 'The grey mass' does not exist other than as an exception to the rules that apply to specific groups. Interest in such a study-object as a facet of the history of everyday life – a nutritional history of the occupation, the impact of Allied bombing or a history of public opinion – is perfectly legitimate, but it then requires the student to distinguish between particular groups in order to define its object. Such research is not part of my concern with the long-term consequences of the occupation. These experiences, like those of soldiers and collaborationists, did not contribute to a distinct post-war ideology, nor were they crystallising points, catalysts, of the crisis of national identity.

In addition to this triple comparison between three groups with a distinct war experience, this study attempts a genuinely comparative international history, adding a second triple comparison between Belgium, France and the Netherlands. Thematically within this book, the international comparison is secondary to the comparison of the three different groups. I have opted to break down the international comparison to the lowest level possible: the three national case studies are unfolded and spread out over the different chapters, and even within each chapter are broken down into the smallest elements possible to allow for a comparison in concrete terms without the repetitions that a threefold national case-study structure would require.

This approach springs from a third fundamental assumption on the nature of the experience of the Second World War in the three countries: that resistance fighters, labour conscripts and victims of persecution are united less as citizens of different states and more by the shared experience of resistance, forced economic migration or Nazi persecution. The assumptions raised by this hypothesis – that the challenge of war was closely comparable for the population of these three countries and that, despite national particularities, so were its consequences – will be put to the test in each chapter.

Is the comparison amongst these three countries, rather than any other set of countries, *a priori* a valid undertaking? In the course of this book, Belgium, France and the Netherlands will often be referred to as 'Western Europe'. In a highly restrictive sense, this is a valid expression. Never in history, except during the Napoleonic wars, did Great Britain's insular position set it more apart from continental history. In Southern Europe, Spain and Portugal stood aside from the war, and Italy's war experience was sufficiently distinctive to keep it separate from any group of countries. Northern Europe, with Sweden remaining neutral and Finland occupied by the Soviet Union, offers perspectives for an interesting comparison with Denmark and Norway. In view of Denmark's privileged situation, a comparison with Norway in particular would certainly be rewarding. Such a comparison, even involving a geographically remote country with a tiny population in a huge and strategically peripheral territory, would probably bring out analogies with the Netherlands, which stands somewhat isolated in this threefold comparison for reasons of cultural and political tradition, in the company of two at least partly French-speaking and traditionally Catholic countries with a Latin political tradition. A comparison with Eastern Europe is beyond the scope of this study. South-eastern Europe was partly a theatre of civil wars (Greece and Yugoslavia), and partly a region of Axis satellite-regimes (Bulgaria, Hungary, Romania), which also lie outside the comparison. Switzerland lived in ambiguous neutrality. Finally, any overall comparison as to the consequences of war between who were (as it may not be superfluous to repeat), after all, the victims, even if sometimes complicit, and who were the perpetrators is, on a logical ground, excluded.

The exclusion of other candidates for comparison does not alone justify the validity of retaining this trio of countries for this analysis. First, there are external reasons that favour the comparison, namely the intentions of the German occupier. The conquered territories of the West were a great prize for the Nazi regime, for the wealth and industrial production capacity that Nazi planners wished to preserve, and also because of the explicit racist hierarchy of the Nazi ideology. Extending eastwards, the German *Lebensraum* had to be emptied of local elites to make room for colonisation by the *Herrenvolk*. Western Europe had to be vassalised, and was considered capable of some degree of Nazification. The occupier did not intend to destroy these countries, nor to decimate their populations. In the institutionalised power struggle that characterised the Nazi regime, this major orientation of the Western occupation policy was translated into different modalities dependent on country or region. Differences in occupation regime that might be crucially important when studying the mechanics of wartime decision-making in the occupied countries – such as the difference between countries subject to administration by the German army, the *Militärverwaltung*, and countries subject to administration by the Nazi Party, the *Zivilverwaltung*; the difference between Vichy France, occupied France and the 'forbidden zone'; or even the discrimination made by the occupier between the 'Germanic' Flemish part of Belgium and the 'Latin' Walloon part – lose much of their relevance when the war experience is approached from the perspective of post-war social consequences (with the exception of the regions annexed to the Reich itself, Alsace-Lorraine and Eupen-Malmédy).[2] The basic dynamics of resistance, economic mobilisation and persecution were not fundamentally affected by these exogenous differences. The chronology of the flow from these three countries to Germany and its Eastern conquests of, for example, Jews destined for mass murder, or workers displaced within the framework of the economy of total war, remained basically the same, independent of the local occupation regime and its technicalities. These differences should not, however, be neglected or glossed over. Dutch historiography in particular tends to attach great importance to the issue of its *Zivilverwaltung* as a justification for some sort of Dutch exceptionalism, yet in my opinion the belated liberation of the Netherlands is much more significant in explaining Dutch differences: that is, its protracted occupation in a context of generalised chaos and war of total attrition when the formal aspects of the occupation regime could make little difference.

Since the object of this research is not the nature of the occupation, but the experience of it by the occupied societies, the commensurability of internal factors characterising these societies is primordial. Jacques Semelin effectively demonstrated the importance of what he calls the 'social cohesion' of a society in explaining its reaction to the Nazi occupation.[3] Waclaw Dlugoborski, in a comparative essay of exemplary lucidity, distinguishes four determining internal factors that help explain the very different impact of German occupation across Europe: first, the stability of social structures before invasion and occupation; secondly, the 'endurance' of different types of society and their ability to preserve their distinct identities in the face of occupation and Nazification;

---

[2] See, for example, Yves Durand, *Le Nouvel Ordre Européen Nazi, 1938–1945* (Brussels, 1990); Gerhard Hirschfeld, *Fremdherrschaft und Kollaboration. Die Niederlande unter deutscher Besatzung, 1940–1945* (Stuttgart, 1984); and Albert De Jonghe, *Hitler en het politieke lot van België, 1940–1944* (Antwerp, 1982).

[3] Jacques Semelin, *Sans armes face à Hitler. La Résistance Civile en Europe, 1939–1943* (Paris, 1989), esp. pp. 93–127; see also Werner Rings, *Leben mit dem Feind. Anpassung und Widerstand in Hitlers Europa, 1939–1945* (Brissago, 1979).

thirdly, the social legitimacy of pre-war domestic institutions and of those imposed by the occupier; lastly, the relative importance of those social and ethnic groups dislocated or massacred by the occupier in the national pre-war society.[4]

In all four areas of typology, Belgium, France and the Netherlands rank in the same narrow band. They are all 'old' nation-states, older in any case than their aggressor and older than any of its other victims to the north, south or east in continental Europe. Ethnically, they were more homogeneous than any central European nation. They share a common Napoleonic past which contributed to their emergence as modern states. Belgium and the Netherlands share a common history before 1580 and between 1815 and 1830 and, for part of both the territory and the political history of Belgium, they share a common language, Dutch.[5] Belgium and France share the experience of the First World War, the formative experience of their twentieth-century history. They share a Catholic (and, in reaction, an anti-clerical) tradition and, despite the affirmation of the Dutch language in Flanders as a vehicle for politics and education since the late nineteenth century, a French-speaking political culture. To a lesser degree, the Dutch share in a minority tradition of Catholicism and, for the social elites and high culture on the eve of the Second World War, they, in common with most European nations, shared French culture to some extent. The fact that Dutch society did not undergo the experience of the Great War does set the Netherlands apart in this comparison. Throughout this book we will be confronted with the fundamental difference between France and Belgium on the one hand, countries with a cumulative experience of modern warfare, and the Netherlands on the other hand, where war was totally unprecedented.

The same is true for industrialisation and the political affirmation of the working class, where Belgium and France were forerunners on the world scene, followed with some delay by the Netherlands. As for the entrenchment of political institutions, Belgium and the Netherlands following their separation are examples of a very gradual evolution, on a European scale comparable only to the United Kingdom or Switzerland,

---

[4] Waclaw Dlugoborski, 'Einleitung. Faschismus, Besatzung und sozialer Wandel: Frages-tellung und Typologie', in Dlugoborski (ed.), *Zweiter Weltkrieg und sozialer Wandel. Achsenmächte und besetzte Länder* (Göttingen, 1981), pp. 25–32.

[5] The concept of 'the Low Countries' is the organising principle of Dutch-language historical journals, textbooks and conferences, the most prestigious of which are the *Algemene Geschiedenis der Nederlanden*, a multi-volume reference work and journal, and E. H. Kossman, *The Low Countries, 1780–1940* (Oxford, 1978). The concept is valid for obvious reasons for medieval and early modern history, but, as this book will illustrate, much less so for the post-Reformation and contemporary period.

and contrasting to some extent with the political instability that characterised France before the establishment of the Third Republic. On a European scale, however, France joins the narrow club of twentieth-century European nations with an old and relatively stable tradition of parliamentary democracy. As for the entrenchment of national identities, France and the Netherlands on the eve of the Second World War came as close to an unquestionable and rock-solid national definition as any European nation ever came. Belgian national identity was beginning to experience the first convulsions of cultural polarisation, but Belgian patriotism had reached its zenith in 1918, and the national attachment was greater than backward-looking contemporary projections would suggest.

A Latin political tradition and an advanced state of industrialisation account for an important degree of social and political polarisation in France and Belgium. During the 1930s in particular, left-wing parties of the working class, periodically tempted by the idea of a popular front, violently confronted recently established fascist movements, a situation which destabilised the political climate. This situation contrasts with the social cohesion of traditional Dutch politics dominated by conservative forces, i.e., neither fascist nor of a popular-front type. The interwar years show a remarkable political stability, with only three different prime ministers in charge over a period of twenty-one years. The Socialist Party entered a government coalition of national unity only after the outbreak of the Second World War. The traditionalism of Dutch politics is not unrelated to Dutch neutrality during the Great War. Dutch society did not undergo that war's radicalising and democratising effects to the same extent, and, in many regards, entered Eric Hobsbawm's 'short twentieth century' only in May 1940.

In terms of scale, Belgium and the Netherlands were very comparable in 1940, both in population and surface area, whilst France's population was almost seven times that of each of its northern neighbours and its surface area almost seventeen times as great. Since our comparison is of a qualitative and not a quantitative nature, this difference of scale is of only secondary importance. Social structures, national identities, the legitimacy of the national institutions and the demographic composition of the population had all become settled in the course of the nineteenth century, and had deepened and become firmly entrenched during the first four decades of the twentieth century through a systematic involvement of the masses in politics. Looked at from a continental perspective, on the eve of the German invasion, Belgian, French and Dutch societies resembled each other more closely than any one of them separately resembled any other European nation.

This convergence of destinies would be strengthened after 1945, when Western European countries set out to modernise their economies and stabilise their political systems in unprecedented and increasingly co-ordinated ways. As this book will argue, the remembrance of the war years was an effect rather than a cause of this convergence. In addition, despite closely identical war experiences, the memories they engendered were quite divergent.

Apart from theoretical preconditions, the validity and feasibility of the comparison depend first and foremost on the availability of comparable source material. Scarcity of sources has never been a problem in describing a period separated from the historian by barely thirty to fifty years. Many witnesses survive, and organisations and administrations created for the care of resistance veterans and war victims still function, the best guarantee for the preservation of their archives. Moreover, no other group in twentieth-century history has devoted more energy to the preservation of their legacy than resistance veterans and war victims; and, as one of the fortunate achievements of their activism, excellent national research and documentation centres have been created in all three of the countries studied here. Without the resources and expertise of the staff of the Centre d'Etudes et de Documentation Guerre et Sociétés Contemporaines/Studie- en Documentatiecentrum Oorlog en Hedendaagse Maatschappij in Brussels, the Institut d'Histoire du Temps Présent in Paris and the Rijksinstituut voor Oorlogsdocumentatie in Amsterdam, my research could never have covered the field it set out to investigate. This is not to say that it has been easy to establish three comparable sets of sources – cabinet archives, parliamentary sources, archives of organisations, associational press, police reports, eyewitness accounts, archives of administrations concerned with war victims, etc. To expect identical types of sources for each strand in such a comparison would be unrealistic.

This holds true initially because of the very different archival circumstances in the three countries and the very different degree to which public access to government archives has been realised. As a statement of optimism and confidence in the future of historical research, it could be said that this is a result of the pronounced backwardness of the Belgian situation and the relative backwardness of the French situation compared to the Dutch model; I hope that it is only a matter of time before the former catch up with the latter.

In the course of this research, access to Dutch public archives has routinely been obtained and indeed greatly facilitated by its archivists. The quality of accessible source materials was very high. This applies particularly to the most precious source of information for this study, the archives of the Dutch post-war prime ministerial cabinets. Unlike Belgium and France, where trucks removing loads of paper are a regular sight at every cabinet change, the open public files in the Netherlands did indeed appear to correspond to the entire cabinet archives, including much personal and confidential material. Censorship was never exercised at the source of this flood of information, and only rarely at its outlet, in restrictions over publishing certain documents emanating from members of the royal family.

In France, access to sources is surrounded by an aura of privilege and confidentiality. A researcher does not even get into the Bibliothèque Nationale without presenting due documents attesting to his or her credentials, and, even if the modernised Archives Nationales are a highly efficient institution and a most pleasant environment for research, access to sources is subject to personal scrutiny. In the course of this research, I did obtain access to fascinating source material dating from the first two years after the liberation, but not to any sources that even come close to those found through the free access obtained in the Netherlands, including sensitive and confidential source materials dating from the late 1960s.

The situation of public archives facing the historian of the post-war period in Belgium is unworthy of a modern industrialised nation. Cabinet archives are considered the private property of the politicians who produced them whilst in public office, and, even if private archive institutions such as the Katholiek Archief Documentatie Centrum or the Archief en Museum van de Socialistische Arbeidersbeweging go to some lengths to recover this archival material, unlimited access as stipulated under the laws regulating the availability of the government archives to the public does not apply to donations bequeathed to these institutions. The historian of the contemporary period faces long delays imposed by politicians' heirs, whose good (or other) graces may allow access only to some historian of their choice. This deplorable state of affairs is illustrated by the sad fate of the archives of, amongst others, Paul-Henri Spaak. The public ethic of the public nature of public archives still has a very long way to go. In the course of this research I did obtain access to the archives of the administration for war victims, de facto access that was only very recently formally regularised by the (recently created) Commission for Access to Public Documents.

Apart from this external insurmountable difficulty, the impossibility of a comparison based on three strictly comparable sets of sources is inherent in the comparison itself. The types of sources relate directly to the type of post-war commemorative policies developed by a specific society. Most prominently, the contrast between a governmental policy of remembrance, striving for a national consensus to the detriment of militant associations in the Netherlands, and the fragmented memories of associational activism in Belgium and France is also mirrored in the sources. The Dutch effort to de-politicise the collective memories of the war can be reconstructed on the basis of the rich governmental archives, but, as the effort was successful in marginalising the veterans' associations, their activity and consequently archival production were negligible and there was virtually no debate in the Dutch parliament. The highly politicised debate in France and Belgium left abundant traces in parliamentary sources, and the associational militancy engendered a rich press and very important archives of associations. In view of the prominent context of memorial and political rivalries between different organisations, an impartial and detached treatment would require multi-focused research based on the archives of all relevant organisations. The dozens of organisations involved, and the difficult and time-consuming effort required to retrace them and obtain unlimited access, make this impossible. Moreover, not all archives are equally well preserved, equally rich or equally systematic.

In the course of these pages the reader will observe my reliance on the excellent archives of two particular associations: the Fédération Nationale des Déportés et Internés Patriotes et Résistants (FNDIRP) in Paris and the Confédération Nationale des Prisonniers Politiques et leurs Ayants-Droit/Nationale Confederatie van Politieke Gevangenen en hun Rechthebbenden (CNPPA/NCPGR) in Brussels, which include descriptions of the internal affairs of other, often rival organisations. The value of these archives results from the organisational history of the two associations, as described in part IV: a large and loyal membership, remarkable organisational stability and rigorous methods of reporting and filing of documents. Nor is this state of affairs unrelated to the particular position of both organisations as inclusive anti-fascist front organisations (chapter 12) and, in the case of the former, a front organisation controlled to an important extent by the Communist Party during the Cold War years (chapter 14). From a purely archival point of view, the influence of the organisational tradition of systematic reporting that characterises communist militants – of regular self-examination and a thorough concern for documentation and analysis, including coverage of political adversaries – has been highly beneficial. The organisational instability of anti-communist associations – characterised by constant mergers, schisms, liquidations and new creations combined with a lack of concern for reporting, documentation and filing and, in general, a more individualistic approach to organisational matters and a lesser degree of a collective ethic – was, from the same technical perspective, highly detrimental for the historian. The same imbalance applies to both the political and the categorical origins of sources, namely organisations of victims of persecution, as opposed to the organisations of resistance veterans. I have tried to remedy this state of affairs by using the associational press of the latter organisations wherever possible, and assessing critically the rich funds of the two cited organisations, to avoid an imbalance that could arise from the origins of the source material.

One of the effects of the choice for a highly integrated comparison is the dispersion of the treatment of sources. Rather than dealing exhaustively with one corpus of sources in one section before moving on to the next source type, I will constantly intermingle Belgian, French and Dutch sources, and, as explained above, sources on a single topic more often than not have a different origin depending on the country. This may leave the reader with the impression of a rather arbitrary mix of sources. Is the national distinctiveness respected when sources and examples from three countries are used to describe phenomena that are common to all? Would it not be possible to cite an equal number of dissonant sources that do not fit into this transnational framework? The flexibility of the structure of this book should serve as an indication of the care with which this issue of national distinctiveness and international phenomena has been approached. Whenever deviant developments or dissonant sources were found on a particular topic in one of the three countries, they have received separate treatment.

The first part (chapters 1–3) deals with the legacy of the resistance, an issue that involves the particular national destiny of each of the three countries much more than a homogeneous social dynamic calling for a collective approach. The second part (chapters 4–6) describes population displacement to Germany and the subsequent repatriation, which seems to offer *par excellence* an identical challenge to each of the three societies. Yet the challenge to the Belgian and Dutch governments-in-exile was wholly different from that which faced De Gaulle and the internal opposition to Vichy, which turned the 'exile' of French prisoners of war into a cornerstone of its policy and ideology. This requires separate treatment.

Forced economic migration, the subject of the third part (chapters 7–10), lends itself to a highly integrated, cross-border analysis, since both its wartime implementation and its post-war legacy were the result of Nazi Germany's devolution of the social costs of total war indiscriminately on to the occupied countries of Western Europe. This part illustrates the unpredictability of comparative research. The first three chapters demonstrate the similarities of the experience of labour conscription and homecoming, whilst the last chapter, on the place of this experience in national collective memories, comes to the most divergent conclusions for each of the three countries. The fourth part (chapters 11–14), on the victims of Nazi persecution, is from the beginning forced to identify them in each of the three countries in post-war society, rather than taking the term at face value and comparing their reception. In the analysis of three different collective memories of national martyrdom, the Dutch case is very divergent from the Belgian and French cases, which show great similarity in the conflict between exclusive patriotic and inclusive anti-fascist memories. Chapter 14, lastly, is not even comparative in its approach, but simply international, since it deals with the commemoration of the war and the legitimisation of the international post-war order: namely, how the reference to resistance and persecution during the Second World War was a core element in the discourse of the Cold War and European integration, particularly in so far as both dealt with the German problem.

This book aims to describe the construction of patriotic memories in Western Europe during the period of national recovery after the Second World War. National recovery implied material reconstruction and economic growth, political restoration and national reconciliation, the reinvention of national identities and the creation of a new framework for European co-operation. As such, this is an open-ended period, with different chronologies for different areas of recovery and for different countries. As far as patriotic memories are concerned, one could advance 1965 as a symbolical end to the period of national recovery. Commemorations staged at the occasion of the twentieth anniversary of the end of the war offer a summary of many of the processes described in these pages, reducing the disturbing plurality of wartime experiences into a singular icon of national heroism and martyrdom. The year 1965 is of course only a rather arbitrary symbolic date in the middle of a decade of change, when patriotic memories reached their most formalised expression, whilst at the same time they started to lose their consensual appeal through the emergence of new memories, incompatible with national glorification. The new fragmentation that set in during the 1960s, the fading of the austere ethic of national recovery, the public criticism of national myths of heroism and particularly the emancipation of a commemoration of the genocide as a distinct tragedy, incompatible with patriotic remembrance, will be touched upon in the last chapters of this book. The analysis of the decay of patriotic memories starting in the 1960s – beginning in earnest only in the 1970s and to some extent continuing to this day – is not however the object of this book, primarily concerned as it is with their construction in the years of the war's immediate aftermath.

Both the approach and the sources of this study define a collective object. The universality of the fashionable terminology of 'national memory' might cause its users to forget the metaphorical and probably even inappropriate use of the word 'memory' in this context.[6] Few human characteristics are more inalienably individual than memory. This book does not seek to cover the proliferation of individual memories of resisters, labour conscripts and Nazi victims in Belgium, France and the Netherlands. It even deliberately disregards the most voluminous and readily available corpus of potential sources on the war experience of these groups, namely eyewitness accounts and autobiographies. The subjective individual character of these sources limits their utility for the study of society as a whole. This does not imply that the very numerous studies that are wholly or partially based on this corpus are not valid or relevant: they simply have another object of study. My object is the construction of collective 'memories', the constraints, additions, transformations or myths that constituted the *Vergangenheitsbewältigung* in these three countries of these three different experiences. That these collective constructions did intervene and mould individual memories to some extent will be shown in connection, for example, with the homecoming of labour conscripts or the powerful narrative of antifascism as a means of interpreting the individual sufferings of Nazi victims. Yet each individual memory remains, despite the obtrusiveness of collective representations, an individual's secret garden. I limit myself to describing the construction of these representations, and, when they are manifestly false, I say so. For example, when female workers from Western Europe in wartime Germany are collectively represented as prostitutes, we can contrast this with wartime statistics on occupational patterns; or, when all concentration camp inmates are represented as arrested resistance fighters, we can compare this to the historical diversity of the KZ population. The question of the adequacy of these collective representations to suit individual experiences will be addressed only in the conclusion of this book.

As such, whilst attempting a history of mentalities and representations, this study demonstrates a thorough methodological traditionalism in the choice and treatment of its sources. Instead of the oral tradition, the memorial production or the representation of the war in literature, cinema and the visual arts, my sources are government archives, the

---

[6] For adequate criticism of the terminological inadequacy of much of the writing on 'memory', see Emmanuel Sivan and Jay Winter's contributions to Winter and Sivan (eds.), *War and Remembrance in the Twentieth Century* (Cambridge, 1999). The author thanks Jay Winter for generously granting access to this manuscript before its publication.

records of parliamentary debates, newspapers and archives of social organisations. Instead of an interdisciplinary methodology borrowing from sociology or anthropology, its method is that of conventional institutional history, focusing on legal terms or the criteria for membership of associations. Wherever 'memory' is used in these pages, its meaning as a metaphor refers to conventional objects of history, such as the political instrumentalisation of the past or the symbolic differentiation of social groups, and not, as the reader must be aware, to any psychologising interpretations of post-war history.[7] In the integrated approach to the history of collective memories and social history, this study attempts a return to the established methods of the historian's craft.

The double comparative method of this study – three social groups in three countries – has evident advantages. An ambitious object of research stated in ambitious terms – conceptually, chronologically, geographically – implicitly raises expectations that the author believes that more is better. Of course, if the scope of a research project gains in width at the expense of its depth, a broadly defined object necessarily leads to superficial results.

I do not share this minimalist prejudice with which practitioners of micro-history condescendingly regard the generalist. First of all, from the perspective of the reader, 'more' does *a priori* indeed seem 'better': why read nine different books on resistance veterans, labour conscripts and victims of persecution, respectively, in Belgium, France and the Netherlands, if it is possible to deal with the subject in just one work? Yet the motive underlying the definition of my object of study is explicit comparison, not encyclopaedic coverage through the addition of case studies. Comparison, from the perspective of the historian, is a methodological tool, both heuristically and analytically. If indeed the shock of war and occupation was similar for these three countries, would a close examination of the ways in which each reacted not teach us more about the nature of the trauma and the characteristics of these societies?

If studied separately, each national narrative would be very different. Developments that on a national scale might have seemed unavoidable, or the only scenario imaginable, become puzzling when compared to the very different outcome of the same issue one or two frontiers away. By broadening the scope in this way, I hope to have achieved greater depth in this study. Each national case study has raised new questions, suggested new sources or even entire fields of research in the others, as a

---

[7] See also the explicit reservations expressed by Rousso, *Le Syndrome de Vichy*, p. 21.

permanent and systematic source of inspiration. Even if the bulk of the research has been realised in a chronological sequence, starting with Belgium, moving on to the Netherlands and finishing with France, each intensive period of research in one country has forced me to return to the two others, in a continuous to-and-fro between countries, sources and hypotheses. Comparative history is certainly not 'a new panacea', as Marc Bloch had already warned his readers in 1928 – merely 'a technical instrument, of common usage, easy to handle and susceptible of positive results'.[8] I hope that this book helps to illustrate its manifest virtues.

[8] Marc Bloch, 'Pour une histoire comparée des sociétés européennes', *Revue de Synthèse Historique* 46 (1928), p. 16.

Part I

Troublesome heroes: the post-war treatment
of resistance veterans

1   Appropriating victory and re-establishing the state

Were the political regimes that followed the downfall of fascism also the product of the struggle against fascism? For the countries that had been fascist it was the inescapable question. The East German regime promoted it insistently; few in West Germany even acknowledged it. Political figures like Willy Brandt – who, as an exile, could invoke with some validity the heritage of opposition to Nazism – were rare, and between the ostracised communists, the naive idealism of the isolated youngsters of the White Rose or the military aristocracy who waited until 20 July 1944 to move against Hitler, the choice of heroic ancestors was problematic. In contrast, the Italian post-war First Republic was very explicitly legitimated as the child of resistance and anti-fascism, and protagonists of the resistance played a prominent role in post-war politics. For both Germanies and for Italy, the post-war state was in any case a completely new start, unrelated to the sinister character of the regime that preceded it. The occupied countries of Western Europe had become part of the fascist order only through military occupation. Domestic fascists, even in France, would never have come to power without the victory of their foreign allies.

For Belgium and the Netherlands, the end of the war logically implied the re-establishment of the pre-war regime, free from the opprobrium of aggressive fascism. At most, the pre-war regime could be held responsible for its innate weakness and for the defeat. During the occupation, the constitutional state had been suspended and replaced by temporary arrangements. The two national administrations continued their activities in a political vacuum, receiving their orders from the occupier, whilst the legitimate government was in exile. Liberation implied the return of the legitimate government and the end of the temporary circumstances of the occupation. For France, the situation was fundamentally different. Pétain's investiture had been a constitutional transition, and the 'French State' he directed from the provincial town of Vichy the creation of a new French regime. Here it was the successor and opponent of the regime that functioned under the occupation that was 'Provisional', until the restoration of the Republican order: on 2 June 1944, four days before the landing in Normandy, De Gaulle's French Committee for National Liberation changed its name to the 'Provisional Government of the French Republic', a name that it would keep until the first post-war national elections in October 1945. The new regime that followed the end of the war was characterised by a sincere desire to re-establish the Republic: not the Third Republic that had preceded the war and was deemed responsible for the defeat, but a new Fourth Republic that drew part of its legitimacy from the Resistance against Vichy, *l'autorité de fait se disant gouvernement de l'Etat français*.[1] In the Fifth Republic that followed it in 1958, elected by plebiscite and tailored by General De Gaulle, the protagonist of the opposition to Vichy, this reference was strengthened even further.

In spite of this fundamental difference, in all three countries the occupation was only rarely presented as an intermezzo in the national political life, or, when it was, it was strongly polemical in flavour. After the ordeal of war, a mere restoration of the pre-war situation implied a slide back into the old weaknesses, that no lessons had been learned from this terrible experience. Except for Dutch Calvinist conservatives, the word 'restoration' was an implicit criticism of the post-war order. The word 'renewal' legitimised the post-war order: lessons had been learned, pre-war weaknesses overcome. The favourable or unfavourable outcome of the comparison between pre-war and post-war depended on the elimination of a set of negative variables – had the purge of fascists and collaborationists, of 'weak' administrators and traitors, been successful?, had the political divisions and instability of pre-war years been overcome?, had the national defence and security policies learned from the collapse of 1940?, had social injustices been reduced? – and on the integration of one positive variable: the Resistance.

The Resistance was the vigorous element of the Nation's moral health, it was the symbol of rebirth, of the fundamentally new. This role it occupied not only in the political discourse of the post-war years, but to an important degree also in historical and memorialist writing, whether framed in the moral wording of restoration or renewal or the more scholarly vocabulary of continuity and discontinuity. In political history the discussion on continuity or discontinuity has a similarly legitimising function, and in the comparison between pre-war and post-war the Resistance is the good, the patriotic, the unassailable feature. Attributing a significant influence to the Resistance legitimates the post-war order; minimising it criticises this order. Academic tradition has

---

[1] The standard formulation to indicate Vichy in post-war legal texts.

often attributed great significance to the Resistance in post-war politics, but not surprisingly another critical current proposes that the Resistance had no impact whatsoever on the course of post-war events.[2] 'The Resistance' was credited in Belgium with accomplishing the Social Pact, which fundamentally revised labour relations in what was quite appropriately considered one of the major innovations distinguishing the post-war period from the pre-war era.[3] In the Netherlands, *ontzuiling* (the reduction of religion as the organising principle in politics) was traced back to the transdenominational contacts in the clandestine movement, equally one of the most significant evolutions of Dutch post-war politics.[4] As mentioned above, in France the Fourth and Fifth Republics themselves were, to an important extent, identified as political legacies of the resistance; in the field of finance and economics the major nationalisations in the sectors of banking, insurance, electricity, coal mining and the Renault company were described as implementations of the programme of the Resistance, as was the creation of social security in the social field.[5]

What or who was this 'Resistance' which did all this? When studies of post-war history ascribe such a pervasive impact to the resistance, they rarely define who or what they mean by the term. For the actual war years, however, no subject has been as frequently studied and examined in such detail as the resistance. Several thousand historical studies on the resistance have been published for France alone. The prolific historiographical activity under the common denominator of resistance covers a wide diversity of subjects, movements and individuals. The largest number of publications concerns the 'technical' resistance: armed guerrilla groups, intelligence networks, escape lines for Allied pilots, sabotage teams. Other important forms of resistance covered are the clandestine press, political agitation against the occupier, underground trade union cells, strikes in protest against the occupation, and symbolic manifestations that defied the occupier, such as the commemoration of

---

[2] See, for example, Joost Van Lingen and Niek Slooff, *Van verzetsstrijder tot staatsgevaarlijk burger. Hoe progressieve illegale werkers na de oorlog de voet is dwarsgezet* (Baarn, 1987), and Grégoire Madjarian, *Conflits, pouvoirs et société à la Libération* (Paris, 1980).

[3] See Dirk Luyten and Guy Vantemsche (eds.), *Het Sociaal pact van 1944. Oorsprong, betekenis en gevolgen* (Brussels, 1995).

[4] For an effective criticism, see Coen Hilbrink, *De illegalen, Illegaliteit in Twente en het aangrenzende Salland, 1940–1945* (Oldenzaal, 1989).

[5] See Claire Andrieu, *Le Programme Commun de la Résistance. Des idées dans la guerre* (Paris, 1984); Charles-Louis Foulon, *Le Pouvoir en province à la libération. Les Commissaires de la République, 1943–1946*, Travaux et Recherches de Science Politique 32 (Paris, 1975); Hilary Foottit and John Simmonds, *France 1943–1945* (Leicester, 1988); and Andrew Shennan, *Rethinking France. Plans for Renewal 1940–1946* (Oxford, 1989).

11 November. Still another category deals with individual acts of resistance such as hiding Jews or refusal to work for German industry. A last group of studies defines resistance as an opinion – notably the whole literature on the resistance of the churches during the occupation.

According to the definition of resistance, each group of studies covers a very different historical reality and a distinct social body. Attempts to identify and quantify the resistance sociologically lead to the most divergent conclusions. Yet there is virtual consensus on one point: the numbers involved in the resistance were very small compared to the total population. This makes it all the more difficult to understand how a small group of people could have had such a formative influence on post-war history. The implicit and imprecise use of the term 'resistance' in many all-embracing theories about continuity and change in post-war societies is a side effect of the legitimising, even ideological, character of the discussion. If 'resistance' ends up meaning everything from a tightly organised sabotage team to the attitude of the Catholic church in the last years of the occupation, it is not used as a description of a concrete historical event or a clear-cut sociological body, but as a value judgement. Resistance then indicates a praiseworthy attitude, the opposite of collaboration or betrayal. Resistance as a key to the appreciation of the post-war evolution is not a workable terminology. How can one measure the impact of a category for which no one can agree on who is included and who is excluded? A historiographical tradition based on this vague and normative terminology is inert for factual criticism. An uncritical acceptance of whatever a certain tradition defines as 'resistance' becomes deeply equivocal when implicated in a comparison.[6]

Each author can, of course, establish his or her own definition, to clarify what he or she intends to study. Jean-Pierre Azéma and François Bédarida, for example, propose as a general definition 'the clandestine action, undertaken in the name of the freedom of the nation and the dignity of the human person, by volunteers organising the struggle against the domination (and most often the occupation) of their country by a Nazi, fascist, satellite or Allied regime'.[7] This definition imposes a permanent value judgement on the historian. Few collaborationists would have denied that they were struggling for the freedom of the nation and the dignity of the human person. The Second World War in

---

[6] See, for example, Bob De Graaff, 'Collaboratie en Verzet. Een vergelijkend perspectief', in *Vijftig jaar na de inval* (Amsterdam, 1985), pp. 95–108. De Graff distinguishes different definitions of resistance but makes a most uncritical use of statistics on resistance fighters: 400,000 for France, 70,000 in Belgium and 25,000 in the Netherlands.

[7] Azéma and Bédarida, 'L'Historisation de la Résistance', *Esprit* 198 (Jan. 1994), pp. 22–3.

general, and the German occupation of Western Europe in particular, indeed faced each individual with a moral conflict, and the choices made by individuals and groups were first and foremost concerned with values that a historian cannot ignore. But the attempts at a general and universally applicable definition of resistance as a tool for the social historian, a definition that would allow us to distinguish the group of resistance veterans as clearly as we can distinguish former labour conscripts or former victims of persecution, are doomed to failure. Moreover, no single definition would cover the present object of study: the legacy of the resistance, that is, the role in post-war society of whoever was considered or claimed to be considered as such.

For the purpose of this study, I will not initially establish our definition of resistance in order to measure subsequently its influence on post-war society, but limit myself to a description of the lively debate on this definition during the post-war years, and through this debate try to assess the role of resistance in post-war society. The most striking characteristic of the post-war vocabulary is precisely the qualification of the term 'resister' by the addition of 'real', 'authenticated', 'bona fide' or the equally frequent terminology of 'the resisters of September [1944]' or of May (1945), the 'false', the 'so-called' resisters. Could 'the resistance' in the weeks following the liberation easily be identified as the groups of armed citizens that suddenly surfaced from a secret existence? Almost immediately, discussion sprang up: whether all of them had really been resisters during the war and whether they were the only ones with the distinction of having resisted the occupier. The definition of what and who had been elements of the resistance, accommodation or collaboration became one of the most vehemently debated political issues of the post-war years until approximately the early 1950s, and continuing less intensively to the present day.

The polemics concerning the war record of political parties and the endless quarrels about decorations, titles and official histories are at first sight amongst the most easily outdated anecdotes of post-war history. Yet they reflect a profound conflict in post-war politics. The brutal suspension of normal political life during the occupation left the occupied populations disoriented, bereft of their habitual structures and references. The future had become uncertain, even the future of the nation as such. After the war came the settling of scores – between those who had betrayed the nation and those whose national loyalty and combativeness had never faltered at the extremes, and, less often mentioned though politically far more relevant, in the nuances of attitudes at the centre – *attentistes* and lukewarm resisters, compromised and not so compromised politicians and political families, converts of more and very recent date. In 1944, what was at stake in this settling of scores was not so much the past as the future. The attitude during the war had to provide legitimisation over who – amongst individuals, and social and political groups – was qualified to take the lead in the national reconstruction. The German withdrawal left a political vacuum, and for the immediate post-war years the crucial political issue was who would fill the gap, occupy the centre stage of the political scene. The immediate power aspirations of resistance movements were quickly settled. The success of resistance parties was very short-lived, and those resistance figures who rose to some political prominence did so only in so far as they rallied behind a traditional political party.

As a theme in the post-war political discourse, however, the notion of resistance was the point of reference, the norm against which to measure patriotic veracity and political merit. To a large extent, in post-war politics too, the notion of 'resistance' led a life independent and deliberately disconnected from its sociological body. The difference between the sociological reality of the resistance and its metaphorical political meaning lay in mythologising the national narrative of the traumatic experience of the Second World War. The urge for legitimisation amongst individuals and groups was mirrored at the national level by the urge for entire countries to identify with the resistance as a means of legitimising their role in post-war international politics. Resistance was crucial to the formation of a national epic. 'Being liberated' was too passive a mode to celebrate the recovery of national independence, and gratitude is a weak basis for national identity. For the three countries concerned, glorification of the contribution of the resistance movements was the only basis available for a true national myth.

France, the Netherlands and Belgium are indisputably the posers of 1940.[8] For France, triumphant in 1918, the unprecedented defeat demolished its status as Great Nation and Empire and plunged the country into a profound national crisis. It had taken the German invader six weeks and 100,000 casualties to impose the armistice on 22 June 1940. In the Netherlands, defeat was equally unprecedented. The country had not been occupied, or involved in any major war, since Napoleonic times. Yet military defeat, imposed by the German army in barely five days, was experienced rather as a moral outrage than as a national humiliation. In Belgium the invasion of 1940 was seen as a

---

[8] Useful entries into the vast fields of the historiography of the war years are, for France, Jean-Pierre Azéma, *De Munich à la Libération, 1938–1944* (Paris, 1979); for Belgium, Etienne Verhoeyen, *La Belgique Occupée. De l'an '40 à la libération* (Brussels, 1994); and, for the Netherlands, Louis De Jong, *Het Koninkrijk de Nederlanden in de Tweede Wereldoorlog* (The Hague, 1969–91), 14 vols.

repetition of the 1914 scenario, for better – belief in the possibility of national resistance and resurrection, even with most of the country occupied – and for worse – the civil population fled the country in massive numbers, fearing a repetition of the atrocities of 1914. Eighteen days after the attack of 10 May, King Leopold III, supreme commander of the armed forces, capitulated to spare his army further useless bloodshed.

Of course, in 1940 the military success of Nazi Germany was not perceived as the prelude to the final defeat which in 1945 it would prove to have been. This perspective required a visionary capacity, or, in contemporary terms, a cruel lack of realism. Accordingly, political evaluation of the events of 1940 recommended resignation first of all. In France the impact of the collapse of 1940 meant that no single pre-war political force – government, parliament, political parties – refused to accept the defeat. In co-operation with Nazi Germany, the Vichy regime continued to exert politically legitimate power. The defeat was evaluated – not only by the regime itself – as the inevitable consequence of national weakness and political chaos during the pre-war years, to be remedied only through acceptance of an unavoidable German domination and a profound reconstruction of the French Nation. In the Netherlands queen and government stayed in the war at the side of the British, more for reasons of timing and coincidence than out of conviction or confidence in the national future. When the queen and her cabinet fled to London to escape German bombing, the war on the western front was far from over. After a few months, the prime minister of the government-in-exile left London to return to the Netherlands and work towards a peace settlement with Germany. In the occupied country a new political movement animated by notorious pre-war politicians, the Dutch Union (Nederlandse Unie), gathered mass support behind a programme of loyal acceptance of the occupation. In Belgium King Leopold III decided to surrender and stay in the occupied country. He envisaged a political future not unlike Pétain's role in France under German acquiescence. His ambitions were never realised only because of a lack of approval by Hitler. The Belgian government had fled to France in the hope of continuing the war; after the French defeat, it fell into despair and tried to organise its return to the occupied country. Coincidence again, and the personal conviction of a single minister, led the government finally to London and the Allied camp. Popular support during these months was on the king's side and the government was largely repudiated.

The Allies supported the cause of the exiled representatives of the occupied countries of Europe neither for what they represented in terms of popular allegiance in their own countries, nor for the contribution to the war effort which these exiles could scarcely deliver, but for the legitimisation of a broad Allied front. This front consisted partly of governments with no pre-war past – first and foremost General De Gaulle and his Free French – and partly of governments with no post-war future, such as the Polish government-in-exile or the Yugoslav king and his government. The legitimacy of the Dutch representation was strong: the head of state and her executive were united in exile. The Belgian representation was constitutionally weaker: the executive broke away from the head of state. The legitimacy of De Gaulle was entirely problematic and indeed unacceptable to the United States until the very last phase of the liberation of France.

In the course of the war it was not only military fortunes that changed. The national destiny of the occupied countries was affected most deeply by the changing nature of the occupation itself. Economic pillage, forced labour and persecution withdrew legitimacy from political forces that collaborated with the Nazi regime and shifted popular allegiance. To military defeat was added the suspension of the rule of law, shortages of food, clothing and fuel, massive deportations and the assassination on an unprecedented scale of political opponents and Jews. The delegitimisation of the foreign occupier and his domestic accomplices did not reduce the national humiliation of military defeat – on the contrary, it intensified the national crisis. The integrity of the national territory, the rule of law and democracy proved defenceless in the face of foreign occupation and domestic treason. This disintegration crowned the process of decay observed by many during the 1930s.

The visionary capacity to believe, in 1940, in the possible defeat of Nazi Germany was not exclusive to the enlightened few or those thrown on the British shores by the hazards of history. In the occupied countries, despite the crushing supremacy of Nazi strength, individuals refused to accept defeat and organised forms of resistance. They often worked in complete isolation, and at first their means of action were limited and symbolic in nature. As the chances of war and the nature of the occupation changed, resistance increased. Opposition was organised along political lines, with a clandestine press as the main means of action, or took the form of economic obstruction with strikes and sabotage. Towards the end of the occupation, these widespread forms of resistance were in line with the opinions of the majority of the public, resentful of the occupation and of collaboration, and awaiting Allied liberation. In France, from the spring of 1943 onwards, the National Resistance Council (CNR, Conseil National de la Résistance) formulated a political alternative to the Vichy regime, based on a broad assemblage of political forces. The Dutch National Resistance Council (GAC, Grote Adviescommissie der Illegaliteit), starting its activities in the summer of 1944, prepared actively for political take-over after the belated liberation, involving all representative social and political organisations. Only Belgium had no such formal body; Belgian society was deeply divided, not least over the royal question. Further, the absence of a Vichy-style domestic political regime crystallising internal opposition prevented the replication of the French scenario. The *Blitzkrieg* liberation, leaving no time for extensive political negotiations, cut short the process of integration which developed in the Netherlands in the following months.

With the exception of isolated areas in France, armed insurrection was rare, and violent action took the form of precisely targeted guerrilla attacks on German or, more frequently, collaborationist personnel and infrastructure. The resistance activities most relevant from the military point of view, intelligence supplied to the Allied services, involved only small specialist cells. Large-scale military involvement of resisters from the 'internal front' was carefully prepared, but started only with the arrival of the Allied troops, when it performed a secondary and supportive role. Though often useful, the 'internal front' was not a decisive factor in the military outcome of the Second World War. Faced with relentless persecution and organised on a spontaneous basis outside the traditional social and political networks, armed resistance required exceptional courage and therefore attracted people with an unconventional profile, inclined to radical high-risk activity. This type of resistance was inevitably the work of a radicalised minority. The national political resistance bodies, involving conventional political forces and striving for representativeness, were first of all concerned with the future reconstruction of their national political life; the fight against the occupier took a much lower priority.

In 1940, the defeat was undeniably a national defeat: more imagination was required to turn the Allied victory of 1945 into a national victory. In 1944 and 1945, the exiled governments chosen as partners by the Allies shared with the resistance forces in the generous vision of a collective victory offered by the Anglo-Saxon liberators. The Dutch queen, whose return to the Netherlands with her government coincided with the German surrender, was the unquestioned champion of the struggle for national liberation. So too, as a *deus ex machina*, was General De Gaulle. France owed its status as an Allied power to his stubbornness and poker-player's bluffing ability. The heroic stature of the Belgian government-in-exile was more open to question. In any case, the nationalisation of the victory required more than the presence, in the Allied centres of decision-making, of the nation's representatives in exile; De Gaulle's *français libres* and their African exploits, the few hundred soldiers of Belgium's Brigade Piron in the British ranks or the Dutch Internal Armed Forces, constituted in the liberated south in September 1944, were all too peripheral to the decisive military events, and to the experience of the occupation in the country, to act as properly national heroes, even though the Allies granted them, as for example in Paris in August 1944, a disproportionately glorious part in the final act.

Resistance in all its forms was the only possibility for a nationalisation of victory and liberation. The identification of National and Resistance had a pressing urgency about it in the first months after the liberation. Governments had to affirm their legitimacy in the face of organised groups of armed citizens and re-establish public order and the constitutional state.

It was undoubtedly in France that this identification mattered most to the protagonists of the months following the liberation. De Gaulle had led a long struggle to impose his legitimacy throughout the empire and facing the Allies, and through his emissary Jean Moulin had established a connection between his *Résistance extérieure* and the *résistance intérieure* in the country. He achieved acceptance of his leadership in the CNR. Yet this formal acceptance was far from a warrant for an agreed and planned political take-over after the liberation.[9] As a true counterstate to Vichy, the CNR had developed a plan for national insurrection, with a parallel structure of departmental liberation committees assuming political responsibilities. Military events made this impossible, but the liberation committees claimed political representativeness until the first post-war elections, and the CNR rhetorically (but only rhetorically) claimed to incarnate the French Republic no less than the provisional government. The second part of the CNR's programme concerned its political platform for the post-war years, some sort of counter-*Révolution Nationale*. The programme pleaded for thorough social and economical changes, in particular the nationalisation of major sectors of economic life. As Claire Andrieu candidly describes, the programme had only limited circulation during the occupation and drew most attention and consensus in the first months of 1945, when the three major national parties – the PCF, the Socialist SFIO and the Christian Democrat MRP – proclaimed their public adherence. Through the major nationalisations of the autumn of 1945, De Gaulle's government, in which the three parties participated, could claim to have implemented the CNR's

---

[9] Philippe Buton, 'L'Etat restauré', in Jean-Pierre Azéma and François Bédarida (eds.), *La France des années noires* (Paris, 1993), vol. II, pp. 405–28; Philippe Buton and Jean-Marie Guillon (eds.), *Les Pouvoirs en France à la libération* (Paris, 1994).

programme at least partially. In post-war French politics, the Conseil National de la Résistance represented a historical reference, for the parties and for government. The unanimous front united against Vichy dissolved as soon as Vichy disappeared, and with the re-establishment of republican legitimacy the CNR had in fact realised its main objective.

De Gaulle's first political acts demonstrated precisely his central concern to re-establish the republican legitimacy, rather than a revolutionary seizure of power. The general declared that the republic had never ceased to exist and that he, as its incarnation, was the only legitimate head of government. As soon as Paris was liberated, De Gaulle publicly identified the whole Nation with the Resistance: Paris liberated itself, sustained by *la France toute entière*. In the first 'government of national unity' under his guidance, members of the Conseil National de la Résistance were incorporated in the enlarged consultative assembly as a sign of recognition. The seizure of power in the centre of the country did not bring immediate control over the periphery, however, where De Gaulle's regional commissioners faced the long and difficult task of establishing republican legitimacy in the face of firmly autonomous liberation committees stemming from the resistance, particularly in the south-west of the country. Even before the end of the war, at the end of April 1945, local elections re-established political representation at the municipal level, followed by national elections at the end of October. The formation of the new French army and its contribution to the final offensive created open opposition between the former leader of the external resistance and the internal resistance. The fighting formations of the FFI (Forces Françaises de l'Intérieur) were dissolved and more than 200,000 of its members enrolled in the army, under the command of regular officers.[10] The Milices Patriotiques, incorporating many last-minute volunteers and officially dissolved on 28 October 1944, would finally be disbanded only in January 1945 after the intervention of the communist leader Maurice Thorez on his return from Moscow. By the end of the European war, the French army consisted of 1,300,000 men, mostly regular draftees, containing resistance involvement in a new republican army and establishing the French contribution to the occupation of Germany.

Belgium presented a different picture. Most of the country was liberated in a matter of days and the government of national unity, formed three weeks later, included communist and resistance ministers in the government team newly returned from London. The symbiosis of traditional forces in Belgian politics, incarnated in the London

---

[10] For the modalities of this integration, see AN F60 374.

government, and the new radicalism of the resistance was short-lived.[11] Insurmountable mutual distrust, deep political divisions in Belgian society and a particular lack of political skill and national stature on both sides led to an open and occasionally even violent conflict over disarming the resistance and integrating it into the regular army. The resistance fighters were gathered in camps, fed and armed, but the government refused to use the resistance troops in the war. This, according to the government, would undermine the stability of the country in the long run, as the resistance movements would establish themselves as private militias. The transition from the clandestine struggle to a new national army was a complete failure. By the end of the Battle of the Bulge, Belgian troops numbered barely 11,000, and by the end of the European war no more than 53,000, only half of them with a resistance background, more particularly from the military nationalist formations. By November 1944, more than two months after the liberation, the government had decided that resistance fighters could enter the army only on an individual basis (as happened earlier in Italy) and, more significantly, that all their arms must be handed in within the next fourteen days, on sanction of arrest. The communist ministers resigned from government and on 25 November 1944 a protest demonstration by the resistance in the streets of Brussels degenerated into a shoot-out. When the crowd headed for the neutral zone round the parliament, the police opened fire on the demonstration and injured forty-five members of the resistance. Only the visible presence of British armoured vehicles in the adjacent streets prevented an escalation. The incidents surrounding the disarming of the resistance inspired a violent speech by Winston Churchill on the situation in Belgium, ostensibly revealing an attempted coup by communist resistance forces. The British historian Geoffrey Warner has since demonstrated that the so-called *coup d'état* was a fabrication, designed mainly as a defence against House of Commons criticism of the British government's support for conservative forces in Greece, Italy and Belgium, but Churchill's rhetorical violence had lasting significance in representations of the Belgian resistance, both abroad and in Belgian historiography.

If there was an erratic political consensus in Belgian politics in the months between the liberation and the end of the war, this was not based on a shared identification with the resistance, but rather on the

[11] See José Gotovitch, *Du Rouge au tricolore. Résistance et Parti Communiste* (Brussels, 1992), pp. 367–441; Pieter Lagrou, 'US Politics of Stabilization in Liberated Europe. The View from the American Embassy in Brussels, 1944–1946', *European History Quarterly* 25 (1995), pp. 209–46; and Geoffrey Warner, 'La Crise Politique Belge de novembre 1944. Un coup d'état manqué?', *Courrier Hebdomadaire de CRISP* 797 (1978), pp. 1–26.

shared absence of any reference to the central divisive element, King Leopold III. As soon as this tacit consensus was lifted by the liberation of the king in Austria, the national coalition fell apart. The Catholic royalists, who defended both the unconditional return of the king and the more compromising attitude of the war years, including leniency in the purge of collaborationists, were forced into opposition. The anti-royalist coalition of socialists, liberals and communists operated an alternative identification with the resistance, not with the aim of a national reconciliation, but in a dialectical logic of polarisation against king, compromise and Catholic opposition. King and resistance were central to the first post-war election in Belgium in February 1946: the latter gathered more support, albeit with only a narrow margin. The Belgian royal question would finally be resolved more than five years after the end of the war. Even though the Catholics formed a coalition government with the socialists in March 1947, after the departure of the Communist Party, the regency by the king's brother Charles was maintained until the summer of 1950. In March of that year, a new Catholic–Liberal coalition government held a referendum on the eventual return of the king in which an overall majority voted in favour of the king, but only a marked minority of French speakers. A homogeneously Catholic cabinet then accepted political responsibility for the king's return in July 1950, but after a week of violent confrontations and rampant civil war tensions, Leopold finally resigned in favour of his son Baudouin.

In the Netherlands, the post-war political situation was determined by its peculiar chronology.[12] Unlike France and especially Belgium, the Netherlands did not benefit from a lightning liberation. The failure of the assault on the Rhine in October 1944 cut the Dutch territory in two very unequal halves. The liberated south was administered by a Military Authority whilst the north, east and centre of the country continued to be occupied until the German surrender in May 1945. The south became a hotbed of political conflicts, with the London government opposing the queen, the Military Authority and the local resistance movements. The occupied part of the country was particularly cut off during the harsh winter of 1944–5. Famine and flooding, strikes and destruction of the infrastructure left it in chaos and destitution. Partly because of this state of disorganisation, the first national elections were not held until May 1946, one year after the German surrender and more than twenty months after the liberation of the south (the previous national elections dated from 1937, almost a decade earlier). Local elections followed another two months later. Yet despite the absence of

---

[12] De Jong, *Koninkrijk*, vol. Xa; F. Duynstee and J. Bosmans, *Het kabinet Schermerhorn-Drees, 1945–1946* (Assen and Amsterdam, 1977).

FEEST TE SINT-GILLIS

— Leopold komt terug : wij zijn gered !...

1 Celebration at St Gillis Prison. Collaborationists exclaim: 'Leopold is coming back we're saved!' From *Front*, 1 July 1945. Photo, Isabelle Sampieri, CEGES/ SOMA.

elections and the division of the national territory, the political legitimacy of the executive was questioned less in the Netherlands than in its southern neighbours. The conflicts that had opposed government, queen and local forces in the months leading up to May 1945 disappeared once the new cabinet was formed after the liberation of the entire territory. The queen was acclaimed and acted as the embodiment of national ardour, and the new government, incorporating political figures of the clandestine home front, achieved a remarkable entente with the urban resistance elites. The national council of the resistance movements was its chief ally in the normalisation of political life.[13] The end

[13] Pieter Lagrou, 'Patriotten en Regenten. Het parochiale patriottisme van de na-oorlogse Nederlandse illegaliteit, 1945–1980', in *Oorlogsdocumentatie '40–'45* 6 (Amsterdam, 1995), pp. 10–47; H. W. Sandberg, *Witboek over de geschiedenis van het georganiseerde verzet voor en na de bevrijding* (Amsterdam, 1950).

of hostilities in Europe had removed all justification for continuing resistance activism, and opposition from rank-and-file resisters to the re-establishment of local administration was quickly marginalised.

In continental Europe, France, Belgium and the Netherlands, together with Denmark and Norway, were successful examples of the re-establishment of democracy and political stability, France with a new constitution, Belgium with a new head of state after six years of 'the royal question'. The occupation had not disturbed the foundations of the occupied societies, nor removed all legitimacy from their institutions. Resistance had proved the endurance and the popularity of these foundations, rather than fostering an alternative political order ready to take over as soon as the enemy had left. Of course, the rapid normalisation of political life in the months following the liberation required the resistance to rein in some of their ambitions. Democracy being a matter of the majority, how could a tiny minority returning from exile, or the more substantial minority involved in the radical choice of resistance, establish legitimacy and allegiance without dramatically broadening its basis? The failure of new resistance parties in all three countries in the course of the first post-war year illustrates this eloquently.[14] After the initial, and often in different degrees discordant, confrontation between the heroic legitimacy of the resistance and the political legitimacy of a majority, a policy of memory gradually reshaped historical interpretation of the occupation and integrated resistance and the nation. The overwhelming majority of the population underwent the occupation and, at many levels, were forced to make concessions and compromises. This was particularly true for the state apparatus working under German supervision in Belgium, and the Netherlands, and in France under French collaborationist supervision in the southern part of the country prior to November 1942 even in the absence of German troops. Furthermore, an important minority had been 'displaced' to Germany, as prisoners of war, deported workers, concentration camp inmates or racial minorities destined for annihilation: they too had to be reintegrated into the national community by way of the national epic. This national epic, the reconstruction of a national identity, was necessarily concomitant with the process of material reconstruction and political reaffirmation.

How did the assimilation of resistance and nation function and, first

[14] For France, see Jean-Marie Guillon, 'Parti du mouvement et Parti de l'ordre (automne 1944–automne 1945)', in Buton and Guillon, *Les Pouvoirs en France à la libération*, pp. 38–59; for Belgium, see Wilfried Beerten, *Le Rêve Travailliste en Belgique. Histoire de l'Union Démocratique Belge, 1944–1947* (Brussels, 1990); for the Netherlands, see Jan Bank, *Opkomst en ondergang van de Nederlandse Volksbeweging* (Deventer, 1978).

of all, did it function? After all, not every citizen, not every political family had the same war record, and those who could claim greater merit were unlikely to allow any expropriation of the resistance merit to the benefit of the nation collectively. The national epic could be a factor of unity only to the extent that such people failed to assert their claims. In this narration, the country had experienced an external aggression, it had suffered collectively and it had resisted, everyone according to his or her own means, collectively. The internal gradations in patriotism – who had resisted more or earlier, who had suffered more – were then secondary. A truly national epic required some form of expropriation of the resistance merits of those groups or individuals that had been more inclined to perilous actions, had taken greater risks, paid a heavier price. The success of a political consensus on the occupation period depended to a large extent on the weakness of the *milieux de mémoire*, those groups that had been more involved in the major events of the national epic, which were capable of incarnating the collective memory of the war. If they were allowed, encouraged or used to display their claims, the effect would disturb the consensus. Instead of some collectively worshipped consensual image of the past, there would be commemorative rivalry and a perpetual settling of historical scores.

The Netherlands provide an example of consensual commemoration, thanks to a consistent policy of the post-war political coalition to limit all kinds of commemorative activism, with only marginal opposition. Government and affiliated elites were the main agents of memory. Belgium and France, on the other hand, are examples of disruptive memories, where contests over wartime merit became a favourite weapon in post-war political confrontations. In Belgium, the polemic over the legacy of the resistance was the reverse side of the polemic over the 'royal question': the war record of individuals, institutions and political parties became one of the major battlefields of post-war history. In France, reference to the war years provided a crucial legitimisation for General De Gaulle, the French Communist Party and the governments that tried to steer the country between these two forces. In both countries there was a tradition of veterans' patriotism. In the interwar years, veterans' leagues had been important political actors, second only to the trade unions and the political parties themselves in membership figures and militancy. In France, veterans' leagues fuelled both fascist militias like La Rocque's Croix de Feu and fervently republican and pacifist movements.[15] In Belgium, veterans of the First World War also

---

[15] See Robert Soucy, *French Fascism. The Second Wave, 1933–1939* (New Haven, 1996); Antoine Prost, *Les Anciens Combattants* (Paris, 1977); and Prost, 'The Impact of War on French and German Political Cultures', *Historical Journal* 37 (1994), pp. 209–17.

animated not only the fascist wing of the Flemish movement and its democratic and pacifist wing but also the hard core of Belgian patriotism.[16] *Milieux de mémoire* had a natural authority in politics and, from the First World War, had inherited organisations, rituals, a discourse and a whole set of legal dispositions – from medals to priority employment – to emulate.

[16] See, for example, G. Provoost, *De Vossen, 60 jaar Verbond van Vlaamse Oud-Strijders (1917–1979)* (Brussels, 1979).

2   Heroes of a nation: Belgium and France

Nowhere was patriotic legitimacy more crucial to post-war politics than in France: it was General Charles De Gaulle's only legitimacy when he returned from exile and declared the constitutionally legitimate heir of the Third Republic, the Vichy regime, null and void.[1] The amalgamation of colonists and exiles that had made up his Free French Forces was not a firm basis on which to build a new regime. De Gaulle was thus forced to promote a generous and collective vision of the French struggle for liberation, to pass over in silence the role of Vichy and of the Allies, and to nationalise the contribution of the resistance movements on the French territory. As provisional head of state between the liberation and January 1946, from the (extra-parliamentary) opposition until 1958 and as president of his self-styled Fifth Republic until 1969, De Gaulle applied a commemorative policy which assimilated the Nation and the Resistance in a symbolism that was simultaneously heroic, emblematic, abstract and elitist. The national honour had been safeguarded throughout the ordeal of the war by the heroes who presided over its destiny, in exile or on French soil, as combatants or as martyrs. Gaullist speeches and rituals staged tributes to the army and the nation through exemplary figures of patriotism and amalgamated the ambiguous victory of the Second World War with the patriotic triumph of the first. Abstract commemoration and its consensual appeal suited the general better than the cult of veteranism as a social movement. De Gaulle opposed the re-establishment of a Ministry for Veterans after the liberation, since he identified it with the political abuse by the Vichy regime (see chapter 10). He resented the organisations of PoWs and labour conscripts, both of which brought together hundreds of thousands of dubious heroes, and he certainly did not

---

[1] See Rousso, *Le Syndrome de Vichy*; Gérard Namer, *La Commémoration en France de 1945 à nos jours* (Paris, 1987); Pierre Nora, 'Gaullistes et communistes', in *Les Lieux de mémoire*, t. III, *Les Frances*, vol. I, *Conflits et partages* (Paris, 1992), pp. 360–71; and Paul Thibaud, 'La République et ses héros. Le Gaullisme pendant et après la guerre', Esprit 198 (1994), pp. 79–80.

favour the attribution of heroic status across the many groups of resistance veterans and victims of persecution.

De Gaulle's theatrical and patriotic leanings were combined in his talent for staging commemorations. On 16 November 1940, with characteristic bravura, he had created his Ordre des Compagnons de la Libération, to be bestowed by him personally on the exemplary heroes who would distinguish themselves in the – at that time still very remote and even unlikely – liberation of France.[2] The medal carried the symbol of the Free French, a sword with the Cross of Lorraine. The chivalric element of an 'Order' indicated that De Gaulle's inspiration lay closer to the Knights Templar than to more contemporary examples of veterans' mass movements. On his own initiative De Gaulle himself elected 1,036 symbolic heroes, a list he closed by a decree that appeared three days after he had resigned from government, on 23 January 1946. The list mirrored De Gaulle's vision of the respective contributions to the liberation of France: 783 combatants of the Free French Forces, 107 intelligence agents assuring the connections between the occupied country and the general's services, and only 157 heroes of the internal resistance on French soil (some nominees fell into more than one category). Of these, 238 had been decorated posthumously. Six of the 1,036 were women. The communist resistance, and left-wing forces in general, were barely represented. Raymond Aubrac, Pierre Villon, Charles Tillon, Pierre Hervé and Maurice Kriegel, amongst the most prominent heroes of the internal resistance, did not figure on the list. At some point in post-war history and particularly during De Gaulle's presidency under the Fifth Republic, thirty-eight *compagnons* would become cabinet ministers, amongst them George Bidault, Jacques Chaban-Delmas, Henri Frénay, André Malraux, Pierre Mesmer, Alexandre Parodi, Christian Pineau, René Pleven, Maurice Schuman and Pierre-Henri Teitgen.

The *compagnons* were the protagonists of the commemorations staged by General De Gaulle, particularly at Mont Valérien, the monument of his own creation inaugurated on 11 November 1945.[3] Not only did the date of the inauguration bear witness to De Gaulle's effort to assimilate the collective memory of World War II into that of a classic military conflict, the First World War, the whole ceremony emphasised it. Mont Valérien had been the site chosen by the Germans for the execution of

---

[2] See Roger Faligot and Rémi Kauffer, *Les Résistants. De la guerre de l'ombre aux allées du pouvoir, 1944–1989* (Paris, 1989), pp. 551–6.

[3] See Namer, *La Commémoration*, pp. 127–41, and Serge Barcellini and Annette Wieviorka, *Passant, souviens-toi! Les Lieux du souvenir de la Seconde Guerre Mondiale en France* (Paris, 1995), pp. 166–75.

probably more than 1,000 French prisoners (resisters and hostages) over the period of the occupation, but the monument, as conceived by De Gaulle, was primarily a memorial to the fallen soldiers of the French army. Fifteen corpses were selected for symbolic burial on Mont Valérien, eleven of them the bodies of men killed in battle. Three fell in the battle of 1940, five in the battle for liberation. Ten had been regular soldiers, chosen from the different military forces – infantry, navy, air force; colonial forces were well represented, with four soldiers of African descent. Only one was a resister killed in action. Four graves contained the bodies of heroes who had not fallen in battle but were resisters executed by the enemy after their arrest. One was a resister-PoW. As with the list of *compagnons*, De Gaulle preserved Mont Valérien for his own commemorative purposes by publishing a decree which kept the direction of the monument in safe hands when he withdrew from power in January 1946, even though the Communist Party or the government itself could not be prevented from visiting the site as part of their own commemorations. At the height of the French colonial war in Indochina, the government of the Fourth Republic added one grave of a French soldier killed in the war against Japan, for rather obvious propaganda reasons. A seventeenth grave awaits the burial of the last surviving *compagnon*. As soon as he returned to power in 1958, De Gaulle undertook the construction of a majestic monument on the same site, which was inaugurated on 18 June 1960.

The Ordre and Mont Valérien illustrate De Gaulle's emblematic and elitist concept of commemoration of the Second World War. The general never favoured the transformation of his former Free French Forces into a powerful veterans' league supporting his political ambitions. The *Bulletin de l'Association des Français Libres* is a repetition of desperate appeals designed to stir even a modicum of associational and commemorative activism amongst the veterans of the Free French. The association claimed 24,000 potential members, but succeeded in selling only 3,200 copies of its journal. In February 1948 it published a list of regional clubs, totalling over 20,000 'members', but only two months earlier it had admitted that no more than 6,000 of them paid membership fees. Most characteristic of the list was the geographical dispersion of the Free French, mostly recruited amongst French citizens who were not living on the continent at the time of the German occupation and who had, to a great degree, remained outside it after the war. In 1948 more former Free French were living in the French territories of Brazzaville or Tahiti, or even in Brazil, than in Lyons.[4] Sixty-eight

---

[4] The *Bulletin de l'Association des Français Libres* (Dec. 1947 and Jan. 1948) listed 14,353 'members' in France itself, 5,399 in the Union Française and 2,247 abroad.

French departments had fewer than one hundred former Free French in their territory, thirty-three fewer than thirty, and about a dozen not even a single potential member. Only the metropolitan area of Paris and the Breton department of Finistère, home of some of the most important French naval bases, exceeded 1,000 members. The Free French felt crushed and marginalised in a social landscape dominated by powerful associations of veterans and war victims. They bitterly complained that they were neglected by the government, comparing their treatment with that of the prisoners and deportees, for whom a special ministry had been created, endowed with huge financial resources and personnel.

The journal complained about local sections 'asleep in a terrible lethargy' or 'an indifference regarding our duties towards the community of Free French which reveals a most dangerous state of mind'. Faced with a crushing deficit, the association announced that it needed to triple its membership figures, phlegmatically adding:

> It is the type of speculation on which the Free French have lived since 1940. Of course, if our efforts in this direction fail, we will be forced to conclude that the Free French are no longer interested in themselves or in what they have been, and, in this case, we won't be able to bring a dead body back to life. Then we will shut down the house in its present form, transform it into a club of older gentlemen engaged in charitable works, and continue to provide a modest and shaky presence at official ceremonies.[5]

This soon turned out to be a fairly accurate prediction of the association's development.

The communist remembrance has often been presented as the mirror image of the Gaullist resistance myth.[6] The national insurrection and partisan war of the internal Resistance took the place of the external Resistance and its classic military feats – the *maquis* instead of Bir Hakeim. The war in the colonies and at the side of the western Allies was replaced by the glorious victory of the Red Army. Instead of De Gaulle's abstract and all-embracing references to the Nation, the French Communist Party (PCF) identified strongly with specific heroes and martyrs. It cultivated its martyrs – 'the party of the 75,000 executed militants' – and successfully organised a whole constellation of veterans' associations for partisans, deported workers and victims of Nazi persecution. The immediate post-war period corresponds with the party's most expansive time. Communist ranks had been decimated by persecution and the party was actively canvassing for new members and voters; the success of this operation was partly due to the appeal of the

---

[5] *Bulletin de l'Association des Français Libres* (Apr. 1948).
[6] See, in addition to the above, Marie-Claire Lavabre, *Le Fil Rouge. Sociologie de la mémoire communiste* (Paris, 1994), pp. 190–219.

resistance aura. Instead of an exclusive narrative, appropriating patriotic merit and stressing the distinction between the historically certified resisters and those who joined the myth *post facto*, the collective memory propagated by the PCF was as open and inclusive as possible. Reference to the Nation, central to the Gaullist discourse, was replaced by reference to the working class, the embodiment of resistance against a collaborating bourgeoisie and its reactionary ideology, and to anti-fascism. The paradigm of anti-fascism was the most inclusive: all political opponents of fascism, and even more all victims of fascism, could subscribe to it and become part of an anti-fascist family in which the party played a central role, contemporaneously and historically, and where martyrdom and heroism, victims and veterans mingled together, fraternally sharing the heritage of victory. I will deal with the issue of anti-fascism as a factor which revised and reconfigured traditional notions of French patriotism in chapter 12. The political debate on the treatment of the resistance was not characterised by innovation – on the contrary, it expressed the integration of the collective memory of the resistance into older patriotic memories.

De Gaulle's resistance to the reinstatement of a Ministry for Veterans created much criticism and resentment in veterans' circles, and particularly in the official representative structure of all First World War veterans, the Union Française des Anciens Combattants (UFAC). The UFAC faced a disruptive challenge after 1945.[7] If it was to rehabilitate the image of the veterans of 1914–18 and continue as a truly representative organisation, it needed to bring in the veterans of 1940–5 as well. The ranks of the UFAC needed a purge, and they needed the new blood of the new *génération du feu*. Almost immediately, the post-war UFAC offered five seats to representatives of the CNR, and it was generally accepted that the place of the resistance veterans was in the UFAC. At the same time, the *poilus* of the Great War hesitated to open their ranks to the new generation, for fear of devaluing their own criteria. As one of its members expressed it in December 1945: 'The UFAC doesn't want any "32nd of August" [1944] resisters.'[8] Belonging to the great patriotic family of the *anciens combattants* of the war in the trenches was a highly formalised matter, expressed by the fetish of the *carte du combattant* which a veteran could obtain only after three months – ninety days – of effective combat, as certified by regiment listings and combat records.

---

[7] See 'Ordonnance no. 45-1181 du 14 mai 1945 relative à la création de l'Union Française des Combattants', *Journal Officiel* (7 June 1945), pp. 3294–8, and the documentation in AN F60 240.

[8] M. Barral in Commission Pensions (13 Dec. 1945), AAsN. The *poilus* or veterans of the Great War were known thus, as 'the bearded ones', because of their rough and manly life in the trenches.

This carried the implication, for example, that soldiers taken prisoner after less than three months of effective combat did not qualify for the *carte du combattant*; yet none of the PoWs of 1940–5 had such a record, for less than six weeks had passed between the German invasion and the armistice. By the same token, if the criteria of 1918 were to be maintained, only the Free French troops or the troops who took part in the final offensive against Germany could qualify. For the resistance, the establishment of a record of ninety days of effective combat was a haphazard undertaking, since this time there were no general orders, regiment listings or combat records. Debate over the integration of new categories of 'combatants' into the great patriotic family of 1914–18 was to animate many of the commemorative gatherings of organisations established to unite 'veterans' of various characteristic experiences of the Second World War, such as concentration camps or forced economic migration.

The new government of Félix Gouin, who succeeded De Gaulle in January 1946, did incorporate a new Ministry for Veterans and War Victims. The precise title of the ministry, which was to incorporate the services of the former Ministry for Prisoners, Deportees and Refugees, had been debated, with propositions for lengthy names such as 'Ministry for Veterans, Prisoners, Deportees and War Victims'.[9] The final name of the ministry confirmed the dichotomy between veterans – that is *anciens combattants*, fighters, heroes – and victims, virtually forcing each group to aim for the honourable division of fighters, rather than falling into the alternative category of losers, the war victims. Laurent Casanova, the communist minister who assumed this new responsibility, represented all the groups gathered under his ministry. He was welcomed by the appropriate commission of the Assemblée Nationale in February 1946 as 'a valorous fighter, a prisoner who escaped, a resister and a man stricken in his dearest affections' – the latter referring to the death in Auschwitz of his wife and communist resistance heroine, Danielle Casanova.[10] Casanova, who would contribute much to the new patriotism of the French Communist Party, saw it as his central task to unify the movement of veterans and victims of both wars, combining a scrupulous respect for the achievements and procedures of the generation of 1914–18 with the inevitable recognition of the fundamental difference of the generation of 1939–45.

In the genuine generational conflict between the two *générations du feu* the resistance played only a secondary role compared to the clash – as described by François Mitterrand, one of Casanova's successors – of

[9] M. Marbrut in Commission Pensions (19 Dec. 1945), AAsN.
[10] Commission Pensions (13 Feb. 1946), AAsN.

two giants: the veterans of the trenches of 1914–18 (two million men) and the veterans of the stalag of 1940–5 (one million men). The *poilus* of the victorious army of the trenches were animated by a particular animosity against the military prisoners of the defeat of 1940, contemptuously known as the 'knights of the raised rifle-butts' (*les chevaliers de la crosse en l'air*), the sign of surrender.[11] In a *fait accompli* manoeuvre which roused indignation amongst the members of the UFAC, Mitterrand, one of the national leaders of the PoW movement before he became minister of veterans and war victims, would give the much coveted *carte du combattant* to all PoWs with the exception of animators of Pétain circles, but including even PoWs who became civilian workers.[12]

A first decree containing a definition of who could be considered 'a member of the resistance' was published shortly before the end of the war, on 3 March 1945.[13] It established five categories: all members of resistance organisations, recognised either by De Gaulle, the Allies or the CNR; individuals who had joined the Free French Forces in London or Algiers, or tried to do so; and individuals who even in complete isolation had committed 'recognised acts of resistance'. The fourth and fifth categories covered all resistance victims of arrest or execution by the Germans or Vichy for reasons other than common law offences. The text carried no reference to the post-1918 definitions of the *combattant*, no notion of effective combat, *carte du combattant* or minimum involvement of ninety days, nor any of the procedural provisions to authenticate applicants. The three proposals submitted to the Assemblée Nationale in the course of 1945, concerning procedures and criteria, no longer referred simply to a 'member of the resistance', but specified instead *ancien combattant de la Résistance, combattant volontaire de la Résistance,* or *combattant de la Résistance,* most explicitly referring to post-1918 notions of veteran soldiers.[14] The joint proposal discussed in the spring of 1946 was presented as a reparation for the discrimination between the regular military formations of the Free French Forces (Forces Françaises Libres, FFL) and the Forces Françaises Combattantes (FFC), who had been in direct contact with London – both of whom were assimilated

---

[11] See the excellent analysis by Christophe Lewin, *Le Retour des prisonniers de guerre français* (Paris, 1986), pp. 177–89.

[12] See ibid. and Commission Pensions (30 May, 9 July 1947, 30 Apr. 1948).

[13] See Serge Barcellini, 'Les Résistants dans l'oeil de l'administration ou l'histoire du statut de combattant volontaire de la Résistance', *Guerres Mondiales et Conflits Contemporains* 178 (1995), pp. 141–65; and Olivier Wieviorka, 'Les Avatars du statut de résistant en France (1945–1992)', *Vingtième Siècle* 50 (1996), pp. 55–66.

[14] *Rapport . . . par M. De Raulin,* in *Documents AsN,* annexe 608 (7 Mar. 1946), pp. 584–5.

with regular soldiers – and the resistance troops of the Forces Françaises de l'Intérieur (FFI), who lacked any such support.

The new law, unanimously adopted by the Assemblée Nationale, stipulated the requirement of ninety days of combat, the *carte du combattant*, and delegated application of the procedure to the Ministry for Veterans, implying a *de facto* assimilation with the post-1918 status and procedures for veterans. Yet these features differed in important respects from the status of Great War veterans. The *poilus* of 1914–18 could decide at any time to apply for the status of combatant, since there was no documentary difficulty in confirming their military record. Many would only do so several decades after the war, particularly when they came to retire. Even as late as 1986, for example, about 1,000 veterans of the Great War would apply for the 'green card' (for the card was indeed the same colour as that other coveted card across the Atlantic).[15] For veterans of the resistance, the documentary evidence was less clear cut – either a declaration of membership by a national leader of a movement, or two declarations by certified veterans of a resistance involvement of which they had been witnesses. As time passed, these declarations were deemed less sure: since the documents were not contemporary with the events, memories might be fallible or organisations might show a tendency to magnify membership figures; or it could be a matter of ingratiating oneself with latter-day applicants. The law therefore specified a period of nine months in which to submit applications, with the due documentation, before the procedure would be irrevocably closed. This law was almost immediately contested and a new version adopted in 1949, largely inspired by a general anti-communist atmosphere, contained fresh dispositions designed to prevent what its enemies perceived as a communist intention to obtain massive and inauthentic certification for its militants. Resistance organisations had to be endorsed by the ministry rather than recognised by the CNR (which would have implied the recognition of the PCF as a resistance organisation), and the active involvement of ninety days had to precede the D-Day Normandy landings. Due to these manoeuvres, the law came into effect only in March 1950, with a foreclosure of one year.

The immediate effect of the law was a revival of organisations for former resisters. As Olivier Wieviorka convincingly describes for Défense de la France, resistance movements barely survived the end of the war and the attempts to set up veteran-type associations based on wartime movements were mostly unsuccessful.[16] Attempts to create

---

[15] Faligot and Kauffer, *Les Résistants*, p. 584.
[16] Olivier Wieviorka, *Une certaine idée de la Résistance. Défense de la France, 1940–1949* (Paris, 1995), pp. 353–410.

national organisations uniting resistance veterans of all types of movement in the face of the legal recognition of the category of 'resisters' were abortive. The procedural battles and, most significantly, the campaign against foreclosure of the procedure gave birth to three national organisations of resistance veterans which explicitly emulated their forebears of 1914–18, all founded in the early 1950s.[17] The Association Nationale des Anciens Combattants Résistants (ANACR), founded in July 1952, was animated by communist resistance figures, recruited primarily amongst former FFI and Franc-Tireurs et Partisans (FTP). Thanks to the significant proportion of non-communists in its membership and leadership, it was highly successful, with over 30,000 members. The Association Nationale des Combattants Volontaires de la Résistance (ANCVR), founded in February 1953, succeeded an elitist Gaullist formation of officers and deputy officers of the resistance – whatever a rigorous definition of military grades might have meant in the conditions of underground action. Its membership did not exceed 1,500. The Confédération Nationale des Combattants Volontaires de la Résistance (CNCVR), founded in October 1953, was the more popular Gaullist formation with just under 10,000 members. Their combined efforts at militancy laid an effective whip on the governments of the Fourth Republic. The 'foreclosure' was postponed annually until De Gaulle's return to power. As the undisputed hero of the resistance, with a profound dislike of veterans' attitudes, the general-president autocratically closed the procedure for new applicants. The effects of the postponement of foreclosure could not be described as marginal: whereas 76,000 cards had been distributed in 1954, by the end of the decade France counted almost 200,000 authenticated resisters.[18] The steady production of new declarations by witnesses and resistance chiefs was perceived with irony, and certainly devalued the aura of the 'green card'. The decision in 1975 by Valérie Giscard d'Estaing to cancel the national holiday of 8 May, commemorating the end of the Second World War, provoked such a wave of protest and associational militancy that the president was forced into an expiatory sacrifice: the foreclosures were lifted, and the number of cards issued soared to reach 260,000. François Mitterrand, this time as president, favoured a generous distribution of *cartes de combattant de la résistance*, including some to his fellow PoWs.[19] The outcome of a debate dominated by an obsession for authenticated heroism achieved the opposite result. Resistance veterans

---

[17] See Barcellini, 'Les Résistants'.
[18] See the graph, ibid., p. 162.
[19] See, in addition to the above, Eric Conan and Henry Rousso, *Vichy, un passé qui ne passe pas* (Paris, 1994), pp. 173–207.

and their organisations were to a certain extent devalued, and the French nation would address itself to other *milieux de mémoire* with a more secure status.

Of the three countries dealt with in these pages, Belgium showed the most outspoken conflict between the returning exiled government and local political forces claiming the inheritance of wartime resistance. In Allied documents, Belgium was even ranked with Greece and Italy as an alarming and unstable democracy.[20] Even though it was a rhetorical exaggeration to represent Belgium as being on the brink of civil war and revolution, it was instrumental both to Churchill in staving off domestic criticism and to the Belgian government as it begged for more Allied support. Government and resistance were indeed in opposition, partly due to the clumsy approach of the Pierlot government as it failed to assimilate the resistance and appropriate its merits, which were achieved very skilfully in France and the Netherlands. On his return to Belgium, Pierlot offered two government posts to communist ministers and one to the leader of the Independence Front, the largest Belgian resistance organisation founded by the Communist Party, but after a month they left the government in protest against its ill-considered methods of disarming the resistance. Allied observers were dissatisfied with the Catholic Pierlot and judged his government too conservative to be in touch with Belgian public opinion. His fall and the succession of the socialist pragmatic Van Acker in February 1945 at the head of a new government of national unity, again including the communists, were welcomed both in Belgium and abroad as something of a new start for Belgium. Apart from foreign affairs minister Paul-Henri Spaak, the new cabinet did not include any of the ministers of the cabinet-in-exile in London. Political figures who had spent the war years in occupied Belgium were deemed less alienated from the population than the exiles. Van Acker's unifying and pragmatist approach was demonstrated by the absolute priority he gave to Belgium's national coal production.

The eruption of the royal question in the summer of 1945 signified the end of national cohesion. The Catholic Party identified with the king and refused to remain in a government that prolonged his exile. The anti-royalist coalition presented itself on the rebound as 'the government of the resistance' and prided itself on the inclusion of seven 'resistance heroes' in a cabinet of eighteen ministers, including two members of the newly created resistance party, the Union Démocratique Belge (UDB). Yet despite this appropriation of the resistance aura, the resistance

[20] Lagrou, 'US Politics of Stabilization'.

movements themselves were very much divided over the royal question. Conservative patriotic movements such as the National Royalist Movement (Nationale Koningsgezinde Beweging) and movements of career soldiers such as the Secret Army (Armée Secrète) were strongly royalist; the Independence Front was profoundly anti-royalist; and other organisations, such as the Belgian National Movement (MNB, Mouvement National Belge/Belgische Nationale Beweging) or Groupe G (a resistance organisation specialising in sabotage during the occupation), refused to take a public stance.[21] In the campaign leading up to the first post-war elections, the issue was often presented by the anti-Leopold camp as a choice between resistance and collaboration. In election week the journal of the Independence Front exclaimed: 'The CVP [the old cluster of the Catholic Party had been transformed in December 1945 into a more centralised "Christian Popular Party"] is our public enemy No. 1, the CVP where all the traitors have found a safe haven.'[22] In parliament, Leopold III was called 'the greatest of all traitors' and 'the only hope of all the collaborators, great and small'.[23]

In September 1945, that is, in the very first weeks of its existence, the 'government of the resistance' translated its identification into political acts: a provisional law establishing financial support for widows and orphans of resistance victims; a law liquidating the debts of resistance movements; an amnesty law for offences perpetrated by the resistance up to forty-one days after the liberation, that is, including the first unruly period of settling scores with collaborators; the law for 'the purge concerning civil loyalty' and the 'Act of Armed Resistance'. All were issued under legal dispositions which gave the government special regulating powers without going through a systematic parliamentary debate on each. The 'civil purge' was a highly controversial political manoeuvre: citizens could be administratively stripped of their voting rights on charges of collaboration. By the elections of February 1946, at a speed which implied arbitrariness, 43,000 names were listed, and in a mere five weeks 18,000 of them were denied the right to participate in the elections.[24] Individuals suspected of collaboration were at the same time suspected of casting a vote for the royalist opposition, and their

---

[21] For the Armée Secrète, see *Pygmalion* (May 1945–Feb. 1946); for Groupe G, see *Pile ou Face* (Jan.–Feb. 1946); for the FI, see *Front* (May 1945–Feb. 1946). See also Francis Balace and Colette Dupont, 'Les Anciens et le roi. Facteurs de cohésion et de divergence, 1945–1950', *Cahiers du Centre de Recherches et d'Etudes Historiques de la Seconde Guerre Mondiale* 9 (1985), pp. 123–74.

[22] Fernand Demany in *Front* (24 Feb. 1946).

[23] Respectively Charles Janssens and Julien Lahaut, quoted in Theo Luykx, *Politieke Geschiedenis van België*, vol. II, *(1944–1985)* (Antwerp, 1985), p. 452.

[24] Huyse and Dhont, *Onverwerkt verleden*, pp. 26–31, 129 and 142–8.

2 The resistance against king, Christian Democrats and collaborationists: 'How so, you're coming back? Of course, I only went to cast my vote for the Christian Democrats!' From *Front*, 24 February 1945. Photo, Isabelle Sampieri, CEGES/SOMA.

exclusion was an urgent priority that could not await the due process of law, with routine sentences. Resistance movements such as the Independence Front and Groupe G called on their members to prevent former collaborators from voting, even those not barred from the election lists, by picketing polling stations.

The 'Act of Armed Resistance' issued on 19 September was certainly not the initiative that could be expected from a government attempting to create a new patriotic front against the king and the Catholic opposition. In this matter, the government could merely act on a proposal elaborated before it came into existence. When the Van Acker government succeeded the Pierlot government in February 1945, one of the criticisms in the motion of non-confidence was dissatisfaction over the way it had treated the resistance fighters. Even after their forced disarmament the first claim of the resistance forces was still the continuation of the war. Indeed, 80,000 resistance fighters had remained in camps for two months, badly paid, inactive, waiting on the government's permission to participate in the war. In the end not only was permission denied, but the government even decided that resistance fighters could be engaged in the army only on an individual basis and not in units under their wartime resistance leaders. To achieve promotion they would have to pass exams, just like any other career soldier. Many resistance fighters saw this as a humiliation, particularly because it meant that they would have to serve under officers who had remained passive during the war. Contemptuously, they called them the old order, the men who were responsible for defeat in 1940, or *les napthalines*, those who put their uniforms in mothballs during the war.[25] It was therefore no surprise that, of the 80,000, only 25,000 volunteered for the army, most of them pre-war career soldiers. The task of the newly formed Belgian units was far from glorious. They served under Allied command as the so-called Liberated Manpower Units, charged with logistics – messenger boys to the Allies.[26] The military frustration amongst the resistance was obvious. Not only had they not played an important role in the liberation of the territory, but after the event they were denied a chance to participate in the final offensive. Their claims were double: moral recompense, and an indemnity for the period of inactivity. To resolve the demands of the resistance the Van Acker government had created a Conseil de la Resistance as soon as it took office in February 1945.[27] The nationalist military groups dominated this council, particularly in the largest formation, the 'Secret Army of Belgium', which was headed by career officers. Because the council was created to remedy the treatment of the mobilised volunteers of September–October 1944, the largest non-armed resistance organisation, the Independence Front, was not even represented, apart from its armed wing, the Patriotic Militia. Under the guidance of the Armée Secrète career officers, the council proposed a 'Statute of Armed

[25] *Front* (25 Jan. 1945).
[26] See Lucien Champion, *La Chronique des 53.000* (Brussels, 1973); *Front* (28 Jan. 1945 and 15 July 1945); and *Parlementaire Handelingen Kamer* (6 Feb. and 7 Aug. 1945).
[27] *Belgisch Staatsblad* (10 Feb. 1945), p. 646.

Resistance', which defined both wartime action and post-war benefits entirely in military terms. Four of the nine organisations represented in the council had voted against the project, precisely because of this narrow military concept, and the Independence Front had immediately claimed a new 'Act of Civil Resistance'.[28] The proposal was nevertheless accepted by the Ministry of Defence and published in the official journal as a concrete sign of governmental good-will towards the resistance.[29]

The beneficiaries of the act had to prove membership of a resistance organisation or an individual resistance activity of a military nature before the Normandy landings on 6 June 1944, deeming the influx of last-minute resisters after the landing unworthy of recognition. The period of resistance activities would be recognised as active military service and the leaders of the resistance movements would be entitled to higher military grades.

The statute foresaw a graduated distribution of ranks: one lieutenant-colonel for every 3,000 members, one major per 1,000, one captain per 250, and so on. The resistance organisations who designed the text also granted themselves maximum independence in the procedures for recognition: every movement had to deal with demands for recognition of their own members. The screening commissions also included one observer from another movement, but the movements made a gentlemen's agreement not to intervene in each other's registration policy.[30] As a result the movements had no formal constraint over recognising whoever they wanted and, further, they had strong motivation to recognise as many members as possible, not only to inflate their own importance but also to attain the quota of military ranks for its executives. A second procedure for individual acts of armed resistance was so demanding in the evidence required that most potential applicants preferred to obtain *post facto* a certificate of membership from a recognised organisation, which was generally very easily obtained. In all, 141,400 demands were recognised and only 12,000 rejected.[31] In their periodicals the resistance movements overtly recruited new members to demand recognition.[32] In 1950 a parliamentary commission revealed a series of fraudulent recognitions, but this was only the official corroboration of popular scepticism over the numbers of recognised resistance fighters throughout the post-war

[28] *La Voix des Belges* (18 Dec. 1949), and Charles Hoste, personal communication, to author (5 July 1989).
[29] *Belgisch Staatsblad* (12 Oct. 1945), pp. 6734–9.
[30] *La Voix des Belges* (18 Dec. 1949).
[31] Numbers as of 1950: *Parlementaire Handelingen Kamer* (13 Feb. 1951), p. 8.
[32] *Pygmalion* (Dec. 1946); *Front* (19 and 28 Jan. 1947).

years.[33] The statute had set a precedent, rewarding resisters for their attitude during the war. In its terms, however, it was too closely phrased in purely military terms: the resistance fighters were *post facto* incorporated in the army. For those military units which, remembering the First World War, entered the resistance for nationalistic reasons, this was the only valid interpretation. This merely military version of the resistance was not acceptable to the other movements, with the left-wing Independence Front (Front de l'Indépendance, the FI) the most important amongst them. The FI was an umbrella organisation founded by the Communist Party but intended as a broad democratic forum. Its many branches were active in hiding Jews, supporting the families of deported members and organising resistance cells in factories and amongst farmers, schoolteachers and lawyers. The FI proposal of a law recognising a broad front of patriots in its own image was one that suited the 'government of the resistance' particularly well.[34] After its narrow victory in the elections of February 1946, it was granted more time to develop its own project. The minister in charge of the project in the new government team, the communist minister of reconstruction Jean Terfve, was himself an FI man. After his escape from prison in August 1941 he had been active in the FI as propaganda leader, as national commander of the partisans, the armed branch of the Communist Party, and finally he even replaced Fernand Demany as secretary-general of the FI. Terfve wanted to succeed where the statute of the armed resistance had failed: a text recognising all meritorious Belgians in one final tribute to the resistance.[35]

His proposal set out three concrete forms of resistance: sabotage, clandestine press and aid to people in hiding.[36] The basic criterion in each case was action against the enemy involving a real risk. A fourth category recognised those who had contributed to 'works of patriotic solidarity, working against the aims of the enemy or his henchmen'. This category, vague enough to be acceptable to the other movements, was basically designed to recognise FI activities, such as its underground trade union cells or its professional organisations for magistrates, teachers and farmers.[37] The procedure was virtually copied from the statute of the armed resistance. Individual resisters would have to prove

---

[33] *Parlementaire Handelingen Kamer* (13 Feb. 1951), pp. 16–27, and *Documenten Kamer* (ordinary session 1950–1), no. 386.

[34] *Front* (25 Aug., 28 Oct., 11 Nov. 1945, 17 Feb. 1946); *La Voix des Belges* (May 1945).

[35] See also ch. 10.

[36] *Belgisch Staatsblad* (16 Jan. 1947), pp. 431–4, and *Front* (1 Dec. 1946).

[37] See the file 'Historique Résistance Civile – Werken van Patriottische Verbondenheid', AO, Brussels, documentation service, RAP 610, TR.237.367.

their activities, but members of the organisations recognised as 'works etc.' simply had to submit a declaration of membership.

Before he could even submit the proposal, Terfve was obliged to make an exception. The unforeseen problem was posed by the 'refractors', or labour draft-evaders. When the Germans first recruited Belgian workers to work in factories in Germany, as I will describe in detail in chapter 7, many workers preferred to go into hiding to escape requisition. Only a minority of them joined the resistance movements. The attitude of the 'refractors' had undeniable patriotic merit: by accepting the hardships of their life in hiding, they withheld their labour from the enemy. Regardless of the motivation of the 'refractors' – as patriots or home-birds – their attitude had been passive and could in no way be accepted on the same footing as the active choice of resistance. Terfve found a somewhat artificial solution for this problem, making a double statute with one preliminary tribute to the nation in resistance and two separate parts, one for active resistance and one for the 'refractors'.

In his statute Terfve had annexed an earlier proposal, that of the clandestine press. This had been one of the main forms of resistance in Belgium, resistance in which the country had a rich tradition dating back to the First World War. The MNB, publisher of *La Voix des Belges*, one of the clandestine newspapers with the largest print-runs and widest distributions, was infuriated at being bundled into a statute that recognised such a diversity of forms of resistance.[38] According to the advocates of the clandestine press, it deserved the same rights as the armed resistance, higher army grades included. The statute of civil resistance was low in status, designed by the FI to win a decoration for the bulk of its adherents, and the dangerous and important work of the clandestine press should not be submerged in this flood of acknowledgements. The statute of civil resistance had been approved by the council of ministers in November 1946, but its opponents assembled a new league of non-communist clandestine newspapers, appealed to the regent and blocked its application.[39] In March 1947 the communists left the government. One year later parliament unanimously approved a separate statute for the clandestine press, wholly inspired by the military vocabulary of the Act for Armed Resistance.[40]

The blocking of application of the statute had one even more serious consequence: Terfve did not have the opportunity to put it into practice.

[38] *La Voix des Belges* (17 Nov. 1946).

[39] See *Front* (19 May, 8 Sep., 1 Dec., 8 Dec. 1946; 12 Jan. 1947).

[40] *Documenten Kamer* (June 1948), no. 536; *Parlementaire Handelingen Kamer* (17, 23 and 24 June, 30 July 1948, 3 Aug. 1949); and *Parlementaire Handelingen Senaat* (23 June 1948).

In March 1947 the Communist and Liberal Parties left the government, and socialists and Catholics came together in a government which prioritised Cold War unity as against divisions over the royal question. Terfve was succeeded by the Catholic minister Robert De Man, who now became responsible for implementing a project designed to gain mass recognition for his party's sworn enemy, the FI. The minister's first step was the mobilisation of all non-communist organisations that could possibly offer some sort of resistance activity to join in a new umbrella organisation which would counterbalance the FI. Baron Tilmans, a Catholic industrialist and ex-resistance fighter, agreed to establish the contacts, whilst De Man urged the different branches of the Catholic labour movement to establish some sort of resistance action and join in the new organisation.[41] As soon as it was founded, the organisation won recognition from the minister on the same footing as the FI. About forty very heterogeneous groups of Catholic, socialist and liberal tendencies joined the new 'confederation', including sixteen clandestine movements and twenty-five clandestine cells inside legal organisms.[42] This made the recognition possible of a number of respectable organisations that maintained official activity all through the war, permitted and approved by the occupier, such as the National Work for War Veterans, the Catholic Workers' Youth and the Catholic Service to War Victim Families, which organised aid to households hit by Allied bombing.

Still, it would require interpretational agility to recognise all these movements according to the terms of the law. The clandestine press had been removed from the text. Aid to those in hiding was the easiest category; many Catholic organisations had been active in hiding Jews and draft-evaders – more than half of the member organisations obtained their recognition for this kind of activity. The two other categories needed more exegesis. Sabotage during professional activities had been adopted by Terfve to reward workers who committed acts of sabotage in factories producing goods for German warfare, and De Man launched a new notion, namely 'administrative sabotage', a category which covered the civil servants who remained at their posts throughout the occupation and, having formally accepted German orders, sought to evade them. Five core points of 'patriotic fraud' in the administration were recognised in this way. It was the fourth category, 'works of patriotic solidarity', which proved to be the most elastic clause in De Man's interpretation. Almost every work of charity, as for example aid to victims of Allied bombing, found its place under this condition. The

[41] Tilmans, personal communication, to author (20 Apr. 1989).
[42] *Belgisch Staatsblad, bijlage Verenigingen zonder Winstoogmerk* (20 Mar. 1948), pp. 681–6 and 309–14, and *Belgisch Staatsblad* (11 Mar. 1948), pp. 1981–3.

FI was bitter in its comments on the distortions of its statute: 'The manoeuvre is obvious. They want to drown the resistance, engulf it in a tide of sundry heterogeneous organisms in order to devalue it. Moreover, surreptitiously they want to sneak a number of individuals into the resistance because they allegedly committed "administrative resistance", when in fact they overtly collaborated with the enemy.'[43]

Still, De Man had to find an administration willing to apply his exegesis. In itself this should not have been a problem, because no staff had yet been appointed to this new department which would deal with all non-military resisters and war victims. According to the Belgian political traditions, all would be loyal supporters of the Catholic Party.[44] The hundreds of thousands of cases were ranked according to priority, and initially the administration would handle only the files of political prisoners. As I will describe in chapter 5, the administration had an important moral and financial responsibility over the fate of individuals who had suffered real hardships. The services for war victims gathered impressive documentation on the concentration camps and examined every personal case closely. By 1950, when the same civil servants turned to the demands of the statute of civil resistance, they had acquired a professional ethic that made them examine every case with the same critical norm of inquiry. They returned to the original text of the law: applicants had to prove an activity implying real risks, directed against the aims of the enemy – criteria that posed problems for the applicants on the list of anti-FI organisations. The procedural provision that members could qualify automatically on the mere basis of a declaration of membership, for which the 'confederation' had been set up, was ignored. Even though the organisations had been recognised by ministerial decree and their list published in the official journal in 1948, the administration ordered a critical investigation into each case to assess which of them could genuinely qualify under the terms of the 1946 law.[45]

The procedure proved to be a disaster for the anti-FI list. All the FI branches were retained as having performed 'works of patriotic solidarity', but only half of the anti-FI organisations. Out of a total of 44,000 individual demands, only 10,000 were recognised. Interrogated about the resistance character of his work during the war, one volunteer of the relief action for victims of Allied bombing answered: 'No, our

[43] *Front* (14 Mar. 1948).
[44] Pierre Potargent, personal communication, to author (15 Feb. 1987); Van Calster, personal communication, to author (22 Dec. 1986).
[45] Note, Van Calster (12 Nov. 1950), 28/GVC/DM, AO, Brussels, documentation service, RAP 610, TR.237.367.

activity had no clandestine character whatsoever. We usually wore an arm-badge to be allowed on the site of the disaster. There was no risk involved and the Germans were quite positive about our action.' Asked why he then demanded the statute of civil resister, this brave man answered: 'Finally it was Miss Baers [the national head of the Catholic Labour Women's Association and president of Aid Action] who asked us to submit a demand, because the fourth condition for "works of patriotic solidarity" was added especially to recognise our action.'[46] The administration rejected the demand on behalf of his relief work, but assured him that he was entitled to the statute under another heading of the law, since he had given shelter to two Jewish clandestines during the occupation. This the applicant refused, since, according to his own declaration, this had nothing to do with resistance, but with sheer humanity.

The procedure became a repeated source of conflict between the minister and his administration. In 1950, on his personal initiative, the minister recognised an organisation of railway personnel from his local electoral district. It had clandestinely sold goods stolen from railway warehouses to railway men, undercutting black market prices, and claimed to have used the profits to finance support for families of railway men who were PoWs or draft-evaders. The administration rejected this decision: the whole scheme might have been a convenient swindle with dubious charitable aims, but as an activity it had not implied real risks and was not directed against enemy aims.[47] The minister ignored the results of the investigation of his administration and the recognition was published in the official journal as an addition to the list of 1948. Subsequently the administration systematically turned down all individual applications by members of the railway committee, embarrassing the minister with a recognised organisation without even one recognised member. Even a Catholic minister, part of a homogeneously Catholic government and facing an administration appointed under a Catholic predecessor on the basis of their political affiliation, could not violate the procedures. Unlike the merry distribution of medals under the terms of the Act for the Armed Resistance, the 'civil resistance' was indeed limited to an authenticated elite, and was, against all odds, reasonably well preserved from political interference.

The one example that contradicts this conclusion throws an interesting light on the continuing legitimisation of resistance titles. Although

---

[46] 'PV of AAC' [code used to protect anonymity] (4 Dec. 1950), AO, Brussels, documentation service, RAP 610, TR 237.367.

[47] 'Dienst Ravitaillering van de NMBS', AO, Brussels, documentation service, RAP 610 TR 237.367, no. 15.

their case was somewhat similar to the failed attempt of the railway men, the applicants in this group had more weight. The whole upper echelon of the Flemish wing of the Catholic labour movement sought recognition for their action during the war. All were close friends of Minister De Man, the author of the 1948 list covering 'the centre for social and economic studies' of which they claimed to be active members. Two of the applicants were also ministers (Paul Willem Segers and Gerard Van den Daele), one a national union leader (August Cool) and several others held senior responsible posts. The Flemish wing of the Catholic labour movement had been heavily compromised by its participation in the collaborationist trade union founded by the occupier in 1940 and they wanted to clear their record with a decoration for resistance acts. Their testimonies were all too obviously concocted: none of them had expected to undergo a real investigation and most were caught out in contradictory declarations. The applicants had effectively met during the war after their unfortunate adventure in the collaborationist trade union in which they had participated despite the refusal of the Walloon wing of the Catholic workers' movement. Even after leaving the German-controlled trade union they had clung to most of the opinions underlying their participation at the start of the occupation – a strong attachment to corporatism and the authoritarian state – and they had even drafted a political platform defending these views. None of this was known to the investigators of the administration, of course, who had enough reasons to doubt the applications through comparison of the inconsistent interrogations on the location, the frequency or even the attendance at the 'Study Centre' meetings. As one of the applicants, Alfons Billion, declared to the present author forty years after the investigation, in which testimony was given under oath, it was a relief to his professional conscience as a judge to confess to what he still regarded as perjury. Billion received a phone call from an old friend, asking him to state on oath that he had been in a resistance organisation with a political heavyweight amongst the Catholic workers' movement, who were facing charges for collaboration and needed a cover (Billion asked not to disclose any names). Billion himself had been inculpated for his participation in the collaborationist trade union, but his case had been shelved:

We Catholics, and particularly people from the workers' movement, felt cornered. After the war, we were not only confronted with a different mentality, but also with different people. The government returned from London and engaged people who had distinguished themselves in the resistance. All at once we had to justify our wartime action to strangers. Almost everyone in our *milieu* did have some trouble, if not with the purge, at the least with imputations. We felt threatened, we felt insecure as to whether we would be successful in life. Afterwards, it all turned out well and most of us had a good career, but at that time it did not look like that. It was in this atmosphere that at a certain time we decided we had to support one another, and someone suggested: 'Couldn't you swear to something that we did together?' This was not an aim of the movement, but a feeling that something had to be done, with the idea that, if we were called to account later, we'd find the arguments. And so we ended up attesting before these commissions I didn't trust very much, let alone that I felt under obligation to. I didn't even know what the criteria were for recognition.[48]

The minister intervened personally with the administration to grant absolute priority to the applications of the 'Centre'. The investigating civil servants were much impressed by their charge to interview a minister or a national trade union leader. Nevertheless, four out of five 'commissars' issued a negative report on the soundness of the applications, advice that was overruled by their superior. All recognitions were forced through the commissions. Ministers deserved a different treatment from railway men who trafficked in stolen goods; yet their medals as civil resisters did not serve them well – afterwards, none dared to display them for fear of reviving old accusations.

The settings for 'civil resistance' are interesting in so far as they show a vigorous attempt by the Catholic Party to counter the appropriation of the resistance legacy by the anti-royalist coalition. The party remained in government for seven long years, between March 1947 and April 1954. Until June 1950, it did so as part of coalition governments with the Socialist or the Liberal Party, but after that date it formed its own CVP/PSC governments, with an absolute parliamentary majority. In such a position of unequalled power a thorough reappropriation of the legacy of the resistance should have been possible, yet this did not happen. On the contrary, it was the opposition that championed the legacy of the resistance as a successful opposition strategy, both in the debate on the purge and the royal question, twice forcing a Catholic minister of justice to resign, and by obtaining the succession of Leopold III by his son Baudouin despite a formal referendum majority. Paradoxically enough, during its seven years in power the Catholic Party accumulated more frustrations than the opposition who were excluded from this power. As I will describe in the conclusion of this book, in 1954 the formerly anti-royalist camp would stage a triumphal return of a 'government of the resistance' when the Catholic Party was forced into opposition. In fact, whilst in power, the Catholic Party gave up the symbolic battle for the legacy of the resistance.

[48] Billion, personal communication, to author (10 Oct. 1987).

3   A nation of heroes: the Netherlands

During the war years the fears of the governments-in-exile had been focused on the transition, the chaotic period between the German withdrawal and the re-establishment of public order, the probably protracted period of liberation struggles when irregularities could occur and subversive forces might be tempted to seize local power. During this period, the military command would take control of the situation and share administrative responsibility with the exile governments according to 'Civil Affairs Agreements'. Conservative resistance movements of career soldiers like the Armée Secrète in Belgium and the Ordedienst (OD) in the Netherlands had also prepared for this period, wanting to impose their own authoritarian conception of law and order, which could only increase the apprehension of the governments-in-exile. The Belgian government was spared the realisation of its worst fears by the hazards of military strategy: the invasion forces had been contained in the Normandy bottleneck from 6 June 1944 until early August, but once the German defence was broken on the Normandy front the Allies rushed forward to the next barrier, formed in the north by the great rivers in the Netherlands, which they reached in less than two months' time. The airborne landing at Arnhem on 17 September 1944 hit a strong SS tank division and ended in costly defeat for the Allies. The offensive had to be postponed until the next spring and the logistics problem forced the Canadian troops to clear the Scheldt estuary downstream from German resistance in a slow and costly operation.

The strategic deadlock of the Allied offensive halfway across the Dutch territory divided the country in two: the liberated south, and the occupied central and northern part. Throughout the whole country the Allied offensive had led to a wave of expectations and panic amongst the German occupation forces and the collaborationists. Rumours of the imminent liberation of the entire country culminated in 'mad Tuesday', 5 September 1944. About 65,000 NSB members (the Dutch national socialist party) and their families fled to Germany and people gathered in the streets with Dutch and British flags to welcome liberators who failed to appear.[1] The part of the Netherlands that lay north of the big rivers was condemned to undergo another hard winter of occupation. Extreme cold, lack of coal, meagre food rations, Allied bombing and increased German repression made this final year of the war harder to bear than its predecessors. The most important feature, however, was that after 'mad Tuesday' the psychology of the occupied country was no longer the same. Part of the country was liberated, the Allied troops were within reach, victory was beyond doubt, liberation only a matter of time. In this context the resistance movements could start preparing for the post-war political situation and anyone who had not chosen sides yet, or who had chosen the wrong side, could use the extra time to clear his or her record.

In the liberated south, the administration was delegated to a Military Authority, operating from Brussels and headed by the young General Kruls.[2] The Military Authority had extensive powers over matters of civil administration – particularly the appointment of mayors and the purge of the police corps – and in arresting people suspected of collaboration with the enemy. For part of this task, Kruls could count on the 'Dutch Internal Armed Forces', a formation incorporating volunteers from the resistance and modelled on the French FFI.[3] The creation of this force brought a halt to the law-and-order adventurism of the OD. It was at the same time an outlet for the resistance enthusiasm of the queen and her son-in-law, Prince Bernhard, who was appointed as their commander. Recruitment of the Forces, about 20,000, had been precipitate and the troops soon stood accused of arbitrary arrests, looting of houses belonging to arrested collaborationists and cruelty to internees in the camps. The Military Authority's administration of the liberated territory was particularly criticised by the government-in-exile in London, whose ministers tried to impose their own policy in a variety of conflicting competencies. In this conflict Kruls sought the support of the queen and of the organised resistance in the south. The queen ran a smouldering conflict with her own government, reproaching it for its legalism and bureaucracy compared with the untamed heroism and moral purity of the resistance which she idealised. The queen resented the 'old politicians' and favoured a thorough constitutional reform that would reduce the role of parliament. For this programme, and against the constitutional scruples of her government, she sought support from representatives of the

[1] See De Jong, *Koninkrijk*, vol. Xa.
[2] See H. J. Kruls, *Generaal in Nederland. Memoires* (Bussum, 1975), pp. 61–145, and De Jong, *Koninkrijk*, vol. Xa, pp. 533–687, 857–907.
[3] See G. J. Van Ojen, *De Binnenlandse Strijdkrachten* (The Hague, 1972).

resistance who had crossed the Channel and naturally favoured the 'vigorous' approach of the Military Authority.

In the field, Kruls and the queen found a useful partner in the Community of Ex-Illegal Workers (Gemeenschap Oud-Illegale Werkers Nederland, GOIWN). This organisation developed in November 1944 out of the demand for a representative body of resisters to express the wishes of the population in the liberated south, and as such was a hybrid combination of a political movement, one of the many 'renewal' movements that emerged in the predominantly Catholic south in this period, and a veterans' association.[4] Dominated by prominent figures of the political elites of the south, it had the future Catholic prime ministers Beel and De Quay (leader of the Dutch Union in 1940) amongst its most active leaders. Many of its proposals recalled elements of the unitarian ideology of the Dutch Union, and bore the mark of the official doctrine of the Catholic church, the most influential political institution in the south. Amongst these influences were immoderate royalism, pleas for social corporatism and a strengthening of the executive powers of government. The GOIWN was clearly not the voice of the militant resistance, but rather that of a socially conservative establishment hoping to direct the discontent of resisters and other protesters. The presence of several former Dutch Union figures obviated claims for a thorough purge. Internal opposition within the organisation criticised the social elitism of its leaders. Protest letters complained about the fact that the board of directors consisted of 'gentlemen with scientific titles and chief executives of Philips' (the light-bulb factory was a major economic and political focal point of the southern provinces).[5] Local units of the GOIWN proved surprisingly militant, denouncing the leniency of the purge and the widespread corruption of the Military Authority. Others even threatened to take justice into their own hands if 'carpetbaggers continued to climb over the backs of the resistance fighters'.[6] As the self-proclaimed representative of the resistance, the GOIWN also sought contact with the government-in-exile in London, where they were welcomed by the queen but ignored by the government. The cabinet reshuffle of February 1945 met some of their wishes: only four ministers of the former cabinet – those whose international experience was indispensable – remained en poste and seven seats were offered

[4] J. Van Oudenheusden and J. Verboom, Herstel- en vernieuwingsbeweging in het bevrijde zuiden. Eindhoven, 's Hertogenbosch en Waalwijk, 1944–1945 (Tilburg, 1977), and Henk Termeer, Het Geweten der Natie. De voormalige illegaliteit in het bevrijde Zuiden, september 1944–mei 1945 (Assen, 1994).
[5] For full reference, see Lagrou, 'Patriotten en Regenten'.
[6] 'Open brief inzake voedselroof door ambtenaren te Tilburg', S. D. District Tilburg, RIOD, GOIWN archive, 197E.

to personalities from the liberated south, including De Quay.[7] All ministers critical of the Military Authority administration were replaced by loyal supporters of General Kruls.

Immediately after the German surrender in Holland on 5 May 1945, the queen charged Willem Schermerhorn and Willem Drees, two politicians who had been politically active in the country throughout the occupation, with forming the new government. Only the traditional Calvinist Anti-Revolutionary Party (ARP) and the Dutch Communist Party (CPN) refused to support the government, the former because the new cabinet did not mirror the pre-war political balance and thus harmed the ARP, the latter because it did not sufficiently reflect post-war opinion and thus, supposedly, harmed the CPN's interests. The choice of Schermerhorn as prime minister rather than a pre-war politician was meant to demonstrate the 'renewal' of Dutch politics. Yet indications that a new wind was blowing through the country could be based only on general impressions. The last elections had been held in 1937 and forty seats of the pre-war parliament were vacant because their occupants were either dead or found guilty of collaboration by a purge committee (eight members of the fascist NSB and three from other parties).

Partly to make up for this lack of democratic control, resistance movements in the occupied part of the Netherlands formed an advisory body at the explicit demand of the London cabinet. The Grand Advisory Commission of the Underground (Grote Adviescommissie der Illegaliteit, the GAC), an institution vaguely comparable to the French Conseil Nationale de la Résistance, adopted its name in May 1945 but was more or less active from the summer of 1944 onwards.[8] In telegrams to the occupied country in February and June 1944, the government had asked for the creation of such a representative body specifically in order to avoid irregularities at the time of the liberation and to represent the government in the period between the liberation and its own arrival in the capital. The very fragmented resistance movements were at that time unable to agree on a common delegation and the government was forced to appoint its representatives on the continent unilaterally for the period of transition; yet even these representatives were ignored by the Military Authority when it moved to the north after the German surrender. More important still, the surrender followed secret negotiations between the Dutch government and the German authorities of

---

[7] See Duynstee and Bosmans, *Het kabinet Schermerhorn–Drees*, and De Jong, *Koninkrijk*, vol. Xa.

[8] See Sandberg, *Witboek*; and De Jong, *Koninkrijk*, vol. Xb, pp. 937–99, and vol. XII, pp. 200–8.

which the GAC was not even informed. The cease-fire agreement implied that the Allies promised not to attack the metropolitan area of the western part of the country across the great rivers (Rotterdam, The Hague, Amsterdam) before the final surrender, whilst the German army agreed to reduce repression and allow food drops into the starving occupied territory. The end of the war in the west was particularly unheroic. The cease-fire and subsequent surrender left the armed branches of the resistance without any combat record, and the council was even ignored in the negotiations that led to the surrender. In the most crucial phase, on which all preparations had been focused, the resistance movement was virtually absent. The role of the GAC would therefore start only with the end of the occupation.

Discussions on the role of the resistance in the post-war period consumed most of the council's attention in the period July 1944–May 1945. The debate was not just on the position to be adopted by the united resistance movements in post-war politics, but also on the principle of whether it should take any position at all. The left-wing movements pleaded strongly in favour of a political 'renewal'. The post-war world had to learn from the period that led to the crisis of the 1930s, to war and defeat, and the resistance movements were the only representatives of the shift of public opinion since 1937. 'Renewal' included in particular a transformation of party politics, that is, a rejection of pre-war fragmentation along denominational lines and a plea for the formation of a new broad Labour Party. The right wing argued against any changes in pre-war political ways, and particularly against any reduction of the role of religion in party politics. Resistance had been a struggle for the restoration of Dutch national traditions and values, with the different religions at the very core, against the interventions of a godless and totalitarian enemy. This line of conduct defended the interests of the Calvinist ARP and, in the south, the Catholic Party. Conservatives argued that if the resistance tried to play a political role it could lead to Polish, Greek or, especially, Belgian situations. 'Self-limitation' was the only proper attitude. The right wing imposed its line of conduct: the government could hardly be expected to grant an important role to the GAC if, for a start, this council could not even agree whether it wanted such a role. The council delivered one-third of the members of a National Advisory Commission, set up to control the government in the absence of a parliament and prepare for the composition of a new parliament. Yet even before the commission started functioning, the government had already decided to restore the parliament elected in 1937 by replacing the purged or deceased deputies with younger colleagues. The formal political role of the GAC was thereby aborted.

The 'restraint' of the Dutch resistance movement, which had allowed such an orderly transition – or, less euphemistically, their failure to play a significant role in the re-establishment of national political life – was a source of national pride and comparative self-satisfaction for the Dutch government. Prime Minister Schermerhorn declared 'that probably in no other European country has the resistance movement imposed such thoughtful restraint on itself as in the Netherlands'.[9] One former resistance newspaper concluded similarly: 'This proves once again that in the Netherlands the men of the resistance were not driven by political or other ambitions, but only by the desire of everyone on his own field, and as much as possible together, to combat the invader of our country and the oppressor of our people. Significantly, therefore, the character of resistance in our country has always been very different from that in, for example, Belgium or France.'[10] These Dutch moral authorities depicted a particularly dreadful vision of the events in Belgium in the autumn of 1944 and regularly referred to the scenario of unruly resistance troops 'in Belgium and Greece', thereby consciously assimilating one isolated unruly protest demonstration into a fully fledged civil war. Powerful leagues of resistance veterans could only degenerate into self-serving interest groups claiming special benefits, or, worse still, into subversive networks of rancorous dissenters, undermining public order and the national consensus.

The GAC was composed of Amsterdam-based leaders of national resistance organisations, mainly in fact editors of underground newspapers. Some organisations, like the relief organisation for draft-evaders, the LO, involved several thousands of contributors, but others, like the committee of university professors agitating against the Aryanisation of Dutch academic life, consisted of a mere handful of individuals. Except for the LO, which continued its relief action after the liberation, all movements had ceased their activities. Even when they continued to appear, former underground newspapers no longer involved the extensive networks of clandestine printing and distribution, operating instead with only a limited editorial staff. The representatives of former resistance movements united in the council were invested with the prestige of their wartime activities, but they no longer spoke from an organised basis that could control their actions. The resistance elites were moreover closely acquainted with government circles and they systematically supported a moderate and pro-government attitude.

In view of the evident frustration of the resistance in the Dutch

[9] Schermerhorn in *Mededelingenblad van de Grote Adviescommissie der Illegaliteit* 4 (12 Sep. 1945).
[10] 'Einde der illegaliteit?', *Je Maintiendrai*, 2 Nov. 1945.

mainland, rank-and-file radicalism was inevitably much stronger than in the south a few months earlier. Dozens of veterans' leagues sprang up all over the country, claiming a role in the purge or the crucial issue of distribution. The Amsterdam Union of Ex-Resistance Fighters, for example, argued in June 1945 that 'through the sudden outbreak of peace [*sic*] the great majority of the armed resistance movement has not been able to engage in the combat against the hated enemy . . . and through this course of events it has not had the chance to contribute on a large scale to the liberation of our country, as has for example been the case in France and Belgium . . . and that the great tension of the active resistance, pushed to the extreme, has as a consequence not been vented and has until now not had a chance to discharge itself gradually . . . and that the resistance in our country has not been able to acquire the prestige of the resistance movements in the aforementioned countries'.[11]

The alarmist attitude with which government and the GAC viewed the lack of 'restraint' in neighbouring countries was an enviable model to rank-and-file resistance enthusiasts. The problem of the containment of resistance troops after the end of the war and the liberation of the entire country in May 1945 was many times greater than it had been in the autumn of 1944 in the liberated south. Membership figures for the 'Internal Armed Forces' had exploded to reach 120,000 recruits, that is, 50 per cent more than the number of resistance volunteers in Belgium in September–October 1944, for a comparable population and in a situation of continuing warfare. Enrolment had inevitably been somewhat uncontrolled, and severe problems of discipline and internal conflicts were rife. Governmental anxieties concentrated particularly on the influx of communist resistance fighters. In the first months of 1946, resistance radicals posted threats against liberated collaborationists and a series of incidents revealed the extent to which former resistance groups still had access to weapons. Resistance groups in Groningen captured the local police chief in order to liberate arrested companions, whilst other groups, particularly in Velsen, operated in a grey zone of black-market activities and common criminality.

In general, violent incidents, let alone subversive or revolutionary events, were rare in the Netherlands. The activities of former resisters and their organisations were of the fairly conventional type of sociability so widespread in most other European countries: the veterans' league. The Netherlands had remained neutral in the First World War and had not been involved in any European war since the skirmishes of the Belgian revolution in 1830. The whole military panoply of medals and

---

[11] *Aan de Oude-Illegale Werkers te Amsterdam*, pamphlet (15 June 1945), ARA, cab. PM, box 128.

banners, parades and the laying of wreaths at monuments to the unknown soldier, which had impregnated civilian rituals in Belgium and France, was unfamiliar to the Dutch. After the Second World War, former resisters in the Netherlands felt a need to invent or emulate precisely this kind of social recognition and the type of manly, patriotic sociability offered by veterans' leagues cultivating the memory of the common combat, organised irrespective of the religious affiliation that determined the rest of Dutch social and cultural life. The 'Union of Former Resisters' of The Hague, for example, developed a dazzling associational life, with chess and table tennis tournaments, and stamp collectors' and pigeon fanciers' clubs. The most important of these veterans' leagues was of course the GOIWN, which had established its paternalist conception of a veterans' league in the south since the autumn of 1944. The GOIWN expanded successfully into the north of the country after May 1945. Most of the rural and popular membership of the LO–LKP joined, encouraged by its Calvinist leadership, which saw the conservative GOIWN as the lesser evil compared to the anarchic explosion of more militant leagues. The Grote Adviescommissie der Illegaliteit of the Amsterdam-based resistance elites could not ignore this success and it was forced to offer half its seats to GOIWN representatives. Yet the fears of the GAC's leaders, that it would be overtaken by a vigorous and conservative veterans' league, quickly led to its dissolution. In November 1945 it was decided that the council would only keep up the appearance of a representative resistance body until the first post-war elections of July 1946, and delegate all commemorative matters to an executive board.

This left the GOIWN alone with the task of imposing the 'restraint' deemed so characteristic of the Dutch resistance. In this challenge, it was seconded by the LO–LKP foundation, the post-war continuation of the resistance movement for draft-evaders. The LO–LKP, described in resistance circles as 'the vicars' club',[12] was profoundly conservative and averse to any form of militant veteranism. At the same time it was characterised by a paternalist concern with the reintegration of its veterans into a lawful society. This concern it shared with the other offspring of the LO, the Foundation 1940–1945 for resistance victims (see chapter 12), and the Dutch Popular Recovery for the former draft-evaders (see chapter 9). The LO–LKP foundation displayed a commemorative activism second only to that of the Communist Party and certainly much more influential. At opposite ends of the political spectrum the ARP and the CPN found themselves excluded from a

---

[12] Hilbrink, *De illegalen*, p. 46.

government of national unity. This government prided itself on the discipline of the national resistance, identified strongly with it and appropriated its merits. Communists and anti-revolutionaries alike wanted to prove that, even if they did not participate in the post-war government, their share in the wartime resistance had been disproportionately important. The LO–LKP created a film, a radio play, a two-volume commemorative book titled *The Great Command* and a national commemorative rally on the eve of the first post-war elections.

The Calvinists soon discovered that commemorative activism was a dangerous opposition strategy. Although criticism of the government was the explicit aim of the commemorative rally, its organisers lost control of events when militant veterans diverted its pious setting into a demonstration against the treatment of resistance veterans in general and appealed for a new veterans' radicalism. The LO–LKP leaders were increasingly aware of their alienation from a radical base, who saw their virtuous moderation as 'sterile resistance'. Meanwhile the GOIWN had to cope with a similar rank-and-file militancy describing it condescendingly as 'an afternoon tea party' or, worse, 'a corrupt gang, because it excludes all lefties and it is dominated by a small clique who only send invitations to one another'.[13] Both organisations were forced into ever closer co-operation to face criticism and marginalisation, merging their respective journals *De Vrije Stem* and *De Zwerver* in 1947. Increasingly unsuccessful in their ventures, both decided in the course of 1948 to draw a veil over their attempt to create a docile veterans' movement, delegating their activities to a phantom 'Consultative Commission of the Resistance'.

Rebellious former GOIWN sections and militant veterans' organisations of North and South Holland now gathered their efforts in a 'National Federal Council of the Former Dutch Resistance' (Nationale Federatieve Raad van het Voormalig Verzet Nederland). The new union, of 3,000–4,000 members, was innately anti-communist, forcing the communist members out of the local sections of North Holland, the only province where they still bore some weight. It was notoriously unpopular with all the post-war governments, at least until the late 1960s, and boycotted at all commemorative occasions. The national leaders were described as quarrel-mongers and whenever the government was forced to deal with representatives of the former resistance, particularly for international meetings, it systematically preferred the

---

[13] Respectively, *Verslag Vergadering GOIWN 23/11/46, AMELO* and *Verslag van de Vergadering VVN [Vereinigung der Verfolgten des Naziregimes] Den Haag, 8/12/47*, both in Ministerie van Binnenlandse Zaken, Archief Binnenlandse Veiligheidsdienst, The Hague, inzagemap GOIWN, CO2148804.

leaders of the organisation of resister-prisoners, ExPoGe, as I will describe in chapters 12 and 14. The only form of official recognition for the veterans came from Prince Bernhard, who cultivated his personal image as head of the Internal Armed Forces, and regularly received their delegations in his Soestdijk Palace. Bernhard also vigorously supported the main demand of the veterans: the creation of a special medal. This princely benevolence towards them was met by the veterans with an unswerving idolatry for prince and monarchy.

The ostracism suffered by the communists was many times worse. Excluded from all the leagues for resistance veterans in 1948, they were also excluded from the organisation of resister-prisoners in 1949, and one year later even from the board of the official charity for resistance victims, the Foundation 1940–1945, as we will see in chapter 12. They were left with no alternative but to unite communist resisters of all types, anti-fascists and war victims in one single organisation, United Resistance 1940–1945. It was the object of countless police and secret service investigations, and interdictions on all public demonstrations from most public authorities.

This organisational development was indispensable in clarifying the Dutch enigma of 'the incredible shrinking resistance'. Whereas in France and Belgium veterans' organisations were the main protagonists of commemoration and social policy, the Dutch situation is characterised by their virtual absence or, at least, the total ostracism in which they operated. By extension, this 'anti-veteranism' came to characterise the way in which Dutch post-war society dealt with labour conscripts and victims of persecution. It is crucial, in this analysis, to demonstrate that there was nothing 'natural' or 'spontaneous' about the weakness of veterans' movements in the Netherlands, as if Dutch veterans did not feel the urge to associate together and claim their legacy as their peers in Belgium and France had done. Veterans' movements were deliberately dismantled, boycotted, covered with moral opprobrium. Post-war governments, seconded by a loyal establishment of prominent resistance figures, both in the GAC and in GOIWN, strove for a political consensus concerning the commemoration of the resistance, and were very well aware of the disruptive effects of veterans' leagues claiming particular merits. The elimination of veterans' associations was indeed the precondition for the consensual commemorative policy pursued in matters such as memorials, medals, memoirs and exhibitions. As a result of the effective side-tracking of veterans' associations, one can indeed describe the commemoration of the resistance in the Netherlands as a coherent policy of memory. The main agent of this policy was the government, and more particularly the office of the prime minister. For

Goed mijn jongen – nu zullen wij het verder zelf wel doen.

3 'Well done, my boy – now we can handle it by ourselves.' From *Metro*, 26 July 1945. Photo, Netherlands Institute for War Documentation, Amsterdam.

as long as it existed, the GAC served as a counsellor or at least as a justification of this policy.

The dirigiste manner in which the erection of monuments was planned, regulated and centralised is an extraordinary example of the Dutch style of commemoration. On 15 October 1945 the Dutch Official Journal published a royal decree subjecting the erection of 'monuments of war and peace on the public road, or on places visible from the public road' to the approval of the minister of education, arts and the sciences.[14] The decree was the result of combined pressure from the

[14] See Wim Ramaker and Ben Van Bohemen, *Sta een ogenblik stil . . . Monumentenboek*

Dutch Circle of Sculptors and the GAC. At one of its first meetings after the liberation, the council had argued that monuments should not be erected without the approval of the local resistance. The GAC had to 'steer' commemorative initiatives to avoid 'bunglers with commercial goals' appropriating them for their own purposes. The representative of the resistance movement De Vrije Kunstenaar (The Free Artist) pleaded at the same meeting for 'some sort of patronage'. The council created a commission for 'publications, monuments and exhibitions' with some of the most prominent post-war Dutch intellectuals as members, such as the historian Jan Romijn, the novelist Anne De Vries and the columnist Simon Carmiggelt. In a press release, the commission invited the submission of commemorative initiatives concerning the resistance for its judgement, with the triple goal of ensuring a correct presentation of the resistance, of respect for regional and political equilibrium in the various components of the resistance, and finally of none of the initiators of resistance commemorations individually having a less than spotless war record.[15] The Dutch Circle of Sculptors had a corporatist motive for their intervention: the Netherlands had a some-what austere tradition over the erection of public monuments and consequently only a limited number of professional sculptors.[16] This situation contrasted with Belgium and France, where the First World War, and in France the war of 1870 before that, had engendered a large number of war memorials. One of the authorities of the Dutch Commis-sion even justified the need for regulation with a reference to 'the chaos that was created in Belgium and France where every hick-town [*negorij*] had some sugar-sweet monument, both in its form and its installation of poor taste'.[17] In any case, it was to be expected that the Second World War would lead to an explosive demand for memorials. It was in the best interests of the corporation of professional sculptors to prevent amateurs from reaping the harvest, and to organise the distribution of proliferating contracts. If every town and village were to organise contests for the best design, sculptors would be overwhelmed by work and exhaust their inspiration. Centralised regulation, setting aesthetic and professional

---

1940–1945 (Kampen, 1980), pp. 23–8, and the discussion in the cabinet meeting, *Notulen Ministerraad* (10 and 24 July and 11 Sep. 1945), ARA.

[15] Undated, RIOD, GAC archive, 184, 4B.

[16] *Concept-rondschrijven van de Nederlandsche Kring van Beeldhouwers*, n.d., RIOD, GAC archive, 184, 4B, and Louk Tilanus, 'Monumenten. Het herdenken in brons en steen van de jaren 1940–1945', in D. H. Schram and C. Geljon (eds.), *Overal sporen. De verwerking van de Tweede Wereldoorlog in literatuur en kunst* (Amsterdam, 1990), pp. 65–77.

[17] Bijhouwer, quoted in Ramaker and Van Bohemen, *Sta een ogenblik stil*, p. 23. See also the correspondence of Dr P. Gunning to the minister of education, arts and the sciences (12 June 1945), ACPM, 351.853, *monumenten*.

requirements, and a rational distribution of assignments would be in the best interests of all parties.

The eleven provincial commissions and one central commission brought together representatives from artistic and resistance circles and screened the designs, both on aesthetic grounds and for the content or message that they carried. The monument in Oss, for example, was rejected because it merely portrayed the afflictions of war without any elevating or edifying message.[18] The discussion in the council of ministers stipulated explicitly that monuments could be banned for reasons of local vulnerability, to avoid memorials which would keep traumatic or divisive local memories alive.[19] The most surprising aspect of this centralised regulation was its rigorous implementation. The first test case was the small town of Koog-aan-de-Zaan, where the memorial, financed through local subscription, was rejected on aesthetic grounds. The mayor of the town ignored the negative ruling of the minister, and the memorial was built and officially inaugurated on Liberation Day 1946. The minister responsible, Van der Leeuw, presented the issue to the cabinet meeting, pleading for the destruction of the memorial in order to avoid any precedent for tolerating violation of the regulation, 'despite the commotion that this was liable to cause in the local community'.[20] The memorial was demolished. To enforce the application and to avoid unfortunate incidents, all cabinet ministers were subsequently ordered to check first with the minister of education, arts and the sciences whether a memorial was authorised before agreeing to participate in an inauguration or a patronage committee.[21] The result of the systematic screening of all war memorials was a very high degree of uniformity in the 1,500 war memorials with which the country is now covered. This includes municipalities which were created on land retrieved from the sea as polders in the decades after the end of the war. References to military events were rare, and the pictorial repertoire was either symbolic, with a wealth of doves, torches and broken swastikas, or social realism, with 'the resisters' portrayed as anonymous common people, nameless heroes with whom the population could identify, rather than a personalised cult of identifiable heroes.[22] The initial idea, favoured by the queen, of a national monument to the resistance with the names of heroes carved in stone, was opposed by the GAC, as part of its general refusal of the distribution of medals (described below,

[18] Ramaker and Van Bohemen, *Sta een ogenblik stil*, p. 27.
[19] Minister Ringers, *Notulen Ministerraad* (11 Sep. 1945), ARA.
[20] *Notulen Ministerraad* (1 July 1946), ARA; and Ramaker and Van Bohemen, *Sta een ogenblik stil*, pp. 25–7.
[21] *Notulen Ministerraad* (17 June 1946), ARA.
[22] Tilanus, 'Monumenten', pp. 71–2.

pp. 74–7), and, as a result, Dutch war memorials, unlike all Belgian and French monuments, rarely carry lists of fallen citizens.[23]

The central commission, whose members formed a catalogue of institutional power in the Netherlands – queen and prince, ministers and generals, provincial commissioners, mayors of the major towns, religious authorities, university rectors, student organisations, resistance organisations, women's organisations, press and artists, trade unions and the major Dutch companies – carefully planned a national memorials policy. In February 1947, the commission reached a conclusion. The subject of the commemoration, according to this note, was 'the suffering of oppression, impotence in the face of supremacy, the irreparable grief that hit so many of us, the lawlessness, the material hardships and the fear for survival; the dogged resistance, the faith and pride of the powerless, the solidarity of all who knew that they were united against the oppressor, the inner certainty of victory, the hope for liberation, the final triumph and the deliverance of the heavy burden, all that we, as a people, want to transmit to posterity, as the experience of this dark epoch that almost ended our existence as a nation'.[24] The proposal for nine national memorials stressed the legacy of the Resistance. The national memorial (memorial 1) was to be on the dam in Amsterdam (see conclusion, pp. 292–5). National martyrdom was to be commemorated in Bloemendaal cemetery (2), where resistance victims of the *Sicherheitsdienst* had been buried and at the sites of the former concentration camps at Amersfoort, Vucht and Westerbork (3). This last choice was proposed 'because, on the one hand, these camps were a characteristic instrument of German oppression in its most cruel form, and, on the other hand, because they brought so much suffering and are so intimately linked to the resistance spirit of our people that a monument is fully justified'.[25] As will be discussed in chapter 11, for most of the inmates of these camps, Jews in transit to the centres of mass death, these sites were linked to the opposite of the 'Dutch resistance spirit'. Execution sites were to be commemorated by plaques with a shared heading. The remaining monuments were to honour the army on the Grebbeberg (4), the navy in Den Helder (5), the merchant navy in Rotterdam (6), the landing in Walcheren (7), the arrival of the queen in Eede (8) and the German capitulation in Wageningen (9). Dutch monuments commemorating the Second World War, from the modest

---

[23] Report, GAC meeting (12 Sep. and 17 Oct. 1945), RIOD, GAC archive, 184, 1C.
[24] Quotes in this paragraph are from note, Commissie voor Oorlogsgedenktekens (15 Feb. 1947), ACPM, 351.853, *monumenten*.
[25] Ibid.

local stele to the major national memorials, were the result of a planned, regularised and disciplined policy of formal and deliberate consensus.

The GAC made an unsuccessful attempt to establish similar control over other commemorative initiatives, one of which was publishing. Its commemorative commission deemed it improper for a commercial editor to reap financial benefits from the heroism and martyrdom of the resistance. One way of establishing an effective monopoly was through the office for paper distribution – paper was a strictly rationed commodity in the early post-war months – but the 'patrons' of commemoration discovered that it was legally impossible to prevent publications of fewer than 5,000 copies. The council further attempted to write an official history of the Resistance and quarrelled with Professor Posthumus who, although not a resistance figure, had been appointed by the minister of education, arts and the sciences to create the State Institute for War Documentation (Rijksinstituut voor Oorlogsdocumentatie, RIOD) with that aim. The relative independence achieved by the RIOD, combined with the unquestionably patriotic figure of Louis De Jong, successor to Posthumus and former broadcaster with Radio Oranje in London, eventually produced in the early 1960s a nationally broadcast series of television documentaries, and in the following two decades the fourteen-volume *History of the Kingdom of the Netherlands During World War II*. They are an example of national historiography that comes as close to an official history – including supervision committees and preliminary presentation of each volume to the approval of the minister – as can be achieved in Western Europe.

The GAC monitored the film industry. The screening in commercial cinemas of documentaries on the discovery of the concentration camps stirred a first debate.[26] Some members of the assembly disapproved of these showings as distasteful sensationalism that could not contribute in any positive way to the education of the Dutch public, but a majority finally favoured their wide distribution.[27] The council's commission also tried to create 'the film of the Resistance' and organised a contest for the best script.[28] The low moral calibre and frivolity of most responses was disappointing, including allusions to adultery, which the commission judged incompatible with the image of the resistance that it wanted to promote, and nothing came of the initiative.[29] Only the LO–LKP produced an official resistance film, one of four very schematically

---

[26] See the correspondence (June–July 1945) in RIOD, GAC archive, 184, 3A.
[27] Report, GAC meeting (18 July 1945), RIOD, GAC archive, 184, 1C.
[28] See the complete file in RIOD, GAC archive, 184, 4A.
[29] *Rapport van de door de GAC ingestelde Film-commissie*, n.d., ibid.

heroised films to appear in Dutch cinemas before 1950.[30] In March 1946 the GAC also set up an official national exhibition on the resistance, 'Combative Democracy':[31] rather than a historical reconstruction, it attempted a poetic-symbolic evocation – frescoes depicted an average Dutch family caught in the nets of the German occupier, with the resistance cutting open the ropes; the occupier as an octopus strangling the Netherlands in its tentacles; Seyss-Inquart (the Austrian Nazi appointed as governor during the German occupation) mowing down Dutch institutions with a scythe; etc. The exhibition attracted 50,000 visitors in Amsterdam, and later travelled to other major towns. Abstract, depersonalised and moralising, it was symbolic of the commemoration as seen by the GAC.

This brings us to the last aspect of Dutch commemoration of the resistance: medals. In a consistent policy of anonymous heroism, of a nation of heroes, where patriotic merit was collective and indivisible, honorary distinctions were disruptive, separating the brave from the rest. As can be seen from the situation in Belgium and France, special distinctions for resistance veterans were not only one of the main objectives of veterans' associations, they also, through the endless procedures and claims for revisions or improvements, provided inexhaustible fuel for the continued militancy of the associations. A ban on medals was a necessary complement to a ban on veterans' movements. Yet for the queen of the Netherlands, a special distinction for the heroes of the resistance was a personal affair. As the 'mother' of the resistance, who had appealed for action from her exile in London, she felt responsible for the award of a special mark of national recognition. If no special distinction was created, the queen would be forced to award the royal *Willemsorden*, traditionally presented to civil servants after years of loyal service – that is, she would be favouring civil servants who stayed in office through the occupation, rather than their colleagues who resigned and took to the resistance.[32] Prince Bernhard equally saw it as his personal task to honour the resistance heroes he had headed after the liberation for their wartime feats, and he willingly acted as a spokesman for the resistance veterans' claim for a medal.[33] According to the GAC, awarding medals would detract from the unselfishness of the resistance, it would create discord and envy in resistance ranks, and a fair distribu-

---

[30] See Egbert Barten, 'Toenemende Vrijheid. De verwerking van de Tweede Wereldoorlog in de Nederlandse speelfim', in Schram and Geljon, *Overal sporen*, pp. 213–51.

[31] See Romijn, *Snel, Streng en Rechtvaardig*, pp. 259–60.

[32] For the general context of decorations in the Netherlands, but which is rather unsatisfactory for World War II, see Kees Bruin, *Kroon op het Werk. Onderscheiden in het Koninkrijk der Nederlanden* (Amsterdam, 1989).

[33] Report, GAC meeting (25 Nov. 1945), RIOD, GAC archive, 184, 1C.

tion according to merit was, in principle, impossible. In more general terms, medals did not match the austerity of the years of reconstruction in the Netherlands. When the issue of decorations for Allied soldiers who had distinguished themselves in the liberation of the Netherlands was raised in cabinet, the minister of defence explained that it was up to the Allied forces to propose the names of their own soldiers, who would then be granted a medal by the Dutch government. Prime Minister Schermerhorn's reaction was indignant: 'So, in fact, the foreigners decorate themselves at our expense!'[34] A proposal to offer Allied soldiers a commemorative dish instead of a medal – not only cheaper, it was argued, but moreover good promotion for the Dutch ceramics industry in Delft – was finally withheld, 'because of the special circumstances'.[35]

Where the Dutch resisters were concerned, torn between royal insistence and rejection by the resistance establishment, the government pursued a hesitant and half-hearted policy. In May 1946, a royal decree establishing the Resistance Cross was published in the Official Journal, just in time for a first decoration ceremony on the first anniversary of the liberation.[36] The government intended to draw up a restrictive list of 250–500 'genuinely national figures' and initially, after a confidential survey, about eighty-five names of deceased heroes were selected for the first (posthumous) decoration round on Liberation Day 1946.[37] The government hoped to break the opposition of the GAC with this precedent, and to complete the list the following year with its approval. Meanwhile Prince Bernhard, frustrated in his role of resistance champion by the ban on medals, sought a way to circumvent it. Members of his staff suggested in November 1945 that he should award regular military medals to the volunteers of his 'Internal Armed Forces', instead of waiting for the establishment of a special resistance medal.[38] The implication of Bernhard's plan to get his medals in through the back door was that the decorations would be issued for the period served after the liberation, as volunteers in the Internal Armed Forces, and not in direct recognition of resistance merit. The former resistance organisations then announced that they would refuse a decoration which primarily rewarded last-minute volunteers and officers who discovered a

[34] *Notulen Ministerraad* (10 July 1945), ARA.
[35] Ibid. (25 Sep. 1945).
[36] *Koninklijk Besluit* (3 May 1946), *Staatsblad*, G107. See, for a short history of the Cross and complete biographical reference of the bearers, C. M. Schulten, *'Zeg mij aan wien ik toebehoor'. Het verzetskruis 1940–1945* (The Hague, 1993).
[37] *Nota Luit. Kol. Six voor MP* (13 Apr. 1946), ACPM, 351.855.23.
[38] Letter, Major Hoogwegen to Prince Bernhard (1 Nov. 1945), ACPM, 354.075.31–9.075.5; *Nota Six voor MP* (15 Apr. 1946), ibid., 351.855.23.

cause to fight for only once the war was over, that is, those who least deserved such a decoration.[39] Bernhard could not take the risk, and instead of distributing medals on a large scale he dispensed a series of military *Willemsorden* and foreign decorations amongst the upper echelons of his former Internal Armed Forces – a move which stirred up obvious envy.

The atmosphere was now poisoned, and General Koot, who was charged with drawing up a new list of candidates for decoration, informed the government at the start of 1948 that he was not able to present an acceptable list of a few hundred people in order of greatness, as required by the government, without stirring up a storm of protest.[40] The government moreover risked a public humiliation, since many on such a list would feel obliged to refuse the Resistance Cross rather than accept the injustice of this discriminatory selection. Koot proposed either to stop issuing Resistance Crosses or to do it on a vast scale, and, in view of the general feeling in resistance circles of a lack of national appreciation for their group, pleaded in favour of the latter solution. In his estimation the broader distribution of medals to all 'genuinely meritorious' resisters would involve 25,000–30,000 individuals.[41] Many prominent resisters, including even the former president of the GAC, supported Koot's plan.[42] The governmental policy had been ill thought-out: once it had decided to issue a resistance medal, it could not limit distribution to a fortunate few. The ministers of defence and of the interior defended the plan in cabinet but failed to convince their colleagues, and particularly Prime Minister Drees. He resorted to the GAC's earlier argument that a distribution of medals would initiate a competition for glory that would tarnish the collective ideal of the resistance. In addition to this earlier argument, there was a new reason to refuse medals: how could one avoid decorating communists, the new internal enemy?[43] Three communists had figured on the list of decorations of 1946, and in particular the posthumous Resistance Cross of

---

[39] Letter, L. G. Van de Haar to prime minister (n.d.); letter, Raad van Verzet to Major Hoogwegen (26 Sep. 1945): both in ACPM, 354.075.31–9.075.5.

[40] Letter, minister of the interior to all ministers (9 Jan. 1948); note, minister of the interior to all ministers (24 June 1948); *Request 43 verzetslieden aan MP* (24 May 1948), *Nota voor de MP* (29 Nov. 1948): all in ACPM, 354.075.31–9.

[41] Koot's estimate of 1948 corresponds with that of historian Lou De Jong thirty years later. See: De Jong, 'Verzet en Illegaliteit 1940–1945', *Mededelingen der Koninklijke Nederlandse Academie van Wetenschappen, afd. Letterkunde* (nieuwe reeks) 39, 6 (1976), pp. 203–21.

[42] Letter, J. J. Brutel De la Rivière to prime minister (3 June 1948), ACPM, 354.075.31–9.

[43] *Nota voor MR* (n.d.), with summary of cabinet meetings (19 Feb. 1946, 19 Jan. and 28 June 1948), ACPM, 354.075.31–911.

Hannie Schaft had been used by the party to promote its heroic past. Now that the government was trying to ostracise the Dutch communists it was impossible to endow them with fresh historical prestige by awarding medals. Even though the supporters of large-scale decoration pleaded that communists could be stripped of their medals on the ground of present 'national indignity' as soon as they received them on the grounds of past merit, the government foresaw only trouble. The stalemate of 1948 would later be presented as 'the decision of 1948' not to award new medals. A few posthumous decorations followed in the early 1950s, but all in all, no more than ninety-three individuals were awarded the Resistance Cross. In comparison, even the *compagnons de la liberation* were a large club. In 1948 Prince Bernhard had obtained a 'war-mobilisation cross' for the rank and file of his 'Internal Armed Forces', the name of which prevented all confusion with the resistance. The patriots and career soldiers of the National Federal Council of the Former Dutch Resistance (Nationale Federatieve Raad Voormalig Verzet Nederland), with the support of the prince, pursued a resistance medal relentlessly. Finally, in 1980, the Dutch government conceded a commemorative Resistance Cross (*verzetsherdenkingskruis*), awarded to about 15,500 applicants. The 1980 debate echoed the debate of the 1940s, and was to a large extent animated by the surviving protagonists of those past times. With thirty-five years' delay, the Netherlands caught up with the ribbons and medals of their southern neighbours.

Resistance veterans proved troublesome heroes in all three countries examined here. The more importance post-war society attached to the national resistance as an honour-saving device, the more divisive it was to identify a social group corresponding to it. The rest of this book will be concerned with an entirely different challenge to post-war societies. Populations displaced to Germany were a social group whose wartime experience had sharp geographical contours, but what honour-saving device was applicable to their case, the comprehensively heterogeneous, miserable and tragic individual trajectories that had left them behind on enemy territory?

Part II

Repatriating displaced populations from Germany

4   Displaced populations

At the end of the Second World War in Europe, the most difficult and urgent challenge facing the Allies was not material damage, but the human distress caused by the colossal mass migrations during seven years of warfare. More than eleven million Europeans were caught up in the territory of the former Third Reich, displaced by war and by the Nazi policies of population, labour and persecution. The total number for the entire European continent was some thirty million individuals, including eight million Soviet citizens and twelve million ethnic Germans.[1] These migrations were an important factor in the strategic planning of the Allied advance across German territory, initially because this human mass could block the entire German road system. The Allied command decreed a 'standstill' wherever groups or individuals would be liberated by the Allied armies. Spontaneous repatriation, on foot or by any 'borrowed' means of transport, would only add to the chaos in the German transportation network, hinder military operations, spread the risks of epidemics and preclude any systematic sorting of repatriates. Governments of liberated countries were ordered to leave the central organisation of the repatriation operations to the Supreme Headquarters of the Allied Expeditionary Forces (SHAEF). SHAEF in its turn delegated the humanitarian aspects of the 'displaced persons problem' to the United Nations Relief and Rehabilitation Administration (UNRRA), founded in November 1943.

During the first months, from May to September 1945, progress was spectacular. An average of 33,000 people were repatriated each day from the western occupation zones, with peaks of more than 100,000 per day in late May and early June. Two million Soviet citizens and 1,500,000 French citizens accounted for more than 60 per cent of the displaced persons (DPs) in the western zone, followed by 900,000

---

[1] See Wolfgang Jacobmeyer, *Vom Zwangsarbeiter zum heimatlosen Ausländer. Die Displaced Persons in Westdeutschland, 1945–1951* (Göttingen, 1985), particularly pp. 23–82, and Michael Marrus, *The Unwanted. European Refugees in the Twentieth Century* (Oxford, 1985), pp. 296–345.

Poles, 300,000 Belgians and the same number of Dutch. A hard core of 'unrepatriable' DPs would remain in camps until the early 1950s, particularly political refugees from Poland and the Baltic states and Jewish refugees from the post-war pogroms in Eastern Europe.[2]

The humanitarian activity of repatriating the dispersed populations of Europe at the end of the Second World War involved the greatest number of individuals ever undertaken, yet in the long term the practical problems of scale were the most soluble. The major miscalculation of the military planners was their underestimation of the operation's political and human implications. The screening of repatriates was a prime political problem with lasting consequences. The reception of a repatriated SS volunteer could not be the same as the welcome for the concentration camp survivor. Through the screening and classifying of repatriates a rudimentary 'Nuremberg of the masses' took place, to determine the experience of each and every repatriate. The human mass that war had left behind in the territory of the loser confronted the Allies and national governments with the lacerating political and ideological heritage of the Second World War in all its aspects.

The displaced populations of France, Belgium and the Netherlands presented significant differences, of which the most important cause lay with the German occupation policies, more particularly its policy regarding the early liberation or protracted detention of PoWs. After the invasion of Poland, the Wehrmacht planning staff outlined a deliberately discriminatory treatment of PoWs following the planned conquest of Western Europe, putting 'Germanic' populations ahead of 'non-Germanic' ones.

Under this policy, only 20,000 of the 300,000 soldiers in the Dutch army were taken to Germany in May 1940, and all were repatriated and demobilised in the first weeks of June.[3] Career soldiers and officers were obliged to swear an oath that they would not engage in any way in the struggle against Germany. Only five generals and about sixty officers, mostly in the colonial army and coincidentally on leave in the Netherlands, refused the oath and constituted themselves prisoners of war. After the discovery in May 1942 of the involvement of career officers in the activities of the OD, a movement of officers preparing for the establishment of a militia to prevent disturbances of public order after the liberation, fewer than 2,000 officers who had registered at the demand of the occupier were taken to Germany. Another year later, between May and August 1943, 240,000 Dutch soldiers were obliged to

---

[2] See Leonard Dinnerstein, *America and the Survivors of the Holocaust* (New York, 1982), and Mark Wyman, *DP. Europe's Displaced Persons, 1945–1951* (Cranbury, NJ, 1989).

[3] De Jong, *Koninkrijk*, vol. VIII, pp. 122–62.

register with the occupier and subjected to deportation and captivity if they could not prove that they were economically indispensable. Large-scale forgery of documents attesting to this condition and massive evasion – combined, no doubt, with a lack of perseverance by the occupier – kept the numbers of PoWs taken to Germany during this roundup at a mere 11,000. Of the 13,000 Dutch PoWs who were held captive (the overwhelming majority of them only from the summer of 1943 onwards), between 2,000 and 3,000 were liberated; 300–400 died in captivity, leaving about 10,000 PoWs to be repatriated in May 1945.[4] PoWs made up 4 per cent of the repatriated Dutch in the summer of 1945.

In Belgium, as early as 1939 treatment of PoWs was seen as a means to re-enact the *Flamenpolitik*, the deliberately divisive policy operated by the German authorities in their occupation of Belgium during the First World War. Its aim was to dismember Belgium into a Flemish part, to be annexed to Germany, and a Walloon part, to be ceded to France.[5] The Belgian army of 1939–40 consisted of 700,000 soldiers plus 200,000 reserve troops. During the eighteen days of the campaign, 50,000 soldiers were captured by the German troops, and in the generalised confusion following the capitulation 145,000 Flemish and 80,000 Walloon soldiers were taken to Germany.[6] On 5 June 1940, precisely one month after the invasion of Belgium, Hitler decided to liberate all Flemish PoWs except career soldiers, and to detain all PoWs from Brussels and the Walloon part except those able to prove their Flemish descent and those exercising a profession of public utility such as medical doctors, technicians, miners, farmers and public transport employees.[7] Flemish soldiers were screened by means of a rudimentary language test before a commission of Flemish activists who had collaborated with the German occupying forces during the First World War. At the end of 1941 almost 80,000 Francophone soldiers were still held captive, whilst over 100,000 Flemish soldiers had been liberated. About 13,000 PoWs were repatriated between 1941 and 1945 for strictly medical reasons, and 1,700 died in captivity, leaving more than 64,000 Belgian PoWs to return from captivity at the end of the war. PoWs made up 21.3 per cent of the Belgians repatriated in the summer of 1945.

Of the 1,850,000 French soldiers captured by the German army,

[4] Ibid., p. 866.
[5] De Jonghe, *Hitler en het politieke lot van België*, pp. 18–32.
[6] G. Hautecler, 'L'Origine et le nombre des prisonniers de guerre belges, 1940–1945', *Revue Internationale d'Histoire Militaire (Edition Belge)* (1970), pp. 949–61.
[7] Jan Velaers and Herman Van Goethem, *Leopold III. De Koning, het Land, de Oorlog* (Tielt, 1994), pp. 331 and 733.

1,500,000 were taken to Germany as PoWs.[8] Of these, 950,000 would only return five years later. Some of them, about 250,000, were employed as civil workers in Germany, but this transformation did not fundamentally alter their condition. The 550,000 PoWs who did return to France very gradually before the end of the war benefited from special liberation measures for specific categories, such as the sick, fathers of families or veterans of the Great War. Official figures state that 70,000 PoWs escaped, most of them in the chaotic first weeks after the invasion. PoWs made up 44 per cent of all French repatriates in the summer of 1945. If an exception is made for the annexed departments of Alsace and Lorraine, whose male population was drafted for the Wehrmacht and ended up in vast numbers as PoWs of the Red Army, PoWs made up more than half (51 per cent) of French repatriates in the summer of 1945.

The differing sizes of the PoWs groups in the three countries are a fundamental obstacle to comprehensive comparison. There is simply no measure between the dominant impact of captivity on French society – because of its sheer volume and duration – the negligible impact of the tiny group of Dutch PoWs and the regionally contrasting situation in Belgium. The very nature of captivity also sets this group apart from the other groups studied here. PoWs are a part of classic warfare, whilst this book is mostly concerned with the distinctive aspects of the Second World War which mark it out as an ideological conflict. This is not to say that the treatment of PoWs by Nazi Germany was free from ideological assumptions, or followed the canons of classic warfare as laid down in the Geneva convention, for example, to the letter. *Flamenpolitik* plus the systematic starvation and later economic mobilisation of Soviet PoWs and the bartering over the French PoWs prove the extent to which Nazi Germany used its mass of captured PoWs to impose its imperialist and racist views on the future of Europe. Yet for the purpose of comparing the specific impact of the Second World War on comparable social groups, the population of PoWs does not offer the required criteria. In dealing with the organisation and the impact of repatriation from Germany to France, PoWs will inevitably be a substantial part of the picture.

The transparency of the PoW population is not the least of the differences that set it apart from the groups we are mainly concerned with here: labour conscripts and survivors of the concentration camps. PoWs were registered, counted and internationally monitored, and enjoyed a status defined by international agreements. None of this

[8] Yves Durand, *La Captivité. Histoire des prisonniers de guerre français, 1939–1945* (Paris, 1980).

applied to the two other groups, as we will see in greater detail in the chapters devoted to each of them. The definition of labour conscripts was blurred by the uncertain distinction between voluntary economic migration to Germany and conscription on legal, socio-economic and moral-patriotic terms. This problem was particularly awkward in the Netherlands, where migrant workers had been encouraged to leave for Germany long before war broke out. Victims of Nazi persecution were even more problematical. As chapters 11 and 12 will illustrate, figures vary enormously, depending on their presentation, according to either the place of imprisonment (KZ survivors) or the reason for arrest (political prisoners). For Belgium, for example, the number of registered repatriated KZ survivors was 9,000. The number of officially recognised political prisoners was more than 40,000. The universe of Nazi persecution, with its diversity of places of detention and disciplinary regimes, its multiplicity of motives for persecution and reasons for arrest, simply cannot be defined in a single phrase. The description of these categories in all their variety, and the motives underlying the exclusion or inclusion of certain categories in the national martyrdom are precisely the object of this study. Statistics that appear in this paragraph are present merely for their phenomenological value, as an illustration and introduction to the problems of interpretation ahead.

Although the statistics for labour conscripts and victims of Nazi persecution lack the transparency that characterised the PoW population, they are – unlike the latter – the result of closely comparable Nazi policies in the three countries in this study. The mobilisation of continental European labour for the German war-machine was implemented far more ruthlessly in Eastern and Central Europe than in Northern and Western Europe. In Belgium, France and the Netherlands, however, as chapter 7 will demonstrate, this centrally planned policy used comparable means, following a concerted time-table and reaching comparable results. The policies of persecution against the ideological enemies of the Nazi occupier had different results in the three countries. This applies particularly to the Jewish population. Comparative figures of equal reliability are not available for repression of the resistance, and must take into account the different realities of anti-German resistance in the three countries. Yet the goals and means of the occupier, again following centralised and similar directives, were, unlike the policy regarding PoWs, very comparable.

A final problem in the comparison of repatriation statistics concerns the presentation of these statistics. One of the core problems of the repatriation, on which the following paragraphs will focus, was the categorisation of repatriates. The political desire to present the mass of repatriates as victims of Nazi Germany indiscriminately, or with only minor categorisation, led to the post-war publication of homogenised or adjusted statistics.

The comparison of Belgian statistics *post* and *ante* reveals this effort.[9] In November 1944, barely two months after the liberation, a survey by the Ministry of Public Health estimated the number of Belgians in Germany at 234,000, which included, among others, 17,915 concentration camp survivors, 62,039 PoWs, 79,000 labour conscripts, 10,353 arrested evaders of labour conscription and 54,141 voluntary workers.[10] In collaboration with the National Institute for Statistics, the Commission for Repatriation gathered slightly different statistics, of a total of 300,000 Belgians missing in Germany, including 140,000 workers (taking all types of engagement together) and 30,000 fugitive collaborators. In the official report published by the commission in July 1945, and in the statistics established by one of its officials in a semi-official publication of 1948, only three categories remain: KZ inmates, PoWs and workers. In the case of the workers, differences between recalcitrant convicts and volunteers have been effaced, and the group of collaborationist refugees has disappeared all together.

Dutch and French statistics do not distinguish between civil workers in Germany, and also drop collaborator refugees from their lists. For the Netherlands, the number of collaborators fleeing to Germany on 'mad Tuesday', the panic of 5 September 1944, when the liberation of the Netherlands seemed imminent, is estimated at 65,000. Even if many of them might have returned to the Netherlands in the following months, it still seems probable that a substantial number remained in Germany until May 1945, or fled a second time at the approach of the German surrender. Dutch repatriation authorities, like the Dutch government's policy towards war victims in general, shunned any form of categorisation.[11] The report of the Hondelink commission, which in December 1943 drafted the fundamental outline of all subsequent Dutch repatria-

---

[9] See the official *Rapport sur l'activité du Commissariat Belge au Rapatriement* (Brussels, 1945), and Maurice-Pierre Herremans, *Personnes Déplacées (rapatriés, disparus, refugiés)* (Ruisbroek, 1948).

[10] *Parlementaire Handelingen Kamer* (12 June 1945), pp. 507–10.

[11] See De Jong, *Koninkrijk*, vol. Xa, p. 203, and the Hondelink Report, annex 4, reproduced in G. F. Ferwerda, *Verslag van den Regeringscommissaris voor de repatriëring* (30 Oct. 1945), RIOD, DOC II, 663a. For the general context of the Dutch repatriation, see Dienke Hondius, *Terugkeer. Anti-semitisme in Nederland rond de bevrijding* (The Hague, 1990), and Connie Kristel, '"De Moeizame Terugkeer". De repatriëring van de Nederlandse overlevenden uit de Duitse concentratiekampen', in *Oorlogsdocumentatie '40–'45* 1 (Amsterdam, 1989), pp. 77–100; De Jong, *Koninkrijk*, vol. XII, pp. 110–30; and the final report by R. A. Wellema on the seach for missing persons (3 Dec. 1951), ARA, cab. PM, box 131.

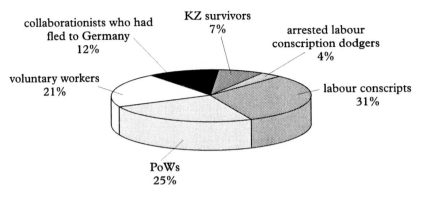

4.1.1 Repatriation to Belgium: estimates, 1944

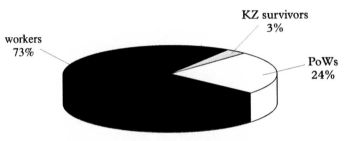

4.1.2 Repatriation to Belgium: government statistics, 1946

tion plans, made one important exception for the Jewish DPs. Its estimate of 400,000 Dutch DPs on German territory included 15,000 Jews, and, of the 140,000 Dutch DPs in German-occupied Poland, 'approximately half' were counted as Jews. This total of 85,000 Jews underestimated the total number of Jewish deportees up to the end of the war (107,000), but in a comparative perspective it was remarkable, since French and Belgian statistics hardly ever took the tragically distinctive fate of their Jewish DP population into account. Yet, when counting repatriates, barely 5,000 Jews survived their deportation, leaving particularly homogeneous repatriation statistics in the Netherlands. The overwhelming majority of Dutch repatriates were workers. The approximately 10,000 PoWs, 5,000 Jews and slightly more than 6,000 non-Jewish survivors of the concentration camps together made up less than 10 per cent of the approximately 280,000 Dutch repatriates from Germany.

The most blatant example of *post facto* politically framed statistics was produced in France by Henri Frénay in his *Bilan d'un effort*, published at

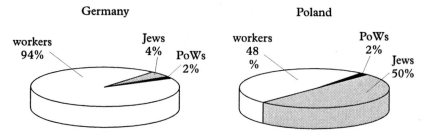

4.2.1 Repatriation to the Netherlands: estimates, December 1943

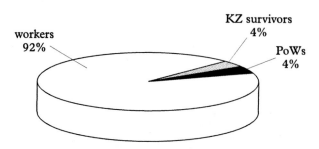

4.2.2 Repatriation to the Netherlands: reconstruction, 1946

the end of 1945. Repatriates were divided into four groups and counted in round – and, for the last group grossly inflated – figures: 950,000 PoWs, 700,000 workers, 300,000 deportees from the annexed departments of Alsace and Lorraine, and 200,000 'deportees', meaning, in this context, victims of Nazi persecution. Previous distinctions between all sorts of workers, as I will develop further in this text – volunteers, transformed PoWs, workers leaving under the *relève* or the STO – had been ironed out and the mass of victims had been homogenised.[12] Repatriation statistics read as a unilateral history of French martyrdom, as if drafted to fit post-war claims commissions.

On the whole, statistics on displaced populations do not offer a clear introduction to our subject of study; they present instead the multiplicity of problems of interpretation and commensurability that face the historian. If one were to establish a *displacement ratio*, that is, the share of

---

[12] For the earlier estimates, see *Enquête sur les problèmes techniques relatifs au retour des prisonniers et plus généralement à l'échange des populations déplacées* (Dec. 1942–Feb. 1943) and *Eléments statistiques relatifs aux prisonniers de guerre travailleurs et déportés français en Allemagne* (May 1944), both in AN, F9 3105. For the general context of the French repatriation, see Lewin, *Le Retour*; François Cochet, *Les Exclus de la victoire. Histoire des prisonniers de guerre, déportés et STO (1945–1985)* (Paris, 1992); and Annette Wieviorka, *Déportation et génocide. Entre la mémoire et l'oubli* (Paris, 1992).

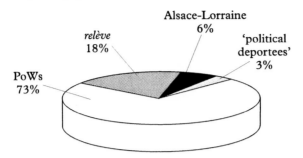

4.3.1 Repatriation to France: estimates, February 1943

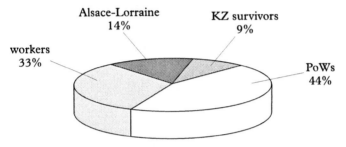

4.3.2 Repatriation to France: government statistics, November 1945

the total population of the three countries displaced to Germany, its value would be very relative. At the time of the German invasion, the Belgian population was 8,400,000, the Dutch population 8,730,000 and the French population 41,980,000. As shown above, the official number of repatriates for these three countries was 300,000 each for Belgium and the Netherlands and 2,150,000 for France. The total population of France is five times the total population of Belgium or of the Netherlands, whilst its DP population in Germany was seven times larger than the DP population in Germany of each of the two other countries. Expressed in percentages, this gives 3.57 per cent of the Belgian population, 3.43 per cent of the Dutch population and 5.12 per cent of the French population. As explained at the opening of our discussion on statistics, this difference can be explained by the retention of vast numbers of French PoWs in Germany, compared with the partial liberation of Belgian PoWs, the total liberation and later the marginal retrieval of Dutch PoWs. Other factors should not be neglected, however, particularly the exceptional situation of the densely populated annexed departments of Alsace and Lorraine (compared with the tiny population of Eupen-Malmédy, the strip of land annexed by Belgium in

1918 and taken back by Germany in 1940), the population of which was partly deported to Germany and forcibly enrolled in the Wehrmacht and partly dispersed as refugees in the rest of France. The relative value of the displacement ratio of DPs in Germany compared to the total population will become even clearer after a closer look at the Dutch situation, where, first, the repatriation ratio was exceptionally low compared with the deportation ratio, because of the volume of Jewish deportations (one-third of the total DP population on exit, 1.66 per cent on re-entry) and where, secondly, the DPs in Germany constituted only a minority of the total population displaced through the belated liberation.

5 The challenge to the post-war state: Belgium and the Netherlands

The sheer scale of the repatriation, its implications for social conditions in the economic reconstruction and its repercussions on the self-image of nations humiliated by an exodus that they had been unable to prevent turned it into a central political challenge. It constituted a test case for the post-war regimes – their organisational abilities, their efficiency and their inventiveness. It enabled governments that promised and projected a new welfare state, that studied Beveridge and domestic variants of plans for social security, to demonstrate the capacity of the state to take care of great numbers of destitute citizens. It magnified the problems of rationing and distribution. It presented the opportunity to experiment extensively with new technologies, most often put at their disposal by the Allies, in matters as varied as disease prevention (DDT, first used on a large scale by the Allies during the typhus epidemic in Naples in 1943) or transport (the air transport of ordinary citizens from Germany had a most spectacular effect, which repatriation officials were quick to exploit through a careful *mise en scène*).

It also created huge opportunities for political recruitment. The repatriates were politically virgin, cut off from political developments in their homeland since their departure – 1940 for the French prisoners of war, many of whom still lingered in the mental atmosphere of the first months of the Vichy regime at the time of their return; 1943–4 for most labour conscripts. They were unfamiliar with the emergence of a large resistance movement and massive public adherence to the Allied cause and to the governments-in-exile that took place after they left for Germany. They had lived in relative political isolation, whatever the claims by resistance movements of all kinds as to the influence of their propaganda amongst their fellow citizens in Germany. In any case, after the Allied landing and the ensuing liberation of France, Belgium and part of the Netherlands, their isolation was complete and they were cut off from the tumultuous start of post-war political life in their countries. Every repatriate moreover represented a whole string of relatives, neighbours, colleagues and friends, whose political sympathies might be affected by their appreciation of their government's repatriation efforts. Governments in general, and the repatriation officials in particular, paid special attention to their public image in brochures and speeches for repatriates, and in lengthy explanations of the repatriation policy in the domestic press.

The Dutch government-in-exile was the first to start preparing for repatriation. This it did in a most unpolitical spirit, recruiting Ferwerda, a technocrat from Unilever, to organise the whole operation. His under-estimation of the highly political nature of the repatriation was largely responsible for his subsequent failure and eventual dismissal once repatriation operations actually started. Local resistance movements, working in the field with the military authorities, refused to recognise the competence of plans elaborated by some technocrat in London. They thereby crystallised the political conflict that set the exile government in opposition to the queen, the military establishment and the resistance forces in the liberated south.

The Belgian commissioner for repatriation, former prime minister Van Zeeland, never hid his ambitions to relaunch his political career through his new charge, and he was indeed severely criticised for what others perceived as his abuse of his position as commissioner in furthering his personal popularity. In liberated Belgium the Catholic trade union, whose president had become minister for war victims, mobilised all its branches for the reintegration and recruitment of repatriates through its numerous charitable and social organisations. It also set up a crypto-Catholic Federation of Deported Workers. When the Catholic ministers went from government to opposition in August 1945, the Communist Party eagerly took their place as protector of the repatriates.

De Gaulle appointed a heavyweight chief of the French resistance, Henri Frénay, as commissioner for repatriation, and explicitly charged him with the task of winning back the mass of expatriates for the Free French cause from the firm hold laid on the French in Germany by Vichy, through its intensive propaganda. Frénay envisaged a political career as champion of a new resistance party, and counted on his merits as organiser of the repatriation to bolster his popularity. His political ambitions were on a collision course with the Communist Party and its self-proclaimed monopoly as the party of the resistance. The PCF was to use a public campaign denouncing the shortcomings of the repatriation to dislodge Frénay as a political rival. Similarly, Ferwerda and Van Zeeland were targets of less vigorous and less successful campaigns by communist organisations and publications which saw the repatriated masses as their own privileged hunting grounds.

The state of preparation for repatriation by the Belgian government in London and the cabinets that succeeded each other in Brussels until May 1945 augured badly for the Belgian citizens detained in Germany. The Belgian Commission for Repatriation was created only on 27 June 1944. Dutch and French preparations had started in the spring of 1943, followed by the nomination of repatriation officials in October and November 1943 respectively. According to a post-war report, the role of the first commissioner, the socialist Max Buset, was 'practically without influence', and preparations only really started after the nomination, on Belgian territory, of his successor Paul Van Zeeland as commissioner and plenipotentiary minister at the beginning of October 1944.[1] Van Zeeland's action inevitably suffered from the instability of Belgian post-war politics. Between the liberation in September 1944 and the repatriation in May 1945, two government investitures and three cabinet reshuffles took place. Four more governments followed in the twenty months that followed the start of the repatriation, with three different ministers in charge of war victims.

The Catholic former prime minister Paul Van Zeeland was a political heavyweight who had extensive powers at his disposal to address the Belgian backlog. Van Zeeland was fully aware of the political opportunities of his important charge. An official of the US Department of State observed after a meeting with him that

the former Prime Minister [Van Zeeland] intended to make the maximum political capital out of his present functions as commissioner for repatriation. He suggested that the successful repatriation under [his own] direction of several hundred thousand Belgian families would earn [him] a popularity which might dispel the cloud under which he resigned the premiership.[2]

Van Zeeland's fondness for public relations issues earned him the nickname of 'the interview-man' and the accusation that, apart from his famous interviews and the ostentatious display of the military and diplomatic competence of his commission, he had 'shown evidence of complete incompetence, he has not anticipated or organised anything'.[3] When compared with the meticulous plans presented by the Dutch and French exile governments, Van Zeeland's preparations do indeed appear slight; yet, when measured by its achievements, the Belgian repatriation operation was remarkably successful.

Statistical assessments provide one indication of the belated but effective Belgian effort. When promulgating the decree to create a

---

[1] Herremans, *Personnes Déplacées*, pp. 118–19.
[2] Interview with Paul Van Zeeland (18 Jan. 1945), US National Archives, Washington, DC, US Department of State Records, 855.00/1–1245.
[3] *Front* (8 July 1945) and *La Voix des Résistants* (15 Sep. 1945).

Commission for Repatriation on 27 June 1944, the Belgian minister of foreign affairs Paul-Henri Spaak expressed his fears that the number of displaced Belgians 'reaches or surpasses one million'.[4] Barely three months after the liberation, the National Institute for Statistics and the Ministry of Social Affairs were able to present statistics calculated on the basis of the German and Belgian administrative documentation that were more accurate than the outdated ones used for Dutch and French repatriation plans – which were calculated in exile and never replaced by more up-to-date figures. The actual speed of the repatriation operation itself was of course the most powerful test of efficiency. In mid-June 1945 an intermediate survey of the repatriation calculated that since late April 1945 on average 4,000–5,000 repatriates per day had arrived in Belgium, including some 7,000 concentration camp survivors.[5] According to the final statistics of SHAEF and UNRRA, 300,000 Belgians returned from Germany. Except for a small minority (2–3 per cent), they did so before August 1945.[6] Almost 600,000 foreigners transited through Belgium, of whom half a million were French. Dutch and, more surprisingly, French repatriates travelling through Belgium often referred to their excellent reception in Belgium, mentioning both the enthusiasm of the population and the efficiency of the repatriation system. Overall, they made very favourable comparisons with their reception in their own country.[7] The key to the Belgian success was improvisation. Traditionally, the Belgian state had always played a minor role in social policy, making up for the minimalist liberal concept of the State with a particularly intense, and officially subsidised, associational network. Compared with the dirigiste plans of Frénay and Ferwerda, Van Zeeland's organisation was similarly minimalist. DPs in Germany had been grouped according to their nationality, on the orders of SHAEF, and encouraged by air-dropped information flyers. Every Belgian DP received 100 Belgian francs for the journey and a simply worded, humane and moving pamphlet, preparing them psychologically for their return: 'Political Prisoners, Hostages, Deported Forced Workers returning from Germany: the entire country greets and welcomes you.'[8] Patriotic appeals were strangely absent, especially when

---

[4] *Rapport sur l'activité du Commissariat Belge*, pp. 115–16, and Herremans, *Personnes Déplacées*, p. 30.

[5] Report by a parliamentary delegation in Germany, *Parlementaire Handelingen Kamer* (12 June 1945), pp. 507–10.

[6] Jacobmeyer, *Zwangsarbeiter*, p. 60.

[7] Lewin, *Le Retour*, p. 290, n. 25; Annette Wieviorka, *Déportation*, p. 85; Kristel, 'Moeizame Terugkeer', pp. 90–1 and 95; Hondius, *Terugkeer*, pp. 87–90. See also *Rapport hebdomadaire de la Direction Départementale de la Haute-Saône*, 12 Apr. 1945, AN F9 3172.

[8] CEGES/SOMA, BrB 11/36.

compared with Frénay's prose in France, and the main thrust of the text was the reunion with their families, estranged through the long separation. In addition, repatriates received a brochure with useful addresses and organisations, most of which were private.[9]

Their reception was organised locally in repatriation centres established in schools, hospitals and other institutions, co-ordinated by the Ministry for War Victims, headed by the former president of the Catholic trade union, Pauwels. The collaboration of the Catholic politicians Van Zeeland and Pauwels certainly contributed to the important role played in the reception by Catholic organisations. Many repatriation centres were even established in Catholic institutions, using their unparalleled property and infrastructure resources. Other active charities included the Red Cross (which was neutral), Solidarity (the charity of the Independence Front) and the National Work for War Veterans.

Official measures helping the repatriates – in matters ranging from free medical aid, subsidised care in sanatoria, rationing of supplements of coal, food, clothing, special recuperation holidays, decrees regulating re-employment by their last employer before their departure to Germany, to the re-enrolment of students in universities and special conditions for taking official exams – were all taken on an *ad hoc* basis. The official administration involved and the qualifying criteria differed for each decree. As a rule, voluntary workers and former collaborationists were excluded from aid, but the procedures to identify the *bona fide* repatriates ranged from a declaration of good faith by the applicant to certificates issued by the local mayor or the local resistance organisation. Without the assistance of some social organisation, repatriates were lost in a bureaucratic forest. The political crisis that erupted in the summer of 1945, when King Leopold III also applied for repatriation, prolonged the confusion. The eviction of the Catholic royalists from the coalition government in August 1945 was accompanied by the liquidation of the Commission for Repatriation by Van Zeeland. His decision was criticised as irresponsibly premature (2–3 per cent of the Belgian DPs were still abroad and their repatriation would prove particularly arduous) and politically opportunistic (the commissioner had reaped the glory of the early mass repatriations and left the most difficult cases to his political adversaries).[10] The left-wing cabinet that succeeded the coalition of national unity promoted state intervention in social policy and during the course of 1946 established a comprehensive corpus of legislation in all matters regarding repatriates, as will be discussed in the following chapters.

[9] CEGES/SOMA, BrB 2151/3, BrB 2151/4 and BrB 18/54.
[10] Herremans, *Personnes Déplacées*, pp. 120–3.

The improvisation and voluntarism of private organisations could only be channelled to good effect because of the time factor. Belgium was liberated in September 1944 and during the eight further months of war the return of the expatriates was anxiously awaited and actively prepared. By the time the first repatriates entered the country the material situation was stabilised and public opinion was ready for compassion and charity. The arrival of repatriation convoys drew un-expected masses of families hoping for the return of a father, son, brother, mother, daughter or sister, interested bystanders and intrusive onlookers. Soon repatriation centres had to be fenced off and protected by the police to restrain the interested crowds.[11] Amongst UNRRA personnel, Belgium was relatively best represented.[12] The presence of Belgian team members in Germany had a very positive effect on the Belgian repatriates and convinced them of their government's concern for their situation. More important still was the presence of Belgian troops in British ranks. In complete violation of the prior agreements that all repatriation operations had to be centrally channelled through SHAEF and UNRRA, from March 1945 onwards, the British 21st army group dealt directly with Belgian military authorities to siphon off the masses of Belgian DPs encumbering the advance of the troops in northern Germany.[13] This whole-hearted improvisation again hastened the homecoming of thousands of Belgian citizens.

Dutch repatriation planners prided themselves on their meticulous preparations. Starting the operation in April 1943 through the creation of an interdepartmental commission, and nominating in October of the same year the dynamic manager G. F. Ferwerda as head of a Commis-sion for Repatriation, the Dutch government-in-exile was a precursor in planning the repatriation. With respect to the uncertain information available to exile governments, the Hondelink Report of December 1943 was an impressive achievement. Ferwerda was nominated as president of UNRRA's Technical Subcommittee for Displaced Persons. Belgian officials declared that his 'name had become synonymous with repatriation' in the exile community in London.[14] Yet the Dutch repatriation was a failure. Dutch repatriates returned home days and weeks later then their French and Belgian counterparts. In the midst of the operation, a conflict between Ferwerda and his London-based operation and Kruls, the military commander in the Netherlands,

[11] Eugene Coine, *Kajottersweerstand in Duitschland* (n.p., n.d. [1946]), p. 85.
[12] See figures in Jacobmeyer, *Zwangsarbeiter*, pp. 34 and 260.
[13] Ibid., pp. 40 and 62–3.
[14] Herremans, *Personnes Déplacées*, p. 126.

exploded, resulting in the dismissal of the former. Ferwerda's plans were rightly accused of excessive bureaucratic rigidity. More to the point, however, Ferwerda was the victim of the same time factor that had saved Van Zeeland.

No scenario could have foreseen the failure of the Allied assault on the Rhine in October 1944, cutting the Dutch territory in two and freezing the front line in a deadlock that would only be lifted by the German surrender in May 1945. Allied troops reached Berlin and the Elbe before they reached Amsterdam and the Waal. Unlike the Belgian government, the Dutch cabinet was forced to stay in London in a prolonged exile, and to entrust the administration of the liberated territory to a Military Authority responsible for all civil matters, under the hierarchy of the Allied military command rather than its own government. The Dutch chief of the Military Authority, the young General H. J. Kruls, exploited his autonomy to the maximum, drawing on the aversion for the London cabinet shown in the Catholic south and by the queen. Kruls' extensive powers were doomed to frustrate the London ministers, who were condemned to continue their paperwork preparations in London, whilst in the liberated territory their directives were high-handedly disregarded on the grounds of 'operational necessity'.

Management of the repatriation was a central focus of conflict. Ferwerda and his officers were refused entry into the liberated territory. Instead of establishing close co-operation, the London offices and the military forces in the field embarked on a disastrous competition for repatriates. Ferwerda's commission had worked long months in exile to establish lists of missing persons in the homeland, and transmitted them to the Allied authorities. Meanwhile, thousands of Dutch DPs were returning to the liberated zone; but the Military Authority, who registered the returns, refused to transmit the names of the repatriates to London, thus causing a tremendous loss of time and credibility in the eyes of the Allies, who were supposed to search for people who might very well have returned to the Dutch south weeks or months before. The Dutch Red Cross, also using logistics in the field, tried to develop a repatriation activity of its own rather than co-operating with either of the other two contenders. Abroad, the Dutch blundering created an unfortunate impression. The Military Authority, the Commission for Repatriation and the Ministry for Social Affairs each had travelling charity ambassadors in Great Britain and the United States raising funds and collecting food and clothing for the Dutch DPs.[15] Each of the three thwarted the others' activities and created permanent confusion in

---

[15] See the file *Regeringscommissariaat voor bijzondere hulpverlening*, ARA, cab. PM, box 130.

the minds of potential donors. When the British government refused to make strained transport facilities available for food collections, the Dutch fund-raisers nevertheless continued to accumulate stocks in New York and London, and rumours started to circulate that donations for the Netherlands never reached their destination.

Once the flood of repatriates was out on the German roads in April–May 1945, the whole Dutch repatriation organisation collapsed. Ferwerda disposed of detailed intelligence on repatriates and elaborate plans to transport them home, but he had no ambulances or trucks, not even to bring home the Dutch concentration camp survivors. The Military Authority had requisitioned the entire transport system, but it was wholly unprepared for the task of repatriating hundreds of thousands of civilians. Pressured by local resistance organisations, Kruls set up commando-style rescue operations for well-known resistance personalities, but these spectacular and isolated actions inevitably only intensified the chaos. At the end of May, the desperate situation forced the minister to sack Ferwerda and trust the entire repatriation operation to the Military Authority. In the public campaign against Ferwerda's commissionership, resistance organisations played a major role. In the south, the Military Authority had co-opted the Community of Former Illegal Workers (GIOWN) and the volunteer militia Dutch Internal Armed Forces, headed by the intemperate Prince Bernhard, and manipulated GIOWN's support for its cause. Yet also in the rest of the country, immediately after the German surrender, the united resistance cried out against the shortcomings of the repatriation.[16] All attention was focused on the delay in repatriating arrested Dutch resistance fighters from German concentration camps. Dutch survivors in the camps were indeed repatriated several weeks later than the French and Belgian inmates and, in contrast, no Dutch officials or military came forward to care for them in the weeks following their liberation. The Dutch liberated in Buchenwald were repatriated by an American convoy four weeks after their liberation, leaving the sick behind. The 900 Dutch evacuated to Sweden, 340 of whom escaped Auschwitz and Ravensbrück, were repatriated, by boat, only in the course of August. In view of the death rate of 20 per cent amongst the severely weakened survivors in the weeks following their liberation, the consequences of this delay were particularly tragic.[17] Other groups of repatriates suffered the same delay, with less grave consequences, but with a similar feeling of abandonment by their government. The statistics for the repatriation

[16] *Mededelingenblad GAC*, 2 and 3 (22 and 29 Aug. 1945), RIOD, GAC archive, 184, 2C. See also GAC archive 15A, and ARA, cab. PM, box 132.
[17] Jacobmeyer, *Zwangsarbeiter*, p. 43.

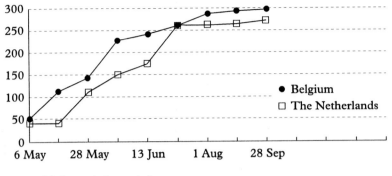

5.1 A retarded repatriation

from the western occupation zone clearly show the effects of the Dutch upheaval: only at the start of July did the Dutch reach the level of Belgium, despite the greater facilities for self-repatriation along the German–Dutch border.

For the repatriation of Dutch DPs from the Soviet occupation zone, the backlog was even worse. Official Dutch anti-communism and the belated diplomatic recognition by the Netherlands of the Soviet Union in 1942 – achieved only after Allied pressure – had never allowed for the establishment of normalised relations. The conclusion by France and Belgium of mutual repatriation agreements with the Soviet Union and the consequent presence of Soviet repatriation officers in Brussels and Paris, combined with the presence of communist ministers in the French and Belgian governments, magnified the comparative disadvantage of the Dutch. Bilateral negotiations over the repatriation of Dutch citizens from the Soviet Union and Soviet citizens from the Netherlands would drag on for years and reinforce the popular impression of Dutch neglect of repatriates, compared with French and Belgian solicitude.[18]

The ineffective Dutch repatriation was the subject of a long political controversy. In January 1946, the government charged its information service to organise a public defence of the repatriation policy. After a preliminary inquiry, the information service recommended total silence on the subject, since a public defence of an indefensible failure could only worsen the government's image.[19] 'It was all too obvious', wrote

[18] See ARA, cab. PM, box 132, and Ingrid Harms, 'Russische vrouwen in Nederland. Portret van de verloren dochters van vader Stalin', *Vrij Nederland* (1 Mar. 1986), pp. 2–36.
[19] *Rapport Regeringsdienst Oog en Oor* (10 Jan. 1946) and *Regeringsvoorlichtingsdienst* (14 Jan. 1946), both in ARA, cab. PM, box 132.

one information officer, 'that there had been no co-ordination in the operation and that not all the officials concerned were competent in the matter.'[20] There was proof of financial carelessness, and several cases of fraud were taken to the military court after repeated press allegations. The sharp contrast between the reception in 1946 of repatriates from the Dutch Indies and the reception of Dutch repatriates from Germany one year earlier would further sharpen the feelings of injustice experienced by the latter. Despite the ensuing policy of official silence, public protest continued on one particular subject, voicing moral indignation over the abandonment of Dutch resistance fighters in German concentration camps.[21] In 1952 the final report of the parliamentary commission of investigation concentrated on the same issue, condemning in merciless terms the internal rivalries and bureaucratic rigidity of the repatriation officials.[22] The commission deplored the failure to implement militarisation of the repatriation earlier, thereby throwing a probably undeservedly heavy share of the blame on Ferwerda. The most important conclusion for what follows is the feeling of abandonment and official neglect experienced by Dutch repatriates, an abandonment and neglect that were denounced in the post-war years on behalf of only a tiny, albeit particularly vulnerable and victimised, proportion of Dutch DPs. And the repatriation, for most Dutch DPs, was only a preparation for the letdown of coming home.

The most important consequence of the strategic stalemate on the Rhine front was that, for most of the Dutch territory, liberation and repatriation coincided. Instead of eight months of liberty, reconstruction and preparation for the homecoming of the DPs, the Dutch heartland suffered the hardest winter of the occupation, with bombing, flooding and famine. The last eight months of the occupation took a higher toll of the Dutch population than the four previous years combined. The Dutch historian De Jong describes the 'hunger winter', as the winter of 1944–5 is known in the Netherlands, as 'one of the major calamities in Dutch history'.[23] Before the start of Allied food drops, the *weekly* calorie ration fell below the minimum *daily* calorie ration recommended by SHAEF. About 16,000 people died of starvation, and in May 1945 a quarter of a million were estimated to be suffering from malnutrition

---

[20] Report, J. H. Kerremans (12 Feb. 1946), ibid. See also letter, minister of justice to prime minister (20 Apr. and 22 May 1946), ibid.

[21] See Ed De Neve, *De Glorieuzen* (Enschede, 1946), and De Neve, *Indien de Nederlandse regering te London . . .* (brochure) (Amsterdam, 1947). For press reactions, see RIOD, KB II, 1171 en DOC I, De Neve.

[22] *Enquêtecommissie Regeringsbeleid 1940–1945* (The Hague, 1952), vol. VI, a–c.

[23] De Jong, *Koninkrijk*, vol. Xb, pp. 160–279, 1440–9; vol. XII, pp. 259, 261, 268, 298.

pathologies.[24] Half a million people lost their houses, and a million and a half lived in damaged accommodation. Eleven per cent of farmland was flooded and 900 bridges were destroyed as well as half of the trucks and river craft and over 80 per cent of railway equipment. Shoes and clothing were so scarce that many city children went barefoot.

The Netherlands in May 1945 had no need to import human distress from Germany. More importantly, displaced persons of all sorts made up almost a quarter of the whole population: 850,000 civilians had fled the theatre of war, 200,000 were evacuated from flooded land, tens of thousands had left the cities for the countryside in search of food, 350,000 workers were in hiding to escape deportation to Germany and 60,000 Dutch citizens had sought refuge in Belgium and France. In the colonies 80,000 Dutch citizens were held prisoner in Japanese camps. The 300,000 Dutch repatriates from Germany were only one of several groups of refugees, estimated by De Jong at 1,900,000 for all categories combined.

In the generalised distress that hit Dutch society at the time of the liberation, everything imaginable was in short supply. At the end of May, the minister of social affairs was so alarmed by the total lack of elementary equipment for the refugees and the homeless that he suggested official military requisitioning of household goods that had been spared by the war.[25] In this context, there was certainly also a shortage of compassion for the extraordinary and extra-territorial suffering experienced by Dutch DPs in Germany. Dutch public opinion in May 1945 had no energy or enthusiasm to spare for welcome parades and outbursts of charity.

After the surrender of the German troops in the Netherlands, the organisers of the relief operations immediately faced a situation of emergency, without any transition period. Many of the ingredients for the catastrophe of the repatriation were again present. The government administration had to organise its return home from London. Even though the Gerbrandy cabinet remained in charge of current affairs until 27 June 1945, Schermerhorn and Drees, two politicians who had lived through the occupation in the homeland, were appointed on the very day of the German surrender to form a new cabinet. Meanwhile the Ministries of Social Affairs and the Interior tried to set up a network of district offices for War Victims (Districtsbureau Verzorging Oorlogs-

---

[24] The figure of 16,000 is Gerard Trienekens's revision of De Jong's official figure of 22,000: Trienekens, *Tussen ons volk en de honger. De voedselvoorziening, 1940–1945* (Utrecht, 1985), pp. 398–407. See also his *Voedsel en honger in Oorlogstijd, 1940–1945. Misleiding, mythe en werkelijkheid* (Utrecht, 1995).

[25] Letter, Minister Wijffels to prime minister (26 May 1945), ARA, cab. PM, box 130.

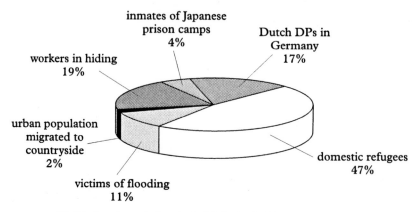

inmates of Japanese
prison camps
4%

Dutch DPs in
Germany
17%

workers in hiding
19%

urban population
migrated to
countryside
2%

domestic refugees
47%

victims of flooding
11%

5.2 Displaced populations in the Netherlands, May 1945

slachtoffers) to operate at a local level. The Military Authority saw its operation zone extended to the whole of the Dutch territory, and in the framework of its task of restoring public order it took charge of rationing and emergency relief, thereby bypassing the government's district offices. The local resistance had tried to set up a relief organisation of its own, the Dutch Popular Recovery (Nederlands Volksherstel), whereby local resistance groups of the LO (the rural and Christian organisation that had organised assistance to workers in hiding) co-operated with local social agencies such as the poor relief for integrated action at the time of the liberation. To make matters worse, even the Red Cross decided to repeat its accomplishment of adding confusion to the repatriation, by putting its oar into domestic relief under the aegis of the Aid Action Red Cross.

As a result, the relief was 'a mess'.[26] The government's district offices, the Aid Action of the Red Cross and the Popular Recovery worked in parallel to each other, but in total isolation. In many localities the Popular Recovery even succeeded in presenting two competing aid committees: one centrally appointed from The Hague and integrating the local poor relief, and one locally founded emanation of the LO resistance workers. Predictably, the consequence was an atmosphere of arbitrariness, official neglect and, worse still, corruption that dominated public opinion. The political opposition did not fail to voice these accusations in parliament.[27] In February 1946, more than six months after the repatriation, the minister of the interior and the minister of

---

[26] Report GAC, n.d., RIOD, GAC archive, 1843B.
[27] *Handelingen van de Tweede Kamer der Voorlopige Staten Generaal* (9 Jan. 1946), pp. 201–2.

social affairs issued a common circular deploring the lack of the most elementary co-ordination between the different providers of assistance and calling for a thorough reorganisation, thus acknowledging the protracted distress of the relief organisation.[28]

In addition to the chaos of actions for relief and charity for repatriates, the Dutch government refused to co-operate with organisations of mutual aid set up by the repatriates themselves. Compared with the crucial role of associations of repatriates in Belgium on a voluntary and spontaneous basis and their officially planned and financed role in France, this is a most striking difference. Faced with widespread destitution, the government decreed that

an apportionment of the landscape of war victims must be avoided at all costs. Naming certain categories in any regulation in this matter will inevitably cause new categories to claim their rights. As soon as the principle of individual assistance is given up, a chain reaction of claims citing the acquired rights of others will cause an explosion of the budget.[29]

Social policy and national recognition were therefore to be separated. This categorical refusal also found roots in the overall rejection of 'veteranism' described in chapter 3. The Dutch government ignored and boycotted all pressure groups, uniting not only veterans but also war victims, as the following chapters will describe in detail. Any group claiming special merit or special suffering not only threatened to be a burden on the national budget; it also endangered the national consensus that heroism and martyrdom had been the collective experience of the Dutch people.

Dutch repatriates came home under grossly unfavourable material and psychological conditions. The coincidence of liberation and repatriation, across most of the national territory, meant the collapse of all the carefully prepared plans. Moreover, the domestic distress caused by the 'hunger winter' overshadowed the extra-territorial sufferings of expatriates in Germany, regardless of the conditions of their detention there. Both in the organisation of the repatriation itself and in the organisation of reception and relief on Dutch soil, ambitious dirigiste plans – as elaborated by Ferwerda or projected in the national network of government agencies for war victims – clashed with competing initiatives from various sides, notably the Military Authority, the resistance organisations and private charity. There was no allowance for improvisation and voluntarism. Whereas the previous years of occupation had been characterised by the suffering of specific groups – communists, deported workers, Jews, etc. – now famine, large-scale material

---

[28] ARA, cab. PM, box 130.
[29] *Notitie voor S. van V.* (17 Jan. 1946), ARA, cab. PM, box 127.

De Hun in Holland.

„Nu pas kunnen ze zeggen, dat hun het water tot de lippen komt"

4 'The Hun in Holland': 'Now they can rightly say they're up to their necks in the water.' From *De Vrije Stem* (journal of Gemeenschap Oud-Illegale Werkers Nederland) 5 (28 April 1945). Photo, Netherlands Institute for War Documentation, Amsterdam.

destruction and massive migrations of civilians to escape hunger, flooding and Allied bombing caused indiscriminate suffering. The very collective nature of the hardship imposed by war in the Netherlands during the last months of occupation, and the generalised scarcity of all forms of re-equipment, created a post-war situation that diverged considerably from Belgium and France and that would influence all subsequent developments.

Despite this fundamental difference caused by the hazards of military strategy, the challenge to the post-war state had been the same for Belgium and the Netherlands. The governments-in-exile faced the problem of preparing the repatriation of hundreds of thousands of their citizens from a distance. In the occupied country, the occupation authorities had refused to envisage their own defeat and consequently had not prepared the return of the populations they held hostage in Germany. The Dutch government-in-exile actively planned to cope with the problem in London, the Belgian government was granted eight months of improvisation in liberated Brussels, but the central challenge was this: to create an entire infrastructure out of nothing. The problem was posed in terms of social policy and relief. The Belgian commissioner focused on co-ordinating private charitable initiatives, and the Dutch commissioner was a technocrat and manager without any previous political experience. Political conflicts emerged only once the repatriation started. Here lies the major difference with the situation in France, where the central challenge to the post-war state was not to create something out of nothing, but to recapture the infrastructure set up by Vichy and to compete for the political allegiance of expatriates who had been at the heart of the ideological endeavours of the *Etat Français* it was preparing to replace. The existence of Vichy, and the central role played by expatriates in the conflict between State collaboration and the Free French, oblige us to return much further back in time and to examine the course of the political and ideological contest between Pétain and De Gaulle, and between two concepts of population displacement: Exile and Deportation.

6   Pétain's exiles and De Gaulle's deportees

Nowhere was the repatriation more central to the post-war political challenges than in France. Unlike Belgium and the Netherlands, where pre-war governments prepared for their return to power after the liberation, the French National Liberation Committee had to struggle for legitimacy with Vichy, the constitutionally legitimate heir of the pre-war Third Republic.

The Vichy regime (and Pétain personally) had turned the exile of 1,500,000 French soldiers into a cornerstone of its ideology of atonement and resurrection, and, more unfortunately still, into a touchstone of the effectiveness of its policy of collaboration.[1] The fate of the French army after its collapse in May and June 1940 had been a major argument for Marshal Pétain, commander-in-chief, to assume the political responsibility of the armistice and the subsequent 'French State', much in the way that the Belgian King Leopold had legitimised his surrender and his refusal to leave the country after the defeat. Philippe Pétain, the soldier-hero of the Great War, acted as the father of his troops, the saviour and protector from further useless bloodshed. One of the immediate consequences of national collaboration with the victors had been that Vichy took responsibility for the protection of its PoWs under the terms of the Geneva convention, instead of reverting to diplomatic representation by a neutral nation, as all other defeated countries had done. As the next chapter will discuss, the regime engaged in lengthy and wearisome transactions to liberate PoWs by promoting the voluntary departure of three civil workers in return for each liberated PoW, the so-called *relève* or relief. It suggested the 'transformation' of PoWs into civil workers, thereby voluntarily abandoning the protection of the Geneva convention. Later, it even defended and enforced the deportation of French workers to Germany. The results of this policy were catastrophic for Vichy's popularity, and for the French PoWs. Whereas Dutch and Flemish PoWs were mostly liberated during the first year of war by

[1] Durand, *La Captivité*, and Durand, *La Vie Quotidienne des prisonniers de guerre dans les stalags, les oflags et les commandos 1939–1945* (Paris, 1987).

unilateral German decision, more than two-thirds of the French PoWs remained captive until the very end of the war. The exile of the French PoWs – who were joined later by hundreds of thousands of civil workers, victims of a generalised labour conscription promoted by Vichy – was a powerful demonstration of the failure of the National Revolution's core values. Despite extensive collaboration, Vichy was unable to retain young French men in their domestic occupations, *Travail*, with their families, *Famille*, or in their country, *Patrie*.

The only political advantage that Vichy drew from assuming the protection of its PoWs was the possibility of organising political propaganda for its 'National Revolution' in the stalags (camps for soldiers) and oflags (camps for officers) through its mission in Berlin, the Scapini mission, which set up Pétain groups, meetings and journals amongst French PoWs. Vichy could deliver its own postal parcels to French prisoners without passing through the International Red Cross, and it made the most of this opportunity for propaganda through these famous *colis Pétain*, containing tinned food, tobacco and official propaganda. Throughout the war the PoWs continued to occupy a central place in Pétain's speeches. In the ideological discourse of the 'National Revolution' the hardships of captivity came to symbolise the theme of national redemption through sacrifice. The asceticism of prison life, separation and forced celibacy, rudimentary meals, manual work and male comradeship were idealised in pseudo-religious terms reminiscent of monasticism or the lay-apostolate of Catholic Action. A whole generation of young French men was physically purged of the weaknesses, temptations and perversions of pre-war France, which Vichy denounced so vehemently as the causes of defeat, and thus prepared for the rebirth of a nation built on moral austerity and spartan discipline. Scapini himself personified his mission, as a hero of the Great War who had lost his sight in battle. In February 1943, Vichy set up a similar mission, headed by Bruneton, for French labour conscripts in Germany.[2]

In France itself the families of prisoners and the repatriates who were allowed to return in dribs and drabs were the object of endless solicitude. Vichy set up a vast social programme, both in its own southern zone and in the occupied northern zone, incorporating on the one hand pro-Vichy charitable organisations for PoWs, such as the 'Prisoner's Family', a branch of the Secours National, the French Red Cross, the federation of prisoners' spouses, prisoners' chaplains, associations of repatriated prisoners and more militant fascist formations such as the

[2] See Henri Rousso, *Pétain et la fin de la collaboration. Simaringen, 1944–1945* (Brussels, 1984 [Paris, 1980]), pp. 331–95.

Légion Française des Combattants, very active in recruiting repatriates.[3] On the other hand, it created a multiplicity of government offices in charge of all matters concerning PoWs in the Ministries of Defence, Agriculture, Education, Food Rationing, Labour etc. The Vichy administration issued a whole series of laws protecting the families of PoWs, such as the reduction of taxes and housing rents and the severe prosecution of adultery involving the spouse of a PoW. For returning PoWs it guaranteed re-employment in the job they had left at the time of their mobilisation. In October 1941 a 'Commission for the Reintegration of Prisoners of War' was set up to co-ordinate all governmental and associational efforts, headed by Maurice Pinot, a liberated officer PoW and formerly on the staff of the president of the Confederation of French Employers. On the local level, the commission established the 'Prisoners' House' (*maison du prisonnier*), at least one per department, totalling over 150 local houses by the end of the occupation. The activity in these local 'houses', staffed by Vichy officials, was redoubled by the organisation of Centres of Mutual Aid (Centres d'Entr'aide), the officially endorsed association of repatriated PoWs. In a context of suspended liberty of association, both the Prisoners' Houses and the Centres of Mutual Aid became important instruments for promoting allegiance to the regime.

In the first year of its existence, incompatibility between the social and the political roles of the commissionership and its local branches scarcely arose. Repatriated PoWs, assailed as they were with Vichy propaganda, shared the admiration for Marshall Pétain that prevailed in the camps. Further, enthusiasm for the 'National Revolution' in no way reduced the chances of an early liberation. Pinot and his collaborators were the incarnation of the traditionalist and paternalistic side of the 'National Revolution' that characterised the early phase of the Vichy regime – a period when even leaders of the French resistance, such as Henri Frénay, were still deeply loyal to the regime and its leader. Yet the Vichy regime was no monolithic bloc, but rather the permanent setting for internal struggles, conspiracies and intrigues. Militant fascist and fervently pro-German factions – the collaborationist parties in Paris with, most prominently, Doriot's Parti Populaire Français and in Vichy the clan around Laval, ousted by a conspiracy in December 1940 but back in power in April 1942 through German pressure – competed with the traditionalists championed by Darlan. The commission and its vast network of social organisations was only an instrument in these larger power struggles. The collaborationist policies of the *Relève*, and the

---

[3] Sarah Fishman, 'We Will Wait'. Wives of French Prisoners of War, 1940–1945 (New Haven, 1991).

concomitant canvassing for voluntary departures, required a steadily increasing pro-German political engagement, and the pressures to politicise the whole organisation mounted. In January 1943, Pinot was fired and replaced by the ideologically more fervent André Masson.[4]

Pinot's dismissal was followed by the resignation of a large section of the staff of his commission and, more importantly, by the organisation of a parallel circuit inside the administration to oppose Masson's political line whilst preserving the social infrastructure and loyalties of the Centres of Mutual Aid and the Prisoners' Houses. Pro-Pinot and pro-Masson elements in the administration of the PoWs ranged on either side of an internal division amongst Vichy adherents, in which both sides initially appealed for the support of Marshal Pétain and called upon the ideology of the 'National Revolution'. They differed, however, over the increasingly collaborationist course of the regime under Laval's guidance at a time when the German armies on the eastern front, encircled at Stalingrad, engaged in total war and required the total mobilisation of the occupied countries of Western Europe. The radicalisation of the regime – and of the war – would gradually shift the internal opposition to outright external resistance to the regime without ever abandoning the infrastructure of the official administration.

The ideological ambiguities of this current are illustrated by the trajectory of the young François Mitterrand.[5] Politically active as a right-wing student before the war, Mitterrand escaped from captivity at the end of 1941. On his return to France he was briefly employed by the Légion Française des Combattants and later worked as a journalist for the pro-Vichy press, where he delivered proof of his attachment to the ideals of the 'National Revolution'. In June 1942 he took office as a close collaborator of Pinot in the Commission for the Reintegration of PoWs and quickly developed his talents as organiser and orator. After Pinot's dismissal Mitterrand somehow became his spokesman, Pinot himself being too exposed to retaliation by Vichy on the one hand, and too suspiciously close to Vichy in the eyes of its opponents on the other. Mitterrand soon established himself as one of the leaders of the internal opposition in the administration against Masson. At the first National Convention of Masson's Prisoners' Movement in July 1943, Mitterrand intervened publicly to criticise the governmental policy of the *Relève* and the new political discipline of the Prisoners' Movement called for by Masson. His public protest was echoed by the BBC's French broadcasts, but was at the same time used by the anti-Laval conspirators in Pétain's

---

[4] Unless indicated otherwise, the following paragraphs are based on Lewin, *Le Retour*.
[5] See also Pierre Péan, *Une Jeunesse Française. François Mitterrand, 1934–1947* (Paris, 1994).

entourage, who would even have suggested offering Masson's post to Mitterrand.[6] Mitterrand's position at that time is again reminiscent of the situation of his later friend Henri Frénay twelve months earlier: his internal opposition to the collaborationist current in Vichy was helpful to the opponents of Laval, who protected him from prosecution and arrest.

As a result of this internal opposition, two parallel circuits existed at the interior of the vast social infrastructure set up by Vichy to care for the exiled – first PoWs but, from 1943 onwards increasingly, labour conscripts as well: an official circuit that followed the radicalisation of the regime and an 'apolitical' circuit, opposing the continuing politicisation. Yet Pinot and Mitterrand also had eminently political goals: to avoid leaving the infrastructure, and with it the important *milieu* of the expatriates, in the hands of the collaborationist faction, to safeguard a precious instrument for their own post-war ambitions. From the start it was obvious that what was really at stake was the future repatriation of PoWs at the end of the war, and of the new exiled groups which had gradually joined them in Germany. Whoever was in charge of the reception of the repatriates, whoever commanded the infrastructure to welcome them, would have a crucial political advantage over other pretenders to political power. The central aim was to preserve the carefully constructed network, the continuing loyalties of local officials, the successful organising of early repatriates: any offensive or perilous activity was therefore shunned. The movement was hostile to the idea of armed *maquis* formations and the risks they implied.[7] It actively prepared the wide distribution of a journal at the time of the liberation, but no earlier. Its sole feat of arms at the time of the liberation of Paris was the immediate occupation of the administrative building of the Vichy Commissionership and of the Prisoners' House in the Place de Clichy.

Inevitably, in preparing for the liberation, the Pinot–Mitterrand movement understood that it had to choose sides in order to ensure its own future. In its hesitant search for new political allies after the break-up with Vichy, it made contacts both with General Giraud, himself an escaped PoW, and with General De Gaulle. The political ambiguities of his movement brought Mitterrand to the rare feat of meeting personally, in the course of only fourteen months, the three protagonists of France during the Second World War: Marshal Philippe Pétain, General Henri Giraud and General Charles De Gaulle.[8] Giraud's part in the drama was short-lived, but De Gaulle's role grew steadily.

De Gaulle and his Free French could not ignore the centrality of 'the

[6] Ibid., p. 284.   [7] Ibid., p. 422.   [8] Ibid., pp. 373, 434.

exile' in Vichy's political and ideological endeavours. First of all, at the propaganda level, the Free French could not fail to exploit the patent failure of the policy of state collaboration adopted by Vichy for the liberation of the French PoWs. Gaullist propaganda denounced the complicity of Vichy with an enemy retaining hundreds of thousands of young French men and its inability to obtain important concessions. It indicted Vichy's highhanded policy of assuming responsibility over French PoWs through its Scapini mission and its later transactions of the *Relève* and the transformation as one-sided concessions which voluntarily delivered fresh French manpower to the German war-machine. Gaullist rhetoric also frontally attacked the ideological flaws in the veneration of 'exile' as a purgative and expiatory sacrifice for national renewal, exposing its euphemistic use and replacing it systematically by 'deportation'. The British historian of the French resistance Roderick Kedward locates the origin of the term 'deportation' to denote French expatriates in Germany during the Second World War in the last months of 1942, as a reaction by the resistance and Gaullist propaganda against the *Relève* scheme. BBC broadcasts called the *Relève* a 'treasonous slave-trade and a savage deportation'.[9] The contemporary Nazi occupation of the southern zone and the beginning of mass deportations of Jewish men, women and, particularly, children greatly contributed to the generalised qualification of Vichy's policy in terms of slavery and deportation.

From the time of its conception, indeed, 'deportation' in the French context acquired a universal implication. It should be noticed that in no country except France were the different forms of exile so linked. Vichy first of all deliberately created the confusion between PoWs and civil workers, since the total mass of French citizens in Germany flowed back and forth between the two groups through the mechanisms of *Relève* and transformation. Gaullist propaganda reinforced this trend by stressing that all French citizens in Germany were victims of deportation, were there against their will, taken by force by the Germans, with the guilty complicity of Vichy, and not to help the German war effort against the Bolsheviks, as Vichy might claim. In the resistance press and in the propaganda produced in London and Algiers the distinctions between deported Jews, arrested resisters, labour conscripts and workers leaving under the *Relève* or even under socio-economic constraints were deliberately blurred. Even the 'exile' of PoWs in captivity, the object of Vichy's mysticism, was assimilated into the universal category of 'deportation'.

---

[9] Roderick Kedward, *In Search of the Maquis. Rural Resistance in Southern France, 1942–1944* (Oxford, 1993), pp. 4–5. Annette Wieviorka links the origin of the word to the STO, which took effect only in February 1943: *Déportation*, pp. 26–30.

This trend would only be reinforced by the creation in November 1943 of a Commission for Prisoners, Deportees and Refugees.

Secondly, next to the political exploitation of Vichy's failures, De Gaulle and the resistance had to counter the successes of Vichy's policy – that is, not in dealing with the Germans but in propaganda inside France and in recruiting adherents in the *milieu* of PoWs and workers. Could De Gaulle, cut off from the territory of metropolitan France, allow the Vichy-tainted infrastructure of the Mutual Aid Centres and Prisoners' Houses to be thrown to the winds, or could there be co-operation with the Pinot–Mitterrand group who offered to recycle the infrastructure?

Not until the end of 1943 did De Gaulle find himself in a position to set up his shadow cabinet in Algiers and to nominate a shadow minister in charge of the expatriates. At the end of May 1943, De Gaulle had transferred his headquarters from London to Algiers to set up the French Committee of National Liberation (CFLN) together with General Giraud, the chosen partner of the American liberators in North Africa after the murder of Darlan.[10] Within a few months the conservative Giraud was first side-lined from political responsibilities to solely military command, and then eliminated from power altogether. As an important element in the strategy of establishing De Gaulle's position, a consultative assembly was created in November 1943, consisting of pre-war parliamentarians and representatives of the internal resistance. At the same time, representatives of the internal resistance entered the shadow cabinet. Henri Frénay, one of the first to have organised a resistance movement in the unoccupied southern zone and editor of an underground newspaper, *Combat*, was appointed to the care of French expatriates.

After his escape from captivity in June 1940, Frénay, a career officer, was employed by the Defence Ministry in Vichy, from which he resigned in January 1941. Using his extensive network of relationships in military and bourgeois circles, he became active in political agitation, mainly by editing a clandestine journal. Frénay denounced defeatism and collaboration but remained loyal to Pétain. His clandestine journal was noted by the intelligence organisation of the internal opposition in Vichy and quite well received in many quarters of the administration. From 1942 onwards the rupture with the regime was complete and Frénay's organisation developed a nationwide network of clandestine press and intelligence. Frénay was its undisputed patron and organised his movement in a military spirit. In September–October 1942 he crossed the

---

[10] See Azéma, *De Munich à la Libération*, pp. 277–97.

Channel to London for a first meeting with De Gaulle, leading to the mutual recognition of both parties. On his second mission to London in June 1943, Frénay joined De Gaulle in Algiers, where in November De Gaulle suggested that he should enter the CFLN as commissioner for 'prisoners, deportees and refugees'. He did not return to France until after the liberation of Paris.

Frénay was disappointed by the offer and was at first inclined to refuse it.[11] At a personal level he struggled with the moral dilemma of engaging in politics in complete safety in Algiers whilst his comrades in France faced the risk of arrest, deportation and execution. More importantly, however, on the political level he resented being side-lined to theoretical responsibility for expatriates and refugees who were out of reach from Algiers and only potentially interesting after a remote future repatriation. Having been deeply involved in the power struggles between the resistance movements in France and particularly apprehensive of the role played by the communists, Frénay would have much preferred to be in charge of the Ministry of the Interior, which would be responsible for restoring order and political authority immediately after the liberation – in Frénay's eyes the most crucial future issue. Frénay finally accepted the offer, judging it even more harmful for his movement not to be represented in the CFLN at all than to be in a post of minor responsibility.

Frénay's appreciation of his nomination in his autobiography may have been coloured *post facto* by his analysis of what followed: the political party of the resistance he dreamed of became a fiasco and his responsibilities during the repatriation made him the personal target of a relentless campaign by the Communist Party. It served two of his main ideas on the course of the history of the resistance: first, that De Gaulle systematically and consciously sapped the best forces of the resistance (beginning with Frénay himself) by calling them to London or Algiers and charging them with entirely theoretical responsibilities in order to weaken the resistance as a rival for post-war power; and, secondly, that all protagonists (except himself) were blind to, or victims of, systematic infiltration and conspiracy by the Communist Party – d'Astier, Mitterrand, Jean Moulin, De Gaulle.

When trying to persuade Frénay to accept his charge, De Gaulle had insisted that the repatriation and reintegration of expatriates and refugees 'conditioned in a large measure the moral health and political future of France'.[12] Frénay seized upon both. First, by his own calculations, four million Frenchmen depended on his commission, trans-

---

[11] Henri Frénay, *La Nuit finira* (Paris, 1973), pp. 383–4.
[12] Ibid., p. 383.

formed into the Ministry for Prisoners, Deportees and Refugees on the eve of the Normandy invasion, when the CFLN was renamed the Provisional Government of the French Republic; this meant, counting their families, one-quarter of the French population.[13] If his rivals and adversaries had meant to park him in a position of harmlessness, cut off from the real levers of power, he had here an alternative reserve in which to construct a solid base for a post-war political career. The second challenge involved the 'moral health of the nation', or patriotism. Frénay worried that, 'inevitably, prisoners must have a mentality of the defeated . . . If we want to be heard by them, won't it be crucial to try to redress their morale, to fight their resignation and, bit by bit, give them back their fighting spirit? Couldn't we, in this way, reduce the gap that separates them psychologically from France-at-war?'[14] He saw it as a central task for his commission to counter the influence of Vichy's propaganda amongst PoWs and workers in Germany, and to implicate them, at least nominally, in the liberation struggle of the Free French and the internal resistance.

Rhetoric concerning *la France combattante* and a concern with post-war political positions were essential to De Gaulle's self-fulfilling prophecy. Frénay would first deal with the rhetoric. From the end of July 1943, even before his own arrival, De Gaulle's nephew Michel Calliau, alias Charette, liberated PoW and self-proclaimed resistance hero, produced a dazzling stream of 'third-front' propaganda. In the name of the 'Resistance Movement of PoWs and Deportees', Calliau distributed grotesque projects of general insurrection by French PoWs and 'stab-in-the-back' fantasies of secret radio contacts and weapons-drops on PoW camps. Calliau's caricature of his uncle's rhetorical style was in line with the mindset of a besieged Gaullist clan, ignored by the Allies in North Africa and challenged by Darlan and Giraud. Yet barely a month after Frénay's nomination, François Mitterrand arrived in Algiers. The prosaic approach of the Pinot–Mitterrand group, to recycle the infrastructure of the Vichy administration and the associations of repatriates set up by Vichy, offered Frénay concrete perspectives for control over an important political tool. Anxious to escape the isolation of speculative and rhetorical responsibilities, Frénay wholeheartedly embraced the realistic Pinot–Mitterrand strategy and would trust its representatives all the more as definite prospects of his ministry's transfer to Paris approached.

Calliau's Manual of the Deportee in Germany, circulated in Algiers in November 1943 – the very month when Frénay took office – was a

[13] Ibid., pp. 395–6, 400, 415, 466.
[14] Ibid., p. 398.

5 'You resisted; they liberated you; they will repatriate you; STAY WHERE YOU ARE.' Photo, AN F9 3169, Centre Historique des Archives Nationales, Paris.

ludicrous example of Gaullist rhetoric and bellicose slogans. 'Civil worker from France, you are not a volunteer, but a convict; you are not a worker, but a deportee . . . As of now, you are present in the ranks of Combatant France, at the side of the Resistance in France, the African Army, the combatants of the liberation, directed by General De Gaulle . . . Create a true mystique of sabotage, a true frenzy of destruction . . . Block up the sewers to flood the roads. Create landslides in the mines . . . Create the reflex of sabotage. Exploit all means of sabotage: iron, fire, theft, terror. Get gunpowder, through the German illegal parties.' Unencumbered by any sense of realism, it incited deportees to 'organise the repression of idiots who "work well": quarantine, conversion, beatings. As for the spies and informers, hang them. One example per factory is enough. Lawful self-defence. We're fighting a war. We'll send you material from France, but don't wait. Once you've destroyed your factory, it will no longer be bombed. Make your results known in France. Generalised sabotage is crucial for victory, for a fast victory and for a French victory.'[15]

The frenzied patriotism of Calliau and the like also inspired some pathetic repatriation plans – plans that would have had tragic consequences had they not subsequently been replaced in full by more realistic assessments of the state of mind of the French expatriates in Germany.[16] Frénay was certainly too well acquainted with the reality of the resistance in occupied Europe, its difficulties and its risks even to consider the possibility of an insurrection by all the French in the territory of the Reich itself. But the theme of the third front made its way into speeches and programmes and to a large extent inspired the discourse of the commission.[17] The 'third front' strategy was not directed so much at the German enemy as at France's allies. The Free French owed their weak position at the side of the Big Three precisely to the fact that they delivered very few troops to the Allied military forces, and that most of those young French men of military age were captives of the enemy and even, in vast numbers, supplying manpower for its war economy. What better device, then, than transforming the two million French men in German hands from France's debt-side to the assets of a fifth column, that would count double in the final battle, attacking the German troops from behind? Reports were sent to the Inter-Allied Committee with the plans and – more problematic – the achievements

[15] *France-Politique. Rapport APN/1/26201* (Algiers, 17 Oct. 1943), AN F9 3106.
[16] See the *Etude sur la psychologie des prisonniers de guerre et des déportés par rapport au problème du rapatriement* (Algiers, Dec. 1943), AN F9 3125.
[17] See, for example, 'Causerie de M. Frénay' (BBC broadcast, London, 24 Feb. 1944), AN F9 3105, and Frénay, *La Nuit finira*, pp. 398–9.

of the PoW and deportee resistance in Germany.[18] Numerous reports
were also send out to the press, where they were surely received with less
scepticism. One Swiss newspaper even stated that the French resistance
in Germany was better organised than the resistance in France, double-
counting the French expatriates in an underground army of four million
men.[19] More surprisingly, these grandiloquent propaganda reports
seem to have stirred some echo in German intelligence offices.[20]

The intelligence that reached Algiers about the attitudes of its PoWs
and labour conscripts was more disquieting than the 'third front'
propaganda suggested.[21] In repatriation plans developed during 1944,
the main psychological factor taken into account was not dauntless
patriotism and pugnacity but disenchantment and cynicism, old loyalties and suspicion of the new authorities.[22] Algiers did not send dyna-
mite, automatic rifles and radio transmitters to the PoW camps in
Germany. It did send, monthly, over 700,000 *colis de Gaulle* to rival the
illustrious *colis Pétain*.[23] If there was any truth to the saying that the way
to a man's heart is through his stomach, it was in this field that the Free
French would try to challenge PoW allegiance to the old marshal.
Winning the political sympathies of French PoWs was certainly a more
realistic priority than the conquest of Germany from the interior.
Chocolate, cigarettes and slogans were surely more effective weapons
than the aforementioned triad.

In the propaganda activities of the commission the offence-minded
heroism of the third front would gradually be replaced by and integrated
into the defence-oriented heroism of deportation and the language of
martyrdom. Given the conditions under which French expatriates lived
in Germany, keeping one's human dignity and internal convictions of
national loyalty was already an achievement of heroic stature. The
'deportation' discourse would promote the centrality of a few unifying
symbols of suffering and oppression: barbed wire, camps, hunger,
imprisonment. In a highly explicit way, this propaganda countered
Vichy's propaganda of voluntarism and regeneration through exile. On

---

[18] *France-Politique, SIF/30503* (20 May 1943), AN F9 3105.

[19] *St Galler Tagblatt* (2 Feb. 1944). In comparison, press coverage in Algiers seemed
almost prudent. See clippings in AN F9 3105.

[20] See Durand, *La Captivité*, pp. 381–2, and Cochet, *Les Exclus*, p. 100.

[21] See, for example, FRENCH PRISONERS OF WAR IN GERMANY. *Notes of a Discussion by
some British Repatriates* (London, n.d. [Summer 1944]), AN F9 3168.

[22] *Note de M. Hicquet* (Algiers, 23 Feb. 1944); *Etude de M. Buton* (Algiers, Feb. 1944):
both in AN F9 3125. See also *Les Conditions en Allemagne. Récits des déportés* (Algiers, 4
Nov. 1943), AN F9 3106.

[23] *Compte Rendu de la Commission Permanente Intercommissariale des Prisonniers, Déportés et
Réfugiés* (Algiers, 10 Dec. 1943), AN F9 3117; *Message de Monsieur André Philip*
(Algiers, n.d. [June–Oct. 1943]), AN F9 3105.

21 May 1944 a 'National Day of Prisoners and Deportees' was organised in Algiers, with a religious service, military parade, speeches by De
Gaulle and Frénay, and the opening of the exhibition 'The Barbed-Wire
Front' (*le front des barbelés*). At its opening, the exhibition was presented
as the antidote to Vichy's exhibition 'The Soul of the Camps' (*l'âme des
camps*):

[In the Vichy show] Our captivity, the suffering of millions of comrades who
have experienced and continue to experience hunger, beatings, painful separation, forced labour, bombing and threats became a joyful fresco of an operetta
captivity full of spectacle and literary conferences; a world apart, a happy world,
without complications, a perfect opportunity for meditation.[24]

Giant posters promoted the assimilation of the fate of all French in exile
in Germany. In one, a PoW, with a soldier's cap and barbed wire in the
background, and a worker, with a worker's cap and a factory behind
him, raise one hand in greeting but have their other hands chained
together with handcuffs. Another poster shows a map of Germany,
black on a blood-red background, covered with the names and codes of
PoW camps, barbed wire, handcuffs, watchtowers and guards with dogs
and automatic rifles, and carries the title, in pseudo-gothic script:
'Germany, concentration camp [*L'Allemagne, camp de concentration*]'.[25]
The map does not locate a single Konzentrationslager.

The discourse of deportation created deliberate confusion between
different categories of French expatriates in Germany, as Vichy's discourse of exile had done, but for opposite reasons: rather than voluntarism and regeneration, all shared the condition of prisoner, of convict,
no matter what the precise condition – PoW, worker or KZ inmate. The
martyrdom of France was one and undivided, the policies of the Nazi
occupation and Vichy uniformly cruel and brutal. It is revealing to
observe that the word chosen for the assimilation and charged with
notions of martyrdom and patriotism did not, at this stage, really
matter. Since forced labour, captivity, internment, prisoner, deportee,
KZ inmate were all interchangeable, one or the other would do the job,
and there was even some debate as to which one would suit best:
prisoner or deportee.[26] In the light of the subsequent sacralisation, the
interchangeability of the terminology deserves special mentioning.

In the debate on categories and terminology, estimates and calculations of Frénay's administration were integrated into much wilder

---

[24] Note, *L'exposition 'le front des barbelés'* (undated), AN F9 3117, and Frénay, *La Nuit
finira*, p. 434.

[25] Both posters in AN F9 3117.

[26] See J.-P. Blessy, 'Un Grand Problème National. Nos prisonniers et nos déportés',
Quatrième République (18 Mar. 1944), AN F9 3105.

IMP. LA TYPO-LITHO & J.CARBONEL. ALGER.   S.G.M.A. 4 - 44.

6 Deportation: worker and PoW handcuffed (May 1944). Photo, AN F9 3117,
Centre Historique des Archives Nationales, Paris.

fantasies on 'the martyrdom of France', often expressed in terms of
Malthusian anxieties. In March 1944 *L'Echo d'Alger* announced
1,500,000 PoWs, the execution of 50,000 hostages, the death in
concentration camps of 100,000 inmates, the death by starvation of

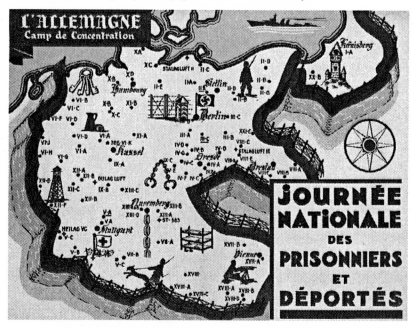

7 'Germany, concentration camp': poster for National Day of Prisoners and Deportees. Algiers, 21 May 1944. Photo, AN F9 3117, Centre Historique des Archives Nationales, Paris.

1,000,000 children in France and the drop in annual births from 700,000 to 450,000.[27] In the same month Frénay declared in the Consultative Assembly, on the subject of repatriation, that: 'the problem is first of all of a sanitary order, since most prisoners will be affected by often serious diseases . . . this question is vital for the future of our race'.[28] In February and March 1945, alarmed by news of the conditions of French citizens in German concentration camps, Frénay issued a warning to all Germans, threatening retaliation against German civilians for each French casualty. In a confidential note to his colleagues, Frénay expressed his anxieties not in terms of human rights or the prevention of war crimes, but in the most explicit demographic terms:

Should we interpret [the living conditions of French expatriates] as the result of an accidentally precarious food supply or rather the implementation of a plan to starve to death a numerically and qualitatively important part of the French elite? . . . It is not excessive to think that Hitler's Germany, driven to the brink

[27] *Echo d'Alger* (8 Mar. 1944), AN F9 3105.
[28] Quoted in *Quatrième République* (18 Mar. 1944).

of a military defeat, takes its revenge in this way at the demographic level, for the benefit of the next generation when it will once more take up arms against us.[29]

When the exhibition 'The Barbed-Wire Front', conceived in Algiers in May 1944, was staged again in the Grand Palais in liberated Paris as part of 'the week of the absent' organised between Christmas 1944 and New Year 1945, the setting was definitely less antagonistic than at the previous showing. Frénay had inherited the huge metropolitan administration concerned with 'the absent' from Vichy and had it staffed with men from Pinot's circle, and with it he had inherited some of the language; instead of dismissing Vichy's rhetoric, he – undoubtedly unconsciously – reproduced it:

It is the soul of the camps [*l'âme des camps* – the very title of Vichy's exhibition] that we have tried to recreate in these rooms . . . In the silence of the camps and through their ordeals, their souls have been enriched. It is an immense moral strength that they will offer to France after their return.[30]

In February 1945, Frénay addressed the 3,000 employees of his central administration: 'You are the Ministry of the Suffering' – a language undoubtedly familiar to most of them.[31] Frénay's discourse had travelled a long road since the early days in Algiers.

Under Frénay's aegis, the Ministry for Prisoners, Deportees and Refugees had become a remarkably successful melting pot of ideological elements: the utopian militancy of the 'third front', the ecumenical language of 'deportation', the revivalist metaphors of the 'soul of the camps'. It proved much more difficult to integrate these different tendencies at the organisational level. Calliau had fomented the suspicion against the Pinot–Miterrand group in Algiers even before Frénay's arrival, describing the group in his memos to his uncle as a bunch of firstly Pétainist and subsequently pro-Giraud turncoats and impostors with no activity whatsoever that could be described as 'resistance'.[32] Calliau cultivated a personal hatred against Mitterrand and even intrigued to prevent his return to France and to enrol him in the army so as to eliminate his influence on the PoW organisations. Mitterrand did succeed in leaving Algiers for London, thanks to the help offered by the services of none other than Giraud, and was later landed on the French coast by the British secret services. Back in France, Mitterrand succeeded in combining two other groups of whose existence he had

[29] *Communication du Ministre des Prisonniers de Guerre, Déportés et Réfugiés* (22 Feb. 1945), AN F60 10.
[30] Frénay, *La Nuit finira*, p. 493. [31] Ibid., p. 494.
[32] Péan, *Une Jeunesse Française*, pp. 321, 367–8, 373–81, 403–6, and *passim*. Charette published an anti-Mitterrand pamphlet in 1987: Michel Calliau, alias Charette, *Histoire du MRPDG ou d'un vrai mouvement de résistance (1941–1945)* (Paris, 1987).

learned in Algiers – the more realistic elements of Calliau's Resistance Movement and the National Committee of PoWs, a branch of the pro-Communist National Front – into a unitary National Movement of PoWs and Deportees. Opening its ranks to all categories of 'deportees' and starting a new activity for the victims of labour conscription in Germany, the movement clearly assimilated the conception of the commission of one over-arching body of French expatriates. Frénay would later accuse Mitterrand of having co-opted the communists against the instructions he had given him in Algiers. It cannot be doubted, however, that Frénay saw the unitary movement as the associational prolongation of his ministry and as the prerequisite for the success of his mission. At Frénay's insistence, Mitterrand was appointed interim secretary-general over all Vichy services in charge of PoWs and labour conscripts for the period between the liberation and his own arrival. Calliau was side-tracked. Frénay himself disembarked in Cherbourg on 28 August 1944 with the remaining members of the government on a warship from Algiers, accompanied by only one collaborator: the representative of the Pinot–Mitterrand group in his ministry.[33] Meanwhile, Mitterrand, in the sole feat of arms in his war record, had taken by force the administrative building of the Vichy services.

The alliance with the Pinot–Mitterrand group not only implied the recovery of the Vichy buildings: it also implied recovery of personnel and legislation. One of the first requests for equipment for Frénay's embryonic commission in the first weeks of 1944 was a complete and up-to-date set of the official journal of 'the pseudo-government of the French State'.[34] To avoid the chaos of a legislative vacuum, all texts promulgated by Vichy were maintained and would only gradually be cancelled, adapted or replaced. It was obviously impossible to build up an administration from scratch and throw away what existed, especially since no one could foresee how much time would be left between the liberation of France and the repatriation following the defeat of Germany. The two might very well coincide. In any case, faced with the urgency of the tasks of repatriation and reintegration, any other choice would have been irresponsible. This strategy, of course, faced Frénay with a major psychological handicap. One anecdote, taken amongst the abundant traces of administrative continuity in the ministry's archive, illustrates this eloquently. In April 1945, the 'psychological service', in charge of converting the spirit of the repatriates from Vichy's submission into the fighting spirits of combatant France, still used order forms for its propaganda material with the heading 'Etat Français', crossed out

[33] Frénay, *La Nuit finira*, p. 453.
[34] Letter, Frénay to Cassin (Algiers, 29 Feb. 1944), AN F60 10.

and with the words 'République Française' inserted.[35] The communist campaign against him would of course not fail to accuse him of having similarly recycled the members of the Vichy clique of Masson, laundering their reputations and allowing them to continue in political life in the new post-war France.

It was at the local level that the problems of recycling the Vichy infrastructure were most acute. In the field, the entire action of reintegrating repatriates was carried out through the Prisoners' Houses that had been set up by Vichy and further developed by the ministry after the liberation, totalling 230 local houses by the summer of 1945.[36] Many houses had served as the meeting point of collaborationist groups and were indelibly identified with Vichy propaganda. The departmental direction of Angoulême reported in February 1945: 'A regrettable doubt persists against the House of the Prisoner and the Deportee in the mind of certain sections of the population who remember the times when the front of that house was adorned with the slogans of the former head of the French State.'[37] The situation in the department of Pas-de-Calais in January was similar:

In general, the Prisoners' House was the target of diverse criticisms, originating in the fact that before the 'liberation' [sic] this house was considered not as an instrument for the welfare of the PoWs and their families, but as an instrument of Vichy's policy of collaboration with the occupier. In Arras in particular, the 'Pétain Youth' movement, which had obtained a meeting-place in the Prisoners' House, held their boisterous gatherings there and some of their members indulged in excessive and for their age unusual expenses. Furthermore, some of the staff were members of the [collaborationist parties] and the Milice and their behaviour upset the population.[38]

In others, the replacement of former personnel took a long time, for lack of new candidates. Many local officials whose activities had showed evidence of only a moderate adherence to the regime were left in place. In their reports to the ministry, some former Vichy officials who had stayed in office did not hesitate to recall the period before the liberation with nostalgia, and made comparisons that favoured the previous regime.[39] In November 1944, the Centres of Mutual Aid and the National Movement of PoWs and Deportees decided on a formal merger. The Centres were historically interwoven with the relief structure set up by Vichy; the National Movement was similarly interwoven

---

[35] AN F9 3125.   [36] Lewin, *Le Retour*, p. 31.

[37] *Extraits des rapports des directions départementales adressés au chef des services de l'information*, AN F9 3172.

[38] Ibid.

[39] See, for example, *Direction Régionale d'Anger* (Jan. 1945), ibid., and *Direction Départementale de l'Eure et Loir* (1 June 1945), AN F9 3173.

with the commission in Algiers. Their union gave the new movement a
semi-official role, expressed functionally by the representation of delegates of the movement on the management board of every 'Prisoners'
House'. The merger was seen by the Pinot–Mitterrand group partly as a
device to contain communist influence by recovering the convertible
conservative elements of the centres, but it only presaged innumerable
local battles to dominate the local committees of the movement and its
delegates on the boards of the Prisoners' Houses.[40]

The ministry staged nationwide propaganda efforts, for example by
providing all Prisoners' Houses with pictures of General De Gaulle to
replace the official portraits of Pétain they had been forced to remove.[41]
The battle against Pétain's influence, however, was only a rear-guard
action. The ministry's true enemy was the Communist Party. Frénay
had dreamt aloud that his position as minister would further his ambitions as protagonist of the political face of the anti-communist resistance. The Communist Party would achieve the opposite: through a
campaign against Frénay as minister responsible for repatriation and
reintegration, it would ruin all his hopes for a political career in party
politics. In the protracted debate during the months between the liberation and the end of the war on the political future of the resistance,
Frénay had consistently opposed the union between his National Liberation Movement and the National Front, fearing that the Communist
Party, which already controlled the National Front, would thus gain
control of all the political heirs of the resistance. This stance could
hardly make him popular with the PCF. The party decided to eliminate
Frénay as a political rival through an orchestrated campaign against his
person and against his direction of the repatriation. The scope of the
campaign was a powerful demonstration of the influence of the party.
The impressive collection of unanimous press articles from all over
France, from the smallest local newspaper to the national communist
press, from the resolutions of communist-manipulated assemblies of
repatriates at all levels, bear witness to what the party could achieve.[42]
The same themes appeared each time: Frénay's connivance with Vichy,
first during the war as a bourgeois and protégé of Pucheu; after the war
as recruiter for the Vichy clique and other traitors in his ministry,
including, unfortunately, René Hardy, accused of having betrayed Jean
Moulin; Frénay's alleged incompetence as a minister, the supposed

[40] Lewin, *Le Retour*, pp. 55–7. See also *Direction Régionale de Toulouse* (12 Mar. 1945);
Direction Départementale de la Vienne (1 Mar. 1945); *Direction Départementale du Hérault*
(2 Mar. 1945): all in AN F9 3172.
[41] Letter, J. Richard to M. Barassin (Paris, 9 Apr. 1945), AN F9 3168.
[42] Clipping files in AN F9 3168; reporting of anti-Frénay agitation in local assemblies in
AN F9 3172 and 3173. See also Lewin, *Le Retour*, pp. 131–6.

cause of the death of neglected survivors of concentration camps and delay in the return of thousands of others; the corruption and squandering of money to the detriment of the destitute repatriates; etc. The campaign effectively destroyed Frénay as a political adversary and he decided not to stand for election as a candidate of the Union Démocratique et Socialiste de la Résistance he had helped to found. A lifelong resentment resulted from the episode, evident on every page of his memoirs.

Did the French DPs benefit from the high political stakes involved in their repatriation? They undoubtedly did, through the volume of finances and logistical effort engaged, the resulting speed of repatriation operations and the triumphalist atmosphere created by the ministry's unrelenting propaganda efforts. Lewin calculated that Frénay's ministry consumed 20 per cent of the government budget for the year 1945.[43] The proximity of relief structures through the dense local network of the Prisoners' Houses and the unparalleled numbers of staff at their disposal provided permanent proof that the provisional government of the French republic genuinely showed even greater concern for the exiles and repatriates than Vichy had done. At the height of the repatriation, Frénay's ministry employed 32,450 people.[44] The massive availability of funds and infrastructure would make up for shortcomings in the preparations.

Frénay's military background, combined with his malthusian anxieties and obsession about epidemics, contributed to the excessive rigidity and authoritarianism of his first drafts of repatriation plans. Timely criticism by some of his collaborators in Algiers allowed for more realistic reassessments.[45] When the high tide of the repatriation wave broke in April–May, the ministry was forced to improvise, because of the rigidity of its own plans. Frénay had decided to avoid overburdened Paris and to dispatch the repatriates after their arrival at the frontiers directly to their region of origin, bypassing the capital.[46] In view of the total centralisation of the French transportation system, this was a naive mistake – as any tourist travelling through France by train could have told him. Once faced with the impossibility of avoiding Paris, repatriation centres had to be improvised in the Gare d'Orsay and the Hotel Lutetia, on the smart Boulevard Raspail, had to be requisitioned to receive concentration camp survivors, to prove the supreme solicitude of the government for

[43] Lewin, *Le Retour*, pp. 83, 87 and 294, n. 97.
[44] Cochet, *Les Exclus*, p. 108.
[45] See René David, *Note sur le projet de rapatriement* (Algiers, 4 July 1944), AN F9 3124. Other critical reports can be found in AN F9 3125.
[46] Frénay, *La Nuit finira*, p. 509.

its returning martyrs. Repatriation by plane created a similar emergency. SHAEF had communicated its decision that military aircraft would not be available for the repatriation of civilians and national repatriation plans had been drafted accordingly. When faced with the chaos of the DP crisis, however, the Allied command decided that the evacuation of DPs from their operation zone was urgent. Besides, military aircraft which carried *matériel* eastwards for the troops were empty when they returned westward. More than 161,000 French repatriates were flown in to military air bases close to Paris, where nothing had been prepared for their reception.[47] Even though this situation created some panic in the repatriation machinery and some initial criticism, it soon proved a most spectacular advertisement for the government's efforts. Local representatives of the ministry enthusiastically reported a reversal in attitudes to the repatriation: 'All families of repatriates are now delighted at the speed with which their absent relatives are being repatriated, and the solicitude that has accompanied them all along their journey. In particular, the repatriations by air have produced a great impression.'[48]

Already in Algiers a careful *mise en scène* of the repatriation had been a major concern. Banners, *Marseillaises* and welcome committees were a crucial part of the repatriation arrangements. In April, the public was prepared through the distribution to 1,600 provincial cinemas of the short propaganda film *Let's Think of Them* (*Pensons à eux*). Ministry officials were sent out to the province to look for suitable repatriation heroes to champion the national effort in nationwide publicity campaigns, phrased partly in deference to communist accusations. In March 1945, one of those emissaries found 'a certain Aimé Dubois in Angers, who returned recently from Germany in what was his fifteenth escape effort' and suggested that the minister should invite him to Paris for a magnificent reception, before the Communist Party appropriated his odyssey for its own uses.[49] On 1 June the return of a symbolic one millionth repatriate, a tall, blond-haired PoW from the Alps, with the very common French name of Caron, was staged with ceremonies, banners and posters all over the country.[50]

The French repatriation effort benefited from the same favourable time factor that saved Belgian repatriates. There were simply more repatriates, more French troops in Germany, more preparation, more money, more infrastructure and more experience with reintegration.

---

[47] Lewin, *Le Retour*, p. 290, n. 24. Some 61,560 were repatriated by boat and 1,500,000 by ground transport.
[48] *Direction Départementale de l'Ain* (15 Apr. 1945), AN F9 3172.
[49] *Rapport de M. Couillard* (21 Mar. 1945), AN F9 3168.
[50] See AN F9 3168, and Frénay, *La Nuit finira*, p. 525.

Ministère des Prisonniers, Déportés et Réfugiés: grand hall de la gare d'Orsay, transformé en centre d'accueil.

8 The Great Hall of the Gare d'Orsay, transformed into a welcome centre. Photo, AN F9 3169, Centre Historique des Archives Nationales, Paris.

The challenge to the post-war state was also immeasurably greater: not to demonstrate that the regime was capable of improvisation, of creating a social infrastructure out of nothing, but a contest with a previous regime that had concentrated its endeavours on expatriates. In this very different setting, there was no room for much private initiative: the post-war state struggled to control all the strings of the machinery, and all logistics bore the mark of the New State, from the repatriation centres at the national borders to the local Prisoners' House in the most remote department. Even the organisation of repatriates into associations was taken care of by the ministry, with its grand design for a unitary National Movement of Prisoners and Deportees, uniting three branches for PoWs, labour conscripts and 'political deportees', the term through which the victims of Nazi persecution were integrated into the family of repatriates. The future of the unifying concept of 'Deportation' and its organisational offspring is the subject of the next two parts of this book.

Part III

The legacy of forced economic migration

7 Labour and total war

Workers constituted the bulk of the populations displaced by Nazi Germany during the Second World War, totalling about eight million individuals. Nine out of ten Dutch DPs and three out of four Belgian DPs were employed as civilians in Germany. For France, if the annexed departments are excluded, more than half of the national DPs were workers, including one-quarter of transformed PoWs. The numbers involved made forced economic migration one of the major social facts of the second World War.

Historians examining war and social change have often attributed a determining influence to the deportation of workers to Germany. Some of them go so far as to explain much of the course of post-war social and economic history through the mobilisation of the work force of occupied countries.[1] As part of their strategy of total war, Germany and Japan decided to spare their own populations as far as possible from hardships and social unrest, and shifted the social costs of warfare on to the populations of their conquered foreign territories. The wartime experience as *Herrenvolk* also spared the German and Japanese population from radicalisation in the post-war era, providing the foundations for a disciplined social climate and an unparalleled economic recovery. In the occupied countries, the brutal exploitation of the work force radicalised the masses, polarised the social and political climate and provided the raw material for the success of powerful communist parties, bringing social unrest, political instability and, in comparison with the German and Japanese miracles, disappointing economic achievements.

Ulrich Herbert's path-breaking research largely substantiates this view.[2] Throughout its time in power, the Nazi regime struggled with the

---

[1] See Gabriel Kolko's 1990 preface to his *Politics of War. The World and United States Foreign Policy, 1943–1945* (New York, 1990 [1968]), pp. xvi–xx.

[2] Herbert, *Fremdarbeiter. Politik und Praxis des 'Ausländer-Einsatzes' in der Kriegwirtschaft des Dritten Reiches* (Berlin and Bonn, 1985); *Geschichte der Ausländer-Beschäftigung in Deutschland, 1880 bis 1980. Saisonarbeiter, Zwangsarbeiter, Gastarbeiter* (Berlin and Bonn, 1986); *Europa und der 'Reichseinsatz'. Ausländische Zivilarbeiter, Kriegsgefangene und KZ-Häftlinge in Deutschland, 1938–1945* (Essen, 1991). For the English translations, see *A*

contradiction between the economic imperatives that faced it and its self-imposed ideological imperative of the racial purity of the German State. The party had come to power in a context of economic crisis and mass unemployment, but from 1936 onwards the demands of the rearmament programme created a labour shortage. Bilateral immigration agreements between the Reich and the governments of Poland, Italy, Yugoslavia, Hungary, Bulgaria and the Netherlands allowed for the employment of 375,000 workers, mainly in the agricultural sector. These immigrants were subject to specific police regulations, containing them in a legislative apartheid to allay fears of an invasion of impure blood. In the Netherlands, emigration to Germany was strongly encouraged by the government, facing massive structural unemployment, even after the European recovery of 1936. By 1938, figures of Dutch workers in Germany had risen to 40,000. About half went on government emigration contracts; jobless workers who refused a contract in Germany lost their unemployment benefits. The Dutch historian Sijes describes this policy, autonomously implemented by the Dutch administration, as an early form of 'forced employment'.[3]

The invasion of Poland in September 1939 created a fundamentally new situation. Nazi planners had calculated two years beforehand that the mobilisation of German soldiers would create a labour shortage of over one million workers, and debated two alternative solutions for this problem: the massive employment of German women or the importation of labour from the conquered territories. Both were undesirable from an ideological point of view: in the Nazi ideology, women were restricted to their procreative role, and the identity of *Blut* and *Boden* required the expulsion and destruction rather than the importation of 'non-Germanic' individuals. Yet the Nazi analysts had studied the experience of the First World War from a strategic point of view, and concluded that the mobilisation of German women would profoundly destabilise the social climate on the home front, drive up wages and damage opinion in that part of the German population whose allegiance was most important to the regime. Foreign labour, if contained and properly policed, would be the lesser evil and in any case the lesser cost. By the summer of 1940, 700,000 Poles were employed in Germany.

The lightning conquest of Western Europe settled all German labour problems. The continuing deportation of Poles, the possibilities for

---

History of Foreign Labor in Germany (Ann Arbor, 1990) and *Hitler's Foreign Workers. Enforced Foreign Labour in Germany Under the Third Reich* (Cambridge, 1997).

[3] See B. A. Sijes, *De arbeidsinzet. De gedwongen arbeid van Nederlanders in Duitsland, 1940–1945* (Amsterdam, 1990 [1966]) (this book has an English summary, pp. 655–97).

voluntary recruitment in the conquered countries in the West – hit by acute unemployment after their defeat – and, above all, the massive availability of PoWs as a work force, created a triple reserve. Further, the conquest of the heavily industrialised Western European countries opened up vast opportunities for importing locally produced goods and equipment. Throughout the war this would remain an alternative to the importation of labour, which threatened to undermine local production. At the end of 1940, the German economy, employing about three million foreigners, seemed to have reached the limits of its capacity. In the euphoric anticipation of a quick and final victory, all Dutch and Norwegian PoWs, and more than half of the Belgians, were sent home and only the French PoWs were put to work in Germany. After the invasion of the Soviet Union in June 1941, Nazi planners decided on the elimination of Soviet PoWs – categorised as *Untermenschen* – by starvation and mass executions. By September 1941, 1.4 million had died, and by the end of the year only 40 per cent of the 3.3 million PoWs were still alive.

At the end of 1941, it became increasingly clear that the prospects for victory were much farther off than first anticipated and that the German economy could not count on the return of demobilised soldiers for many months to come: on the contrary, almost two million additional soldiers were drafted between May 1941 and May 1942. All at once the labour shortage again became a pressing concern for the Nazi planners. The recruitment, by any means, of workers from occupied territories or *Reichseinsatz* was centralised under the direction of Fritz Sauckel, the former Gauleiter of Thüringen. By the time that the decision was taken to use Soviet labour, most PoWs were dead. In February 1942, massive deportations began of Soviet civilians, under even worse conditions than had been the case for the Poles. After its defeat at Stalingrad in February 1943, Germany's offensive war was reversed to become a defensive westward retreat. What had started as *Blitzkrieg* turned into a war of attrition, requiring the total mobilisation of all occupied societies. The war economy had to tap new labour reserves and find new means of recruitment. This included the economic exploitation of KZ inmates, whose forced labours had previously been merely disciplinary,[4] and the exploitation, in dreadful conditions, of 600,000 Italian soldiers, captured after the Italian change of alliance in September 1943. At the same time, propaganda minister Goebbels embarked on a new discourse, turning from cynical and triumphant racism to a neophyte Europeanist anti-communism. Europe had to join all its forces with

[4] See Ulrich Herbert, 'Labour and Extermination. Economic Interest and the Primacy of *Weltanschauung* in National Socialism', *Past & Present* 138 (1990), pp. 145–95.

Germany, fighting to save the continent from the Bolshevik menace. Increasingly, the *Reichseinsatz* turned westward too, to apply its ruthless methods to populations it had so far spared'from outright deportation. Yet even in Western Europe, Sauckel's actions exhausted the available labour surplus and the results of its successive drafts fell drastically in the course of 1943. Speer, the Reichsminister responsible for the war economy, protected the work force in vital industries in Western Europe which worked for the German war effort, whilst in the occupied societies themselves resistance against deportations was increasing, and increasingly organised.

In Western Europe, labour policies initially remained a national sphere of competence and German demands were channelled through the national labour administrations. This made labour recruitment fundamentally different from the conquered territories in the East. The initial design of local German authorities in the West – Nazification for the Dutch *Zivilverwaltung*, pacification and efficiency for the *Militärverwaltung* – was incompatible with the deportation of workers, and they would try to fend off the first demands from Berlin. As German demands increased in the course of the war, national labour administrations were faced with a permanent dilemma: compliance with German demands was the only way to prevent direct German intervention. Gradually more and more civil servants would resign, be fired or caught in acts of administrative sabotage, and be replaced with collaborationist personnel. With the advent of total war, German occupation authorities would manage labour requisitioning directly, but even then they could not do without the vital help of local administrations to track down recalcitrant workers.

The evolution of national labour policies, from relative independence to complete subordination, was matched by the universal distinction, often presented in manichean ways, of the individual workers subject to these policies as 'volunteers' and 'deportees'. With regard to the wartime experience, Ulrich Herbert states that the form of engagement – voluntary or enforced – was disregarded by the German authorities and did not fundamentally affect either the terms of the contracts or the living conditions of the workers.[5] With regard to the post-war experience, the distinction between voluntary labour and forced labour was charged with moral and patriotic meaning and became central to the experience of homecoming and reintegration.

Forced employment and employment in Germany were by no means synonymous. Both started immediately after the defeat. The economic

---

[5] Intervention in the discussion on the CEGES/SOMA-sponsored symposium on forced labour in Brussels, 6–7 Oct. 1992 (not published in the proceedings).

chaos resulting from military collapse, demobilisation and continental blockade created large numbers of unemployed in Belgium and the Netherlands, who were put to work in an increasingly dirigiste manner, primarily by suspending unemployment benefits when a mandatory job offer was refused. At the same time, large-scale propaganda incited workers to accept job offers in Germany. In the first period, forced employment was limited to the national territory and employment in Germany was, in principle, offered on a voluntary basis. The breakdown of work in Germany into a voluntary period and a subsequent period of forced labour, so prevalent in the historiography, mirrors the concern for a value judgement according to patriotic measures. In 1966 the Dutch historian Ben Sijes introduced a more adequate periodisation of employment in Germany: a first period of the export of jobless workers lasting until the spring of 1942, and a subsequent period of forced employment in Germany, including for employed workers.[6] Unfortunately, Sijes has not been followed by later authors. Sijes documents convincingly the way in which the precarious position of jobless workers created de facto a situation whereby work in Germany was the only alternative. Worried by mass unemployment and under pressure from the German authorities, the Dutch administration even intervened with the organisations of charity and poor relief to withhold any form of relief from the families of workers who refused employment in Germany (and had consequently lost employment benefits). This policy only reinforced the pre-war government emigration schemes to Germany. In these cases, the choice between work in Germany or starvation was not merely a matter of rhetorical exaggeration. In Belgium, the suspension of benefits from workers who refused a German contract was formally forbidden, but in reality many local labour administrations used it as a means of getting jobless and 'anti-social' elements to work, most often under German pressure.[7]

Sijes's distinction also helps to explain the different statistics for the three countries. In the Netherlands, where unemployment was worst, 227,000 workers left for Germany before the formal implementation of labour conscription to Germany in March 1942.[8] In Belgium, 120,000 workers were counted as 'volunteers'.[9] In France 'only' 184,000

[6] Sijes, Arbeidsinzet.
[7] Bart Brinckman, 'Een schakel tussen Arbeid en Leiding. Het Rijksarbeidsambt (1940–1944)', Bijdragen van het Navorsings- en Studiecentrum voor de Geschiedenis van de Tweede Wereldoorlog 12 (1989), pp. 111–15. See also, for figures on departures, Pierre Potargent, Déportation. La Mise au travail de la main-d'oeuvre Belge dans le pays et à l'étranger durant l'occupation (Brussels, n.d. [1946]).
[8] Sijes, Arbeidsinzet, p. 117 (table, p. 140).
[9] Fernand Baudhuin, L'Economie Belge sous l'occupation, 1940–1944 (Brussels, 1945).

workers left before the *Relève* took effect.[10] French historians who infer from these figures a particular French resistance to employment in Germany thus overlook the labour situation created by the totally different policy regarding PoWs.[11] One and a half million French PoWs were retained, and for the most part employed, in Germany, creating a labour shortage in several branches of the French economy.[12] 'Voluntary departures' stand inversely proportional to the figures of PoWs in captivity and proportional to unemployment figures.

During this first period, until the spring of 1942, when resolving local unemployment was the main concern, different forms of forced labour were established. Forced labour in the national territory was established formally in the Netherlands at the end of February 1941 and one year later in Belgium. Dutch measures were not only implemented earlier, they were also more stringent, including disciplinary camps for workers who left their job before the end of their contract – a Dutch breed of Arbeitserziehungslager. Forced labour in Germany was also first imposed in the Netherlands, on 23 March 1942. France followed on 4 September and Belgium on 6 October of the same year. The sooner conscription was organised, the sooner resistance against it rose, and the sooner deportation figures dropped.

In the year following the proclamation of forced labour in the Netherlands, between April 1942 and April 1943, seven successive national campaigns screening factories and administrations for surplus labour forced 163,000 workers to accept employment in Germany – that is, 64 per cent of the 254,000 workers Sauckel had claimed. A closer look at the departures shows that the rate dropped quickly after mid-December 1942: until then 86 per cent of German demands had been fulfilled (111,000 of 129,000). The Dutch administration was increasingly Nazified and consequently mistrusted by the population. Repeated German attempts at a tighter registration of workers met with failure. In April 1943 the German authorities tried to strike a significant blow by recalling the 300,000 Dutch soldiers and officers they had liberated in

---

[10] Figure quoted by Philippe Burrin, *La France à l'heure Allemande, 1940–1944* (Paris, 1995), p. 289, and Azéma, *De Munich à la Libération*, p. 210.

[11] See Roger Frankenstein [Robert Frank], 'Die deutschen Arbeitskräfteaushebungen in Frankreich und die Zusammenarbeit der französischen Unternehmen mit der Besatzungsmacht, 1940–1944', in Dlugoborski, *Zweiter Weltkrieg und sozialer Wandel*, pp. 211–23, and Jacques Evrard, *La Déportation des travailleurs français dans le IIIe Reich* (Paris, 1971), pp. 21–32, who both quote the figure of 82,000 'volunteers'.

[12] See Alan Milward, *The New Order and the French Economy* (Oxford, 1970); Jean-Marie d'Hoop, 'La Main-d'oeuvre française au service de l'Allemagne', *Revue d'Histoire de la Deuxième Guerre Mondiale* 81 (1971), pp. 73–88; and A. Laurens, 'Le STO dans le département de l'Ariège', *Revue d'Histoire de la Deuxième Guerre Mondiale* 95 (July 1974), pp. 51–74.

May 1940. The measure was answered by a massive strike of the Dutch population, followed by brutal repression. On the whole, the action was a failure: only 11,000 soldiers left for Germany. Obstruction came not in the first place from civil disobedience, but from the German *Rüstungsinspektion*, Speer's local commissioners, whose priority was to safeguard local Dutch production capacity for the German army and who systematically delivered exemption certificates to its employees. From May through September 1943, Sauckel's offices then launched the draft-year actions that had proved successful in France and Belgium from February of the same year, targeting three age groups per month of the 18- to 35-year-olds. This time, it was the increasing opposition from the Dutch population that obstructed the levy. From mid-1943, networks of assistance to workers in hiding developed, and draft evasion was promoted as a patriotic duty. The LO, the most widespread Dutch resistance organisation, specialised exclusively in this task. In the first nine months of 1943, more than 140,000 workers were rounded up. In the following ten months, until August 1944, the figure was fewer than 22,000. The failed liberation of the Netherlands in October 1944 added a particularly tragic last chapter to the labour deportations. The forced construction of defensive installations on the new front line was fuelled by unprecedented mass roundups. On 10 and 11 November alone, 50,000 male inhabitants of Rotterdam were deported. Similar actions in other cities procured at least 120,000 trench-diggers for the Wehrmacht.

In Belgium, the implementation of forced labour in the territory of the *Militärverwaltung* in March 1942 was answered by the resignation of the secretary-general of the labour ministry.[13] The subsequent imposition of forced labour in Germany of 6 October 1942, applying to all male workers between eighteen and fifty years old and single female workers between twenty-one and thirty-five, set off even wider protests in the Belgian establishment, who recalled with horror the traumatic deportations of 1917.[14] Belgian protests obtained just one concession to its moral indignation: from 22 March 1943 onwards, women, with the exception of domestics, were no longer deported to Germany. In France and the Netherlands, 30,000 to 40,000 workers had been forced to leave for Germany during the summer months of 1942. In Belgium, forced

---

[13] See Mark Van den Wijngaert, Els De Bens and J. Culot, 'De verplichte tewerkstelling in België (1940–1944)', *Bijdragen van het Navorsings- en Studiecentrum voor de Geschiedenis van de Tweede Wereldoorlog* 1 (1970), pp. 7–68; and *De Verplichte Tewerkstelling in Duitsland/Le Travail Obligatoire en Allemagne, 1942–1945* (published proceedings, CEGES/SOMA conference, Brussels, 1993).

[14] Albert De Jonghe, 'Aspecten van de wegvoering van koning Leopold III naar Duitsland (7 juni 1944)', *Bijdragen van het Navorsings- en Studiecentrum voor de Geschiedenis van de Tweede Wereldoorlog* 11 (1988), pp. 5–19.

employment in Germany started only in October of the same year, but during the last quarter of 1942 the slightly fewer than 50,000 Belgian departures almost equalled the Dutch figures. During the first six months of 1943 100,000 workers were levied – that is, half of all departures in the course of the two years of forced labour in Germany. Of the remaining 50,000 workers, only 20,000 were drafted in the course of 1944. As in the Netherlands, departure rates did not increase as the German needs grew more desperate: they plummeted. In February 1943, at the same time as the STO legislation in France and three months before similar actions took effect in the Netherlands, the draft-years of men born in 1920 and 1921 had been levied, extended in April to the classes of 1922 through 1924. Resistance plans for financial assistance to workers in hiding, on funds advanced by local banks with guaranteed reimbursement by the government-in-exile, only really functioned from April 1944 onwards.[15]

The French situation was determined by two particularities: the captivity of the PoWs in Germany and the desire of Vichy to sustain at least the appearance of holding the initiative in German–French relations, to demonstrate that the *collaboration d'Etat* was a beneficial trade-off, rather than a systematic bowing to German ukazes.[16] The *Relève*, or 'relief', was the combination of both. Sauckel's demands for labour from Western Europe were staved off in France by Prime Minister Laval's plan to provide Germany with skilled workers whilst recovering PoWs, primarily those needed in the agricultural sector in France. The exchange rate was unfavourable: for every liberated PoW, three skilled workers had to leave for Germany, but the plan allowed Laval to launch an appeal for voluntary departures on multiple grounds. There was an economic rationale: France's soil needed its farmers. There was a sentimental motive: families had been without a father and a husband for two years now, and it was only fair and human that others should take their place and allow the reunion of families ripped apart. There was, lastly, an ideological context. In his radio speech of 22 June 1942, calling for the *Relève*, Laval crossed the Rubicon of collaboration by declaring that he wished for a German victory. Laval's initiative was suicidal for the popularity of the regime. The plan proved to be a huge swindle: the return of PoWs was given much publicity, but the actual exchange rate was around seven departures for every single return, and

---

[15] Etienne Verhoeyen, 'Le Gouvernement en exil et le soutien clandestin aux réfractaires', in *De Verplichte Tewerkstelling*, pp. 133–64.

[16] See Milward, *The New Order*; Frank, 'Arbeitskräfteaushebungen'; d'Hoop, 'La Main d'oeuvre'; and Evrard, *La Déportation*. The last is more complete, though uncritical (Evrard was himself drafted for the STO in Germany).

in some areas the rate was even less favourable.[17] The principle of voluntary departures was also in shreds, and screening commissions toured factories to force individual workers into German contracts. Deportation of workers began in the occupied northern part of France, and local factories were closed on German orders.

On 6 September, an obligatory labour service was proclaimed by Vichy, 'in the higher interest of the nation' (and not 'on German orders'), for the same group designated by the German decree in Belgium one month later: men aged from eighteen to fifty and single women aged from twenty-one to thirty-five. By December 1942 the *relève* and accompanying actions delivered 240,000 workers to Germany, almost fully fulfilling Sauckel's demand. In January 1943, Sauckel and Laval agreed on the delivery of another 250,000 workers. This time the 'concession' obtained by Vichy was even less than through the *Relève*. The delivery of fresh French workers would not liberate PoWs; it would only allow the 'transformation' in Germany of an equal number of PoWs into free civilian workers, receiving the same salaries as German workers, rather than working as unpaid captives. This measure was introduced by the Germans to increase motivation and productivity. The French PoWs themselves lost more in the operation than they gained. Without the status of PoW, they lost the international protection of the Geneva Convention and were subject to the same persecutions as any civilian in the Reich. They also lost the esteem of their home country, and when they finally came home they were suspect as collaborators (see below, p. 162). The transformation was presented as a free and individual choice, but by the time of the Allied landing 250,000 PoWs had been transformed into civilian workers with or without their consent and most often in groups. The *Relève* and the 'transformation' show how, for France, labour conscripts and PoWs constituted two interchangeable bodies, or communicating vessels, in the minds both of the Germans and of Vichy. This fact contributed to the homogeneous view of all French in 'exile', later in 'deportation'.

On 16 February 1943, the Obligatory Labour Service in Germany or STO (Service du Travail Obligatoire) established compulsory service for two years for all men born in 1920, 1921 or 1923. This measure surpassed even its own targets: from January through April 1943, 250,259 workers left for Germany. During the summer of 1943, the STO was further extended, levying an additional 105,610 workers. In September 1943, an agreement between Vichy's minister Jean Biche-lonne and Albert Speer, establishing privileged companies working for

---

[17] Frank, 'Arbeitskräfteaushebungen', p. 213.

the German army and employing between them two million workers, stopped further deportations, as had happened a few months earlier in the Netherlands. Sauckel's last levy in the first half of 1944, targeting one million workers, rounded up fewer than 50,000 additional conscripts. Evasion of the labour draft was generalised, and thousands of workers went into hiding. Contrary to the traditional assimilation of labour draft-dodgers and resistance fighters, only a minority of the clandestine individuals crossed the line from self-protection to counter-attack. Even where draft-evaders were grouped in remote regions in the so-called *maquis* and obtained financial support from the organised resistance, opportunities for armed resistance – weapons for a start – were scarce and subversive activity often suicidal.

Despite specific national features, the overall picture of labour requisitioning in the three countries is very similar. Requisitioning primarily took two forms: first, the screening of the labour force in factories and administrations and the forced departure of workers judged as surplus, and, secondly, the levy of entire age groups for labour service in Germany, based on the principles of pre-war military service. Forced labour in Germany was imposed in the second half of 1942, with a few months' advance for the Netherlands, and the draft-year moves started with the defeat at Stalingrad early in 1943, with a few months' delay in the Netherlands.

The three national case studies point to two conclusions. First, the voluntary departures in the first phase were less voluntary than is assumed in most literature. Secondly, the forced departures, with the exception of the last period of massive man-hunts in the Netherlands, were often less forced than is usually portrayed. Statistics indicate that deportation figures dropped as the means of constraint were strengthened. In the Netherlands, the massive departures in the second half of 1942 diminished markedly during the first half of 1943 and almost ceased between the summer of 1943 and the summer of 1944. In France and Belgium, departure rates remained high until April 1943, then halved during the summer of 1943, and dropped very sharply during the last year of the occupation. The difference between the mandatory contracts offered to the jobless on sanction of losing their unemployment benefits and the call-up for work in Germany issued to workers in the second period was in real terms very small. The individual worker, economically dependent, was left with no choice but to accept. Only once defence mechanisms developed – on the part of the employers and their German business partners and subsequently on the part of the resistance – was the refusal to leave a concrete alternative.

This is not to say that the experience of Western European workers

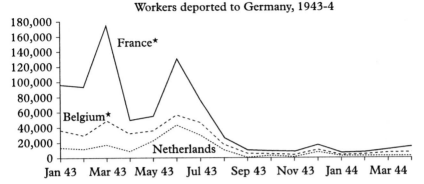

*The workers from the French departments of Pas de Calais and Nord are included in the Belgian figures.

7.1 Departures of Belgian, French and Dutch workers, 1943–4

was homogenous and that the individual condition of workers did not matter; on the contrary, other distinctions, not of a moral nature, mattered far more: the type of employment, and the time factor.[18] In principle, West European workers were employed on the same terms and salaries as German workers. None of the discriminatory regulations for Eastern European workers applied to them. Workers employed in small family enterprises – farms, bakeries, shoemakers – often shared the life of the family, enjoyed better material conditions than at home and established a good relationship with their employers, whose businesses depended on their aid.[19] The overwhelming majority of workers, however, worked in factories in the industrial centres of the Reich. Their main complaints concerned housing: barracks had to be improvised for their shelter, sanitary installations were often inadequate, the food provided by collective kitchens was unsavoury. The constraints of collective and rudimentary life in dormitories and the separation from

[18] See Helga Bories-Sawala, *Franzosen im 'Reichseinsatz'. Deportation, Zwangarbeit, Alltag* (Frankfurt, 1996). See further the fine mosaic of interviews by Jean-Pierre Vittori, *Eux, les STO* (Paris, 1982); Karel Volder's militant *Werken in Duitsland, 1940–1945* (Amsterdam, 1990); Evrard, *La Déportation*; Carine Hurtekant, 'De verplichte tewerkstelling van Bruggelingen', in *De Verplichte Tewerkstelling*, pp. 93–105; Erik Pertz, 'La Mise au travail des Coutraisiens en Allemagne (1940–1945)', *Cahiers d'Histoire de la Seconde Guerre Mondiale* 4 (1976), pp. 181–200. Amongst the numerous autobiographies, see especially J. L. Quereillhac, *J'étais STO* (Paris, 1958), and Bertie Ham, *Arbeider in Moffenland* (Laren, 1945).

[19] See Lucien Ranson's published letters home in *De Gedeporteerden* (Kortrijk, 1983), and the nostalgic souvenirs of shoemaker Frans Hahn in Berlin in Bert Coenen, 'De Bierkaai van de vergetelheid. Leuven, 1944–1995', unpublished MA thesis (Leuven, 1995).

home and family were, not unlike military service, ill supported by some of those subjected to it, as the next section will discuss. The large concentrations of worker accommodation, often called 'camps', were closely supervised. Discipline was imposed by German managers from the factory that employed the workers, assisted by local police. The consequences of indiscipline were draconian, considering the conditions of internment in the Arbeitserziehungslager and prisons. In cases of serious and repeated offences, foreign workers could end up in concentration camps. The most traumatising experience for most workers was the continuous bombing of the industrial centres in which they were concentrated, the permanent alerts, the massive destruction and fires, the injuries, and the casualties. The German population had priority access to the shelters and in the vicinity of the barracks often nothing was prepared for the protection of foreign workers. If labour conscripts were war victims in a narrow, traditional sense, it was from Allied warfare that they suffered most. The living conditions of foreign workers deteriorated severely after the Allied landings, and the workers found themselves *de facto* hostages: holidays at home were suspended, correspondence was impossible, bombing intensified. Those workers who remained behind the front line between the summer of 1944 and May 1945 all lived through terrifying months up to their repatriation. However, not all labour conscripts did stay until the end, nor were all those who did conscripts – an ambiguity that would weigh heavily on their return.

What were the post-war social consequences of these experiences for the occupied countries? Was the working class radicalised as a result of the burden piled upon it by the occupant, of the costs of total war? The 'move to the left' which transformed the political landscape in the occupied countries has often been observed in literature. Communist parties entered government in France and Belgium, and agitated against the government through radicalised unions in the Netherlands. Socialist parties radicalised (except again in the Netherlands) and increased their share of the national vote. Yet, first, the precise nature of the social radicalisation from which these political changes developed is not clear. Gabriel Kolko asserts the emergence of a revolutionary mass consciousness, but refuses to identify it with any political movement, least of all the communist parties, which he describes as anti-revolutionary, bureaucratic and subservient to Soviet imperialism.[20] Robert Frank even goes so far as to assert that 'war and the German occupation contributed more to the strengthening of French capitalism than libera-

---

[20] Kolko, *Politics of War*, pp. 428–56.

tion and the subsequent period to the establishment of labour organisations'.[21] Secondly and more importantly, it has nowhere been empiri-
cally established whether or not this move to the left was the result of the
particular wartime experience of labour exploitation in general, and of
the deportation of a large section of the working class in particular.
What is therefore needed is an analysis of the post-war behaviour of
deported workers as a social group.

Did deported workers act as the militant vanguard of a suppressed
and radicalised working class? A narrow social and economic interpretation of the experience of forced economic migration ignores the
context of the post-war reintegration of deported workers. Ideologically,
these workers returned to societies that identified retrospectively with
the victors of the war and were embarrassed by this mass of losers, who
had been forced to work for their enemy's war industry. Morally, the
liberated societies were alarmed by the return of these victims of crude
proletarianisation, contaminated by the promiscuity and amorality of
the downtrodden slave labourers gathered from all over the continent in
the industrial centres of the Reich. As things stood, repatriated workers
already faced a difficult task in pressing ahead with their own narrowly
defined claims of reparation and rehabilitation. Rather than operating as
a vanguard, the labour conscripts could achieve reintegration only by
maintaining a low profile in the modest role of war victims in their
associations.

---

[21] Frank, 'Arbeitskräfteaushebungen', p. 221.

8   Moral panic: 'the soap, the suit and above all the Bible'

The archives of Frénay's services in Algiers offer a fascinating window on how Western European workers in Germany were perceived.[1] A voluminous report reached Algiers on 25 August 1943 – that is, even before Frénay took office – consisting of edited excerpts from correspondence with French and Belgian workers in Germany (part 1) and French workers working in France for the German organisation Todt (part 2).[2] The report was probably transmitted by Gaullist agents in Vichy. It offers a balanced view of the workers' material living conditions, pointing out the very favourable conditions enjoyed by workers employed in family businesses or on the land, and adding that even for workers in the industrial centres material conditions were often 'very adequate'. In its section on the nature of the forced labour it goes to great lengths to show that the main complaint of the workers was not physical exhaustion due to the strenuous nature of the work, but rather the boredom of long and idle hours in the factory and the frustratingly slow pace. The main, and in many cases obsessive, focus of attention for the authors of the report is the moral conditions. In the introduction they warn that, even if the material conditions are satisfactory, 'this mass of more than one million – or, including the foreigners, more than ten million – workers is doomed to an extraordinary moral decay, the consequences of which are incalculable'. The report, because it is so representative of widespread opinions on labour conscripts, and because it had such a profound influence on the perceptions of opinion-makers, deserves ample quotation:

Morality. Here the degeneration of this mass of millions of workers is truly appalling. It has its roots in this barrack-room life of a promiscuous crowd of

---

[1] The concept of 'moral panic', applying to the context of the social trauma of liberation and repatriation, is borrowed from Herman De Liagre Böhl and Guus Meershoek, *De bevrijding van Amsterdam. Een strijd om macht en moraal* (Amsterdam, 1989), pp. 81, 157–9.

[2] *France Politique, BIP 8/25704* (9 Oct. 1943), AN F9 3106.

men, women, youngsters, young girls, of all races (French, Spanish, Czech, Polish, Russians etc.), a mass which is completely cut off from all its natural links: home, town or village, neighbourhood, parish etc. . . . which are so important for morality. Depression, human respect [*sic*], boredom, tiredness, malnutrition all encourage the coarsest of satisfactions. One should add the extreme shamelessness of foreign women, even Germans, and the abundance of contraceptive devices, available to all (there are vending machines on metro and railway platforms, in public toilets), all this creating a climate of sexual excess, which surprises even many French workers. 'France is a monastery, compared to Germany', wrote one of them . . .

Arriving in Germany, we were directed towards a sorting centre, in a camp of Russian prisoners (civilians) . . . I can tell you about an orgy in this camp. At night, they had organised a party in one barrack room. There were two accordions, and mass obscenities, and whilst some danced others spent their time in bed with the women. Still others took their mattresses to the toilets and took the women with them. With all this, there was great drinking. I assure you, I have a strong stomach, but this was too much. I wept, seeing this low behaviour, or rather, this human decay . . .

In one camp, where a youngster spent two nights, the second night, in this dormitory of 30 guys per group, there were three Belgian girls who spent the night with the guys taking turns on them. One of them received '16 stings' [*piqûres*] in the course of the night. (Excuse my expression, but I don't know how to explain to make you understand.) The next day, during the whole day, it started all over and sometimes two at the same time. It is unfortunately all too true . . .

Nudity is excessively common here. Without Christ, there is no way to resist . . .

German propaganda would say that we are rotten people. That may be true, but they are even more so. Morality is dreadful. Since many men go around bare-chested on the days of coal distribution, the camp intendant caresses them like a woman. Of course, the guys let him have his way, since it means that they get a double ration . . .

Besides, I must have told you already of the slot-machines for condoms [*capotes anglaises*] and tubes of Vaseline you find in all public toilets.

In Hamburg, in certain pubs, you can get addresses of young girls. It is an organised service. You pay a subscription. In our village, the major pub has toilets that are a real brothel, and it's the girls who make the advances. At night, you can see some who do it on the pavement, against a wall . . .

The report goes on for many pages with similar extracts. With repeated vigour and matching moral indignation, it describes incidents of mixed sanitary installations, availability of pornography, music-hall spectacles in worker camps with strip-tease acts, indecent pictures on the walls of dormitories, coarse language and dirty jokes.

A careful reading of the otherwise unidentified excerpts reveals that they originated in the follow-up action of the Jeunesse Ouvrière Chrétienne (JOC), the Catholic Workers' Youth movement, for its members who were dispersed in Germany.[3] The JOC was founded in Belgium and France in the 1920s as one of the most dynamic branches of Catholic Action, sharing its missionary spirit for the re-Christianisation of the working classes under strict clerical guidance.[4] The movement was characterised by feverish spirituality and moral ardour. In the moral-religious world view of Catholic Action, Catholicism was eroded through the disappearance of a rural and Catholic society, characterised by stable local 'organic' communities with the parish at its centre. The advent of the Popular Front and the success of fascist movements, recruiting predominantly Catholic grass-roots support but impervious to clerical guidance, had further weakened Catholic influence in society. In this view the moral and spiritual decay of pre-war society had inevitably contributed to the defeat of 1940. This vision it shared to a large extent with Pétain and his ideology of atonement and rebirth through asceticism, together with purely religious anxieties, as expressed, for instance, in the influential publication of *La France, Pays de Mission* during the first years of the occupation.[5] The entire action of the JOC was aimed at a reconquest of the working class through the build-up of local organisations, creating durable loyalties in a core of devoted and devout lay activists supporting the clergy, who in their turn had to exert their influence over the wider working class through various recreational, social and religious activities. The massive dislocation of workers was in this perspective a true catastrophe. In Germany, Catholic workers would be torn from their sheltered *milieux*, cut off from all forms of social control and spiritual guidance, exposed to the influences of anti-clerical compatriots, moral temptations and, as illustrated in the excerpts above, with only a slight touch of xenophobia, the pernicious influences of promiscuity with 'other races'. Forced economic migration of individual workers was a pure form of 'crude proletarianisation', the

---

[3] The report circulated widely and became a most popular read in clerical circles, perused with a combination of moral horror and pornographic fascination. The first cleric to quote it extensively was Jean Pelissier, *Si la Gestapo avait su! Un prêtre à l'opéra de Munich et dans la haute couture* (Paris, 1945), later reproduced by Evrard, *La Déportation*, p. 325, and Vittori, *Eux, les STO*, p. 193. Charles Molette, *'En haine de l'Evangile'. Victimes du décret de persécution nazi du 3 décembre 1943 contre l'apostolat catholique français à l'oeuvre parmi les travailleurs requis en Allemagne, 1943–1945* (Paris, 1993), reproduces the first part of the report on pp. 304–21, based on a copy in the archives of the French church, identical to the Algerian copy in the National Archives. The report was also published in *Archives de l'Eglise de France* 30 (1988), pp. 14–30.

[4] See Louis Vos, 'La Jeunesse Ouvrière Chrétienne', in Emmanuel Gerard and Paul Wynants (eds.), *Histoire du Mouvement Ouvrier Chrétien en Belgique* (Leuven, 1994), vol. II, pp. 425–99.

[5] For the impact of the book and its author, see Emile Poulat, *Naissance des prêtres-ouvriers* (Paris, 1965).

cause of the secularisation of the masses which Catholic Action sought to resist.

The JOC was particularly hard hit by the draft-year levies, which were aimed at the younger age groups that constituted its membership. At the same time, the movement was convinced that its mode of functioning was particularly well suited to the mission of evangelising disoriented workers in Germany. Its militants had volunteered for work in Germany long before the imposition of forced employment, to carry their missionary zeal to the exiles. With the draft-year actions of February–March 1943, the JOC militants who were forced to leave for Germany received detailed instructions for their future missionary activity, and were mentally supported by correspondence to keep track of all departing members. Through this intense correspondence, following partly pre-established questionnaires, the JOC also obtained detailed reports of the situation in the field.[6] These reports mirrored their preoccupations: first, an obsession with all matters regarding sexual morality, and secondarily a concern with the opportunities for 'evangelising' – primarily the promotion of church-going, at the very least for Easter. As things stood in Germany, the first task alone seemed insurmountable enough to the Catholic militants.

The moralising and missionary activities of Catholic militants amongst the workers in Germany have inspired a staggering volume of historical and hagiographic publications and given birth to a specifically Catholic resistance myth.[7] According to this myth, the main objective of Catholic action amongst the workers in Germany was to combat Nazification and to promote their loyalty to church and country. As such, this Catholic action was perceived as a major threat by the Nazi authorities, and its protagonists were mercilessly persecuted. Some of these authors, including in the most recent publications, do not hesitate to assimilate the persecution of Catholics with the persecution of Jews:

---

[6] See Henri Bourdais, *La JOC sous l'occupation allemande* (Paris, 1995), pp. 127–59, for a reproduction of instructions given to militants leaving for Germany.

[7] All the following publications show an astonishing continuity. Almost literal continuity exists between Coine, *Kajottersweerstand*, and Frans Selleslagh, 'De clandestiene KAJ in Duitsland (1942–1945)', in Frans Hugaerts (ed.), *De KAJ, haard van verzet (1940–1945)* (Ghent, 1989), pp. 199–230. See also Bourdais, *La JOC sous l'occupation*; Molette, *'En haine de l'Evangile'*, pleading for the 'collective beatification' of French Catholicism as a victim of 'Nazi atheism from 1940 to 1945', p. 37; *Jocistes dans la tourmente. Histoire des jocistes (JOC–JOCF) de la région parisienne 1937–1947* (Paris, 1989); G. Cholvy and J. P. Bonthal (eds.), *JOC–JOCF. Efficacité et postérité d'un mouvement d'action catholique de jeunesse, de 1927 à 1950* (Lyons, 1991). Poulat, *Naissance des prêtres-ouvriers*, includes a bibliography of hagiographies published in four languages. The best reference is Charles Klein, *L'Aumônerie des barbelés, 1940–1947* (Cachan, 1967), and Klein, *Le Diocèse des barbelés, 1940–1944* (Paris, 1973) (with a preface by Abbot Rodhain, the protagonist of the work).

in both cases the atheist Nazi regime persecuted its worst enemies, the world religions. Another recurrent theme in the description of the action of Catholics in this 'pagan German Empire' is that it reincarnated early Christianity in the 'pagan Roman Empire': 'the same dangers, the same clandestine reunions, the same faith, the same friendship, the same charity, the same persecution, too'.[8] Corresponding to the martyrs of early Christianity, this more recent Catholic resistance myth is adorned with hagiographies of the martyrs of Nazism whose Calvary had been the concentration camp. Martyrologies differ considerably according to the time and place of each publication, but the most recent Catholic author claims to have retraced up to fifty French 'victims of anti-religious persecution', all Catholic militants from various backgrounds, victims he offers as candidates for beatification.[9] These figures, which can, on all accounts, be considered absolute maxima, are not the only reason to reject radically any comparison of the misadventures of some isolated priest or Catholic militant in Germany during the war with the Nazi persecution of any other group, least of all the Jews.

Spiritual care for the workers in Germany had, particularly in Vichy France, a completely official context, very unlike the claimed clandestinity of catacomb Christianity.[10] During the first months of 1942, even before the implementation of the *Relève*, French clerical authorities were alerted by reports on the moral and spiritual decay amongst French exiles in Germany through the correspondence of Catholic voluntary workers. The French church assured a vast chaplaincy service in Germany for all French PoWs, whose right to spiritual care was stipulated in the Geneva convention, and the idea was simply to extend this assistance to French civilian workers, benefiting from the same official diplomatic recognition. Cardinal Suhard and his emissary Abbot Rodhain took every official step to this effect through correspondence and official visits to Rome, Vichy and Berlin. Ecclesiastical anxieties at the loss of influence over the workers increased dramatically with the implementation of the *Relève*, transformation and STO. The Nazi regime in Berlin was not inclined to extend any specific protection enjoyed by PoWs to civilian workers, but the principle of an official chaplain service was favourably received by the Auswärtiges Amt (the German Foreign Office), because a guarantee of spiritual assistance by French priests would stimulate workers to leave for Germany. Berlin maintained its official opposition to formally accredited chaplains, because it did not intend to allow the development of a parallel

---

[8] Klein, *L'Aumônerie*, 40.
[9] Molette, '*En haine de l'Evangile*', passim.
[10] The official side of the story is dropped from all accounts, except Klein's.

immigrant church with religious services in foreign languages. Nor did the Deutsche Arbeitsfront intend to give up its monopoly over social and cultural activities for the workers for the benefit of exclusive Catholic organisations. The French church, for its part, increased the pressure on Vichy. It is not beyond imagination that some of the moral panic expressed by the report of the summer of 1943, quoted above, was manipulated to this end.[11]

Catholic activism flourished amongst workers in Germany, partly to compensate for the absence of an officially recognised chaplaincy service – a success reflected, amongst others ways, in JOC membership figures reaching their peak in 1945. Much as Pétain and De Gaulle competed through postal parcels for the political allegiance of French people in Germany, the Catholic church competed for their souls. There were 835,000 bibles mailed to Germany, along with 185,000 litres of sacramental wine, and countless do-it-yourself liturgy packages and prayer books. Up to the very end of the occupation, Abbot Rodhain was officially accredited to Pétain, which earned him a warrant of arrest on charges of collaboration at the time of the liberation. The JOC had its official representative with Vichy's Scapini mission in Berlin, and Rodhain encouraged his congregation to work in harmony with Vichy's fervently collaborationist Commission for Labour in Germany, citing his own close collaboration with Bruneton as an example.[12]

What then of the martyrs? The brief detention in prison of French and Belgian JOC leaders during the occupation and the internment in Arbeitserziehungslager and concentration camps (though the distinction is rarely made in the Catholic publications cited above) of a few dozen Catholic militants and priests was mostly concerned with territorial competition with collaborationist youth organisations, and with a series of errors. The latter explanation appears in the memoirs of most of the militants who later asserted their surprise at being interrogated over subversive activities by the Sicherheitsdienst (the SS secret police), when all they ever strove for was piety and puritanism.[13] That fewer than fifty Catholic militants were victims of persecution at a time when hundreds of thousands of others were victim of arbitrary arrest, deportation and murder singles them out more as a group particularly spared from persecution than targeted for it.

The establishment of Catholic organisations amongst the workers in

---

[11] On 30 June 1943 Pétain addressed a note to Prime Minister Laval to support the chaplaincy service, pointing to the terrible moral and physical dangers that threatened the French youth in Germany; it was probably motivated by similar, if not the same, alarmist reporting. Cardinal Suhard had expressly asked Pétain to do this: Klein, *Le Diocèse*, p. 220.

[12] Ibid., pp. 324–5.   [13] Ibid., p. 225.

Germany and the systematic correspondence and reporting make them the most important source on the conditions of the workers, apart from the official collaborationist organisations whose only interest lay in presenting a rosy picture of life in Germany. I have reconstructed here one line of documentation from Catholic militants through Vichy to Algiers. Yet Catholic catastrophism was not the only, nor the most important, message conveyed through these channels. Even more lasting in its effects was the implicit moral grading of the workers, a categorisation that infiltrated its way into the general perception of this group. One particularly representative publication grades them as follows. French workers in Germany arrived in three waves, each stemming from a different social class and accordingly of a very different moral value. First of all volunteers: 'Amongst them a majority of anti-social and unstable elements, men in search of adventure and illicit profits, fleeing from the social constraints of their families, men from the underworld, delinquents, former prison inmates.' Next came the qualified workers of the *Relève*, who 'offer a fairly representative image of the French working class, from which they have been extracted by force . . . Formed (over many generations) by their upbringing, their social environment, their journals, their political and union leaders, the French conscripts have, for the most part, not the "slightest spiritual anxieties", not the slightest question mark. Their lives are self-sufficient.' The third group consisted of the draft-year levies of the STO, which targeted all social classes indiscriminately: 'The young Frenchmen of the STO who do not stem from the working class are as bewildered by this plunge into the life of the worker, the common life in the barracks, as by the contact with this Germany at war, rigidly attentive to its task, stoical in spite of the terrifying Anglo-Saxon bombings.'[14]

Catholic militants found themselves faced with 'the transgressive individualism, the selfishness, the greed for profit, the filthiness, the automatic grumbling, the lack of morality and the spiritual indifference of the majority of their compatriots'. They very explicitly based their moral contempt for their compatriots on social prejudice. Although their vocation was directed at the working class, the militants of Catholic Action were themselves mostly from a middle-class background. The trauma of STO was for them primarily caused by their social 'deportation' into a working-class environment, with its rough manners and crude language, and only in the second place by their geographical deportation to Germany. This different experience of young men from a

---

[14] Ibid., pp. 289–93.

sheltered *milieu*, unaccustomed to material hardships, to the cultural values of the working class and to community life (dormitories, canteen food and communal showers are the most recurrent complaints), was to be decisive after the war in the labour conscript organisations. Particularly in Belgium, as I will discuss in detail further on, the organisation of deported workers was entirely animated by young labour conscripts from a middle-class background.

The effects of social prejudice became wholly terrifying when combined with sexual prejudice. No single group was more, and more unequivocally, morally demonised than the women workers in Germany. The same author writes of them:

The women voluntary workers (about 50,000) are partly recruited from the dregs of the major French cities, but amongst them are also a good number of young girls and women who came to try their fortunes: victims of unemployment, victims of propaganda in favour of work in Germany, victims most often of the incapacity or disorder of their parents from whom they wished to escape . . . These women workers, placed in conditions of promiscuity and indescribable misery, are practically condemned to concubinage or prostitution. The women's Lager are often a true 'hell' of immorality and misery: one finds corpses of new-born babies, thrown in toilets and garbage cans and, in the rooms, neglected babies in wooden crates next to bunk beds. The behaviour of the French women in Germany profoundly humiliates most French prisoners and workers and the Christian militants of Berlin will have trouble recognising as their 'sisters' the ones whom [their chaplain] will try to draw out of their quagmire.[15]

The overall condemnation of women workers was not only the product of clerical misogyny. A report of September 1943 by Vichy's Commission for Labour in Germany repeats almost verbatim the diatribes cited above.[16] Every single mention of French women workers in Germany in sources emanating from Vichy's services shares the same overall moral condemnation. According to the ideology of the 'National Revolution', this is hardly surprising: women were in principle not supposed to work outside the home, let alone to travel abroad unaccompanied.[17] The same moral indignation had focused protests from the Belgian establishment against forced work in Germany for women, and obtained their

---

[15] Ibid., p. 290. Futher derogatory comments on 'filles douteuses' and misogynist action, inspired by inordinate puritanism, can be found in Herni Perrin, *Journal d'un prêtre-ouvrier en Allemagne* (Paris, 1945).

[16] See the reports *Etat d'esprit des prisonniers de guerre* (Vichy, Mar. 1943), AN F9 3105; *La situation de la main d'oeuvre française en Allemagne. Rapport du Commissariat à la Main d'Oeuvre au Ministère de la Production Industrielle* (Vichy, Sep. 1943), and *Conditions de vie des travailleurs français au camp de Strathof (Vienne)* (Algiers, 28 Mar. 1944), both in AN F9 3106.

[17] See Francine Muel-Dreyfus, *Vichy et l'éternel féminin* (Paris, 1996), esp. pp. 123–7, and W. D. Halls, *The Youth of Vichy France* (Oxford, 1981), pp. 369–70.

exemption after a few months, with the notable exception of workers in domestic service, seen traditionally as the only decent occupation for single women. Yet misogynist prejudice was not only restricted to clerical circles and the Vichy old guard: it also permeated the thinking of Frénay's ministerial planners for repatriation. The frequently reproduced categorisation of workers in Germany ran as follows.[18] For male workers, there were three periods. The first period ran until March 1942. All workers who left before this date, when Vichy merely tolerated German propaganda but did not itself promote departures, were 100 per cent volunteers. The second period, until September 1942, was still one of voluntary departures, but the workers of the *Relève* were less culpable than their predecessors, because they were the victims of Vichy propaganda. All departures after September 1942, the third period, were 100 per cent conscripts. However, as the next section will discuss, Frénay adopted a courageous attitude in defending the voluntary male workers. Guy De Tassigny, responsible for the workers in Frénay's ministry, described the voluntary workers as follows, in a number of reports and speeches: 30 per cent are really voluntary workers; 40 per cent are attracted by the financial benefits; 30 per cent want to escape legal prosecution of some sort in France. Ideology, greed and common criminality are the triple forces of male motivation. Sometimes the desire to travel, to see a different country, learn a different language or a purely adventurous spirit are added as possible motives for men. Women are targeted differently: 'There are two categories of women who left for Germany: those who left to join their PoW husbands and those of low morality.'[19] Spouses or whores: even the services of the Provisional Government of the French Republic in Algiers handled rather primitive analytical tools when describing the female DP population. The pedigree of documents reporting on the moral conditions of the workers in Germany, from Catholic militants through the church hierarchy to Vichy and finally Algiers, might create the erroneous impression of a straightforward causal relationship. If Catholic alarmism, fuelling social and sexual prejudice, found fertile soil in much wider circles, this is because these wider circles initially shared much of these prejudices.

There is scant documentary evidence as to the actual figures and conditions of female workers from Western Europe in wartime Germany. Herbert observes that women workers were victims twice over

---

[18] See the file *dossier travailleurs*, composed of pieces emanating from the Service Psychologique in AN F9 3168, especially the transcripts of Guy De Tassigny's speeches.
[19] *Plan*, ibid. See also De Tassigny's *Travailleurs Français en Allemagne*, ibid.

– in their condition as workers and in their condition as women.[20] The forced transfer of women was an expression of ultimate racial contempt. The importation of foreign labour was a means of avoiding the employment of German women, and the lower a nationality figured on the racial hierarchy, the higher was its percentage of deported women workers, from 51 per cent of Soviet workers, to 3 per cent of workers from the former ally Hungary.[21] Statistics for Western Europe are approximate: between 40,000 and 50,000 for France and half as many for the Netherlands, each time described as 'volunteers'.[22] Only for Belgium are the statistics more precise, citing 15,000 workers for the period prior to October 1942 and 21,826 for the period of formal labour conscription – that is, 11 per cent of the total number of workers.[23] Women workers constituted the overwhelming majority of Belgians employed in Germany as domestics, the only profession where conscription was maintained after March 1943, and were also well represented in the textile industry. This occupational pattern illustrates the economic vulnerability of the female workers compared to the situation of male skilled workers in other areas. The best illustration of the exposure of women to economic constraint is provided by the departure rate. The percentage of women was low when the total volume of departures was high, in the last quarter of 1942 and the first half of 1943, yet when the male departures diminished sharply, female departures remained relatively high. In November 1943, one-third of the workers leaving for Germany were women and in December 1943 and January 1944 their proportion was almost half. These figures seem to suggest that forced economic migration – on formal grounds or as a form of subsistence – affected a limited group of – single? – women who lacked opportunities for the alternative solutions adopted so massively by male workers as the German military prospects worsened during the last year of the occupation.

The consistently derogatory or demonising representation of women workers in Germany was responsible for a series of repatriation tragedies. Reports from the Gendarmerie Nationale in the department of the Vosges in April 1945 relate two incidents, on the 26th in Thaon and on

---

[20] Herbert, *Geschichte der Ausländer-Beschäftigung*, p. 164.

[21] Ibid., p. 144.

[22] Hélène Eck, 'Les Françaises sous Vichy. Femmes du désastre, citoyennes par le désastre?', in Françoise Thébaud (ed.), *Histoire des Femmes. Le XXe siècle* (Paris, 1992), pp. 185–211; Burrin, *La France*, p. 290; Klein, *Le Diocèse*, p. 290; and Vittori, *Eux, les STO*, p. 24. Sijes, *Arbeidsinzet*, p. 504, estimates the number of Dutch women workers in Germany at 25,000, observing 'the appalling occurrence of venereal diseases and illegitimacy amongst women', compared to the irreproachable behaviour of Dutch men.

[23] See the statistical annexes in Potargent, *Déportation*.

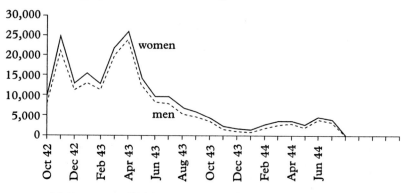

8.1 Departures of Belgian workers, male/female

the 30th in Charmes, in which angry crowds attacked repatriated young girls on the arrival of their repatriation convoy in the local railway station 'returning from Germany, after a voluntary departure, to take them apart and brutalise them'.[24] A Jewish woman who was active in Frénay's resistance movement Combat was repatriated in May 1945 in a convoy of French officer PoWs after her liberation from Litomerice concentration camp, together with other female survivors of the camp. The group travelled in open cattle wagons and the PoWs had to support the women, who were too feeble to sit up alone. The first words which met them after crossing the French frontier, shouted by French peasants along the railway line, were: 'Long live the officers, down with the whores!'[25] The fact that concentration camp inmates had their hair shaved off, the popular punishment for women who had given sexual favours to German soldiers (the *tondues*), contributed to the association repatriates–prostitutes. Another incident in the Gare de l'Est in Paris was reported to Frénay's Ministry on 2 April.[26] Here a woman was rescued from a vengeful crowd by the convoy of PoWs with whom she travelled, who persuaded the crowd to let her go only after an announcement over the station loud-speakers that she was the legitimate wife of one of the repatriated PoWs who had gone to Germany to join her husband and had been the mascot of the whole PoW camp.

[24] *Synthèse pour la période du 15/04 au 15/05 1945* (Paris, 13 June 1945), AN 72 AJ 384.
[25] 'Vive les officiers, à bas les putains!': Yvette Bernard-Farnoux, 'Interview with "IN"', in Marie-Anne Matard-Bonucci and Edouard Lynch (eds.), *La Libération des camps et le retour des déportés. L'Histoire en souffrance* (Brussels, 1995), p. 143. Rita Koopman in Amsterdam was similarly insulted as 'moffenhoer' after her repatriation, because of her shaved head: Hondius, *Terugkeer*, p. 94.
[26] Letter, Clément Legrand to the minister for prisoners, deportees and refugees (Paris, 2 Apr. 1945), AN F9 3168.

It is difficult to assess the scale of collective violence against repatriated women workers on the basis of the isolated cases that were reported. There is, however, another indication of the incidence of moral panic in the general climate surrounding the repatriation of workers from Germany: the contamination-psychosis. Repatriates were portrayed as carriers of all sorts of disease, from which the physically weakened liberated populations had to be protected by all possible prophylactic and legislative means. The epidemic-psychosis revealed the malthusian anxieties of defeated, occupied and humiliated societies, such as those expressed by Henri Frénay and described in chapter 6.[27] Typhus, and to a lesser degree dysentery and meningitis, loomed like phantoms over the whole continent, whilst some hysterical reports evoked smallpox, cholera, malaria, yellow fever and even plague.[28] Typhus did not occur, and the most serious pathology of the DP population, tuberculosis, was a chronic affliction that could not be dealt with in this type of contingency planning.[29] Yet epidemics were not the only scare in the summer of 1945.[30] The medical predictions were to a large degree the result of moral fears: venereal diseases were reckoned to be the main threat to public health imported by the repatriates.[31]

The religious authorities did not fail to contribute to the psychosis. In the Netherlands local information sessions for the spouses and fiancées of future repatriates were systematically organised all over the country by spouses of clergymen, social helpers and district nurses.[32] The meetings were to familiarise the women with the symptoms of venereal diseases and help them to re-educate their male partners. Elementary hygiene, table manners, matrimonial fidelity, family life and, above all,

[27] See *Vue générale sur les opérations de remise en place et de rapatriement à l'intérieur de la métropole*, n.d.; *Note relative aux problèmes sanitaires du rapatriement des prisonniers et déportés français* (Algiers, 14 Mar. 1944): both in AN F9 3125; and *Avant-projet d'ordonnance relative à la création d'un Service Médico-Social en faveur des rapatriés* (Paris, 12 Apr. 1945); *Décret rélatif à la réquisition des médecins, pharmaciens et chirugiens-dentistes* (Paris, 29 Mar. 1945); *Ordonnance instituant le contrôle médical des Prisonniers, Travailleurs et Déportés rapatriés* (Paris, 29 Mar. 1945): all in AN F60 10.

[28] *Note relative aux problèmes sanitaires* (Algiers, 14 Mar. 1944), AN F9 3125; and *Circulaire Staatstoezicht op de Volksgezondheid* (The Hague, 9 June 1945); *Ministerie van Sociale Zaken, directeur-generaal van de volksgezondheid aan de artsen in het bevrijd gebied van Nederland* (Eindhoven, 6 June 1945): both in RIOD, DOC II, 673A.

[29] Jacobmeyer, *Zwangsarbeiter*, pp. 43–4.

[30] See also Hansje Galesloot and Margreet Schrevel (eds.), *In Fatsoen hersteld. Zedelijkheid en Wederopbouw na de oorlog* (Amsterdam, n.d. [1987]), and De Liagre Böhl and Meershoek, *De bevrijding van Amsterdam*.

[31] See, for example, the draconian 'Verordening gewijzigde vaststelling besluit bestrijding geslachtsziekten. Verordening van den Chef van den Staf Militair Gezag', *Publicatieblad* 10 (24 Nov. 1944), RIOD, DOC II, 673A.

[32] Dr C. P. Gunning, *Circulaire aan de Kerkeraden namens de Commissie Bijzondere Kerkelijke Gezinszorg* (19 Sep. 1944), RIOD, DOC II, 673A.

religious beliefs and practices would all have vanished during the long years of absence. Briefly, the recommendation was: 'soap, his suit, but above all the Bible should lie ready to hand on his return'. Similar recommendations concerning the work ethic of repatriates even reached cabinet level – where a report predicting the 'degeneration of part of our population into a permanent *lumpenproletariat*' as a consequence of the 'morally pernicious circumstances in the country of the enemy' and recommending the organisation of work camps for their re-education – were seriously discussed, and eventually dismissed.[33] Yet the requisitioning of jobless repatriated workers for clearing rubble and war damage was implemented on a large scale – camps were impracticable due to lack of space – at least in Amsterdam, and lasted throughout the summer of 1945.[34]

Had they known of the discussions about them in the cabinet meetings of their own government two months after the liberation, the vocabulary labelling them 'anti-social elements' and calling for 'labour camps' and 're-education through conscription' – echoing the phrases of the Nazi authorities during the war – these facts would certainly have come as a shock to Dutch repatriated workers, who thought of themselves primarily as war victims. Yet the 'moral deficit' diagnosed in deported workers, which caused such panicky concern in the summer of 1945, would have transitory consequences compared to the 'patriotic deficit' of which they were simultaneously accused.

[33] *Memorandum betreffende de inschakeling in het normale leven van de repatriërende arbeiders. Stichting het Nationaal instituut aan de Minister-President* (The Hague, 4 July 1945), ARA, cab. PM, box 92; and *Nota Drees voor de Ministerraad* (25 July 1945), ARA, cab. PM, box 130: both reproduced in Pieter Lagrou, 'De terugkeer van de weggevoerde arbeiders in België en Nederland, 1945–1955. Mythen en taboes rond de verplichte tewerkstelling', in *Le Travail Obligatoire en Allemagne, 1942–1945* (Brussels, 1993), pp. 225–6.

[34] De Liagre Böhl and Meershoek, *De bevrijding van Amsterdam*, pp. 101–9.

9　Patriotic scrutiny

Chapter 4 mentioned briefly the rudimentary 'Nuremberg of the masses' which occurred during the repatriation from Germany. Repatriation brought back an explosive mixture of the most wretched victims of the Nazi regime – the concentration camp survivors – and its most detested accomplices – collaborators who had fled with the Germans, volunteers for the Wehrmacht and the SS. Indignation over Nazi crimes, personified in the returning martyrs, was channelled on to the black sheep in the DP herd, creating a generalised atmosphere of suspicion. Screening in the transit centres was alleged to be inadequate, letting through Gestapo agents, miliciens and even ordinary German citizens trying to obtain the repatriation grant, returning to Germany and in some cases repeating the same operation several times.[1] It is interesting in this context to observe that transfer to Germany and repatriation were not always a straightforward round trip, and that some cross-migration occurred. Belgian collaborationists, fearing to return to an environment reminiscent of their wartime behaviour, migrated to France instead and bought farms vacated by their occupants, benefiting from the rural exodus that was itself accelerated by the wartime population displacement. Their concentration in particularly deserted departments – reports in some localities indicate that they took over 50 per cent of the farms – caused resentment in the local population and suspicion as to what had made them flee their own country.[2]

It can be assumed that, at the national level, the reasons for very many repatriated collaborationists not to return to their original region were all too strong. The same reports stipulate that, for those who did, lynching by the crowds in the railway stations upon arrival could often

---

[1] *Gendarmerie Nationale. Synthèse pour la période du 15 mars au 15 avril 1945* (Paris, 22 May 1945); *Synthèse pour la période du 15 avril au 15 mai 1945* (Paris, 13 June 1945): both AN 72 AJ 384.

[2] Notably the department of the Eure, *Gendarmerie Nationale. Synthèse pour la période du 15 septembre au 15 octobre 1944* and *Synthèse pour la période du 15 octobre au 15 novembre 1944*, both in AN 72 AJ 384. In my personal observation, I came across several similar cases in the department of the Ariège.

be avoided only by their immediate transfer by the gendarmerie to the local prison. In the region of Nantua, where only 20 per cent of those deported returned from concentration camps, the tension was such that all prison inmates were evacuated from the local prison to Bourg.[3] On victory day itself, 8 May 1945, not even the military security could prevent the expression of popular justice: at Annemasse a crowd of 1,500, waiting to welcome a repatriation convoy, stormed the police station to seize a milicien and an informer who had been apprehended upon arrival, to execute them in public.[4] As the American ambassador in Brussels cabled home, explaining similar disturbances in Belgium in April and May 1945: 'When a man returns from Buchenwald and points to a prominent citizen of his city and says, "That man is responsible for my deportation to Germany and should be arrested immediately and shot", his words are not easily ignored.'[5] Compared to the outburst of popular vengeance following the liberation, when resistance movements had moderated and disciplined popular rage, such movements now took the initiative in punitive activity, liberating accumulated frustration over the slowness of the purge in the eight months since the liberation.[6]

Popular ire was partly provoked by the *mise en scène* of the repatriation. In April 1945, the Belgian commission had invited the population of Brussels and mobilised the children in state schools to welcome home the first survivors of concentration camps, arriving on Allied aircraft landing at the military airfield in Evere, a Brussels suburb. Through an error in scheduling the convoys, the gathered crowd witnessed the arrival of entire families of collaborationists, with all their luggage and some even accompanied by their pets.[7] In France, the organisation of welcome committees was a central concern of the departmental directions of the repatriation ministry.[8] As explained in chapter 5, repatriation planning in the Netherlands did not allow for welcome committees.

What was the place of the workers in this atmosphere of confusion

---

[3] *Direction départementale de l'Ain* (31 May 1945).

[4] *Gendarmerie Nationale. Synthèse pour la période du 15/04 au 15/05 1945* (Paris, 13 June 1945), AN 72 AJ 384. The report for the previous period mentions the lynching of a repatriated Frenchman working for the German police in Maizières-les-Metz exactly one month earlier.

[5] Lagrou, 'US Politics of Stabilization', p. 219.

[6] See Martin Conway, 'Justice in Post-War Belgium. Popular Passions and Political Realities', *Cahiers d'Histoire du Temps Présent* 2 (1997), pp. 7–34. See also the FI's own reporting in *Front* (27 May, 10 June and 15 July 1945).

[7] Herremans, *Personnes Déplacées*, p. 39.

[8] *Direction Départementale des Hautes-Alpes* (15 Apr. 1945); *Direction Régionale de Bordeaux* (25 Apr. 1945); *Direction Départementale des Basses-Pyrénées* (16 Apr. 1945): all in *Extraits de rapports des directions départementales adressés au chef des services de l'information*, AN F9 3172.

and suspicion? Mostly employed in the industrial centres of the western part of Germany, workers returned earlier than the anxiously awaited survivors of the concentration camps, who had been deported *nach Osten*. This chronological sequence, the result of the geography of wartime population displacements rather than priority rankings of who suffered most, or who most deserved the nation's attention for their patriotic merits, stirred indignation. Resistance movements in Belgium protested that their deported comrades were still living in terrifying conditions in Germany, whilst large numbers of 'voluntary workers, their wives, their children and even their pets, their harmonicas and their luggage' were returning home.[9] In the Netherlands the National Advisory Council of the Resistance protested officially, and claimed priority for survivors of the camps 'not only because of the suffering they endured, but also and chiefly because the reason for their deportation to Germany entitles them to this distinction'.[10] In the course of March and April 1945, local repatriation officials in France complained at the repeated confusion created by the press announcement of repatriation convoys of 'deportees', causing continual false alerts for the welcome committees to greet the 'political deportees' when there were only 'labour deportees' to welcome.[11] As a result, the central administration in Paris decided to distinguish in each of its press announcements between 'political' and 'labour' deportees, to enable suitable welcome committees to be prepared.

Although the workers were definitely considered less worthy of a glorious reception than the survivors of the camps, their classification remained confused. Victims or traitors? – the whole question was inextricably linked with the answer to the next question: volunteers or conscripts? The confusion that reigned here in the public mind had been carefully cultivated by the occupation authorities, who had presented the labour draft as a spontaneous rush of the peoples of Europe to support Germany's titanic struggle with Bolshevism. For propaganda purposes, labour conscripts had even been presented with 'voluntary contracts'; signature or refusal did not affect the outcome of the summons but it might offer the draftees some material reward. All workers had, after all, worked for the German war industry and thus against the liberation of their own country. 'They only had to go into hiding' was an oft-heard objection to any claim of *force majeure* by

---

[9] *Front* (8 July 1945) and *La Voix des Résistants* (15 Sep. 1945).
[10] Petition (Amsterdam, 11 June 1945), RIOD, GAC archive, 15A. See also *Mededelingen-blad GAC* 2 (22 Aug. 1945), RIOD, GAC archive, 2C.
[11] *Direction Régionale Rhône-Alpes* (Lyons, 13 Mar. 1945) and the reply by Richard (Paris, 22 Mar. 1945), both in AN F9 3168.

the conscripts, referring to the heroised life of the underground, the *réfractaires* and the *maquis*.

The distinction between volunteers and conscripts was not merely of psychological or moral importance. Upon arrival in Belgium and the Netherlands it was decisive, immediately, in all matters regarding the reintegration and re-equipment of repatriates, including, crucially, the distribution of food stamps in the generalised rationing. In France, Frénay's ministry would actively combat discrimination amongst workers and particularly defend those workers who left under the *Relève*, but it would discriminate between workers on the one hand and PoWs and 'political deportees' on the other.

In Belgium, government decrees regulating priority access for repatriates to food stamps, re-equipment goods, medical care, subsidised recuperation holidays and government jobs were issued by different ministries, requiring different conditions, all contributing to an incoherent legislative body. Voluntary workers were generally excluded from all measures, but their definition varied.[12] Some decrees were based on chronological criteria – all workers repatriated after January 1945 were eligible, whilst other orders concerned only workers who left after October 1942, the date of the proclamation of forced labour in Germany; this excluded a vast category of 'volunteers' on a most rudimentary basis. Most often, the *bona fide* workers were distinguished from their suspect colleagues on the good faith of a declaration by the local mayor or the municipal police, who could inquire amongst neighbours and relatives as to the conditions of their departure to Germany. In one decree by Edgar Lalmand, the communist minister for supply, additional food stamps for repatriated workers were delivered only to those workers who could submit a resistance movement certificate attesting that they had been forced to leave for Germany only after having attempted all means of draft evasion.[13] Voluntary labour as a form of economic collaboration was punishable by law. There were 58,784 suits filed and subsequently shelved – individual workers could hardly be prosecuted for economic collaboration if even the employers of factories producing for the German army went free.[14]

The Dutch opinion on workers in Germany was to a large extent determined by the resistance organisation LO, the rural and religious network for draft evasion. The LO was the largest Dutch resistance

---

[12] See *Belgisch Staatsblad* (14, 21, 28, 30 June and 11 July 1945) and *Le Travailleur Déporté* 2 (Sep. 1945).

[13] *Belgisch Staatsblad* (13–14 Aug. 1945).

[14] J. Gilissen, 'Etude statistique sur la répression de l'incivisme', *Revue de Droit Pénal et de Criminologie* (1950–1), p. 531.

organisation, and assistance to draft-dodgers had been the core objective of the movement, in a spirit of patriotism and charity. It wished to extend this support in the post-liberation period. Local 'underground offices' (*onderduikbureaux*) helped former draft-evaders who had lost their job or their belongings by going into hiding, by distributing re-equipment goods and offering the services of an employment agency.[15] The official labour offices had been thoroughly discredited by their collaboration with labour conscription, and former draft-evaders in particular could not be expected to have any confidence at all in their services. The LO therefore launched 'labour booklets', certifying that the bearer had been a draft-evader or resistance fighter, and listing all temporary work experience since then. This initiative was supported by the National Labour Council and recommended priority for the em-ployment of those who 'during the occupation undermined attempts to Nazify the Dutch people'. This patriotic virtue made up for the fact that draft-evaders lacked professional experience and technical skill 'com-pared to those workers who left more or less voluntarily to work in Germany'. The LO protested that special measures for repatriates, attributing additional food stamps or priority for the official commercial exam, discriminated against the 'principled draft-evader' who had chosen a more patriotic attitude than those who left for Germany.[16]

The systematic campaign for the defence of the draft-evaders stressed, directly or indirectly, that on patriotic grounds workers in Germany were inferior; but this discrimination was not translated into different legal treatment. The government refused to assimilate draft-evaders with PoWs, which would provide them with an indemnity for each month spent in hiding to compensate for the loss of salary they had incurred.[17] The most obvious reason was the modesty of the budget: the Dutch PoWs were a numerically small group, and any extension would trigger off an avalanche of claims by other groups. Benefits for draft-evaders would also be uncontrollable. Hadn't many of them been employed, and received salaries under a false identity? How could the sums distributed to them during the war through the National Support Fund be taken into account? When refusing preferential treat-ment for draft-evaders, the government also bore in mind that, if the patriotic virtue of repatriated workers was inferior, so was their material

---

[15] See the correspondence between the GAC and the prime minister (Oct.–Nov. 1945) and its response (The Hague, 6 Nov. 1945), ARA, cab. PM, box 127, and *Communiqué Raad van Bestuur in Arbeidszaken* (29 Nov. 1945), RIOD, GAC archive, 12C.

[16] *Mededelingenblad GAC* 5 (12 Oct. 1945).

[17] *Nota Minister van Oorlog over tegemoetkomingen aan onderduikers* (The Hague, 21 Sep. 1945), ARA, cab. PM, box 97.

situation.[18] Government circulars insisted that 'repatriates who were taken to Germany against their will' should not be excluded from relief activities, but it left total autonomy to the local agencies to determine who exactly could be considered as such.[19] On the local level, the discrimination against voluntary workers was sometimes very sharp. In Amsterdam, municipal authorities introduced a yellow DP card, supplementing the white DP card given to all repatriates in the transit centres, specifically for the distribution of relief aid.[20] After a short examination by the local judiciary police, these cards were marked, for all workers, with a 'V' (*vrijwillig*) for voluntary or an 'O' for involuntary (*onvrijwillig*). Those workers who, rightly or wrongly, were stigmatised with a 'V' could have no hope of aid.

Any such categorisation was much more difficult in France. Where did the workers of the *Relève* end up, those who left voluntarily on principle, but under moral pressure from the Vichy regime, which presented it as a patriotic and charitable act enabling PoWs to return? Workers leaving under the *Relève* could have done so for the most noble reasons, but they had been duped by Laval's propaganda. The same applied to the PoWs who agreed to be transformed into workers. Would they be considered volunteers, traitors, after five years of exile?[21] The official line of conduct of the ministry excluded any discrimination against transformed PoWs, but regionally they were sometimes assimilated with workers in the distribution of relief.[22] Striking regional differences in the reception of workers in general were frequently reported to the repatriation ministry in Paris. A report from the department of the Basses-Pyrénées observed of the homecoming: 'Very different depending on whether the repatriate was a PoW, political deportee or STO. First of all, the latter are kept at a distance. They are almost considered as collaborationists, especially in the Basque country, where almost all young persons designated for forced labour crossed the frontier or took to the *maquis*.'[23] A report from Chambéry, capital of the Alpine department of Savoie, stated:

All workers who left for Germany did so as volunteers. Indeed, they refused to join the *maquis*, in spite of a clear enough appeal, and they are seen as traitors.

[18] *Notitie voor S. van V.* (The Hague, 17 Oct. 1946), ibid.
[19] *Rondschrijven Landelijk Nederlands Volksherstel* (July 1945), RIOD, GAC archive, 12C, and *Mededelingenblad GAC* 1 (30 July 1945).
[20] Minister Drees to prime minister (18 May 1946), ARA, cab. PM; box 132; Volder, *Werken in Duitsland*, pp. 87 and 510.
[21] See the moving letter by Mme Veuve Leurquin to Frénay (Douai, 5 Mar. 1945) on behalf of her son, a PoW *transformé*, AN F9 3168.
[22] Richard to Leurquin (Paris, 19 Mar. 1945) in AN F9 3168, and *Direction Départementale de la Gironde* (31 Jan. 1945) in AN F9 3172.
[23] *Direction Départementale des Basses-Pyrénées* (4 Aug. 1945), AN F9 3173.

In this department, where the resistance was particularly active, the purge is handled most severely by the purge committee, whose members were appointed by the departmental liberation committee. Several members of the purge committee and the liberation committee approach the situation of the allegedly deported workers with harshness, and they wish to treat them as suspects on their return and purge them mercilessly.[24]

Evasion was more difficult in more industrialised regions, and the judgement less harsh. In one of the French repatriation ministry's radio talks in February 1945, before the repatriation really started, the question was posed:

Is there any pronounced hostility in the country against the workers in Germany? There have been very few public demonstrations. In a very working-class region, such as the Sambre valley, no one seeks sanctions against them. People generally think that even most of the 'volunteers' were forced by moral pressure or material necessity, and it seems that the population is ready to welcome them. Besides, this is the official position of the General Confederation of Labour.[25]

Frénay devoted much of his action to the defence of unity amongst all the French who suffered 'deportation', and he would insistently resist any categorical discrimination against repatriates. In a circular addressed to the prefects of all French departments in November 1944, Frénay wrote with the utmost vigour that voluntary work in Germany had 'been supported by some fanatics, notoriously known to all', but that

the Relève was an immense deportation which was voluntary only in name, and that no single distinction is possible between those who have been forced through the material constraint of requisition and those who have been forced by the moral constraint of a whole policy of deceit . . . Every distinction between 'conscripts' and 'volunteers' is contrary to the interests of the Nation and would be treason to Frenchmen now absent and who will be united even more powerfully by their long months of combat, which will continue until their liberation, shoulder to shoulder with their comrades, prisoners and political deportees, against the German oppressor. When Germany falls and when our absent ones return, France will not have the right to make a distinction in their reception that was never made in combat. I attach the utmost importance to the organisation in parallel, united associations in the Houses of the Prisoner and the Deportee, of all those who should already have been united through the same fact of deportation or captivity.[26]

Frénay repeated similar pleas on the public radio.

Compared to the 'O' and 'V' stamps in the Netherlands and the

---

[24] *Note pour M. Richard* (Paris, 13 Feb. 1945), AN F9 3168.

[25] Minister for prisoners, deportees and refugees, Bureau Presse and Radio, Service Psychologique, Paris, 27 Feb. 1945, AN F9 3168.

[26] Frénay, to all *préfets* (Paris, 13 Nov. 1945), AN F9 3168.

ostracism affecting voluntary workers in Belgium, Frénay's courageous defence of the voluntary workers proved remarkably successful. The consequence of treating all workers together, which avoided negative discrimination against volunteers, also had a reverse aspect: since all workers were received on an equal footing, there should be no preferential treatment for particular groups of workers either. More particularly, in contrast to Belgium and the Netherlands, French repatriated workers were not entitled to a double ration of food stamps to help their physical recovery. *Reconnaissance nationale* and *reconnaissance du ventre* were inseparable in a period of food-rationing and preferential treatment. Voluntary workers were stigmatised on patriotic grounds in Belgium and the Netherlands and, in their anxiety not to attract even more attention to their less than heroic cause, would not have dared to protest against their discrimination. Workers in France were collectively rehabilitated, but as a result they also collectively resented the minor privileges of PoWs.[27] In the assimilation of all workers as conscripts also lies one of the origins of the future rivalry between the organisations of *déportés du travail* and *déportés politiques*.[28]

The ambiguous position of repatriated workers who lay between the extremes that caught the main public attention over repatriation – traitors and martyrs – together with the general atmosphere of moral panic, constituted a double challenge to any organisation which sought to undertake the rehabilitation of all or some of the workers who had been employed in Germany. Before we go on to the next section, a last group should be mentioned which was targeted by the combined obsessions of patriotic scrutiny and moral panic: the 'matrimonial collaborators'.[29] As in every economic migration, even in a state obsessed with racial purity, the forced transfers of Western European workers to the Third Reich inevitably led to intermarriage between (mostly male) migrant workers and the local (mostly female) population. The establishment of legitimate marital unions, in the midst of what was perceived as a high tide of illegitimate sex, should have delighted the moralists described in the previous chapter, were it not for the absolute unacceptability – on patriotic grounds – of these unions with enemy subjects. Sources mention 'a genuine invasion', a statement that gives the measure of the indignation they stirred, rather than an

[27] See Allier (11 Apr. 1945), Gironde (31 Jan. 1945), Hérault (2 Mar. and 6 Apr. 1945), Haute Garonne (15 Mar. 1945), Bouches du Rhône (16 Jan. 1945), all in AN F9 3172 and 3173.
[28] See, for example, the reports from the department of the Drôme, 15 Dec. 1945, and 8 Jan. 1946, AN F9 3173.
[29] M. P. Heuse in *Annales Parlementaires de la Chambre* (12 June 1945), p. 508.

estimate of the numbers involved.[30] Many of the PoWs and a great majority of the conscripts, particularly the youngest generation levied by the draft-year actions, were single, and the mobilisation of German men as soldiers for the Eastern front had created a demographic deficit of males on the home front. Even for the married PoWs and workers, five, three or two years of separation was a very long time.[31] Search actions for missing DPs often revealed that they had founded a family in Germany or Eastern Europe and refused repatriation. Others returned to discover that their wife had left them; still others returned with their German wife to find that their French wife refused divorce, and stood accused of bigamy.[32]

The influx of German women was partly the result of the early repatriation convoys entirely organised by the Allied military forces, before national repatriation officials arrived in Germany to screen repatriates on departure. Once they had delivered their load in Belgium and in France, the Allied military authorities understandably refused to ship back to Germany the legitimate, albeit German, spouses of Belgian and French citizens. Belgian repatriation officials reluctantly admitted that their policy in this matter had been 'liberal', especially when compared with the Netherlands.[33] Newspapers in France reported the internment of German spouses in special camps in France, from which they were liberated only after a painstaking examination by military security.[34] Many PoWs and workers preferred to wait until the patriotic storm had calmed down before sending for their wives and, in some cases, their children. Even then, the reception was often acrimonious. Historian Christophe Lewin relates a wedding ceremony in France of a PoW with his German wife, celebrated by the local mayor, resister and survivor of the concentration camps. The mayor was dressed in his striped KZ outfit, over which he carried the tricolour shawl to demonstrate his disapproval of this unpatriotic wedding.[35] In the Netherlands, anti-German feelings were in proportion to the destruction caused by the German occupation, and they were long lasting. (Up to the late 1950s, stones were thrown at German tourist buses crossing the

---

[30] Herremans, *Personnes Déplacées*, p. 111.

[31] See Lewin, *Le Retour*, pp. 70–7.

[32] See also *La Cuisine au beurre*, the burlesque, if not wholly improbable comedy of 1963 directed by Gilles Greangier with Bourvil and Fernandel in the main roles, on the return of a bigamist French PoW to Martigues.

[33] Herremans, *Personnes Déplacées*, p. 111.

[34] Quoted by Lewin, *Le Retour*, p. 298, n. 28. See also 'A la porte, ces Bochesses', *La Voix des Belges* 7 (May 1945).

[35] Lewin, *Le Retour*, p. 298, n. 28.

frontier.)[36] Resistance organisations demanded to send back to Germany, or to prison, not only the German spouses but also their Dutch companions.[37] The government, benefiting from the delay in repatriation, effectively refused to allow German women to enter Dutch territory.[38] The next chapter will return to this.

[36] See *Argwaan en Profijt. Nederland en West-Duitsland 1945–1981*, Amsterdamse Historische Reeks 6 (Amsterdam, 1983), and Friso Wielenga, *West-Duitsland. Partner uit noodzaak: Nederland en de Bondsrepubliek, 1949–1955* (Utrecht, 1989), pp. 345–6.

[37] GOIWN to prime minister (22 May 1945), ARA, cab. PM, box 132.

[38] See *Notulen Ministerraad* (15 July, 11 Sep. 1945, 20 Dec. 1946), ARA. The measure was lifted at the end of 1947 (11 July 1947, 12 and 1 Dec. 1947), ibid. See also *Raad voor Binnenlands Bestuur* (Aug.–Sep. 1945), ARA, and M. D. Bogaarts, '"Weg met de moffen". De uitwijzing van Duitse ongewenste vreemdelingen uit Nederland na 1945', in P. W. Klein and G. N. Van der Plaat (eds.), *Herrijzend Nederland. Opstellen over Nederland in de periode 1945–1950* (The Hague, 1981), pp. 159–76.

10 'Deportation': the defence of the labour conscripts

Had they been united by working-class solidarity and supported by organised networks of patriotic resistance, the individual workers – crushed by war and occupation, abandoned to their fate by collaborating labour administrations – would not have left for Germany in the first place. Did their common experience in Germany offer them greater unity? Their geographical dispersion and the great variety of individual working and living conditions made it wholly improbable that the workers would have set up some form of self-help association before their return. Who then would take on their defence, undertake their rehabilitation in the face of moral and patriotic suspicion? In Belgium it was the JOC; in France, Frénay; in the Netherlands, some regrettable clusters of bad advocates who associated their particular cause with that of the workers in Germany at large.

The Belgian JOC had been very active during the war through its 'Service for Workers Abroad', organised in 1942 to shield Catholic workers from moral temptations and spiritual loss, as described in chapter 8. After the repatriation, the post-war challenge was to reintegrate, re-educate and re-Christianise the workers who returned from Germany. A local JOC chaplain declared that the post-war vocation of the organisation was 'to turn them back into the neat human beings they were before they left for Germany three years ago'.[1] Given the loss of Catholic influence resulting from the exile in Germany, an explicitly Catholic organisation would find it almost impossible to retrieve these repatriated workers. In addition to this, the post-war challenge was not only a moral and spiritual *reconquista*, it was also a political *reconquista* of the working class from the mushrooming Communist Party. The JOC therefore decided to channel all its efforts for the reception of repatriates through an externally neutral National Federation of Deported Workers (the FNTDR). The FNTDR can indeed be described as a 'crypto-Catholic' front organisation, a genre communists were experienced in,

---

[1] Van Oostveldt (the local chaplain of the JOC in Leuven; he was involved in the reception of workers from Germany), quoted in Coenen, 'De Bierkaai', p. 131.

but mostly untried by the traditionally very 'pillarised' Belgian Catholic Movement, that is, a movement so solidly established in Belgian society that it could easily afford to concentrate all its efforts on the defensive construction of a Catholic state-within-the-state and regally neglect the sheep lost from the flock. The fact that the powerful Catholic movement felt the need to go undercover and to create a neutral interface for its action for repatriated workers reveals the scale of its anxieties as to its loss of influence over the workers in Germany. The federation was set up by the services of Cardinal Van Roey in the midst of the high tide of repatriation, in May 1945, bringing together a dozen JOC militants and appointing as its president Auguste Roeseler, president of the Brussels section of the JOC, who was still in Germany at the time.[2] The federation was run by full-time JOC militants, employed by the JOC for their work in the federation, some of whom had never been to Germany. The neutral disguise of the JOC action was essential in French-speaking Belgium, where the position of the Catholic workers' movement was much weaker than in the Dutch-speaking part. The national congresses of the organisation and its press were at first uniquely French-speaking, as was its membership.[3] In Flanders, the action was still indissolubly linked with the JOC, which renamed its 'Service for Workers Abroad' the 'Service for the Return' and offered a wide variety of services of social assistance to repatriates.[4] These Catholic initiatives were not absorbed into the FNTDR until the end of the 1940s.

Notwithstanding its neutral disguise, the efforts at 'moral re-education' continued to bear the heavy mark of Catholic Action. The 'family column' of *Le Travailleur Déporté* promoted the image of the 'true' woman, so different from the women the workers had known in the Lager: the devoted and caring housewife, mother of her children, an ideal that was most explicitly propagated in the party programme of the Christian Social Party (CVP/PSC) of 1945.[5] The organisation also inherited the paternalist tradition of the Catholic workers' movement

---

[2] *Le Travailleur Déporté* 1 (Aug. 1945), 6 (Jan. 1946) and 7 (Feb. 1946); Auguste Roeseler, personal communication, to author (29 Nov. 1988). For an angry reply by the secretary-general of the FNTDR to the version set out here, see *Verplichte Tewerkstelling*, pp. 241–4 and 251–4. See also Rudi Van Doorslaer and Etienne Verhoeyen, *De moord op Lahaut. Het kommunisme als binnenlandse vijand* (Leuven, 1985), pp. 147–9, 181–3 and 189.

[3] *Le Travailleur Déporté* 1 (Aug. 1945). In the course of 1946 some special issues were badly translated into Dutch in *De Gedeporteerde*. In 1949 the French and Dutch editions became fully equivalent. Membership soared from 23,000 in December 1945 to 40,000 after the implementation of the act of November 1946.

[4] Coine, *Kajottersweerstand*, pp. 85–9; address listings in *Le Travailleur Déporté*; Theo Delgoffe, personal communications, to author (22 Feb. 1989 and 24 Jan. 1994); Coenen, 'De Bierkaai', p. 139.

[5] *Le Travailleur Déporté* 10 (May 1946).

from which it stemmed. Judging by the social origins of its executives, the federation was organised more for workers than by them. Its president was a leading executive of the powerful Belgian holding Brufina, and a representative on the board of the union of Belgian employers. Its local branches were run by civil servants, retailers and other representatives of the middle class. Class solidarity was certainly not what held the organisation together – indeed to some extent it operated to the contrary. A local study in Leuven revealed contempt of the executives of the organisation for its foundation.[6] Rank-and-file members, according to the declarations of the animators, were interested only in the material benefits derived from their membership. The whole 'moral action' of commemoration and rehabilitation left them largely indifferent. The commitment of the federation animators resembled middle-class charity of a paternalist tradition: they described the rank-and-file membership as 'the common workers' and created a parallel 'circle of friends' for the like-minded alone, with separate social activities and a separate internal journal. Not only did they not have the same contemporary interests, they most probably did not even share the same kind of wartime experience. For the young men of the middle class who were drafted for work in German industry, the impulse to organise a *milieu de mémoire* of their own was not working-class solidarity – it was, on the contrary, the social trauma of the forced confrontation with working-class life, a confrontation that incidentally took place on enemy territory.

The most important challenge to the FNTDR was the patriotic rehabilitation of the workers. Repatriated workers suffered from a patriotic inferiority complex. An initial defensive reflex was to point out that the workers had not been contributors to the Nazi war-machine, but its victims. Any appreciation of their fate must give more weight to the suffering they endured than to the work they performed for the enemy.[7] A second defensive reflex contained a social argument: workers had a duty not only towards their country, but also towards their families. When there was no financial support for their families, a refusal to leave would have been irresponsible. When there was no infrastructure for evasion offered by a resistance organisation or by family wealth, draft evasion was impossible.[8] The third argument went on the offensive: workers in Germany had bearded the lion in its den, and fought the enemy on his own soil with incomparable courage. The resistance myth propagated by the federation was not quite as ludicrous as the one

[6] Coenen, 'De Bierkaai', pp. 145–52.
[7] *Le Travailleur Déporté* 1 (Aug. 1945), 2 (Sep. 1945).
[8] *Le Travailleur Déporté* 3 (Oct. 1945).

invented by De Gaulle's cousin in Algiers during the war. Though *Le Travailleur Déporté* announced, 'Do you really believe that we worked over there for the Prussian victory? Do we need to show you that our labour in Germany was one gigantic labour of sabotage?', the stories in its columns were much more modest.[9] According to these stories, the main object of sabotage was not aircraft engines or power plants, but the individual labour of every worker. The most heroic stories involved overt refusal to work, sit-ins and provocation of German superiors, inevitably ending in work- or concentration camps. Here, stripped of all references to Catholic hagiographies, the FNTDR echoed some of the themes of the JOC myth and even succeeded in listing the resistance by the Belgian workers in Germany in the official resistance annals, the Resistance Roll of Honour.[10] More modest versions involved techniques for developing false symptoms of disease (a pulverised aspirin in a cigarette to provoke violent heart palpitations, 15 minutes of hammering with a spoon on the back of the hand to create an impressively swollen wrist), artificially slow working rhythm (a true ordeal for the supposedly naturally industrious Belgian workers) or long card-playing sessions at work.[11] At the first congress of the federation, the president of its French sister organisation, George Beauchamps, summarised perfectly the campaign of both organisations: 'Every hour that we stole from the enemy was one step towards victory.'[12]

The patriotic discourse of worker heroism in Germany was a matter of tactics. If the federation wanted to achieve the rehabilitation of the workers, it had no choice but to join the patriotic bidding-up that seemed to have suffused Belgian society since the liberation. The organisation had no intention of rehabilitating conscripts at the expense of voluntary workers, rather the contrary. In all matters concerning the purge, its voice was one of moderation. Of course, *Le Travailleur Déporté* sought exemplary punishment for the German executives of the *Werbestellen* (recruitment officers for work in Germany) and their Belgian accomplices in the man-hunt for workers, the *Zivilfahnder*, but its thirst for revenge stopped there. The journal even distanced itself from the outbursts of popular justice, prompted by the repatriation, some of them staged by resistance organisations.[13] In its officially promoted patriotism, the federation defended not the hero but the average citizen who had tried to survive the occupation years, swimming with the

---

[9] Ibid.   [10] *Guldenboek van de Weerstand* (Brussels, 1948).

[11] *Le Travailleur Déporté* 4 (Nov. 1945).

[12] *Le Travailleur Déporté* 6 (Jan. 1946).

[13] *Le Travailleur Déporté* 1 (Aug. 1945). See also Auguste Roesler's preface to Potargent, *Déportation*.

9 The labour conscripts: 'Every hour we stole from the enemy was one more step towards victory.' From *Le Travailleur Déporté*, October 1945. Photo, Isabelle Sampieri, CEGED/SOMA.

current rather than against it, settling for everyday compromises without losing his honour or betraying his country.

Yet the patriotic boasting about collective worker heroism in Germany was responsible for a major misunderstanding between the federation and the minister for war victims. The communist Jean Terfve was delighted to hear that the workers in Germany had collectively and heroically combated Nazism. Nothing fitted better into his grand unitary project of a law for 'Civil Resistance' which would recognise all patriotic agitation, including by Belgian workers on German soil. Terfve's *chef de cabinet* declared in a meeting with federation executives that the minister fully supported its claims to patriotic recognition, but that there was no point in creating a separate act for labour conscripts. 'If we continue in this way, we will soon have acts for all Belgians who did not work for the enemy. The Act for Civil Resistance, full stop, that's all. And we'll use it for all categories of Belgians who deserve it.'[14] Seeking to rehabilitate the mass of deported workers by associating their cause with that of the heroic few now proved counterproductive. Integrated into an Act for Civil Resistance, workers would have to prove active resistance, which the overwhelming majority could not.

The FNTDR was very ready to settle for fewer honours for more workers, and achieved an orderly way out of the patriotic contest.[15] Terfve, who had already agreed to distinguish between the passive attitude of draft-evaders and the active attitude of 'civil resisters', granted a separate act for deported workers, promulgated by the government under the provisions of plenary power contemporaneously with the two other acts on 22 November 1946.[16] According to the wording of the act, the working classes had been the first victims of fascism, and the deported workers deserved the recognition of the nation for that reason. The material benefits were limited: the years in Germany would be counted in the social security contributions and jobless repatriates could apply for subsidised job training. In contrast to the two other contemporaneously issued acts, the deported workers were not eligible for a medal. Even though the act was a pyrrhic victory compared to the claims of the federation, it was acclaimed by the organisation as a major success because it was the official confirmation that workers in Germany who had left as conscripts were free from patriotic blame. As for the

[14] *Le Travailleur Déporté* 11 (June 1946).
[15] *Le Travailleur Déporté* 12 (July 1946).
[16] 'Besluitwet houdende de inrichting van het statuut der gedeporteerden voor den verplichten arbeidsdienst tijdens de oorlog 1940–1945', *Belgisch Staatsblad* (16 Jan. 1947), pp. 429–34; *Le Travailleur Déporté* 16 (Nov. 1946).

medal, the FNTDR sold a homemade insignia for 10 francs in all its local offices.

Application of the law, i.e., the procedure recognising the individual workers, was somewhat slow in coming. The deported workers were at the bottom of the priority listing drawn up by the administration for dealing with applicants in every category. The 'political prisoners', whose act was published, after a long controversy, two months later than the act for the deported workers, enjoyed absolute priority, based on both their patriotic standing and their indigence. In 1948, the administration established its doctrine, the internal administrative guidelines for the interpretation of the act. Carefully prepared, it listed the documentary evidence required to establish a forced departure to Germany. The administration was able to draw on the meticulous archives of the German labour administration in Belgium, which, in particular, contained all the 'voluntary contracts' offered to conscripts for signature. Signatories were rewarded with 750 francs, a pair of shoes and vague promises of better employment. All those workers who had signed this formal document – which in any case had no effect on the outcome of the summons, since even those who refused to sign were forced to leave – had to be excluded from the benefit of the act.[17] Again a vast majority of the workers would be excluded on narrow patriotic criteria of principle. During the war nobody had been fooled by the German propaganda trick that tried to convert conscripts into volunteers, yet was the Belgian administration now using these worthless documents as the ultimate criterion?[18]

After a long campaign and a difficult parliamentary round, the federation obtained a new act on 7 August 1953, including the 'signatories'.[19] The new act was no longer one of national recognition, but an act for war victims. The patriotic virtue of workers who were forced to work for the enemy, but who were willing to sign a formal document of voluntary departure in exchange for a pair of shoes, was wholly problematic for the legislators. Much like the Act for the Political Prisoners, which made a distinction between the beneficiaries of the law – the victims – and the bearers of the title – the heroes – the Deported Workers Act of 1953 distinguished non-signatories, who through their principled refusal of a pair of shoes had shown proof of courage and patriotic abnegation. The signatories received a grey 'deportee card', since their war record was obviously neither white nor black. The non-signatories received a plain white 'deportee card' and, in addition to the benefits of the law of 1946,

[17] *Le Travailleur Déporté* 35 (Aug.–Sep. 1948); *dossier WG*, AO, Dienst Statuten.
[18] *Le Travailleur Déporté* 37 (Nov.–Dec. 1948).
[19] *Belgisch Staatsblad* (3–4 Aug. 1953), pp. 4810–13.

they were entitled to the rewards of national recognition: priority employment in the public sector, exemption from military service (which, in 1953, was somewhat ironic as a benefit), and support from the National Work for War Veterans, and, most importantly, they were entitled to have the statement shown on their grave and death certificate that they 'Died for Belgium'.

In the Netherlands, the first protest committee to speak out on behalf of the labour conscripts, and to denounce their undeserved assimilation with unpatriotic and even collaborationist citizens, was the result of the repatriation controversy, the political debate on the belated repatriation of Dutch citizens from Germany in general and from the Soviet zone in particular. In April 1946, eleven months after the liberation, the parents of 'SS front workers', young workers who had been sent to the Eastern front as conscripted civilian construction workers, addressed a petition to the prime minister to protest against the incompetence and systematic obstruction of the repatriation services over the repatriation of their sons.[20] One year after the end of the war more than 1,000 out of a total of about 5,000 'SS front workers' had not been repatriated.

Requisitioned by the SS-Wirtschaftsverwaltungshauptamt for construction work on the Eastern front, they had lived at the heart of military confrontation and in the extreme cold of the Russian winter.[21] Even though they formally retained civilian status, all were dressed in Wehrmacht uniforms, which exposed them to partisan attacks and made the Soviets reluctant to repatriate them after their capture as PoWs. Moreover, strong pressure was exerted on them in the labour camps to join military formations and carry arms. All requests to Dutch repatriation authorities for news of the absent men were met with the rebuke that no one cared to repatriate former SS members – and in any case, the workers in question would do better to stay abroad for a while if they did not want to expose themselves to prosecution or popular vengeance. The conscripts were systematically confused with farmers who emigrated voluntarily to the East and with NSB volunteers for the SS and Wehrmacht. Those workers who had been repatriated had met with understanding from the French Red Cross, but in the Netherlands they were greeted with suspicion and treated as political suspects. They were systematically stigmatised with the 'V' stamp of 'voluntary worker' on their repatriation documents, and were thus excluded from all relief activity and even from the labour market.

In spite of its small size, the protest committee was very militant. In

[20] Actie-comité Oostbouw to prime minister (11 Apr. 1946), ARA, cab. PM, box 132.
[21] See Sijes, *Arbeidsinzet*, pp. 477–87.

the press it declared that the Dutch repatriation officials were a 'bunch of malevolent, incompetent brats', and very much against the explicit advice of the ministry it negotiated directly with the Soviet embassy to advance the repatriation of workers from the front.[22] The Dutch cabinet was heavily embroiled with the Soviet embassy over the repatriation issue and Minister Drees was infuriated by this parallel diplomacy, favoured, according to reports of the secret service, by the fact that many of its members were communists.[23] The ministry reported to the prime minister that 'most of the East-company-men had a screw loose. This is generally known and was confirmed by the results of interrogations by the judiciary police.'[24] It conceded that the consequences of the 'V' stamps for access to elementary relief might have been too far-reaching, but the stamps themselves were in general perfectly justified. Some individual acts of discrimination might be revised, but a general rehabilitation of the workers on the Eastern front was excluded, since this would imply 'a general rehabilitation of the worst elements'. The few thousand labour conscripts on the Eastern front, drafted by the SS, working in Wehrmacht uniforms on military construction sites, were a narrow and strictly defined group. Their rehabilitation, in a general context of suspicion even regarding 'ordinary' conscripts employed in the German industrial centres, was never very realistic. The militant campaign on their behalf certainly did nothing to improve the image of labour conscripts in general, either in the press or in the eyes of the officials that it targeted.

The second rehabilitation campaign was aimed at a much larger target group. The Dutch Union of Repatriates first appeared in August 1946 as the organiser of the Congress of the International Confederation of Deported Workers. The 'International Federation' was a French–Belgian venture and at the time of the congress the Dutch union had not yet developed any national activity. The Eindhoven congress was probably an attempt to export the Belgian FNTDR across the border, and it is not impossible that its location in the Catholic province of Limburg was the work of the JOC. The name of the union was noticeably different from the Belgian and French sister organisations: no reference to 'deportation' or 'forced labour', but simply to 'repatriates' in general. The union addressed an invitation to the prime

---

[22] Report, Minister of Social Affairs Drees to prime minister (18 May 1946), ARA, cab. PM, box 132.

[23] *Notitie voor MP* (12 June 1946), ARA, cab. PM, box 132.

[24] Report, Minister of Social Affairs Drees to prime minister (18 May 1946); letters, prime minister to Ministry of Social Affairs (17 Apr. 1946 and 13 May 1946); letter, secretary of prime minister to Actie-comité Oostbouw (17 Apr. 1946 and 24 May 1946): all in ARA, cab. PM, box 132.

minister, declaring that 'the hundreds of thousands of deportees have the feeling that the government does not show the slightest concern for the countless problems faced by this important group of the Dutch population', but the prime minister was unimpressed and did not even send a delegate to the congress.[25] In January 1947 the union engaged in national action for the first time, denouncing in a petition to the prime minister the unalleviated distress of the repatriates eighteen months after the end of the war and protesting against the 'unfairness of the existing regulations, which rely too much on the discretion of the administrations and their officials', concluding accusingly: 'These administrations should not forget their responsibilities towards this numerous group of around 400,000 Dutchmen!!!'[26]

The Dutch organisation distinguished itself from its southern neighbours by its very inclusive approach to wartime economic migration. The union vigorously condemned the Dutch policy to refuse entry to the national territory to the German spouses of Dutch workers as 'contrary to all standards of morals and virtue'.[27] The separation of families created by the governmental decision enticed men into amoral relationships and whipped up feelings of hatred against the German people. During the war, had not the government itself declared from London that the conflict was against the system, and not against the German people? 'The governmental decision evokes the racism that it condemns so ardently, as seen in its past and present declarations.' However courageous this defence of the German spouses, this was not a position likely to endear the union to the government or public opinion. Even more suicidal, but equally courageous, was its outright rejection of the stigmatisation of 'so-called "voluntary" workers' and its *mise en cause* of Dutch pre-war labour policies.[28] 'Already before May 1940 workers were forced by the government of the time to work in Germany, because of the prevalent unemployment . . . During the occupation too, people who depended on the poor relief because of their unemployment were left no choice but to accept work in Germany, because these institutions excluded them and their families from all aid. Besides, many Dutch people had to work for minimal wages which were simply insufficient to feed them and their families. They accepted a job offer in Germany out of sheer necessity. All these people are now stigmatised as "voluntary Germanisers" [*Duitslandgangers*], which is, in view of these and other

[25] Letter, Nederlands Verbond van Gerepatrieerden to prime minister (27 July 1946), and his refusal (8 Aug. 1946), both in ARA, cab. PM, box 132.
[26] Letter, Nederlands Verbond van Gerepatrieerden to prime minister (24 Jan. 1947), with annexe, *Sociaal Rapport*, ARA, cab. PM, box 132.
[27] Ibid.   [28] Ibid.

facts, not wholly justified.' The organisation abstained from appealing to some sense of heroism or martyrdom and rejected any form of internal patriotic hierarchy. As a result, after elaborate internal consultation by all ministers and government agencies, the union was seen as a suspect organisation and completely boycotted.[29] The government refused to recognise its representativeness and even excluded it from the long list of organisations in the four-volume handbook for aid to war victims.[30] The Dutch Union for Repatriates slowly bled to death in solitary confinement.

Killing the messenger was of course not sufficient to eliminate the message, a truism that applied particularly to the pre-war Dutch migrant workers in Germany. Since repatriation in the spring of 1945 returned displaced persons to where they had lived at the outbreak of the war, this group had stayed in Germany. As the economic situation deteriorated in Germany during the winter of 1945–6, many of them wished to return to the Netherlands. This comprised not only the approximately 40,000 recent emigrants of the second half of the 1930s, but also far more numerous groups, including those of the pre-First World War waves of emigration. Government estimates put the number of candidates for re-migration at between 70,000 and 240,000, mainly concentrated in the frontier region of Düsseldorf, Münster and Duisburg.[31] Post-war Germany was not a friendly setting for migrant workers: wartime transfer workers had been repatriated and an equal number of ethnic Germans arrived as refugees. German society was ethnically more homogeneous than it had ever been, unemployment ran high and the food supply was insufficient. Dutch migrant workers suffered from hostility simultaneously both from the local German population and from the Allied authorities, for whom all unrepatriable displaced persons were suspected of having good war-related reasons not to return to their own country. From January 1946 onwards, a few thousand migrant workers returned each month to the Netherlands, and in May of the same year 14,000 of them were concentrated at the Dutch–German border whilst they waited to be admitted to the Dutch territory. This the Dutch government did not intend to allow. The local relief infrastructure was still under great strain, and the housing shortage was very acute because of the return of repatriates from the Dutch

---

[29] See the correspondence between the union and the administration (Feb.–Apr. 1947), ARA, cab. PM, box 132.
[30] Annexe to letter, Nederlands Verbond van Gerepatrieerden to prime minister (17 Sep. 1947), ibid.
[31] Report, Ministry of the Interior, *Nederlanders in Duitsland* (4 Feb. 1946); report, interministerial meeting (9 Apr. 1946); letter, Ministry of Social Affairs to prime minister (1 May 1946): all ibid.

Indies. In addition to the practical problems and contrary to the case of the returning colonialists, there was a strong psychological antipathy against these strongly Germanised compatriots, many of whom did not even speak Dutch. A government report added political objections: 'Many of them are so imbued with their national-socialist environment that they would only constitute an element of unreliability in our country, which is all the more true of the children, who have been educated in the Hitlerjügend and the Bund der Deutschen Mädchen.'[32]

The Ministries of the Interior and Social Affairs wanted to hold back this new wave of repatriates at all costs. The simplest way would be to cancel their passports and refuse them at the border. Dutch citizens in Germany would then need a visa to enter the country – a visa that would be granted only after a local investigation in Germany as to their political reliability.[33] This proposed measure, objected the Ministry of Foreign Affairs, was clearly unconstitutional – in no way could Dutch citizens be excluded by administrative decree from entering the national territory. If indigent Dutch citizens were sent back to the chaos they sought to escape, it would moreover embroil the government with the Allied occupation authorities in Germany. The better solution would be to tackle the problem on the spot and provide indigent Dutch citizens in Germany with Dutch poor relief. During the official emigration scheme of the 1930s, government emissaries for the poor relief (*armenbezoekers in rijksdienst*) had toured Germany to assist Dutch workers in need.[34] The Foreign Office supported this idea enthusiastically because it fitted nicely into its plans for claiming the annexation of German territory as reparation payment for war damage, much as Belgium had gained Eupen-Malmédy after 1918.[35] The main problem with annexation was that the government wanted the territory but not the German population that went with it. If the Dutch immigrants could be kept in Germany through an adequate relief structure, they could later be moved to populate the annexed territory as Dutch pioneers. Even if the Netherlands obtained only a mandate or an occupation zone in Germany, these migrant workers could still 'deliver a not insignificant contribution to the strengthening of Western solidarity, *à l'encontre* of all imperial aspirations or Prussian military spirit and propagate the

---

[32] Report, meeting (9 Apr. 1946), ibid.

[33] Report, Ministry for Foreign Affairs (4 May 1945); letter, minister of foreign affairs to prime minister (15 Apr. 1946); note, minister of foreign affairs to prime minister (20 May 1946): all ibid.

[34] Report, Ministry of the Interior (4 Feb. 1946); letter, minister of the interior to prime minister (22 Oct. 1948): both ibid.

[35] Report, Ministry of Foreign Affairs, Germany Section (15 Nov. 1946), ibid. For the Dutch annexation plans, see Wielenga, *West-Duitsland*, pp. 385–414.

Western concepts of humanity and democracy which would constitute the vector for Germany's re-education to become a civilised nation once more'.[36]

The whole context of pre-war emigration from the Netherlands to Germany certainly played down the significance of wartime forced migration, compared to Belgium and France, two countries with a tradition of labour immigration. After the abolition of the Dutch Union of Repatriates, a new 'Committee of the Foundation of Repatriated Dutchmen Resident in Germany Before May 1940' would petition for official attention, stressing that, for chronological reasons alone, their members could not be suspected of a spirit of collaboration.[37] Had this activity met with any success, it would still not have contributed to the cause of rehabilitating wartime labour conscripts.

The care of the repatriated workers in France had a long pre-history, as described in chapter 6. Frénay saw his ministry as a 'movement' which would not simply administer repatriates, but would unify them, organise them, transform them into New Citizens, rehabilitate them in their own eyes and in the eyes of the home front. As described above, during the preparation in Algiers he relied strongly on the National Movement for PoWs and Deportees (the Pinot–Mitterrand group) – a movement initially exclusively for PoWs, but gradually and secondarily for labour conscripts too. In the logistics of their reception Frénay also allotted a central role to the associational movement, as part of his wish to create a triple set of organisations for PoWs, workers and 'political deportees', i.e., in this context, concentration camp survivors. This grand design also implied the reappropriation of the infrastructure created by Vichy, the first to build up an extensive network of co-operating administrations and associations. Vichy's infrastructure for the workers in Germany was best known by the name of its chief, Bruneton. The Bruneton mission in Germany, operating from Berlin, co-operated closely with the Deutsche Arbeitsfront and had even less autonomy than the Scapini mission, its predecessor concerned with PoWs. In France itself, Bruneton's services were supported by a National Federation of Committees of Mutual Aid, whose departmental, cantonal and local sections were effectively headed by the *préfets* of each department. The centres were supposed to prepare for the reintegration of repatriated workers, but in the absence of repatriates they developed a reasonably effective pattern of assistance for the families of workers in Germany, in

---

[36] Report, Ministry of Foreign Affairs, Germany Section (15 Nov. 1946), ARA, cab. PM, box 132.
[37] Letter, prime minister to minister of the interior (15 Sep. 1948), ibid.

particular advances in the transfer of their breadwinners' German salaries. Compared again with the PoWs, this network was much less developed: the workers were less homogeneous as a group, their exile was of a more recent date and their presence in Germany had a less conventional and consensual character. This was the last difference between Vichy's action in favour of PoWs and that in favour of the workers: Vichy did not share any responsibility for the former group's presence in Germany, but its part in the fate of the latter was much more ambiguous.

Frénay's interventions in favour of the repatriated workers can only be understood in the light of this continuity. It was to the *préfets* that Frénay addressed his instructions condemning the discrimination against voluntary workers and his recommendation to set up Committees of Mutual Aid, because they already held this responsibility before the liberation. The distinction between voluntary and forced departures had of course been anathema under Vichy, who had presented all French labour in Germany as a voluntary engagement in the fight against Bolshevism. Frénay did not subscribe to this propagandist design in any way, but he shared the social concern shown by Vichy for the workers whose departure it had guaranteed. The intentions of Frénay and Vichy were completely opposed – all volunteers and thus supporters of Vichy, for the latter; all 'deportees', victims of Vichy, for the former – but the end result was the same. Vichy's 'Federation of the Committees of Mutual Aid for the French Workers in Germany' was renamed the 'National Federation of Deported Workers' (the Fédération Nationale des Déportés du Travail or FNDT), but for as long as Frénay's ministry existed, its relationship to the State remained basically the same as under Vichy.[38] Departmental responsibilities remained with the *préfet* and both the central administration of the federation and its departmental secretaries were paid by, and accountable to, the central government offices. The social tasks of the FNDT as it had functioned under Vichy were all the more indispensable after the liberation, which cut off all financial transfers by breadwinners in Germany to their families in France.

Local officials in the Prisoners' Houses were required to recruit secretaries to run a local section for the repatriated workers, or at the very least, in small localities, to integrate workers into social activities for PoWs or victims of persecution. For its part, the ministry promised subsidies, which were earmarked for the committees for repatriated

---

[38] Guy De Tassigny, *Rapport sur le problème 'Travailleurs Déportés'* (Dec. 1944), AN F9 3168. De Tassigny moved his services into the buildings previously occupied by Bruneton as Mitterrand and Frénay had done for the ministry before.

workers. The take-over of Centres of Mutual Aid and the promotion of the National Movement of Prisoners and Deportees, described in the previous chapter as a political take-over from the pro-Vichy PoW circles, had at the same time to reinforce the worker element in the associational cluster around the Prisoners' Houses. The department of the Somme reported:

We have finally, it seems, attained the goal set forth by M. le Ministre, that is to welcome all deportees without distinction, whether prisoners, political internees or workers, disregarding the role of dispenser of justice, which is not ours. The directors of the Centres of Mutual Aid have finally understood this necessity.[39]

The department of the Basses-Pyrénées, where such marked hostility against the repatriated workers had been reported (see p. 162), related how

the STO try to react against this ostracism, but without much success. Our press service tries to help them, notably by recalling the vast sabotage campaigns undertaken by large numbers of workers. But it requires considerable tact, and it will take much time to overcome this prejudice.[40]

A unifying discourse corresponded to this 'governmental' stage in the life of the federation of deported workers, manned by civil servants from Frénay's ministry, reintegration militants and recycled Vichy officials. Guy De Tassigny, appointed secretary-general, insistently repeated Frénay's condemnation of any discrimination against voluntary workers. On 15 February 1945 he declared on French public radio:

And besides, who, apart from the *maquisards*, the pure resistants, who did not work directly or indirectly for the enemy during those terrible fifty months, in France as well as in the German retreat? Who then? It is true that since September 1944, it has been revealed to us that the whole French nation belonged to the Resistance. A comforting surprise! Well, to all those who need to find scapegoats to justify themselves, I'd say that amongst the voluntary workers there were patriots who left to sabotage the production of the Reich. I will tell them that the factories were surrounded by the Feldgendarmerie and that thousands of workers were left manacled or threatened with automatic guns.[41]

The liquidation of Frénay's ministry also meant the end of this associational structure for the repatriated workers, and created the need for the former labour conscripts to sustain their own federation. As a mass organisation, it was highly successful. Public membership figures varied, in the course of 1946 alone, between 400,000 and 540,000 –

---

[39] (15 Mar. 1945); see also *Allier* (27 Jan. 1945) and *Basses-Pyrénées* (1 Feb. 1945): all in AN F9 3172.
[40] (4 Aug. 1945), AN F9 3173.
[41] *Allocution prononcée à la radiodiffusion française par monsieur Guy De Tassigny* (15 Feb. 1945), AN F9 3168.

which seems very high, compared with the total figures for labour conscription. The transformation was far from smooth: many people involved in the first phase were not themselves former labour conscripts, but former staff members of the Chantiers de la Jeunesse (young men's work brigades established by Vichy to replace military service) or trade union militants. Departmental committees, animated by secretaries appointed from Paris, accountable to Paris and dispensing subsidies from Paris, were now replaced by elected presidents of departmental associations, which were financially autonomous.[42] This organisational transformation was simultaneously a political transformation. The last remnants of functionaries nominated under Vichy disappeared to make room for militants from the parties of the working class: socialists and communists. Both parties seemed to have worked out an effective partitioning of influences in the FNDT.[43] In its parliamentary initiatives, communist and socialist politicians loyally supported the federation (whilst Gaullist politicians loyally, and less loyally, resisted them). The communist minister Laurent Casanova became the unrivalled hero of the cause of the labour conscripts, whilst François Mitterrand, one of his successors, bought the benevolence of the federation by co-opting its leaders on to his staff.

More important, in the context of the formation of a collective memory of labour conscription, was the transformation of a welcome committee assisting the authorities in the reception of repatriated comrades into a veterans' organisation. As such, it became part of an associational universe deeply rooted in French society since 1918, with firmly established codes, rituals and discourses to which it had to conform, particularly because it entered this universe with a tremendous inferiority complex. This was all the more true because this transformation coincided with the creation of a new ministry for 'Veterans and War Victims'. Following the dissolution of Frénay's ministry there had been some political debate as to the form of its successor. As described in chapter 2, De Gaulle had personally opposed the revival of a Ministry for Veterans, in view of the connivance of veterans' movements with Vichy, and Vichy's exploitation of the veterans' administration.[44] His hostility towards the movements of what he saw as the less than heroic PoWs has often been described, suggesting that he had no higher opinion of labour conscripts.[45] A secretary-general for veterans and

---

[42] Le DT 4 (Apr. 1946).
[43] See, for example, the double opinion–editorial page by Guy Mollet and Jacques Duclos in Le DT 7 (July 1947).
[44] See Commission Pensions (30 Nov. 1945, 5, 13 and 19 Dec. 1945), AAsN.
[45] See Lewin, Le Retour, pp. 37 and 136–42.

another for war victims were integrated into the population ministry, much to the (anti-Gaullist) resentment of both groups.[46] After De Gaulle's withdrawal from power on 20 January 1946 the communist resistance hero Laurent Casanova became the first post-war minister of a new Ministry for Veterans and War Victims. The combination in one ministry of the services formerly depending on Frénay's ministry and the services for veterans would be of lasting importance. Henceforth, the paradigm of the combatant would be applied to the war victims as an administrative matter of fact.[47]

The labour conscripts had vested their hopes in Frénay's project of a unified repatriates' organisation integrating the workers in the community of suffering of all victims of exile with the PoWs and the martyrs of Nazi persecution. Yet the integration that did take place was between the latter two groups in the glorious family of patriots, together with resistance veterans and, most of all, with the *anciens combattants* of the Great War, in which there was no room for the workers. Associations of deported workers were not invited to participate in commemorations of 11 November or to join the Union Française des Anciens Combattants, unlike the PoWs and victims of Nazi persecution. They resented being treated in the patriotic family like 'little boys in a gathering where we are not given the place we deserve'.[48]

In order to win their own place in this patriotic family, the FNDT adopted an increasingly patriotic discourse of martyrdom and heroism. Yet the social and practical tone of a federation of Centres of Mutual Aid was only gradually replaced by veterans' rhetoric in the course of the spring months of 1946:

Yesterday, tracked down by the Gestapo, by the police of a Government in the pay of the enemy, 750,000 French were forced and compelled to leave their Fatherland, victims of spiteful blackmail and threatened by very serious sanctions. Their attitude, as much on the national soil as in the foreign countries to which they were taken as captives, has never ceased to be a constant struggle against foreign domination and fascism. The heroic behaviour of some of them even brought them into the torture camps where the Political Deportees were already imprisoned; others were executed; and we have more than 50,000 dead to mourn. A great number of other comrades returned in such physical and moral conditions that they could not be rapidly reintegrated into the life of the Nation.

This discourse betrayed its sentiment of inferiority by its obsessive reference to other, more esteemed patriotic groups: 'You know how much this collective suffering has created in all our comrades the desire

46 Commission Pensions (21 Dec. 1945), AAsN.
47 See Casanova in Commission Pensions (13 Feb. 1946), AAsN.
48 *Le DT* 12 (Dec. 1946).

to unite together on their return in France. This problem is comparable to that of the former Prisoners of War and to that of the former Political Prisoners.'[49]

The price of the entrance ticket into the patriotic club was an internal purge of all voluntary workers. Purge committees on the national and departmental level had to oust 'voluntary workers who may have infiltrated the federation and those who have had a characteristically anti-national attitude'.[50] Departmental associations voted resolutions protesting 'against the fact that the government has not taken any measure to prevent the French who left voluntarily to work for the enemy from voting in the next elections, and demand that they suffer immediate official disgrace and loss of civic rights'.[51] The departmental congress of the Vosges even addressed a petition to the *préfet* in February 1946 which sought to strip all voluntary workers of their hunting and fishing licenses.[52] Local sections staged ceremonies to inaugurate their flag and lay wreaths at the local war memorial – the veteran's highest place of honour – and on these occasions declared, in an ultimate effort to conform to interwar republican rituals: 'Now, comrades, I ask you more than ever to remain united behind our flag, as we were in the factory and in the camps.'[53] The commemorative rivalry obliged the FNDT to be referential, but it gradually crossed the boundary and became outright mimicry of the memory of the other two groups.

In April 1946 *l'esprit des camps* makes its first appearance in the columns of *Le DT* (*Le Deporté du Travail*, the federation's official press organ) – a mythical concept that was difficult enough for PoWs and survivors of the concentration camps, but wholly inappropriate for the heterogeneous group of workers.[54] At the FNDT's second national congress, President Beauchamp opened his speech with a reference to 'the memory of the camps, of all that we have known or suffered' to appeal to 'our social mystique or our fraternal mystique' and the unity 'amongst those we have left behind over there, in the unity of mass graves and the camps, in the unity of the same shroud of earth, that German earth in which so many of our own are buried'.[55] In its rituals,

---

[49] *Le DT* 4 (Apr. 1946).

[50] *Le DT* 12 (Dec. 1946); see also *Direction Départementale des Landes* (10 Dec. 1945), AN F9 3173.

[51] *Le DT* 3 (Mar. 1946).

[52] *Le DT* 6–7 (June–July 1946).

[53] *Le DT* 15–16 (Mar.–Apr. 1947), relating the ceremony in Dieppe-Neuville. See also *Le DT passim* on flags, monuments and ceremonies in Trignac, Beaugency (Loiret), Bèziers, the Gare des Brotteaux in Lyons and Bergerac. See other STO monuments, with illustrations, in Barcellini and Wieviorka, *Passant, souviens-toi!*, pp. 437–50.

[54] *Le DT* 4 (Apr. 1946).

[55] *Le DT* 12 (Dec. 1946).

the federation perpetuated the unifying symbolism of the resistance propaganda and of Algiers. The front page of *Le DT* showed factories and chimneys behind barbed wire, guarded by a German soldier and a long train with freight cars, an imagery reminiscent of Frénay's *ils sont unis, ne les divisez pas!*, even if the barbed wire and the military surveillance were more appropriate to describe the PoWs' living conditions, and the freight cars symbols of deportation to the concentration camps. The imagery of wartime propaganda, with its desire to level out differences and present a homogeneous picture of the suffering inflicted by the enemy, was much more problematic in the post-war setting, when the very different experiences of different groups could no longer be glossed over. When the FNDT branch of Breteuil-sur-Iton in the Eure organised a caravan at the local fair in March 1947 representing 'the symbolic departure of the cattle trucks carrying off the deportees', they may have created some not wholly unintended confusion. The same could be said of the 'sympathetic caravan' entitled 'Labour Deportation' in the procession in Verpillers in the Isère during the celebration of the second anniversary of the town's liberation in 1947, representing 'a miniature camp barrack-house, similar to those in which the deportees lived in Germany'.[56] This very explicit imitation of the rituals described in the next chapter was interpreted, with lasting consequences, as an usurpation of exclusive symbols of unparalleled suffering.

To a lesser degree the labour conscripts also emulated the heroism of the resistance. The federation vaunted the patriotic credentials of all its executives. All the elected members were presented with some additional heroic title: escaped from Germany, joined the FFI, arrested draft-evader, or at the very least 'combatant '39–'40'. The serial novel in *Le DT* in the course of 1946 was about 'Jacques, a young labour deportee, who succeeded in escaping from Germany and joining a *maquis* group' – a rather atypical *parcours* for its readers to identify with. The ambitious programme of the International Federation of Deported Workers – a cosy Belgian–French club that exchanged invitations for each others' meetings – planned the creation of 'an international Roll of Honour' to chronicle 'the brilliant actions, feats of arms, acts of resistance, sabotage and demoralisation accomplished by the Labour Deportees' plus an inventory of fallen martyrs.[57]

No commemoration synthesises better the traumas, the anxieties, the projections, the rituals and the symbolism of the memory of the Second World War in France than the grandiose four-day-long demonstration

[56] Respectively *Le DT* 17 (May 1947) and 13 (Jan. 1947).
[57] *Le DT* 8 (Aug. 1946).

staged by Laurent Casanova in Compiègne in August 1946.[58] The occasion of the ceremony was the triumphal return of the 'ledger of Rethondes'. On the very spot where the German delegates had signed the armistice in front of Marshal Foch on 8 November 1918, the 'glade of the armistice' in the forest of Rethondes, a village near Compiègne, a stone ledger had been placed with the inscription: 'Here, on 11 November 1918, the criminal pride of the German Empire succumbed, vanquished by the free people it sought to enslave.'[59] This sanctuary of patriotism was completed with an exhibition of the historic railway carriage in which the armistice had been signed, and a statue of Foch. Hitler, always fond of theatricality, had staged the signing of the French surrender on 22 June 1940 in the same carriage, in the same forest. The stone ledger was broken to pieces and carried off to Germany and the railway carriage exposed as a trophy under the Brandenburg Gate in Berlin. Only Foch, so the commemorators claimed later, Hitler dared not touch. It was only to be expected that some ceremonial revenge would follow on 8 May 1945. The railway carriage was destroyed during the battle of Berlin and had to be replaced by an identical copy, but the pieces of the stone ledger had resisted better, and were brought back from Berlin on French trucks, arriving in Compiègne on Saturday 17 August 1946.

Casanova and his masters of ceremony aspired to more than a replay of patriotic triumphalism. For those with imagination, Compiègne was dense with symbolism. The camp of Royal-Lieu had been one of the main transit centres on the way to the Nazi concentration camps, the military camp Quartier Olivier a major demobilisation centre for repatriated PoWs and the station of Compiègne – *faute de mieux* – had been the setting for the first exchange of *Relève* trains, with one train-load of workers leaving for Germany and another arriving with returning PoWs. The practical organisation respected the hierarchies: on 15 August, the rally of veterans of the Great War in Rethondes; on 16 August, in the spirit of the Fêtes de l'Huma, sports displays, air show, concerts and open air cinema; on 17 August at 10:00 a.m., a ceremony for the 'Political Deportees' inside Royal-Lieu camp, in the presence of ministers Marcel Paul and Edmond Michelet, survivors of Buchenwald and Dachau respectively; at 3:00 p.m. a ceremony for the PoWs at Quartier Olivier, and another at 4:00 p.m. at the station for labour conscripts. At 7:00 p.m. the stone ledger arrived from Berlin and, to conclude it all, on 18 August the first stone of a new memorial was laid. According to the

[58] *Le DT* 8 (Aug. 1946) and 9 (Sep. 1946). See also *Le Patriote Résistant* 11, 12 and 13 (1, 20 Aug. and 1 Sep. 1946), and Namer, *La Commémoration*, pp. 172–5.
[59] Barcellini and Wieviorka, *Passant, souviens-toi!*, pp. 78–9.

sculptor and architect of the monument, this would be 'a symbol of the struggle of all French patriots against the Nazi invader and the imperishable testimony of the sufferings of those who have preferred honour to enslavement. It will also recall the losses in human lives and destruction. Political deportees, STO deportees, prisoners, resisters and fighters will thus be associated in one tribute.'[60] Understandably, the artists chose a very abstract structure, a tower 12 metres high with holes in it: one for the suffering of every department (that at least was an indisputable administrative subdivision of martyrdom) and one long cleft, 'symbolising hope'.

One all-embracing assimilation of all the martyrs and all the heroes of both wars: what better adoption into the patriotic family could the National Federation of Labour Deportees dream of? Compiègne would obliterate the affront inflicted by Gaullist heroic elitism in excluding labour conscripts from the tribute to the national martyrs on Mont Valérien on 11 November 1945. Casanova's initiative was hailed in Le DT under the title: 'Compiègne, Pilgrimage of Unity'. And a pilgrimage indeed it was, with its attributes of ritual which elevated Deportation to a civil religion.[61] Twenty niches, each 3.5 metres high, were set up on the road from Paris to Compiègne, each one evoking some form of French martyrdom – like so many Stations of the Cross. Five niches outside Compiègne represented the five categories of patriot.[62] The labour conscripts' niche symbolised a worker 'crushed between the Nazi hammer and the anvil of the French milice, chained by the Gestapo'.[63] The display was promoted with equal enthusiasm by the FNDIRP, the organisation of survivors of the camps closest to Casanova's undertaking. Casanova greeted the labour conscripts explicitly, but prudently: 'I insisted on greeting you, like all the others, because you deserved it. You too, within the limits of what was possible and under the conditions of the time, you helped France to defend its honour against the traitors . . . Down with slave-trading Capitalism! Shame on the traitors who called for it! Long live the peace of free nations!'[64]

Unfortunately it rained, for four days on end. The air show had to be cancelled and the number of participants was too disappointing to be published. The magnanimous spirit of unity was equally absent. When members of the Gaullist organisation of resistance victims FNDIR put up their banner, contrary to the previous agreement to put aside all

---

[60] Le Patriote Résistant 11 (1 Aug. 1946).

[61] The manifestation was described as 'un pieux pélerinage', adding 'c'est la France tout entière qui viendra *communier* en ce lieu plusieurs fois historique': ibid. The same journal mentioned on 20 Aug. 1946 'la purification de Rhetondes'.

[62] Le DT 9 (Sep. 1946).

[63] Ibid.   [64] Ibid.

organisational propaganda, a fight broke out with the representatives of the far more numerous FNDIRP. Much more serious were the protests from some participants over the presence of labour conscripts on an equal footing. Despite the FNDT's efforts to cover up the incidents, press coverage of the display focused its attention on them. Rémy Gourdon of *Combat* – ironically the former clandestine paper of the father of unity, Henri Frénay – and Rémy Roure of *Le Monde*, neither of them light editorialists, denounced the amalgamation perpetrated at Compiègne. The latter wrote: 'To exalt the Labour Deportees is a way of praising collaboration. There were conscripts, forced for most of the time by material reasons to go and work for the Great Reich in Germany. We can forgive this shortcoming, on condition that it is not treated as heroism. Many were only half-forced. There were volunteers who responded to the sentimental posters of the Boches, "my daddy is working in Germany". No Political Deportee or Deportee of the Resistance can accept the assimilation of approximately 25,000 survivors of the camps of slow death with those who collaborated, through their work, with the enemy. The "conscripts" make up the number, and one can understand the reasons for the demagoguery.'[65] The federation tried to reply that the labour conscripts never posed as heroes or martyrs, but immediately contradicted this by producing entirely fantastic statistics of martyrdom: 15,000 workers executed or dead in concentration camps in reprisal for resistance acts, 80,000 workers in disciplinary camps, more than 4,000 workers tried and incarcerated for sabotage, 10,000 escapees – of whom 2,000 joined the *maquis* – and altogether 62,000 dead. Compiègne was the culmination, the zenith of what had started during the occupation as a unified mythification of Deportation for all French in Germany, but the controversy that followed it signalled that those times were gone for good. Even Guy De Tassigny, quoted earlier in this section, secretary-general of the federation under Frénay and a propagandist of a social and low-key profile, who had been forced to leave his position after the transformation into a veterans' league, joined in the chorus of criticism. With a certain degree of *Schadenfreude*, De Tassigny argued that the FNDT had been wrong to abandon his line of conduct, to pour scorn on the volunteers and pose as heroes.[66]

Only three weeks later traditional religion succeeded with traditional rituals where Casanova's attempted civil religion and invented patriotic

---

[65] *Combat* and *Le Monde* (19 and 20 Aug. 1946). The 'pieux pèlerinage' was, in Roure's words, 'une kermesse'.
[66] Guy De Tassigny, *Les Merdophages* (Paris, 1946); *Le DT* 12 (Dec. 1946) and 15–16 (Mar.–Apr. 1947).

rituals had failed. On 8 September 1946, in response to an appeal from Abbot Rhodain, between 60,000 and 90,000 pilgrims flocked to Lourdes, all French repatriates from Germany (with the exception of 300 widows and female survivors of the camps, no women were allowed).[67] Niches set up in front of the basilica evoked life in the PoW camps, concentration camps and the camps for workers. In particular, specially adapted Stations of the Cross symbolised the sufferings in exile. A gigantic map of Germany enabled all the repatriates to retrace the chaplain for the region where they had lived. The rally, which lasted for several days, had the symbolic title of 'The Camp of the Return' and was presented as the fulfilment of the promise made by many Catholic 'exiles' to the Virgin Mary, to go to Lourdes if they returned alive from Germany. An open-air mass was celebrated in the presence of twenty-three 'clandestine chaplains', worker-priests in Germany, and the officiating bishop exhorted all repatriates: 'You, prisoners and deportees, remain faithful from now on to this watchword: United as in Lourdes'[68] – which must have sounded more convincing to the audience than the many calls of 'United as in Germany' that they had heard before. Greeted by the minister of war, Michelet, the crowd marched fraternally in the traditional candle-light procession. No fights, no rain, no critical commentaries in the press on amalgamations of sorts and – Lourdes wouldn't be Lourdes without one – a miracle to conclude it all. Raymond Dufoulon, a former PoW suffering from terminal tuberculosis – the classic illness of repatriation – had received extreme unction on the very morning of his miraculous healing, 'after which he joined his comrades of Stalag 4B in the afternoon ceremonies, without any sign of fatigue, chatting and smoking'.[69] No civil religion, no patriotic high mass could have achieved any of this.

Just as for the Belgian FNTDR, for the French FNDT the supreme symbol of rehabilitation was the law. Through the legislative activism of Frénay's ministry in favour of all repatriates, much had been done by the end of 1945 to improve the legal situation of the labour conscripts, even to the point of provoking the jealousy of other categories. This applied to the guaranteed re-employment for repatriates, the recognition of victims of industrial injuries in Germany as war victims and the indication of 'died for France' for workers who died in Germany. As in the Netherlands, the draft-evaders were the first to protest against this discrimination which favoured the patriotically less meritorious citizens who left for Germany over those who had refused to go. The national union of draft-evaders and *maquisards*, each claiming a membership of

---

[67] See Klein, *L'Aumônerie*, p. 73, and *Le Monde* (22 Aug., 7, 8–9 and 10 Sep. 1946).
[68] *Le Monde* (10 Sep. 1946).   [69] Ibid.

400,000 (that claims for the organisation of French workers who had refused to leave for Germany counted as least as many members as the organisation of those who actually left must have seemed patriotically axiomatic) claimed a 'liberation grant' exactly equivalent to the 'repatriation grant' received by labour conscripts, guaranteed re-employment and reduction of military service – in short: 'In all official texts, draft-evaders and *maquisards* should be ranked behind the deportees of the Resistance, but ahead of the conscripts of the STO.'[70] The *maquisards*, of course, considered themselves *combattants volontaires de la Résistance*, to be distinguished from those draft-evaders who had not crossed the line of active resistance but merely gone into hiding, but they similarly insisted in their claim that they should be given precedence over the labour conscripts.[71]

It was only in June 1948 that a proposal for a law recognising the 'Labour Deportees' was submitted by the communist parliamentarians, joined by the socialists after the summer. This was undoubtedly to allow time to redress these forms of discrimination and to respect the patriotic hierarchies – that is, in particular, to wait until the survivors of the camps had obtained their law, before submitting one for the labour conscripts.[72] The two proposals showed an interesting difference. In their introduction, the communists stressed that many labour deportees had also been resistance fighters (which was perhaps tactically unwise) whilst the socialists, referring to the Hague Convention, stressed that they had been war victims. Yet, in the legal references, the communist proposal was definitely the less patriotic. Whereas the communists considered labour conscription as 'a fact, resulting from the state of war', for the socialists it was simply 'an act of war', and they assimilated the time spent in 'deportation' with time spent in military service (*temps passé sous les drapeaux*). With perhaps even greater symbolism, the communist proposal specified no minimal period spent in Germany, whereas in its third article the socialist text indicated a minimum of three months; this referred to, and probably even anticipated, recognition of the token ninety days of 'effective combat' required for recognition as an *ancien combattant* for veterans of the Great War. The parliamentary commission adopted a joint version by the end of 1948, maintaining the 'combatant' references of the socialist text, but until May 1950 the Gaullist opposition manoeuvred to postpone discussion

[70] Commission Pensions (23 Jan. 1946), AAsN; *Documents AsN* 842 (2 Apr. 1946), annexe 842; 181 (18 July 1946), annexe 188; 241 (26 July 1946), annexe 286; 514 (3 Sep. 1946), annexe 660; 1269 (5 June 1947), annexe 1601.

[71] *Documents AsN*, annexe 205 (26 Dec. 1945), pp. 226–7.

[72] *Documents AsN*, annexe 4597 (17 June 1948), pp. 1230–1; annexe 54281 (Sep. 1948), p. 2119.

of the text on the parliamentary agenda.[73] Finally, on 23 May 1950, the National Assembly voted unanimously in favour of the text. Three weeks later, the Conseil de la République, the Senate of the Fourth Republic, vetoed the title of 'Labour Deportee' in the text, and substituted 'conscript for the STO'. The ensuing never-ending legal battle over *déporté* and *Déportation* as Appellation d'Origine Contrôlée, which was to end in a formal interdiction by decision of the supreme court (Cour de Cassation) against the labour conscripts calling themselves 'deportees', can only be understood in the light of the next chapters and the appropriation of the term by concentration camp survivors.

At the Nuremberg trial, deportation of workers from the occupied countries constituted one of the four main charges against the Nazi regime, reflecting the wartime outrage of labour deportation as one of the worst violations of national sovereignty. In terms of the number of individuals involved, forced economic migration was one of the major social facts of the occupation years, but already by the time of their repatriation the integration of the workers and their ambivalent history into the national memories proved problematic. The experience of the millions of displaced workers is only faintly mirrored in contemporary collective memories, receiving much less attention than the experiences of victims of genocide, concentration camp inmates, resistance fighters and even, finally, the collaborationists, when they are presented as 'victims of the post-war purge'.

The labour conscripts form a particularly interesting point of crystallisation in the collective memories of the Second World War, because their fate personifies the difficult interpretation of the experience of the occupation. Shuffled to and fro between the stereotypes of hero and traitor, they remain, finally, anonymous victims. For no other group was the dividing line harder to draw between individual and collective responsibilities, between compliance and *force majeure*. A brief look at the Italian situation clarifies this ambiguity even better. Bruno Mantelli observes on behalf of the Italian workers in the Reich that 'forced economic migration' is a tautology, since some form of coercion is always implicit in the concept of labour emigration.[74] Mantelli prefers the terminology of 'organised migration', stressing the importance of officially promoted economic migration from Italy to Germany in the period of the alliance of Axis powers, from 1938 until 1943, which

---

[73] *Documents AsN*, annexe 5919 (23 Dec. 1948), pp. 2778–9; Commission Pensions (22 Dec. 1948–17 May 1950), AAsN.

[74] Mantelli, 'I lavoratori italiani transferiti in Germania dal 1938 al 1945. Un tema dimenticato', *Passato e Presente* 38 (1996), pp. 101–11.

involved 500,000 workers, only 100,000 of whom discovered themselves to be emigrants from a nation at war with Germany after 8 September 1943. Italian workers were forced to emigrate for a variety of reasons – the traditional economic pressure that made Italy a country of emigration for most of its modern existence, much in line with the Dutch situation; the administrative constraints of corporatist labour policies; the ideological pressure of the fascist regime, in some way comparable to Vichy's *Relève* policy; and, finally, the physical coercion by occupying forces. In a country with a long-standing tradition of emigration, this particular group was ostracised by a suspicion of pro-fascism and as an embarrassing reminder of Italy's position in the war. Mantelli also observes that, unlike the victims of Nazi persecution and the PoWs, the emigrants had no intellectuals in their ranks; also that no political or cultural force in the post-war republic chose to favour the creation of an organisation for the victims of 'organised migration'. That the Italian case most closely resembled the Dutch circumstances in this respect is probably the most unexpected conclusion of this Italian excursus.

Two other conclusions can be drawn from the experience of labour migration during World War II in these four countries. First of all, the status as victims of warfare and foreign occupation of migrant workers in the German Reich was linked to the status of emigration as such in the national experience of each society. The banality of emigration in economically underdeveloped countries with a long-standing tradition of employment abroad in more industrialised neighbouring countries (or across the Atlantic), such as in the Netherlands and Italy, precluded commemoration of wartime migration, even under physical coercion by the occupying force, as an extraordinary and fundamentally unacceptable fate for the national working class. Emigration had always been a possible alternative for domestic economic hardship, that is, as much a potential choice for each individual as a constraint for the working class collectively. For countries that had a tradition of economic immigration, such as France and Belgium, the experience of population displacement for economic reasons, or rather, the experience of the reversal of the economic migration flow, was, in its sheer novelty, much more traumatic. That workers could be forced to live abroad to earn their living was a blow to moral sensibilities in these countries. Emigrants were, *ipso facto*, victims. That they had been forced to emigrate by the enemy occupier only heightened their victimisation.

A second conclusion is that the place occupied by labour conscripts in national collective memories was a result of post-war political economies in the societies to which they were repatriated. Who was affected by the legacy of forced economic migration? Who championed the labour conscripts as a social group in order to gain their allegiance? No political force could allow this in post-war Italy. In the Netherlands, the isolated initiatives failed to win political support. In Belgium, the Catholic workers' movement threw all its weight into rehabilitating and uniting the labour conscripts – for reasons of electoral strategy, to appease an important social group in which it feared communist influence; also for moral and religious reasons, to reintegrate into the local community workers uprooted by the experience of displacement; and, finally, as part of a policy of memory, whereby the Catholic Party defended a generous and lenient interpretation of patriotism against the partisans of a thorough purge and against the self-proclaimed 'governments of the resistance'. It did so by defending the attitude of the king, of the secretary-generals, of members of collaborationist formations (most of whom stemmed from a Catholic background), by defending the 'voluntary' workers and the labour conscripts. The deported workers as a *milieu de mémoire* personified the stance of the Catholic labour movement much as the executed militants symbolised the Communist Party. With a modicum of heroism and a large dose of generosity towards the ambiguous experience of labour conscription (over the issue of the signatories and non-signatories, for example), the National Federation of Deported Workers (FNTDR) established a mild consensual version of the national narrative with which a large midstream of the population could identify. No communist minister could object to that. In France, French expatriates in Germany, of whom the labour conscripts constituted roughly one-half, were crucial to the political economy of the wartime rivalries between Vichy, De Gaulle and the internal resistance. In the post-war years this political economy changed dramatically. The supreme solicitude for the workers shown by Frénay and the provisional government of the French Republic soon gave way to Gaullist contempt and hostility. The Communist Party and, more equivocally, the socialists defended the conscripts, despite the tide of heroic patriotism that moulded French post-war representations of the war. The initial strategy, of swimming along with this tide in a vociferous mythology of resistance and martyrdom, proved counterproductive. The labour conscripts had to adopt a lower profile and were finally dispossessed of what years of militant propaganda had turned into the cornerstone of their group identity, namely 'Deportation'.

The problematic position of labour conscripts in France, their successful adoption into the patriotic family in Belgium and the complete ostracism suffered by labour conscripts in the Netherlands reveal a paradox in the legacy of the occupation years. The better society as a whole succeeded in creating a consensual myth of patriotism, the worse off were the *milieux de mémoire*. The unified national myth of collective heroism and martyrdom in the Netherlands left no room for such an ambiguous group as the labour conscripts. In France, the *bataille de mémoire* degenerated into a patriotic bidding-up between *milieux de mémoire* of different war experiences and different political allegiances. The next chapter will illustrate more fully the deep disruption over sacred icons of national memory. In Belgium, the state never became an agent of unifying symbols, but was the dispenser of partisan tributes for private uses. The very absence of a national myth – even the wartime attitude of the supposed symbol of national unity, the king, was a protracted source of discord – allowed for the establishment of custom-made national recognition for every group: that is, regarding both their war experience and their political obedience. The respective icons of national memory were much less envied or contested, because each had its own frame of reference.

Patriotism, or rather the particular configuration adopted by patriotism after the war in each society, was much stronger than working-class solidarity. Of all the very different reactions amongst labour conscripts and their organisations described in this chapter, none even remotely resembled that of a militant working-class vanguard, radicalised in its proletarisation by the occupier. Those described as 'the work-slaves of the Nazi war-machine' bore the social costs of warfare individually and did not collectively rise up in revolt, either during or after the war. In France and Belgium it can even be observed that the rehabilitation of labour conscripts was stimulated by the opposite of class solidarity. Middle-class youngsters, drafted in draft-year actions (in contrast to Italy) and traumatised by their 'exile' in another social class at least as much as in another country, were most militant in defending the legacy of labour conscription.

Does this mean that the migration, as experienced by hundreds of thousands of labour conscripts, was without aftermath, without any influence at all in post-war society? Paradoxically, it seems that the patriotic scrutiny which so effectively impeded any collective post-war role for the labour conscripts was more ephemeral in its consequences than the individual impact of the social changes that stimulated moral panic. The dislocation of hundreds of thousands of workers under the exceptional circumstances of war, far from their familiar environment, from a life characterised by limited mobility and social control by family, neighbours, social, political and religious organisations, undoubtedly had a profound impact at the individual level. This impact could indeed be traumatising – the loss of all familiar references, the isolation, chaos and destruction in the industrial centres of Germany in the last phase of the war. It may also have been a form of emancipation, of liberation from social control, of contact with people of different opinions, from different backgrounds, of experiments with untried behaviour, of adventure and travel. This chapter has looked at the collective legacy of forced economic migration in the context of the configuration of national memories of the war and not the impact at an individual level of the experience of such a radical change, yet in the author's many conversations with former labour conscripts, even though all were active members of organisations claiming the martyrdom of the deported workers, together with the grief and the suffering of exile, of comrades lost under the debris of a night of bombing, some underlying degree of nostalgia often appeared for a period of liberty, discovery and adventure, somehow a golden age of youth and unlimited possibilities. Whether traumatising or emancipating or more often both at the same time, the person who returned could not be exactly the same as the one who had left. In that respect, the panicky moralists of the 1940s were right. Massive dislocation inevitably modified post-war behaviour and mentality.

A different line of research, with a different aim and a different methodology, inquiring into the legacy of wartime economic migration as an individual experience, would certainly be most rewarding. The result would probably be a very different evaluation of the relation between wartime migration and social change. There are indications that some 'proletarisation' did develop from labour conscription, in the sense that the displacement accelerated the rural exodus and modified occupational patterns. Several reports in 1945 and 1946 from the French administration responsible for the reintegration of repatriates in rural areas repeatedly observed such changes. Many repatriates who were employed in agriculture before their forced departure to Germany, which most often also entailed a forced occupational switch towards industry, did change trades after their repatriation. Jobs in government administration, the police, the national railroad company or the postal service, for which they benefited from preferential recruitment as war victims, were particularly in demand, intensifying secular French anxieties over rural depopulation.[75]

In spite of the oblivion of patriotic memories, the demonising of moralist discourse, in spite of legal disputes over the correct use of the word 'deportation', the exclusion or inclusion of those who signed a

[75] See 'Rapport de Mr. STEPHAN, inspecteur général en mission dans la région de Poitiers du 24 septembre au 5 octobre 1945', AN F9 3168. See also the reports *Direction départementale des Basses-Pyrénées* (16 Apr. 1945), AN F9 3172; *Hautes Alpes* (31 May 1945) and *Basses-Pyrénées* (4 Aug. 1945), both in AN F9 3173. See also the 'Ordonnance relative aux rapports entre bailleurs et repreneurs de baux à ferme, prisonniers et déportés' (draft document, 1945), AN F60/10.

piece of paper before their departure, the consequences of the mobility imposed by the Nazi Germany on the workers of the occupied countries constituted a wholly individual and inalienable experience which no collective representations could efface.

Part IV

Martyrs and other victims of Nazi persecution

11 Plural persecutions

The first part of this book showed how resisters were awkward heroes and how the recognition of who fought the enemy, and for which reasons, was a disruptive issue for the liberated societies. The second part described the heterogeneity of the population displaced to Germany during the war and the third part the ambiguity of the legacy of forced economic migration involving the greatest population displacement. What strength could a traumatised national consciousness draw from the experience of hundreds of thousands of individuals who had been forced to work for the enemy against their own country? This part deals with the memory of Nazi persecution.

The victims of Nazi persecution could at least, so it would seem, constitute a group, personify an experience, behind which all liberated societies could rally. There was nothing ambiguous in their status as victims; the Nazi methods of persecution were more ruthless and involved greater numbers of individuals than any other persecution seen in Europe in modern times: systematic and mechanised mass murder, arbitrary executions, mass deportation, torture, internment in appalling and murderous conditions. Yet the afflictions suffered by tens of thousands of citizens of the occupied countries in the hands of the enemy did not in themselves create a consensual commemoration of martyrdom. There are two reasons for this. The first is the multiplicity of persecutions: the Nazis persecuted different groups with different goals and with very different means. Any cult of the martyrdom of the victims of Nazi persecution had to accommodate the disparity and gradations of persecution. The second reason concerns the nature of national memories of the occupation. These memories were patriotic, proposing the paradigm of the combatant, the hero. This implied a selective memory. When coupled with the heterogeneity of the victims of Nazi persecution, it became divisive. To overcome these difficulties, the commemoration focused on one rallying symbol of martyrdom as metaphor for all forms of Nazi persecution: the concentration camp. In its turn this assimilation created confusion: not all patriotic martyrs, by any stretch of the current definitions, had been interned in concentration camps, nor were post-war societies ready to consider all concentration camp inmates as patriotic martyrs. Rather than being more straightforward than the previous groups, the legacy of Nazi persecution presents national memory with more inextricable problems.

A limited history of the policies of Nazi persecution would be a less than inadequate introduction to this part of the book. Chapter 4 indicated that the value of post-war statistics on victims of Nazi persecution is primarily phenomenological: they reveal those whom post-war societies were willing to recognise as victims rather than detailing the numbers involved in the various forms of Nazi persecution in the occupied countries of Western Europe. I mentioned two elementary representations which functioned in the post-war period, either through the place of detention (that is, as survivors of the concentration camps) or by reason of arrest, as political prisoners (Belgium and the Netherlands) or political deportees (France). These two representations became symbolically merged, though they only partially designate the same population.

The difficulty of representing the victims of the Nazi occupation originates in the particular character of this occupation. If occupation had been merely a military venture, the occupier would have limited himself to the repression of resistance activities. This first of all involved arresting or executing people involved in activities that threatened the occupier's military security. It could also, and secondarily, involve the repression of political activities operating against the occupation in the administrative or economic field – clandestine press, illegal association, sabotage of orders given by the occupier. More controversially, but still fairly current in traditional warfare, it could imply retaliation – for every soldier of the occupying force or collaborating individual hit by resistance acts, a greater number of civilians were taken hostage or executed. This method of repressing resistance was often combined with a fourth method, the preventative arrest and/or deportation of people suspected of hostile opinions against the occupier and liable to undertake resistance activities in the future. The selection of victims for retaliation was frequently not purely arbitrary; it targeted the latter category – the difference between *Wahlgeisel* (hostages taken in immediate reprisal for resistance acts) and *Haftgeisel* (the reserve pool of political prisoners already detained). The Nazi occupation forces in Western Europe used all four means of repression extensively, particularly the last mentioned.

Preventative arrest even serves as a theoretical legitimisation, put forward by both victim and perpetrator, of what was in fact political persecution of pre-war anti-fascists and communists for an offence of opinion. Here, repression of resistance for the purpose of military security spills over into persecution of an ideological nature. The degree of political polarisation in occupied societies intensified the effects of the foreign occupier's intentions. The combat waged by collaborationist forces against their political enemies often continued pre-war political rivalries through murderous means, radicalised but not caused by the war. This was of course particularly true for Vichy France, where the military collapse facilitated ideological revenge for the years of Popular Front policies.

Ideological persecution as a form of political violence must in its turn be distinguished from ideological persecution in its most pure form, of individuals not for their deeds or opinions but on the basis of characteristics attributed to them externally, by the persecutor. Here we are faced with the most specific characteristic of the Nazi occupation during the Second World War: 'racial' persecution leading to mass murder. The systematic assassination of Jews was conceptually unrelated to the strategic imperatives of military occupation; indeed, it more often ran counter to it. It originated in the anti-Semitism of Nazi ideology, fanatically implemented by the Nazis in almost all of the European territories that they occupied. This is an indication of the absolute priority of genocide in the Nazi programme. Other Nazi policies which were partially implemented in the territory of the Reich itself – for example, forced sterilisation as part of the eugenic programme or the persecution of homosexuals – were not exported, or only incidentally, to the occupied countries of Western Europe.

Lastly, there is the ordinary context of repression of offences against common law, involving those who would have been part of their national penitentiary system in times of peace but now ended up in the extraordinary context of Nazi persecution. Some were recidivists, 'anti-social elements' and other individuals whose marginality in society in normal times was now sanctioned with incalculable suffering in concentration camps under appalling conditions.

These distinctions between the different policies of Nazi persecution in Belgium, France and the Netherlands were not simply theoretical. Each form of persecution targeted a different population, implemented different means and followed a different chronology. In Belgium, those recognised as victims of Nazi persecution under the heading of 'political prisoner' comprised both the Jewish child gassed with his or her family in the second half of 1942 and the 66-year-old bartender's wife who spent forty days in prison in 1941 for having insulted the girlfriend of a German soldier as *moffenhoer* ('kraut's whore'); the seventeen-year-old boy shot in retaliation for German losses during the liberation fighting on 3 September 1944 as well as the newspaper editor known for his anti-German feelings before 1940 and sent to Sachsenhausen in 1943. Even the unfortunate man caught violating the curfew after missing his last train in Charleroi and badly beaten by SS soldiers was labelled a 'political prisoner' on the basis of his maltreatment by the enemy.[1] Rather than the distinctions, it is the assimilation of all these different cases that proceeds from a theoretical post-war construction. This is not to doubt the status of victim of Nazi persecution in any of these cases – on the contrary, there were many more victims than those who were caught by the 'political prisoner' designation, notably the last category of victims listed above. Common law criminals are the black hole, not only in the post-war perceptions and policies, but in the historiography as well – the black marketeers, the petty criminal recidivists, the thieves and prostitutes, and even the workers arrested in Germany for genuine resistance acts but excluded from all measures benefiting 'political prisoners' because of their 'voluntary' departure. Only Gie Van den Berghe's superb publication of *De Zot van Rekem*, the poetic and moving account by a Belgian 'anti-social element' who spent full five years in German concentration camps, does justice to this group.[2]

Moreover, these are distinctions from the perspective of the perpetrator, and not from the perspective of the victims' self-assessment. As will appear further in these pages, victims quite legitimately refused their categorisation by the enemy and showed a general tendency to interpret enemy hostility against them as a consequence of their own original hostility to the enemy. Political opponents often preferred to consider themselves victims of the repression of resistance acts, rather than of persecuted opinions; and victims of racial persecution often preferred to see themselves as being victimised for their opinions rather than for what the persecutor had defined as their 'race'. The more 'rational' the reason for persecution (the perpetrator persecuted the victim because the victim was a threat to him, rather than in the pursuit of some fanatical and irrational idea that targeted the victim for absolutely arbitrary reasons), the more the victim retained some initiative in his own destiny. Paradoxically, persecution seemed more acceptable if it was somehow occasioned by a choice, an action or an opinion made or held by the victim. The more rational the persecutor, the more dignified its victims?

[1] The examples above are drawn from the analysis of 200 personal files for the recognition as 'political prisoners' in the archives of the service for war victims of the Belgian Ministry of Public Health by the students of the University of Leuven participating in my 1995–6 research seminar.

[2] Gie Van den Berghe (ed.), *De Zot van Rekem* [of Louis Nauwelaers] (Antwerp, 1995), pp. 7–87.

In view of the impossibility of comparing experiences, and the arbitrary variations in minimum time limits for legal recognition (the Belgian law required thirty days, the French law deportation or ninety days), it would be impossible to draft a comprehensive inventory of all forms of persecution and all sorts of victims, and to compare this afterwards with post-war perceptions.

The relevance of these introductory remarks will become even clearer through the statistics of victims of Nazi persecution – that is, by demonstrating that there simply are no reliable statistics that permit a valid comparison. This applies as much to the comparison between the three countries as to the comparison of different categories of victims. Reliable statistics exist only for Jewish victims. As will be described in chapter 13, historians played a major role in the developing awareness of the very particular fate of the Jews. I will even suggest that a reversal occurred, from the marginality of the Jewish tragedy in the social memories of the first two post-war decades to their prominence in the historical memories that emerged later. Thanks to the pioneering research of Jacques Presser for the Netherlands, Maxime Steinberg for Belgium and Serge Klarsfeld for France, and due to the accurate Nazi bookkeeping of their own crimes, the victims of the Nazi genocide of the Jews are known by name and individually counted.[3] The Nazis deported 107,000 Jews from the Netherlands, 25,475 from Belgium and 73,835 from France, over 95 per cent of whom were murdered. Of the more than 200,000 Jews from these three countries, 150,000 were deported to Auschwitz. Two-thirds of them were immediately murdered in the gas chambers upon arrival, that is, before even entering the adjoining concentration camp. The Nazi genocide murdered 73 per cent of the Jewish population in the Netherlands, 40 per cent in Belgium and 25 per cent in France. Comparisons between these three figures and attempts to account for the baffling difference in the extermination rate have been undertaken to good effect.[4] Maxime Steinberg in particular is

---

[3] See the name lists published by Serge Klarsfeld and Maxime Steinberg, *Le Mémorial de la déportation des juifs de Belgique* (Brussels and New York, 1982); Serge Klarsfeld, *Mémorial de la déportation des juifs de France* (Paris, 1978); and the comprehensive histories (without a name list) by J. Presser, *Ondergang. De Vervolging en verdelging van het Nederlandse Jodendom, 1940–1945* (The Hague, 1965), 2 vols., and Maxime Steinberg, *L'Etoile et le fusil* (Brussels, 1983–6), 4 vols.

[4] See Bob Moore, *Victims and Survivors. The Nazi Persecution of the Jews in the Netherlands 1940–1945* (London, 1997); Pim Griffioen and Ron Zeller, 'Jodenvervolging in Nederland en België tijdens de Tweede Wereldoorlog. Een vergelijkende analyse', in *Oorlogsdocumentatie '40–'45* 8 (Amsterdam, 1997), pp. 10–63; Maxime Steinberg, 'Le Paradoxe Français dans la solution finale à l'Ouest', *Annales ESC* 3 (1993), pp. 583–94; Hans Blom, 'The Persecution of the Jews in the Netherlands. A Comparative Western European Perspective', *European History Quarterly* 19 (1989), pp. 333–51; and Helen

effective in showing how the chronology and the mechanism of mass murder proceeded from central and concerted directives and how the systematic assassination of Jews in each of the three countries was part of a continental programme, even if this had to cope with different national reactions.

This situation contrasts with our knowledge of non-Jewish victims. Whether defined as concentration camp inmates or as 'political prisoners', the statistics are problematic. In any case, the definitions should be not be confused.[5] In Belgium, the terms of the law recognising 'political prisoners' did not require deportation to a concentration camp, but a minimum of thirty days of detention for reasons other than condemnation for common law offences (including in Belgian prisons), severe maltreatment or execution.[6] As a result, statistics on survivors of concentration camps differ to a baffling extent from figures of 'political prisoners'. The official report published by the Belgian Commission for Repatriation at the end of July 1945, at a moment when the repatriation was not yet wholly completed, estimated the number of 'political prisoners and hostages' to be repatriated at 15,000, adding cautiously that it was in sincere doubt over who to include in this number, and in particular whether common law offenders could figure in these statistics.[7] Obviously, this number does not incorporate the 25,000 Jewish deportees. In 1948, when the repatriation was virtually complete, a semi-official publication of the statistics of repatriates up to 31 December 1946 counted 9,033 'political prisoners and hostages'.[8] This figure comprised the survivors of German camps and prisons, minus the common law criminals, as far as repatriation officials could identify them. The difference between this figure for repatriates and the number of repatriates anticipated in July 1945 can be explained by death rates, which are estimated in most literature on concentration camps at around one-third of inmates.

Under the legal dispositions of the law recognising 'political prisoners', about 60,000 applications were filed with the administration.

Fein, *Accounting for Genocide. National Responses and Jewish Victimisation During the Holocaust* (New York and London, 1979).

[5] As happens in Maxime Steinberg's otherwise remarkable *Les Yeux du témoin et le regard du borgne. L'Histoire face au révisionisme* (Paris, 1990).

[6] A careful use of comparative statistics of Jewish and non-Jewish victims in Belgium can be found in Gie Van de Berghe, *Getuigen. Belgische Bibliografie over de Nazi-kampen* (Brussels, 1995), 2 vols. Still, even Van den Berghe resorts in the final analysis to the arbitrary estimate of 40,000 recognised 'political prisoners' plus 10 per cent of the rejected applications to calculate the number of non-Jewish concentration camp inmates.

[7] *Rapport sur l'activité du Commissariat Belge*, annexe 21.

[8] Herremans, *Personnes Déplacées*, pp. 252–7.

Some of these applications were unfounded, whilst others were rejected on the basis of insufficient documentary evidence, failure to respect the deadlines or interrupted correspondence with applicants abroad. Some of them involved concentration camp survivors, excluded on legal grounds, for membership of collaborationist formations, voluntary work in Germany or common law offences. Rejections amounted to one-third of all applications: finally only 41,000 applicants were recognised as 'political prisoners'. Yet even the number of 60,000 applications does not include all possible Nazi victims. Many applications were never submitted – either personally by the victims or posthumously by their heirs. This must apply particularly to the Jews, who were systematically murdered in entire families, leaving no heirs to claim their recognition. It also applies to foreigners, many of whom were Jews, and who were discouraged from submitting their demand by the very restrictive clauses concerning foreigners living in Belgium at the time of their arrest, assassination or deportation. The last group that is most probably underrepresented is that of common law offenders, some of whom may have applied the same mechanism of anticipatory self-exclusion. A pioneer statistical study of 4 per cent of the 60,000 files produced some remarkable results.[9] First of all, 30 per cent of all files concerned internment on Belgian territory and not deportation to German concentration camps, as explicitly specified in the law. Secondly, and more surprisingly, 12 per cent of applicants in the statistical sample were identified as Jewish. If this figure is correct, one could estimate by extrapolation that about 7,000 of the 60,000 files concern Jewish applicants. Compared to the 1,335 survivors of the 25,475 Jews deported from Belgium to Germany, this figure is very high, yet one should relate it to the figure for all Jews deported or interned during the Nazi occupation, including in camps and prisons in Belgium, France and the Netherlands. According to Maxime Steinberg, this was as high as 34,800. Of this total, about 5,900 survived. Only the Belgian nationals amongst them could be recognised under the terms of the law, except for those with a resistance record (only 941 foreigners obtained this recognition). For the Belgian statistics this indicates two conclusions. First of all, neither repatriation records nor post-war administrative files contain all victims of Nazi persecution, nor all survivors of concentration camps. Secondly, the two series of figures are not incompatible, if we take into account people imprisoned or tortured without deportation to Germany and the group of Jewish victims, for whom precise figures are known, but not the extent to which they are included

[9] See the intermediate report: Patrick Temmerman and Bert Boeckx, *Deportatie en Verzet. Een eerste globale statistische analyse op basis van erkenningsdossiers* (Brussels,1995), 2 vols.

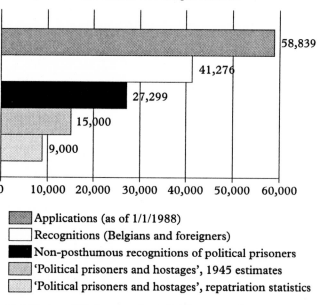

58,839
41,276
27,299
15,000
9,000

0   10,000 20,000 30,000 40,000 50,000 60,000

Applications (as of 1/1/1988)
Recognitions (Belgians and foreigners)
Non-posthumous recognitions of political prisoners
'Political prisoners and hostages', 1945 estimates
'Political prisoners and hostages', repatriation statistics

11.1 Victims of Nazi persecution in Belgium: some figures

in the figures of post-war applicants. The statistics from the Belgian administration are probably very reliable; that is, the investigation to ascertain whether a person came within the terms of the law was scrupulously executed, but any assimilation of concentration camp inmates and 'political prisoners' is wholly unwarranted.

Statistics for the Netherlands originate not in post-war administrative procedures but in the historical research by Louis De Jong and the team of researchers of the State Institute for War Documentation (RIOD) in Amsterdam.[10] Starting from their findings, it would not be possible to reconstitute a set of data comparable to the figures of the Belgian administration. De Jong estimates the number of Dutch citizens in German concentration camps at 11,000. About 2,500 Dutch were sent to German prisons, and 4,000–6,000 Dutch workers were given prison sentences or sent to concentration camps in Germany itself. An unspecified number of the various groups of inmates cited above were condemned as common law offenders. Elsewhere, based on eyewitness accounts of other KZ inmates, De Jong estimates their proportion in the Dutch KZ population in Germany at 30 per cent. In addition, in the Netherlands itself, 53,000 people were interned in concentration camps

[10] De Jong, *Koninkrijk*, vol. VIII.

(Vucht and Amersfoort in particular), many of them foreigners, and of these 53,000, 41,000 were liberated and 570 died in captivity. Of the 100,000 Dutch prosecuted by German courts, only one-fifth were charged with resistance acts, and of the 60,000 arrests only 15,000 involved resisters. The occupier executed 2,000 Dutch. One post-war report, drafted in answer to the Dutch repatriation controversy, mentioned in December 1947 the figure of 29,000 'political prisoners' in Germany, of whom 7,000 were repatriated, 18,000 registered casualties and 2,400 missing. The report also mentioned the reasonably accurate figures of 110,000 Jewish deportees, of whom 6,000 were survivors, but it is not clear whether these figures were estimates or the result of individual tracing and registration.[11] Intuitively, it seems that, if broken down properly, the different groups of Dutch victims of Nazi persecution, with the exception of the Jewish victims, are in the same numerical range as in Belgium, that is, more or less comparable in absolute terms (and consequently, in view of the almost identical figures for the total population, also in relative terms). But much more research is required before this conjecture can be replaced with empirical data.

The status of the French statistics stands around midway between Dutch and Belgian statistics: half administrative, half product of historical research. They are in any case surrounded with considerable secrecy. Annette Wieviorka, whose doctoral thesis on 'deportation and genocide' was published in 1992, mentions that 'according to the currently most reliable figures, 63,085 people were deported to the concentration camps: resisters, hostages, people rounded up in razzias, political [prisoners], common law offenders'.[12] Of them, 37,025 survived. Like Steinberg, Wieviorka adds this figure to the figure for Jewish victims. Only in a cryptic reference in an article of 1995 do we learn the controversial nature of these statistics, that they originate in research by the departmental correspondents of the Historical Commission of the Second World War, whose publication was blocked for twenty years by protests from the FNDIRP, the largest organisation in France of victims of Nazi persecution, and that they virtually coincide with the figures produced by the Ministry of Veterans, namely 65,123.[13] Annette Wieviorka, who discusses the political debate on the two laws recognising victims of Nazi persecution in France, with lengthy quotes, does not

[11] *Rapport van de Commissie van onderzoek inzake het verstrekken van pakketten door het Rode Kruis en andere instanties aan Nederlandse Politieke Gevangenen in het Buitenland gedurende de bezettingstijd alsmede inzake het evacueren van Nederlandse gevangenen kort voor en na het einde van de oorlog* (1 Dec. 1947), p. 12, ARA, cab. PM, box 92.

[12] Annette Wieviorka, *Déportation*, pp. 20–1.

[13] Annette Wieviorka, 'Déportation et Génocide. Le cas français: Essai d'historiographie', in Matard-Bonucci and Lynch, *La Libération des camps*, pp. 234 and 237 (n. 14).

even mention who precisely is included.[14] This is a crucial fact, especially if the only figure that she quotes on non-Jewish victims originates in, or at least coincides with, the figures of the Ministry of Veterans, which can only be established, as in Belgium, according to the terms of the law. If the Historical Commission's local research comes to the same conclusion, this most probably implies that it handled the same criteria.

These criteria were, first, deportation, without limitations as to the duration of internment, to a prison or concentration camp in a territory under German control, in certain camps and prisons of the annexed departments of Alsace-Lorraine and under similar conditions in Indochina; secondly, internment, independent of the place of detention, for a minimum duration of three months or severe maltreatment, illness or torture; thirdly, execution by the enemy. These conditions applied to the 'deportees and internees of the resistance', in cases of arrest or execution for 'a recognised act of resistance' and to 'political deportees and internees' for any reason for arrest except common law offences. The usual restrictions applied to both groups, of exclusion of all those who would have acted before, during or after their internment 'against the spirit of the Resistance'. A major difference from the Belgian legislation was that no time limit applied in cases of deportation (which did not really matter, since no early return was possible for deported persons), whilst the time limit for internment on the national territory was three months (the token ninety days of 'effective combat'), rather than thirty days. This means that the French legislation was more severe, and excluded the category of those who in Belgium obtained recognition for internment of between thirty and ninety days. The most important difference was the possibility of application by foreigners living in France before the outbreak of the war on the invasion in Poland on 1 September 1939.

If the figures of the Historical Commission and the Ministry for Veterans do indeed coincide, how can they then include common law offenders? How can they not constitute that proportion of Jewish victims who filed an application for recognition as 'political deportee', to which they were perfectly entitled under the terms of the law? Are 'deportees' and 'internees' distinguished? Are the figures for executed hostages included? Faced with such a lack of elementary information on the criteria used to establish the figure of 65,000, no valid comparison is possible with the Dutch and Belgian statistics.

A reconstruction of reliable statistics would require the replacement of the administrative and legal concept of 'political prisoners' and

---

[14] Annette Wieviorka, *Déportation*, pp. 141–57.

'deportees and internees' by historically more accurate categories. If we take, for example, the concrete category of concentration camp inmates, two essential preliminary questions would have to be addressed. First, who was in the camps but not in the statistics of 'political prisoners' and 'deportees and internees'? This covers the common law offenders, who were excluded under the terms of the laws, and Jewish victims, who were included in the terms of the law, but for only a minority of whom applications can have been filed for recognition, because of the exceptionally low survival rate. Secondly, who was in the statistics but not in the concentration camps? This covers the inmates of local prisons for an internment of more than thirty days in Belgium and ninety in France, executed hostages and victims of torture. The post-war statistics we have at our disposal today and the vocabulary on which they are based are post-war representations of national martyrdom, involving crucial choices on inclusion and exclusion of specific groups. In the next chapter, I will analyse the emergence of these categories of martyrdom and the debates they involved.

Victors of military conflicts often retroactively legitimise their war effort by denouncing the particular atrocities committed by the defeated enemy. After the First World War charges of the use of poison gas, the destruction of the library of Leuven in Belgium or the brutal murder of civilians in Dinant singled out the German enemy as much more than an ordinary military enemy. Extraordinary deaths and destruction weighed heavier in post-war representations of the enemy than the millions of casualties and victims of conventional warfare, particularly in Belgium and in neutral countries. Since after the Second World War the liberated countries of Western Europe had few of the latter to mourn, it could be expected that the weight given to extraordinary, civilian victims would be even greater. Yet reactions to the experience of persecution of tens of thousands of their citizens expressed much more than the predictable level of moral indignation and victor's justice. France, Belgium and the Netherlands had a tradition of individual liberties, rule of law and *habeas corpus* that was even older than the progressive adoption of political democracy. Despite national collaboration and complicity, the persecutions were a brutal import by the Nazi occupier that wounded the moral sensibilities of the indigenous populations much more than, for example, the progressive establishment of persecution and terror in Nazi Germany itself since 1933, in a country with, moreover, an illiberal tradition even before that date compared to its western neighbours. This accounts for the very different reactions of these populations to the persecution when they were actually confronted with it, from the Dutch strike of February 1941 to official protests by national moral authorities, to the large-scale assistance to persons in hiding. It also accounts for reactions to the persecutions afterwards, to the legacy of what had been a profoundly traumatic experience for the whole of society.

During the war, the local population had been the direct witness of persecution, mostly in the form of deportation, the point of departure of a long trajectory. Public executions – mostly by firing squads in inaccessible locations and only exceptionally by public hanging – affected numerically a marginal proportion of the total figure of individuals murdered by the Nazis in occupied Western Europe. This implies that the moral shock of confrontation with Nazi atrocities would be administered in three phases: first during the occupation, as witnesses of brutal roundups and arrests or occasional public executions; next after the liberation, through the partial discovery of atrocities committed on the national soil. The third and most important shock came only once the war was over, or almost over – when the Allies conquered those regions of the Reich and the occupied East European countries that had been the destination of the deportations and where the victims had either been imprisoned in appalling and homicidal conditions, or, for most of the Jewish victims, immediately massacred.

Immediate reactions to the discovery of the atrocities varied from outbursts of popular vengeance, as described in chapter 9, to a state of moral shock or even morbid voyeurism. The object of this chapter is not so much a description of these immediate reactions as the interpretation of the atrocities and the identification of victims that imposed itself, or was imposed, in the post-war years, that is, through the prism of national martyrdom. I have described the power of patriotism in moulding the memories of resistance, population transfers, labour conscription; inevitably, patriotism similarly moulded the memory of Nazi persecution. Again, the paradigm of the combatant emerged, but those who were imprisoned, deported or murdered as a consequence of their struggle against the occupier did not form a clear-cut group for national memories to deal with. Many were foreigners and even more were communists, who fought for an ideal that was viewed as anti-national by traditional patriots. As explained in the previous chapter, combatants of all sorts constituted only a minority of all victims of persecution. For all others, national memory imposed the paradigm of the martyr.

Martyrs, from the Greek μαρτυρ or 'witness', are no ordinary, innocent and arbitrary victims: they suffer or die, in the original sense of early Christianity, because of their faith; their faith is both cause and effect of their suffering. Martyrs are targeted as victims of persecution because of their witnessing of their faith, but through their ordeals they also deliver the most powerful proof, or witness, of their faith. (Suffering, in early Christianity and Counter-Reformation Catholicism – and in Islamic fundamentalism – is, like material success in Calvinism, a sign of divine predestination.) In the secularised meaning of the word, in which it is systematically used in the sources dealt with here, it denotes victims who suffer or die for a noble cause. The noble cause gives meaning to their suffering in two ways, as mentioned for the Christian martyrs: on the one hand, they are victimised because of their own adherence to this noble cause – an adherence that is a matter of personal choice and, in circumstances of persecution, of heroism – and on the other hand, through their suffering, they deliver the proof of their dauntless personification of this cause.

The paradigm of national martyrdom was imposed by exclusion or by assimilation. A narrowly defined patriotic memory recognised victims of persecution only as a consequence of the combat they waged, and excluded all other victims from recognition. Vehemently defended by patriotic associations in the post-1918 tradition of veteranism in Belgium and France, such an exclusive memory was finally only imposed in the Netherlands, where this tradition did not exist. The inclusive memories of persecution in France and Belgium integrated all victims, except common law offenders, but they identified their experience with that of martyrs of noble causes, be the cause Resistance, Patriotism or Anti-Fascism, and distinguished between them. I will discuss the impact and representation of Nazi persecution, and the imposition of collective interpretations, with particular attention to the inclusion, exclusion or assimilation of different groups of victims in organisations, in the law and, finally, in national memories.

The discovery of Nazi atrocities followed immediately after the withdrawal of the German troops. In France there was the village of Oradour-sur-Glane, the prisons of Eysses and Fresnes and the camps of Struthof and Natzwiller, to mention only a few.[1] In Belgium there was above all the fortress of Breendonk, where resisters and political opponents had been detained in conditions described by many survivors who were subsequently deported to concentration camps in Germany as their worst ordeal, including systematic torture. A brochure circulated, even before the end of the war, on 'The Full Truth About the Concentration Camp of Breendonk. An Illustrated Report on the Atrocities Committed There by the Nazi Torturers'.[2] Associations uniting survivors of camps and prisons on the national territory with the families of victims executed or deceased on the national soil were set up in the last months of 1944. Organisations of hostages of the First World War also immediately opened up their ranks to their companions of the continuing war. Breendonk was officially proclaimed a national memorial.[3] Yet the occupier had not left much evidence of his crimes: most camps

---

[1] See Sarah Farmer, *Oradour. Arrêt sur mémoire* (Paris, 1994), and Barcellini and Wieviorka, *Passant, souviens-toi!*

[2] (Antwerp 1945), CEGES/SOMA, BrB 7/16. For eyewitness accounts on Breendonk, see the exhaustive bibliography by Van den Berghe, *Getuigen*, vol. II.

[3] *Documenten Kamer* 114 (11 June 1946); *Belgisch Staatsblad* (19 Aug. 1947); *Kracht* (Oct. 1948).

and prisons had been emptied at the approach of the Allied armies, and the last convoys taking prisoners to Germany left in the midst of the liberation fighting. For most of the Dutch territory the chronology was very different: most concentration camps would be liberated even before the home front, following the German surrender. The consequences of this peculiar chronology for the general context of the repatriation have been described in chapter 5, and its impact on the return of the workers in chapter 10. This course of events sets the reception of victims of persecution in the Netherlands wholly apart from France and Belgium, and requires us to consider the Netherlands separately.

During the eight months between the liberation of Paris and Brussels and the German defeat, little was known of what had become of the tens of thousands of individuals taken to Germany as victims of the various Nazi policies of persecution. Reporting on the fate of the Jewish victims was very accurate, but was often met with disbelief.[4] By September 1943, reports drafted in Algiers mentioned explicitly: 'Arrested Jews are sent to the camp of Auschwitz, in Silesia, via Drancy. Healthy Israelites will be employed in the salt-mines in Poland and the invalids and the children . . . will purely and simply be eliminated.'[5] Yet official estimates continued to be very vague as to the number of casualties when calculating the numbers of expected repatriates. Nor did accurate reporting on the fate of the Jewish population of Europe automatically stir compassion and sympathy for the Jews in North Africa. An article on the persecutions in occupied France published in *Alger Républicain* in May 1944 referred to the 'anti-Jewish repression', adding: 'There is certainly in North Africa a delicate "Jewish problem". We know that the Germans claim that there was likewise one in Europe, notably in France.'[6] In the view of *Alger Républicain*, the Germans had located the right problem in the wrong place. As described in chapter 6, the administration, both in Vichy and in Algiers, depended for its information primarily on reporting by PoWs. Yet even through these channels, information on the mass murder of Jews trickled in intermittently. In particular, French PoWs interned in Rawa Ruska in occupied Poland, a disciplinary camp for PoWs captured when trying to escape, witnessed

---

[4] See Dinnerstein, *America and the Survivors of the Holocaust*; Robert H. Abzug, *Inside the Vicious Heart. Americans and the Liberation of the Concentration Camps* (New York and Oxford, 1985); Jon Bridgeman and Richard Jones, *The End of the Holocaust. The Liberation of the Camps* (Portland, OR, 1990); Stéphane Courtois and Adam Rayski, *Qui savait quoi? L'Extermination des juifs, 1941–1945* (Paris, 1987); Olga Wormser-Migot, *Le Retour des déportés. Quand les alliés ouvrirent les portes* (Brussels, 1985); FNDIRP, *Le Choc. La Presse relève l'enfer des camps Nazis* (Paris, 1985).

[5] *France Politique. Les Persecutions Raciales et politiques* (Algiers, Sep. 1943), AN F9 3106.

[6] Michel le Troquer in *Alger Républicain* (7 May 1944), AN F9 3106.

massacres of the Jewish population of surrounding villages. They also reported with horror on the daily transports of thousands of Jews in cattle-wagons, on the despair, suicides and executions, adding that several convoys consisted of French, Belgian and Dutch Jews.[7] For the Dutch exile government in London, Dienke Hondius describes how the accurate information by H. Denz on the extermination camps in occupied Poland was deleted from the Hondelink report by the repatriation commissioner Ferwerda, because in his opinion the unbelievable atrocity involved would have discredited the report.[8]

As for the individuals arrested on suspicion of resistance or as political opponents, the expectations of both repatriation administrations and public opinion oscillated between optimism and despair. Apocalyptic fears of a systematic massacre of all 'political deportees' existed not only in Frénay's mind, but were to a large extent shared by very many inmates themselves.[9] In April 1945, the French repatriation ministry was flooded with indignant letters on the very explicit reporting on the cruelties committed in the concentration camps and the resulting death rates, creating alarm and despair in the families of KZ inmates.[10] Frénay intervened with the information ministry in the first days of May and obtained censorship of reporting on death rates and maltreatment in the camps.[11] The very vague public estimates of the numbers of survivors by the ministry – between 40,000 and 160,000 – were not only the result of defective information but also of a deliberate policy which allowed for ample psychological margins of hope for the worried families. One thing was certain: the victims of persecution were greatly outnumbered by the other categories of repatriates, but their return was more anxiously awaited in the light of the reporting in the last months of the war on the murderous conditions they had experienced.

Chapter 9 described the central place survivors of the camps played in public perceptions, concentrating feelings of compassion and indignation on their miserable physical condition and on the news they brought home of comrades who had been murdered or died from generalised maltreatment. The patriotic *mise en scène* of the repatriation – the *marseillaises* and *brabançonnes*, the banners and speeches – heightened

---

[7] *Camps de représailles. Rapport fait de renseignements divers. Régime à Rawa Ruska* (12 Nov. 1943), AN F9 3105. See also the report *11/Les juifs* (11 June 1946) in AN F9 3106.

[8] Hondius, *Terugkeer*, p. 50.

[9] See also Gie Van den Berghe, 'Het einde van de kampen en van een mythe', *Spiegel Historiael* 29, 3/4 (1994), pp. 156–60.

[10] See the distressing correspondence in AN F9 3168 and samples of newspaper reporting in April 1945 in FNDIRP, *Le Choc*.

[11] See letter, J. Richard to radio-distribution (Paris, 8 May 1945), AN F9 3168. See also Edouard Lynch, 'Les Filtres Successifs de l'information', in Matard-Bonucci and Lynch, *La Libération des camps*, pp. 163–75.

this effect. If the nation wanted to turn the return of its lost sons and daughters to the national soil into an indictment of the enemy and a glorification of national martyrdom, no group of victims could perform this role better than the survivors of the supreme sites of national suffering, the concentration camps. Many survivors of the camps were also willing to perform this role of martyrs and heroes, to some extent, and to participate in the *mise en scène*. François Cochet observed several cases of concentration camp inmates who had received new clothing on their way to France, but put their concentration camp clothes on again for the arrival home, precisely to distinguish themselves from the ordinary repatriates and to claim their unique martyrdom.[12] The crowds that flocked to the railway stations and jammed the access to the reception centres wanted to see first-hand who of their relatives and neighbours, PoWs, workers, or victims of persecution was coming back, but they also wanted to witness the return of, as they were then often described, the living dead, the walking skeletons, to check the reality of the reporting on the discovery of Nazi atrocities in the concentration camps. In Belgium at least, the impact of the discovery of the camps was such as to change the vocabulary. At the time of the liberation, the moment of patriotic triumph, the repetition of 1918 had been stressed, with the accompanying national stereotypes of *moffen* and *boches*, of 'teutonic hordes', 'huns', of the 'Prussian military spirit'. With the discovery of the camps, the enemy became much more Nazi than *boche*, the worst war crime no longer the violation of national sovereignty, but inhuman persecution. The war against the traditional enemy of the nation had, *post facto*, grown into the war of mankind against inhumanity.

The impact of regular reporting through the press or cinema newsreels, and the physical impact of the return of the survivors, was driven home by a tremendous determination to inform the whole population about the Nazi crimes. The French Ministry of Information organised a major national exhibition in the Grand Palais in Paris on 'Hitler Crimes' in the summer of 1945.[13] In 1946 it travelled to London and Brussels, where a monumental replica of the gate of the fortress of Breendonk was added, and in 1947 it toured the whole of France, exhibiting in twenty major cities.[14] In Belgium a 'political prisoners' exhibition train', with information on the camps, artefacts from inmates and an urn with ashes

[12] Cochet, *Les Exclus*, p. 75.
[13] *Compte-rendu de la Réunion Interministérielle . . . Service de Recherche des Crimes de Guerre* (14 Apr. 1945), AN F9 3168.
[14] See the brochure *Ministerie van Wederopbouw. Hitleriaanse gruwelen* (Brussels, 1946), CEGES/SOMA, BrB 11/5 and BrB 11/6; *Front* (26 May and 2 June 1946).

10 Repatriation and retribution: 'And now . . . what shall we tell them now?'
From *Front*, 6 May 1945. Photo, Isabelle Sampieri, CEGES/SOMA.

from the crematoria, toured the country, with stops in seventy-one
stations, to carry the knowledge of the camps to even the remotest
regions.[15] The train was an initiative shared by the national organisation
of political prisoners (CNPPA/NCPGR) and the national railway
company. The French organisation FNDIRP even outdid the Belgian
dynamism, by organising a colossal and very effective system of information stands about the camps at local fairs in almost every provincial
centre in the course of 1946 and 1947.

The precursor, a very successful exhibition in Clermont-Ferrand
which, according to its organisers, drew 50,000 visitors in a town of
100,000 inhabitants, inspired an article in the organisation's journal to

[15] See the brochure *Expositietrein der politieke gevangenen en weerstanders van 't spoor*
(Brussels, 1947), CEGES/SOMA, BrB 8/54; *L'Effort* (Nov. 1947); *Compte-Rendu du
Conseil National de la CNPPA* (10 May and 3 Aug. 1947), archives of CNPPA,
Brussels.

serve as a guideline for followers: 'How to make a success of a Week of the Deportee':

On the central square of Clermont-Ferrand we have reconstructed the tower of Buchenwald, flanked by its buildings. This reconstruction, as complete as possible, was based on our memory . . . with the material help of twenty-five German PoWs. The tower, 6 metres by 6, consisted of: on the ground floor, the guard post; on the first floor, the look-out post with its gallery for the patrol rounds. It was covered by a four-sided sloping roof. Its clock was set at 16.05, the moment of the liberation of the camp on 11 April 1945 . . . Next, the visitor entered the second barrack-hut, the door of which carried the inscription: 'here one enters through the door and leaves through the chimney'. Inside the barrack were reconstructed the bunk beds of the camps – with their true dimensions – the beating machine – a copy of the one in Buchenwald – and the crematorium. On one wall a fresco represented the journey with 100 people in a cattle wagon. In showcases on the other walls, our comrades had displayed personal souvenirs, such as, for example, the watch that belonged to the first SS guard to be killed when the camp was liberated, one bread-ration (genuine), a knife and a spoon manufactured in the camp, the pennant of the SS car, etc. . . . In a special showcase the instruments of the Gestapo were displayed: helmet, bull's pizzle truncheon, iron truncheon, manacles etc. . . ., etc. . . .[16]

The Buchenwald tower was also shown at the fairs of Bordeaux, Nancy, Bourges and Vierzon, in August, September and October 1946, and in the first two towns a reconstruction of the hanging of a prisoner was added, with stuffed dummies in original uniforms.[17] In Mulhouse three camp barracks were reconstructed, drawing 50,000 visitors, and the 'great exhibition-fair on the horrors of Nazi barbarism' in Tarbes, in the Pyrénées, drew a crowd of 100,000.[18] These were monumental examples for the federation of labour conscripts (the FNDT) to emulate. The demand for 'the pedagogy of horror' in the organisers, and the element of horror tourism and voyeurism amongst the spectators was not always clear-cut.[19] Nor did patriotic organisations have a monopoly in the representation of the horror of the concentration camps at local fairs. Already in August 1945 a commercial chamber of horrors entitled 'Buchenwald' was organised at the traditional summer fair in Brussels near the south station, exploiting popular voyeurism. Gaston Hoyaux,

[16] *Le Patriote Résistant* 5 (15 Apr. 1946).
[17] *Le Patriote Résistant* 13 (1 Sep. 1946); 15 (1 Oct. 1946); 16 (15 Oct. 1946). The stand in Bourges drew 90,000 visitors in one week, the one in Bordeaux 50,000 and the one in Vierzon 40,000.
[18] *Bilan d'un an d'activité. Deuxième congrès national de la FNDIRP* (Paris, 12–14 Dec. 1946), Serdoc FNDIRP, *dossier Congrès*. See further *3e Congrès National* (Jan. 1948), ibid., and *Le Patriote Résistant* 14 (14 Sep. 1946); 31 (30 May 1947); 41 (31 Oct. 1947); 71 (28 Feb. 1949).
[19] The expression is Marie-Anne Matard-Bonucci's in Matard-Bonucci and Lynch, *La Libération des camps*, p. 61.

socialist parliamentarian, survivor of Buchenwald and himself the author of *32 Months Under the SS Truncheon*, which appeared in November 1945, protested against this exploitation of the concentration camps as fun-fair attractions: 'If this goes on, yesterday's zebras [referring to the striped uniform of KZ inmates] will soon be regarded in the same way as toad-men or bearded women.'[20]

The interpretation of the legacy of Nazi persecution was already implicit in the presentation of the atrocities. Buchenwald dominated all these initiatives as the symbolic camp. The description of the fair in Clermont-Ferrand is illuminating in this respect: the exhibition focused on the red triangles from France and celebrated the heroic myth of the liberation of Buchenwald by the international prisoners' committee, guided by the communists. The exhibition of the atrocities – with its explicit details and instruments – was not intended to provoke only horror or compassion: the inmates were not presented as innocent victims but as martyrs who suffered for a noble cause, and as heroes who fought back. The watch on display, belonging to the first SS guard killed by the inmates, is a highly symbolic trophy: the victims of Nazi persecution did not insist that they had been mere innocent passive victims; on the contrary: they struck back, as soon as they had a chance. The return of the survivors, chronologically coinciding with the final triumph over Nazi Germany, was more an outburst of patriotic pride and combativeness than an outburst of collective commiseration and pity. On 13 June 1945, the Gendarmerie Nationale described the mindset of the French population in its general report for the period from 15 March to 15 May as follows:

The announcement of the victory, the massive return of the prisoners and deportees and the elections have been the three most striking facts of the period in question. The prisoners had known a prosperous and a fortunate France; they discover a poor country where everyone is assailed by the sorrows of the next day. The disenchantment is profound. As for the deportees, 'the best of the Nation', their clandestine struggle has enabled them to measure the depth of the gulf into which France has sunk; as a whole, the dreadful experience they suffered has not blunted their abnegation and courage.[21]

All 'deportees' are the best of the Nation, all of them have been engaged in the underground struggle, all excel in abnegation and courage. The Gendarmerie Nationale reduced the national martyrdom to a very restricted group of deported resisters, omitting the hundreds of thousands of 'deportees' of wartime terminology (all the potential recruits

---

[20] *Annales Parlementaires de la Chambre* (7 Aug. 1945), p. 641.
[21] *Direction de la Gendarmerie. Synthèse pour la période du 15 avril au 15 mai 1945* (Paris, 13 June 1945), AN 72 AJ 384.

for the millions of soldiers of the fifth front) and omitting, or assimilating, the tens of thousands of 'deportees' who returned from concentration camps, to which they had been deported for a variety of reasons other than clandestine struggle. I will now analyse how this interpretation was translated into the social realities of organisations, laws establishing reparation and relief and how, through them, the legacy of Nazi persecution was integrated into national memories, for Belgium, France and the Netherlands respectively.

In Belgium, political recognition for the victims of Nazi persecution was the political jewel in the crown of commemoration for the anti-royalist coalition that governed the country from August 1945 until March 1947. The first minister for war victims, Baron Adrien Van den Branden de Reeth, was part of the coalition's effort to extend its basis to a Catholic electorate, counting on the appeal of the legacy of the resistance. De Reeth was a rather atypical figure: left-wing, anti-fascist, Catholic, a nobleman and a magistrate. During the occupation he had led a resistance group within the Belgian judiciary and contributed to the fake newspaper *Le Soir* of 9 November 1943, a hilarious exploit attracting international attention.[22] De Reeth was a member of the Independence Front, of which he became national secretary at the liberation, and of the Patriotic Militia.[23] Even though he never formally belonged to the party, he was identified as a supporter of the resistance party UDB.[24]

De Reeth's central accomplishment was the reconciliation and unification of the organisations for Nazi victims, who had previously been divided between different national and regional organisations, some of them stemming from the First World War, and the *amicales*, uniting survivors of particular camps.[25] Central to these negotiations was the adoption of a common definition of who could be considered a 'political prisoner'. In October 1945 the participants agreed on a text adopting 'the criterion of suffering', that is, the principle that the law had to take into account the shared affliction of imprisonment (a minimum of one month), torture or execution for all except the common law offenders and those accused of an unpatriotic attitude. This very inclusive project was immediately criticised in traditionalist patriotic quarters. The

---

22 *Front* (17 Oct. 1946).
23 Personal file, Adrien Van den Branden de Reeth, PM IV/00041-16-7746, archive of the Independence Front, Anderlecht (Brussels); *Justice Libre. Affilié au FI* (Apr. and June–July 1945).
24 Paul M. G. Lévy to Jean-Claude Ricquier, *Revue Générale* (Nov. 1987), pp. 21–31.
25 *Bulletin Officiel de la CNPPA* 1 (May 1946); Brunfaut in *Parlementaire Handelingen Kamer* (25 Oct 1945), p. 1182; *Front* (25 Nov. 1945).

vocabulary of 'political prisoner' dated from the First World War. Already after 1918 the victims of German repression of 'franc-tireurs' had been recognised and decorated with the same honour as those members of the regular army who had fallen in the trenches. Great figures of Belgian patriotism, such as Camille Joset, had even been condemned to death twice by the German occupiers on behalf of his resistance activities, in both 1914–18 and 1940–4. This reference to a traditional patriotic notion stirred protest:

> When after the war of 1914–1918 it was said of a person that 'he's a political prisoner', the public knew that this person had committed an act of patriotism. There was no other meaning. Today things are no longer the same. Now, when one says 'political prisoner', public opinion – and our adversaries should have the courage to admit this – immediately asks the question: 'communist? Jew? hostage? or resister?' It's not we who seek the distinction, it is public opinion. Of course, there is no shame in belonging to one category rather than another. Yet it is reasonable for a prisoner to be indignant if he is suspected of having acted during the German occupation out of purely political motivation, when his acts were always inspired by the purest patriotism. You don't have to be anti-Semitic to be troubled if someone wrongly suspects you of having been arrested as a Jew . . . There is no more pettiness in claiming the distinction between a hostage and a political prisoner arrested for patriotic acts than in the distinction between the draft-evader and the labour conscript.[26]

In the first debates in parliament – the project was not even formally submitted to the assembly – the communist deputy Brunfaut pointed out what would be at the very centre of the debate in the following year: 'Do not give the impression that you are animated by ulterior motives: exclude the Jews and the communists arrested on 22 June 1941 from the title of political prisoner.'[27]

The first post-war elections of 17 February 1946 signalled the end of the Catholic-progressive experiment, UDB. The party won only one seat. The Liberal Party was halved. The protagonists in the debate over the royal question were the indubitable victors: the Catholic Party was only one seat short of a majority in the Senate. The communists did not achieve the breakthrough they had hoped for, but the anti-royalist coalition, headed by the Socialist Party, continued its homogeneously anti-clerical composition. With the UDB, De Reeth disappeared from the government. He was succeeded by the communist minister Jean

---

[26] *L'Effort* (Apr. 1946), p. 27. See also *Bulletin Officiel de la CNPPA* (June–July 1946 and Nov. 1946); *L'Effort. Bulletin Officiel de l'UNPP [Union Nationale des Prisonniers Politiques] 1940–1945* (5 Nov. 1945); *Front* (4 Nov. 1945). See, further, Borremans in *Parlementaire Handelingen Kamer* (25 Oct. 1945), p. 1185, and the archives of Albert Régibeau, delegate from Liège and one of the main proponents of the patriotic clause in archives of the CNPPA.

[27] *Parlementaire Handelingen Kamer* (25 Oct. 1945), p. 1183.

Terfve.[28] Terfve had been arrested on 22 June 1941 and imprisoned in the citadel of Huy, from where he escaped by climbing out of a window on 25 August. Terfve initiated the underground struggle of the party in the Borinage, and soon became one of the leaders of the Independence Front and the partisans. His wife was repatriated from Ravensbrück in May 1945. Terfve naturally became involved with care for the victims of Nazi persecution.

On 6 April 1946, barely a week after his installation as minister, Terfve reaped the benefit of the work of his predecessor with the creation of a single national association for all survivors of the German camps and prisons, the Confédération Nationale des Prisonniers Politiques et Ayants-Droits/Nationale Confederatie van Politieke Gevangenen en hun Rechthebbenden (CNPPA/NCPGR). Consequently Terfve vehemently defended the 'criterion of suffering'.[29] The reason for arrest was irrelevant to the law – there was a sufficiency of other laws recognising all kinds of patriotic activism during the occupation. What really mattered was the dignity and courage with which the victims of the Nazi persecution had endured their ordeal. It was this suffering, this sacrifice at the hands of the enemy, that elevated all victims to the rank of heroes of the Nation. This definition stressed the particular character of Nazi persecution during the Second World War: it incorporated very many victims who had not taken part in the military conflict. It refused to make a 'patriotic' distinction, with reference to World War I, which many, including in some of the formally dissolved associations that were now merged in the CNPPA, continued to claim.

Despite opposition from some patriotic groups, the act was approved unanimously (minus two abstentions) in the House of Representatives on 31 October 1946. The Catholic deputies Raymond Scheyven and Louis Kiebooms, who introduced an amendment to restrict recognition to authenticated resistance fighters, were persuaded to withdraw their amendment by their party members of the 'political prisoners' parliamentary group.[30] Thirty-seven members of the pre-war House of Representatives had been political prisoners: twelve socialists, eleven Catholics, ten communists and four liberals.[31] After the elections of February 1946, in both houses taken together, forty-eight

[28] See Gotovitch, *Du Rouge au tricolore*, pp. 562–3, and *passim*. See also *Front* (7 Apr. 1946 and 10 Mar. 1946).
[29] *Bulletin Officiel de la CNPPA* (Nov. 1946) and *Front* (3 Nov. 1946).
[30] *Dokumenten Kamer*, no. 187.
[31] Bruno De Wever and Petra Gunst, 'Van Kamerleden en burgemeesters', in Luc Huyse and Kris Hoflack (eds.), *De Democratie heruitgevonden. Oud en nieuw in politiek België* (Leuven, 1995), p. 74.

parliamentarians were former victims of Nazi persecution.[32] This group operated collectively for the defence of their comrade prisoners, disregarding political divisions. The only discord in the debate was the crusade by the conservative Catholic deputy Carton de Wiart against the recognition of 'concubines' as legal widows of deceased prisoners, an insistence on public morals and legal marital unions that demonstrated the mental alienation of conservative Catholicism from the life of the persecuted and the clandestine.[33] Quite unexpectedly, after unanimous support in the House, the proposal was blocked in the Senate, where the Catholic opposition was only one seat short of the absolute majority.[34] The Catholic opposition criticised the role reserved for the unitary confederation in the application of the law. The national confederation was depicted as a communist front organisation and the Catholic opposition feared that Catholics would be submerged in a unitary organisation.[35] The same apprehension also prompted the reappearance in January 1947 of a 'patriotic' amendment in a modified version.[36] The statute had considerable financial implications – the survivors would be entitled to free medical care, lifelong indemnities, grants for their children's education, etc. – but this time the amendment was not concerned with the costs. Indeed, in the Belgian context no one could afford to exclude victims arrested for reasons other than resistance from the aid program. The subtlety of the Catholic proposal was that every one would have equal rights to aid, but that only resisters would be entitled to national recognition and to the honorary clause of the statute: the title and the medal of 'political prisoner'.

The Catholic attitude had another rationale. If – as public attention and respect indicated – the survivors of the camps, now called political prisoners, deserved national appreciation for their sacrifice and patriotism, then they represented key symbolic and political capital. As a consequence, it was important that each party secured a proportionate share of it. In the total category of survivors the Catholics were a small minority. Those who suffered preventative arrest and those taken as hostages were chosen for their pre-war anti-fascism and were almost without exception Freemasons and atheists. The racial deportees, mostly Jews, were not Catholic either. In short, only amongst the arrested resisters were a fair number of Catholics to be found. Thanks to

---

[32] Somerhausen in *Parlementaire Handelingen Kamer* (13 Oct. 1946), p. 16.
[33] *Parlementaire Handelingen Kamer* (31 Oct. 1946).
[34] Ibid.; *Dokumenten Kamer* 187 (1946); *Parlementaire Handelingen Senaat* (14 Jan. 1947).
[35] *Parlementaire Handelingen Senaat* (14 Jan. 1947).
[36] Ibid.

its virtual majority in the Senate and strict party discipline, the amendment was accepted.

The unyielding attitude of the Catholic opposition forced the minister to seek a new compromise. The final text stipulated that the honorary distinction was to be attributed to: (1) arrested resisters; (2) all those arrested for their political or philosophical convictions; (3) all those who could prove to have shown a truly heroic and patriotic attitude during their imprisonment.[37] Cleverly formulated, this compromise meant that only the Jewish survivors of the camps were not entitled to this national appreciation (apart from the heterogeneous group of genuinely arbitrary victims). The Jews were deported for something they could neither deserve nor choose: their race. Today this is precisely what is seen as the ultimate transgression of Nazism, but this message was politically impotent in the immediate post-war years. The Jews were used as pawns in a political trade-off. Moreover, the statute dealt only with national merit. The Jews who were denied this merit but who still received aid were a small minority. Only about 5 per cent of the Jews deported from Belgium during the occupation had Belgian nationality. For foreign political prisoners, there was a second law, under which only deported foreigners who fought in the resistance could receive aid and naturalisation.[38]

Even though the governing majority incidentally denounced the 'anti-Semitism' of the Catholic manoeuvre, the Catholic boycott drew little criticism and the compromise was welcomed with ecumenical satisfaction. Debates in the national confederation itself on the new proposal had been disconcertingly explicit. Catholic members protested against what they perceived as the inclusion in the initial project of 'Jews arrested simply for a racial motive or other people imprisoned for reasons other than patriotism, for example black marketeers', setting Jews and black marketeers in the same suspect category.[39] Others tried to mediate with assurances that 'the Jewish problem will find its solution in the selection commissions' without stirring any reaction to this decidedly macabre vocabulary.[40] More decisive than the anti-Semitism had been the anti-communism of the Christian Popular Party: the 'criterion of the suffering' was, in their eyes, no more than a trick to smuggle into the statute's coverage those communists who were arrested on the night of the German invasion of the Soviet Union, after a year of

---

[37] *Parlementaire Handelingen Senaat* (30 Jan. and 6 Feb. 1947); *Parlementaire Handelingen Kamer* (13 Feb. 1947); *Belgisch Staatsblad* (16 Mar. 1947), pp. 2703–8; *Officieel Bulletijn van de NCPGR* 2 (Feb. 1947).

[38] *Belgisch Staatsblad* (15 Feb. 1947), p. 1507.

[39] *Compte Rendu de la réunion du Conseil National Elargi tenue à la CNPPA* (2 Feb. 1947), archives of CNPPA.

[40] Ibid. (29 Jan. 1947).

anti-Allied propaganda under the slogan *ni Londres ni Berlin*. Forced to concede over the inclusion of the governing communists, the Christian Popular Party settled for the peace offering which the marginalisation of the Jewish survivors constituted.

The trauma of the concentration camps made a deep impact on the post-war years in Belgium, and the special moral heritage of the survivors was universally respected. The quarrels concerning the statute ended in the 'national' compromise to exclude the Jews from the honorary distinction. In a way, the introduction of the patriotic distinction heightened the national prestige of the 'political prisoners' and introduced an awkward discourse of veterans' patriotism ill suited to this supreme group of civil war victims. In the midst of the Cold War debates, when the confederation was permanently threatened by schisms, its president routinely appealed to 'the will to keep one and indivisible the army of the political prisoners'.[41] The communist vice president thanked the president as the 'fervent defender of the spirit of the political prisoner, which is the cause to which we devoted our life'.[42] The 'spirit of the political prisoner' became the perfect prolepsis by which the patriotic unity was legitimised. No matter the political opinion or the reason for arrest for which each prisoner had been imprisoned: retrospectively unified by the terrible experience of the concentration camp, all shared the same 'spirit', as if it were the conviction resulting from the camp experience that had predestined them for deportation. This complex discourse mingled martyrdom with heroism and, in so doing, transformed the group of political prisoners from victims *par excellence* to the heralds of persecution and resistance and, in the final analysis, of Belgian patriotism *tout court*.

The unity of the survivors, bridging the fragmentation of the 'pillarisation' and the regional divide, was a unique accomplishment in post-war Belgium. The common experience of the camps and the solidarity that developed there enabled the survivors to surmount the deep divisions in Belgian post-war society. The confederation was the instigator of the Committee of Action and Vigilance and its successor, the Committee of Appeal to the Country, militant pressure groups claiming a rigorous purge. Its activities obtained the resignation of two ministers of justice: Paul Struye in November 1948 and Joseph Pholien in September 1952. Its most spectacular intervention as guarantor of the national unity came in 'the royal question'. When the return of Leopold III after his

---

[41] Léopold Ros in *Compte-Rendu de la Réunion extra-ordinaire du Conseil National de la CNPPA* (24 Apr. 1948), archives of CNPPA.

[42] Luc Sommerhausen in *Compte-Rendu de la séance plénière du Conseil National Elargi* (19 Dec. 1948), ibid.

regionally uneven victory in the referendum threatened to set off a civil war, the confederation lent its moral prestige to a peaceful compromise between the parties, leading to the abdication of Leopold and his succession by his eldest son.[43] Even if the cumulative effect of the Cold War disputes and the frustration of the pro-Leopold faction in the confederation led to a temporary schism between 1952 and 1957, the confederation retained an unequalled prestige and authority. It still continues its activities today, particularly in the defence of the unity of Belgium against federalist and separatist claims and against the rise of the extreme right.[44]

For a sound understanding of the French situation, we have to return one last time to Frénay's organisation of repatriation and reintegration. This action was based on two associational axes: the National Movement of PoWs and Deportees, the organisational offspring of the activities of the Pinot–Mitterrand group agitating against Vichy – or at least separate from it – on the one hand, and the Centres of Mutual Aid, the associational support of the Prisoners' Houses set up by Vichy, on the other. Frénay planned to reintegrate and purge the latter structure with the help of the former. Apart from the political change, Frénay transformed these two networks primarily interested in the PoWs to incorporate all the repatriates under his responsibility. In reality this involved the development of two additional branches: one for the labour conscripts, and one for the 'political deportees', that is, the victims of persecution who had been deported to German prisons and concentration camps. The centres of mutual aid, the associational branches of the ministerial action (as described above for the labour conscripts), were organised in three federations. The Federations of Centres for Mutual Aid and the respective branches of the National Movement of Prisoners and Deportees merged in the last quarter of 1945, and survived the liquidation of the repatriation ministry in November 1945 as independent organisations, even though they had originally been the result of governmental policy.

The policy for the labour conscripts and 'political deportees' derived from the existing situation for PoWs, a very large group whose absence dated from the beginning of the war, and who had been at the heart of many Vichy initiatives. The build-up of a parallel infrastructure for

---

[43] See Jules Gérard-Libois and José Gotovitch, *Léopold III. De l'an '40 à l'effacement* (Brussels, 1991), pp. 287–302.
[44] See also Pieter Lagrou, 'Welk vaderland voor de vaderlandslievende verenigingen? Oorlogsslachtoffers en verzetsveteranen en de nationale kwestie, 1945–1958', *Bijdragen tot de Eigentijdse Geschiedenis* 3 (Dec. 1997), pp. 91–109.

labour conscripts was a more difficult challenge: it never acquired the importance and all-encompassing nature of the infrastructure Vichy had developed for the PoWs in Germany from the end of 1942 onwards. In addition, the conscripts were a less conventional group, and initiatives to organise them originated in the existing movements for PoWs. The ministry encouraged the creation of associations and tried to motivate trade unions to support the organisation of returning workers. The situation for the victims of persecution was of course wholly different. Vichy had actively contributed to the deportation of individuals to Germany, seeing them as terrorists, Bolsheviks, Jews and other undesirable foreigners, or at least publicly assimilating them with these categories. Resistance organisations, which had lost many members through Nazi repression, had organised their own clandestine relief structure for the victims and their families, the COSOR (Comité des Oeuvres Sociales de la Résistance), assembled within the Conseil Nationale de la Résistance. Other organisations that were particularly interested in helping the victims of Nazi persecutions, because they counted many victims in their ranks, were the Communist Party and organisations of the French Jewish community. The establishment of committees of mutual aid for the victims of Nazi persecution, the *déportés politiques* in Frénay's terminology, in all major Prisoners' Houses after the liberation, demanded an extra effort from Frénay's ministry, since there was no pre-established associational network. As with the labour conscripts, Frénay promoted the creation of a national federation with local representatives. He also instructed the *préfets* of every department to nominate *animateurs* of departmental COSORs, in an effort to formalise and generalise the assistance to victims of the resistance.

The Federation of Centres of Mutual Aid for Political Internees and Deportees was housed in a building formerly occupied by the services of the Gestapo, 10, rue Leroux, in the XVIth arrondissement in Paris. Like its counterparts for PoWs and labour conscripts, it had a mixed status: associational arm of the ministry, dispenser of governmental aid, on the one hand, and organisation to unite repatriates on the other. Its first and immediate objective was social. It was, as the name 'mutual aid centre' indicated, an associational relief organisation, and, as such, was concerned with all victims of persecution who needed help. 'Rue Leroux' became a habitual point of reference amongst former victims of persecution, if not through the federation, at least through the activities of the *amicales des camps*, which had their headquarters in the same building and co-operated closely with the parent federation. Each *amicale* united survivors of one specific camp – Buchenwald, Mauthausen, Dachau, Ravensbrück and Auschwitz were amongst the most important – and the concrete solidarity of the shared experience in the same place proved a strong link. Even when conflicts over patriotism and the Cold War divided the national organisations of survivors, the *amicales* continued their role as a meeting point.[45] As described in chapter 6, Frénay, who had himself planned a central role for this type of federation, later came to regard them as Trojan horses, reproaching François Mitterrand amongst others with having admitted the communists to his 'National Movement' during the war, which later enabled them to take control of these associations and lead the campaign against him in person. The communists were indeed well represented amongst the 'political deportees', and well organised; they contributed an astounding dynamism to the federation. The federation, very critical of Frénay, was militant in matters regarding the purge and the political fate of Germany, and many of its leading executives were party members.

The Federation of Centres of Mutual Aid and the COSOR, both supported by the ministry, separately developed similar activities, but whereas the former included all victims, the latter was exclusively for resistance victims. Moreover, compared to the important role played by communists in the former, the latter was often more Gaullist in its political allegiance. This was particularly true in those departments where the COSOR was created after the liberation by nomination through the *préfets*, De Gaulle's local emissaries, who often saw it as their central task to contain the influence of communism. The federation accused the COSOR of favouritism and of discrimination against deportees who did not belong to resistance organisations.[46] It even questioned the legitimacy of the departmental COSORs, referring to 'anti-democratic nominations' by the *préfets* on Frénay's order.[47] For their part, the Gaullist resistance circles of the COSOR soon accused the federation of abusing its dominant position in the relief and soon set up their own rival organisation, exclusive to former resistance fighters: the Fédération Nationale des Déportés et Internés de la Résistance

---

[45] See, for example, Claude Lévy, 'Une Association de déportés en son temps. L'Amicale des déportés d'Auschwitz et des camps de Haute Silésie', in Alfred Wahl (ed.), *Mémoire de la Seconde Guerre Mondiale. Actes du Colloque de Metz, 6–8 Octobre 1983* (Metz, 1984), pp. 149–60; and, on Mauthausen, R. P. Riquet in *Le Déporté (UNADIF)* (Nov. 1985).

[46] *Le Patriote Résistant* 7 (15 June 1946); *Les Rapports entre la Fédération et le COSOR, Deuxième Congrès National* (Paris, 12–14 Dec. 1946), SerDoc FNDIRP, *dossier Congrès*. Protests against the neglect by the COSOR of orphans of deported parents not belonging to the resistance were voiced even in the congress of the FNDIR itself. See *FNDIR, Congrès National* (Paris 15–16 Dec. 1945), *dossier organisations françaises*, SerDoc FNDIRP.

[47] *Le Patriote Résistant* 7 (15 June 1946).

(FNDIR).[48] In October 1945, as the liquidation of Frénay's ministry approached, the Federation of Centres of Mutual Aid transformed itself into the Fédération Nationale des Déportés et Internés Patriotes (FNDIP). In spite of its delegates' initial agreement to take part in a new unitary movement for all deportees and internees, the FNDIR finally refused to participate.[49] To show clearly that the FNDIR did not have a monopoly in the resistance, and avoid the impression that one organisation united only resisters and the other only non-resisters, the FNDIP changed its name in January 1946 to Fédération Nationale des Déportés et Internés Résistants et Patriotes (FNDIRP).[50] The name in itself covered a whole commemorative programme. The FNDIRP was as inclusive as possible, that is, open to all victims of Nazi persecution, in French territory and in German concentration camps, excluding only common law offenders. The inclusion assimilated all victims with national martyrs. All were patriots and as such participated in the 'spirit', if not the battles, of the resistance. The organisation claimed over 30,000 members, survivors of Nazi persecution or their heirs.[51]

The FNDIR, the exclusive organisation of resistance victims, claimed to have been founded in Buchenwald. Its activity, initially limited to the Paris region alone, began in the summer of 1945. In the course of its existence its published membership figures oscillated between 5,000 and 10,000. Its relationship to the Federation of Centres of Mutual Aid and its successor, the FNDIRP, was a mixture of political animosity and patriotic contempt. It denounced its rival systematically as a communist front organisation and produced some of the crudest anti-communist propaganda in its journal and at its meetings. Its vice president, De la Baume, declared publicly in December 1945 that he 'infinitely regretted that in 1939 Daladier had not ordered the execution of 55,000 communists, which would have rid France of all the quarrels it has today'.[52] Its Gaullism was equally immoderate. The title of the journal of the FNDIR, *18 Juin*, was eloquent enough (the title later changed to *Le*

[48] *Congrès départemental de l'association des déportés et internés de la résistance* (Lyons, 24 Nov. 1945) in *dossier organisations françaises*, SerDoc FNDIRP. The FNDIRP was well informed on the internal affairs of its rival through infiltration reports. See, for the functioning of this system, letter, Joineau to Duhourquet (18 June 1953), ibid.

[49] *Le Patriote Résistant* 1 (Jan. 1946), and *2e Congrès National de la FNDIRP* (Paris, 12–14 Dec. 1946), *dossier Congrès*, SerDoc FNDIRP.

[50] *Le Patriote Résistant* 2 (15 Feb. 1946).

[51] Roger Bourderon, 'Principes Fondateurs et mise en oeuvre. L'Activité de la Fédération Nationale des Déportés, Internés, Résistants et Patriotes (FNDIRP)', in Wahl, *Mémoire de la Seconde Guerre Mondiale*, p. 137.

[52] *Congrès départemental de l'association des déportés et internés de la résistance* (Lyons, 24 Nov. 1945), in *dossier organisations françaises*, SerDoc FNDIRP; *Le Patriote Résistant* 2 (15 Feb. 1946).

Déporté, and was again a bold statement in the struggle for the exclusive right to the appellation). The journal adopted a disenchanted attitude towards 'politicians' in general, and the government in particular.

In spite of its very public allegiance to Gaullism, politics was not the driving force behind the FNDIR, but patriotic contempt. The same delegate who wished that Daladier had shot all communists in 1939 explained his hostility to an organisation which included all victims, through his experience in the camps:

In Buchenwald – I mention Buchenwald, because I was there, but it was the same in Ravensbrück, in Dachau – we were there as poor unfortunates, we saw comrades dying around us. But, nonetheless, there were some around us who did not know why they were there. Is this true, or is this not true, gentlemen? Because you are resisters, you have known this. I remember. One day, a comrade, in 1943 – in October 1943 – it was icy weather, we were pushing a wagon of stones. One exhausted guy, who couldn't stand it any more, turned to me and said: 'If there hadn't been cretins like you throwing bombs, I wouldn't be here.' I answered him: 'My poor old chap, if only you had done something, at least you would know why you are here, you wouldn't have regrets.'[53]

On its first national congress in December 1945, one delegate declared:

Deportees and internees of the resistance, you who do not make up the quantity, we know this perfectly well, but – I apologise to the other federation – the quality, you will disappear and you will have the same card, the same insignia as those who left for Germany for possibly lofty motives, as racial deportees, victims of raids, people rounded up during the razzia of the Vieux Port [in Marseilles], but also the same insignia as the black marketeers and those who, in 1939, sabotaged the national defence. We must, once and for all, dot the i's and say it.[54]

In the same vein of exclusive combatant patriotism, the Association Nationale des Anciennes Déportées et Internées de la Résistance (ADIR) united some 2,000 women resistance fighters, victims of Nazi repression. The ADIR shared most of the FNDIR's positions, particularly 'in defence of the title', but it seems that the female solidarity at the basis of the organisation provided a stronger cohesion, across the political divide, than the querulous activism displayed by the FNDIR.[55] The ADIR always maintained a fierce organisational independence.

The conflict between the FNDIR and the FNDIRP was, finally, a conflict over the interpretation of French patriotism in the light of events in the Second World War. In this, the FNDIR was defending the

[53] *Congrès départemental de l'association des déportés et internés de la résistance* (Lyons, 24 Nov. 1945) in *dossier organisations françaises*, SerDoc FNDIRP.

[54] Beltrami, *Congrès National de la FNDIR* (Paris, 15–16 Dec. 1945) in *dossier organisations françaises*, SerDoc FNDIRP.

[55] See Dominique Veillon, 'L'Association des Anciennes Déportées et Internées de la Résistance', in Wahl, *Mémoire de la Seconde Guerre Mondiale*, pp. 161–79.

traditional post-1918 interpretation, the paradigm of the combatant, whilst the FNDIRP defended a new anti-fascist version of patriotism, inclusive of non-combatant victims, of 'all the members of our great family'. One of the battlefields was the French Union of Veterans, the UFAC. To be formally adopted into the family of the veterans of the Great War and the heroes of the last war was, as discussed in chapters 2 and 10, a central aim for the organisations of resistance fighters and labour conscripts. It could only be the more so for a federation that had adopted resistance and patriotism in its name. In March 1946, the FNDIR succeeded in being admitted to the UFAC and manoeuvred to have the application of the FNDIRP turned down. *Le Patriote Résistant*, the journal of the FNDIRP, reacted: 'The accusations against us are always the same: our organisation accepts common law offenders and non-combatant Jews.'[56] Whilst violently rejecting the allegation that the FNDIRP admitted the former, the journal defended its inclusion of the latter group: 'Those who today still practice racism and use the arms of Hitler and Goebbels can only be considered as wholly contemptible individuals.'[57] By June 1947, the FNDIRP was unanimously admitted to the UFAC, and afterwards no one questioned its admission.[58] The FNDIRP had contributed to a transformation of French patriotism from a traditional veterans' patriotism to a more inclusive patriotism of which civilian victims were an integral part.

The president of the FNDIRP, Frédéric Manhès, colonel and *compagnon de la libération*, defended the inclusive position of his organisation in an open letter to the members of the FNDIR by insisting that, in the end, all victims of persecution had paid for the resistance: the hostages first of all, victims of direct retaliation for resistance attacks in their region; next came the *raflés*, victims of arbitrary raids, who, precisely because they were arbitrary, could very well have included authentic resisters whose identity was unknown to the persecutor, or people who in their hearts supported the resistance, or people arrested in 1942 who would undoubtedly have become resisters by 1944. Manhès went on:

Why not the 'racials'? Yes, why not them? Of course, they are Jews, but will we in 1946 start the wars of religion all over again? . . . rather than taking note of the fact that the Jews were humans who were hounded more fiercely by the Nazis, humans tracked down like poor animals – as much by the *boches* as by the *vichyssois* – humans who paid the price the experiment of 'Hitlerian civilisation' with millions of dead. According to you, should we forget the brothers of so many of our companions of the Resistance, those millions of human beings who were our comrades in adversity in the German camps and who suffered more

[56] *Le Patriote Résistant* 25–6 (22 Mar. 1946).
[57] Ibid.
[58] *Le Patriote Résistant* 33 (30 June 1947).

than us? . . . Should we reject them too, deeming them unworthy of a place in the organisations of French deportees? When you list the victims of Nazism, to present the bill to the torturers, will you deduct the Jewish victims? . . . In that case, no, because they too, they have paid for the Resistance.[59]

The conflict between an exclusive patriotic memory or an inclusive memory taking into account the diversity of Nazi persecution was most explicit, even if the discourse of the inclusive memory assimilated various types of victim with victims of the Resistance. The conflict would only become more outspoken as it moved from the organisational level to the level of the legal definition of the 'deportees'.

It is somewhat strange that Laurent Casanova and his *chef de cabinet* Maurice Lampe did not submit a unified law for all deportees, as proposed by Jean Terfve in Belgium. The communist faction in the National Assembly submitted a proposal for 'the internees and deportees of the Resistance' in May 1947, that is, the very month in which their party resigned from the government.[60] The FNDIR was also well represented in parliament and in the competent commission, through its own executives Lambert, Devemy and Michelet, and it contemporaneously submitted its own proposal, insisting on the 'hierarchy of urgencies' and the crucial distinction between certified resisters, victims of deportation, and all others:

Without underestimating, not in even the smallest degree, the merit of the unfortunate victims who have suffered for whatever reason, from the terrible scourge that hit our cruelly afflicted country, everyone will nonetheless measure the full difference between fatality in adversity and risks taken deliberately. It was precisely with deliberate purpose and with a spontaneous feeling of abnegation that the volunteers of the resistance accepted, in advance, all the consequences of their acts.[61]

Except for the distinctive criteria of the reason for arrest, both proposals offered a similar definition, as outlined in chapter 11: first, all people deported to German camps, without a minimum period of detention; secondly, people interned elsewhere for a minimum of ninety days, or tortured; thirdly, victims of execution by the enemy. Yet in the debates comparing the two proposals, much of the discussion focused on a rather small but symbolically important group: communists arrested in 1939, who once the war broke out had been held in prison beyond the end of the sentence imposed on them under the Third Republic, and were eventually deported. Recognising them would imply a symbolic assimilation of the persecution of communists by the

---

[59] *Le Patriote Résistant* (1 Jan. 1946).
[60] *Documents AsN*, annexe 1411 (22 May 1947).
[61] *Documents AsN*, annexe 1263 (8 May 1947); annexe 1518 (30 May 1947); annexe 3271 (5 Feb. 1948).

Daladier government with persecution under Vichy. Moreover, argued the anti-communists, these individuals had been arrested as potential saboteurs of the French war effort. For the Communist Party their inclusion was worth many battles. The description by Annette Wieviorka of the debate in parliament – ignoring the more fundamental discussions in the commission and in the associational press – focuses uniquely on this aspect and creates the erroneous impression that the exclusion of other categories was not part of the debate.[62] The vice president of the FNDIRP, the Jesuit priest Michel Riquet, preacher in the cathedral of Notre-Dame in Paris and survivor of Mauthausen, was at the forefront of the campaign against the FNDIR project.[63] Exactly as with the CNPPA in Belgium, Riquet argued that many other laws recognised the resistance, but that a law for deportees recognised the suffering and the dignity with which it had been endured. The suffering, independent of the reason of arrest, had been the same for all (even though Manhès had earlier underlined that, for example, the Jews had suffered more than the resisters) and the dignity, contrary to what De la Baume had claimed, had certainly not been the prerogative of all resisters, nor of resisters alone. The FNDIR proposal committed a 'grave injustice' and Riquet, when heard by the parliamentary commission, even directly threatened Lambert that if the assembly voted for his project 'the deportees would remember the treason of which they have been victim', before walking out of the meeting.[64]

The fact that the inclusion of victims of arbitrary arrests and racial persecution was linked to the inclusion of the small group of communists arrested under Daladier did nothing to improve the FNDIRP proposal's chances of success. The FNDIR proposal for the 'internees and deportees of the resistance' was adopted by the assembly and published on 6 August 1948, but protests against the injustice of it obtained the promise that a law for 'political internees and deportees' would soon follow, as indeed it did on 9 September.[65] The difference lay in the word 'Resistance' – that is, the two laws were almost identical, except that the reason for arrest in the first law was narrowly defined as 'a recognised act of resistance' and that this earned the beneficiaries some benefits of a military nature. The traditional patriots had not only obtained exclusive recognition of the honour, but, through this, as a

[62] Annette Wieviorka, *Déportation*, pp. 141–57.
[63] See *dossier Riquet* in SerDoc FNDIRP, and Riquet's letter to all deputees (18 Feb. 1948) in *dossier statuts*, ibid.
[64] Commission Pensions (3 Mar. 1948).
[65] Respectively, 'Loi no. 48-1251' (6 Aug. 1948), *Journal Officiel* (8 Aug. 1948), and 'Loi no. 48-1404' (9 Sep. 1948), *Journal Officiel* (10 Sep. 1948). See also *Le Patriote Résistant* 59 (17 Aug. 1948) and 61 (18 Sep. 1948).

matter of fact, also of their putative 'hierarchy of urgencies'. The recognition of the 'deportees of the Resistance' was treated with absolute priority over the other deportees, who had to wait another two years before the practical procedure was decided. The separate recognition commissions also allowed the FNDIR to fight its own little war against the rival federation. Debeaumarchais, the machiavellian secretary-general of the FNDIR, boasted at its national congresses that he had personally obtained the rejection of 75 per cent of applications by members of the National Front, the resistance umbrella close to the Communist Party, and turned down the applications by arrested participants in the 'housewife-demonstrations', organised by communist women's organisations to protest against distribution deficiencies under Vichy.[66] Communist parliamentarians protested against the *préfets* meddling in the composition of the commission attributing *déporté résistant* cards, evicting communist members. In the department of the Pas-de-Calais, a communist stronghold in the mining region, the departmental commission was composed of members from the neighbouring department of the Nord. The preliminary screening of candidates by the local police systematically asked about political leanings, and communists were discarded on the assumption that their arrest was occasioned by their party membership, rather than by resistance activities.[67]

The conflict over patriotism had brought the partisans of inclusive and exclusive definitions into violent opposition, but the memory of the 'treason' and the 'grave injustice' of which, in the words of Riquet, non-resistance deportees and internees had been the victims, was overtaken by a new conflict only one year later. The Cold War, as will be described in greater detail in the next chapter, broke out in the FNDIRP and divisions over contemporary issues of international politics proved stronger than the unity over definitions of patriotism. Riquet, as leader of the non-communist faction in the FNDIRP, opposed the organisation's participation at a pro-Soviet peace congress in 1949. According to his own version of the facts, his strong friendship with Lampe and Manhès – dating back to their time in Mauthausen – helped him to persuade them to abstain from such a participation, a 'weakness' on their part to which their party responded with their dismissal.[68] The new secretary-general, Charles Joineau, proved a hard-liner and a dauntless party man with whom it was impossible to co-operate. Riquet

[66] Report, FNDIR congrès (1950), in *dossier organisations françaises*, SerDoc FNDIRP, and *Le Patriote Résistant* (15 Jan. 1953).
[67] Rose Guérin in Commission Pensions (21 Feb. 1951).
[68] *Le Déporté (UNADIF)* (Nov. 1985); letter, Riquet to Monseigneur Moussaron (10 Jan. 1950) in *dossier Riquet*, and *Mise au Point* by Debeaumarchais and Riquet (1950), in *dossier organisations françaises*, both in SerDoc FNDIRP.

now waited for an opportunity to break with the communists, an occasion soon conveniently offered by the *affaire Rousset* (see chapter 14). Riquet, who only one year earlier had sworn that he would never join the FNDIR, now operated a dubious merger of the non-communist departmental associations of the FNDIRP, who quit the organisation with him, under the flag of Union Nationale des Associations des Déportés et Internés et Familles de Disparus (UNADIF), together with the super-patriots of the FNDIR. The two organisations held joint congresses, and had a joint budget and a joint journal. Riquet tried to keep up at least the appearance of independence from the FNDIR, all the more so since much of the same political animosity and patriotic contempt still applied to the former FNDIRP turncoats, in the eyes of the FNDIR hard core.[69]

The importance of the intricacies of organisational history and political strategy in what follows should neither be over- nor underestimated. The patriotic divide was replaced, a year later, by the Cold War divide. The practical consequence of this reshuffle of the organisational cards was a truce in the battle between *déportés de la résistance* and *déportés politiques*, since both were now fraternally united in the anti-communist camp too. As a result, patriotic resentment and agitation moved on to a new battlefield and chose a new target: instead of the *déportés politiques*, the previously disregarded non-combatant victims of persecution, all animosity was now directed at the *déportés du travail*, that is, the labour conscripts. The symbolic target of the battle also changed: from safeguarding the exclusive attribution of the title of The Resistance, the goal was now to safeguard, or rather to acquire, the exclusive title of Deportation. There was an additional political motive behind this new commemorative battle: the Communist Party championed both the labour conscripts and the victims of persecution, and played a dominant role in the major organisations of both the FNDT and the FNDIRP. If, through partisan activism, the two groups became opposed to each other, the party would be in a most awkward position, and, forced to make a choice, would lose the allegiance of either or both of them. So much for the *petite histoire*. The thrust of the argument developed in this book places this commemorative battle in quite another perspective, namely the growing appeal of Deportation as a mythical concept depicting the collective experience of French society during the Second World War. Deportation and Resistance had consistently been conceptually related, from propaganda on the fifth front, from the *mise en scène* of the repatriation to the unfortunate heroism of

---

[69] *Compte rendu de la première journée du congrès de la FNDIR* (Compiègne, 1950), in *dossier organisations françaises*, SerDoc FNDIRP.

the organisation of labour conscripts and the rather murky debates over aid and recognition for victims of Nazi persecution. The general line that can be distinguished in the dialectical relationship between 'Deportation' and 'Resistance' is the rampant ascendancy of the former concept, increasingly the object of sacralisation, over the latter, subject to devaluation and delegitimisation. In addition, there was a change of focus in the symbolism of 'Deportation', from the all-embracing notion of the war years to the extraordinary atrocities of which the KZ inmates had been victims. This shift had been acknowledged by the labour conscripts themselves in their self-representation, which conformed to the paradigm of the KZ symbolism with cattle wagons, camp barracks and barbed wire. In this case, *petite histoire* and *grande histoire* are perfectly compatible, and neither should conceal the determining influence on the course of events of the other.

We take up the thread of the story of the legal recognition of the labour conscripts where we left it at the end of chapter 10. For two years Gaullist opposition had frozen the discussion in parliament of the proposal for a law for the *déportés du travail*. On 23 May 1950 the proposal was finally approved by the National Assembly, unanimously. On 15 June, the Conseil de la République, the senate of the Fourth Republic, on the initiative of the minister of war veterans – himself pressured by the UNADIF – modified the first article of the proposal, replacing *déporté du travail* by *requis pour le STO* (conscript for the STO).[70] All of a sudden, the term *déporté du travail*, in common usage, stirred controversy. The very long debate in the Conseil de la République is in many regards illuminating, and the arguments of the defence of the original proposal were of a high quality.[71] As for the opponents, their argumentation had a strong air of *déjà vu*, repeating the debates over the laws for political and resistance deportees as if these had not already taken place. One cannot avoid noticing the chronological coincidence of the creation of the UNADIF and the redirection of patriotic animosity towards the labour conscripts. The opponents again staged the 'hierarchy of sacrifice'[72] and apparently ignored the 1948 distinction between political deportees and deportees of the resistance.[73] Other speakers ventured into long-winded elaborations and quoted dictionaries, or argued in favour of the protection of the proper meaning of words in the French language, 'even if a recent usage has moulded them

[70] Commission Pensions (17 and 19 May 1950).
[71] *Conseil de la République* (15 June 1950), pp. 1702–18.
[72] M. Héline, ibid., p. 1702.
[73] M. Le Basser, ibid., p. 1710.

into this tragically exceptional meaning'.[74] They mentioned the exceptional character of the 'extermination camps' and of 'those days that
became part of a legend of terror'.[75] The distinction they called for was
not 'offensive' for the labour conscripts, since it confirmed the simple
observation that 'they were lucky enough not to experience hell on
earth'. 'We recognise all war victims. Not all are martyrs. Especially
since the martyrs in this new sense, which they have received by the
German ferocity, join the very meaning of the golden legends when
martyrs were also heroes.'[76]

Under the new appellation the proposal returned to the assembly,
where the FNDIR deputy Devemy, one of the few not to suffer from
amnesia, whilst agreeing on the need to distinguish between 'easy prey
and heroic victims', reminded his colleagues of the decisions of 1948:

I think we have to say to the deportees of the Resistance that we wanted to
create an important difference between those who have undergone the same
suffering by attributing two different types of status: the status of deportees of
the resistance and the status of political deportees. The commission and the
Assembly have noted that the glorious title was not in the noun, but in the
qualification added to the noun, that is, the quality of resistance . . . It would
really be a Byzantine quarrel, it would really be of the worst kind to endanger
the status of the labour deportees for the sake of the name.[77]

The commission of the assembly nevertheless proposed the appellation
of *travailleur déporté*, whereby *déporté*, figuring as adjective rather than
noun, constituted an important concession, and later victims of labour
deportation, where *déporté*, qualifying a person, did not figure in any
grammatical configuration, but only the action of *déportation*: all to no
avail.[78] The law was finally voted as 'conscripts of the obligatory labour
service' (*requis du STO*) on 14 May 1951. All through the debates, the
issue had been presented as one of preventing the labour conscripts
from appropriating the aura of 'Deportation'. Historically speaking, the
act expropriated from them, as concluded in chapter 10, what years of
militant propaganda had turned into the cornerstone of their group
identity.

Even after this victory, labour-conscript bashing continued to be a
ritual part of all UNADIF and FNDIR gatherings. A new goal was set:
even though it was explicitly stipulated in the debates in 1951 that the
whole issue was not to inscribe the word 'deportee' into the law but that

---

[74] Léo Hamon, ibid., p. 1711.   [75] Ibid.   [76] Ibid.
[77] Commission Pensions (21 Feb. 1951).
[78] Commission Pensions (4 Aug., 25 Oct., 8 Nov., 15 Nov., 6 Dec. 1950; 26 Jan., 21
Feb., 21 Mar., 11 Apr. 1951); and *Documents AsN*, annexe 11090 (20 Oct. 1950);
annexe 1168 (3 Nov. 1950); annexe 11551 (7 Dec. 1950).

'the title will remain consecrated by common usage',[79] the activists now wanted to forbid all common usage of the word, even in the very name of the FNDT, the National Federation of Labour Deportees. In the national congress of 1955 the action against the appellation by the STO was proclaimed 'Objective No. 1'. Delegates of the department of the Bas-Rhin wanted the FNDIR to quit the UFAC if the latter did not join its campaign against the conscripts. The delegation of the Vaucluse announced its refusal to participate in official commemorations where the conscripts were represented, and the department of Pas-de-Calais reported that a deputy who had voted in favour of the conscripts in parliament had been sacked from its section.[80]

The 'defence of the sacred title, symbol of the sufferings endured for the liberation of the Fatherland',[81] degenerated into rhetorical aberrations, in which the self-proclaimed 'real deportees' appropriated a historical reality that was, much like forced economic migration, historically distinct from the *univers concentrationnaire* to which they claimed to belong, that is, extermination. Routinely, the FNDIR claimed to unite 'the victims of deportation to the Nazi extermination camps', a claim that could be very partially valid for the rival FNDIRP, which included Jewish survivors, but certainly not for the exclusivist FNDIR. The bidding-up of martyrdom drew the militants into distasteful metaphors. The president of the UNADIF, Eugène Thomas, declared at its congress in June 1960: 'Inevitably, the term "Déporté" equals the crematorium [*four crématoire*], but we will never admit that it smells of the blast-furnace [*hauts fourneaux*].'[82] On 2 December 1979 Jacques Limouzy, Undersecretary in the Prime Minister's Office, in Charge of the Relationship with Parliament, declared in the National Assembly that 'the survivors of the former deportees have the supreme merit and their dead are the sacred dust of France, France the friend of Liberty, of the eternal France', and added that the 'extension' of the term 'deportation' to the labour conscripts would 'diminish the moral value of our victims' and 'justify the campaign trying to deny the existence of the crematoria and the extermination camps'.[83]

In spite of, or, alas, perhaps because of, the rhetorical transgressions of the commemorative activists, the action had a wide resonance and 'Deportation' in the highly sacralised version propagated by the

[79] FNDIR delegate and deputy Devemy, Commission Pensions (21 Mar. 1951).
[80] *Rapport du Congrès de la FNDIR* (Marseilles, 24 June 1955), in *dossier organisations françaises*, SerDoc FNDIRP.
[81] *Le Déporté (UNADIF)* (May 1980).
[82] *Congrès National de l'UNADIF* (Rouen, 10–11 June 1960), in *dossier organisations françaises*, SerDoc FNDIRP.
[83] *Assemblée Nationale* (2 Dec. 1979).

UNADIF–FNDIR became a national icon, including, and probably even especially, in intellectual circles. In 1952, the commemorative activism of both organisations was centralised in Le Réseau du Souvenir ['The Memory Network'], a veritable lobby uniting influential anti-communist personalities supporting the cult of the memory of deportation, under the guidance of Riquet and Edmond Michelet.[84] The network effectively challenged the commemorative hegemony of the FNDIRP and christened the commemoration of the concentration camps, with the creation of a 'Deportation Chapel' in the Paris church of Saint-Roch, dedicated to the 'Holy Virgin of the Seven Sorrows' and the systematic incorporation of religious services in all its commemorative ceremonies. On the political agenda, the creation of the network coincided with the preparation of the amnesty laws of 1953, of which the animators were central defenders. In the campaigns against amnesty and against the European Defence Community, actively supported by the FNDIRP, the Réseau had to provide an effective counterweight to the use made of the memory of the suffering inflicted by Vichyssois and Germans respectively on the déportés. In 1952 the Réseau obtained the official declaration of a National Day of Deportation on the last Sunday of April and in 1953 it launched a campaign for the creation of a 'National Memorial to the Martyrs of the Deportation' in the very heart of Paris, on the Ile de la Cité behind the cathedral of Notre-Dame, a memorial inaugurated by President De Gaulle in 1961. In these commemorative initiatives, the Réseau effectively monopolised the entire organisation. At first, the FNDIRP ignored the National Day of Deportation, but was soon forced to join the demonstration, which it had not initiated. In 1954, the Réseau transferred an urn with ashes from the concentration camps to Mont Valérien, an initiative described by Serge Barcellini as an attempt by the government of the time, to which to the Réseau was closely affiliated, to reappropriate this Gaullist *lieu de mémoire*.[85] The lobby also campaigned against the appellation of labour deportees. In 1956, it even brought Fernand Braudel, Albert Camus, Vercors, Lucien Fèbvre, Ernest Labrousse, Pierre Renouvin, René Cassin, Jules Romains, George Bourgin, Claude Bellanger, Bishop Salièges and a whole set of other personalities, including the widows of Marshals De Lattre de Tassigny and Leclerc de Hauteclocque, to sign the following declaration it had itself drafted:

These transplants are no Deportees. There is more at stake here than a simple quarrel of words. The 'Deportation' did not enter History as merely displace-

---

[84] See Serge Barcellini, 'Réflexion autour de deux journées nationales', *Bulletin Trimestriel de la Fondation Auschwitz* 38–9 (1993), pp. 25–43.
[85] Ibid., p. 37.

ment and forced labour: it implies torture, the insane convoys, the gas chambers and the crematoria; the dehumanisation and the extermination of millions of human beings. It is inseparable from an ethic – which should be condemned for ever – by which the 'superior' being arrogates to itself the right to degrade, before killing, those it judges inferior. It constitutes the greatest crime ever perpetrated against man, and whose repetition should be prevented at all costs. To diminish its horror by extending to others the sad aureole of the name of Deportee is to commit at the same time a historical nonsense, a denial of justice and an insult to the memory of all those who were also thrust into forced labour, but whilst waiting for an inescapable death. The draftees, victims of the Forced Labour Service [STO] do not gain much by claiming the title of Deportee. But, through their revindication, which creates a regrettable confusion, they weaken the understanding, the resonance, the enormity of the crime. In this way, they render themselves unconsciously accomplices to oblivion. They cause a great loss to the sacred cause of the defence of Man.[86]

Rejecting a possible amalgamation between forced labour and concentration camp, these French intellectuals, for all their prestige, subscribed to an amalgamation of a different kind. Deportation was a common and inevitable point of departure. The concentration camp – where death was very probable, but by no means 'inescapable' – and extermination – genocide, gas chambers, mechanical devices for mass killing, as opposed to crematoria, mechanical devices to treat dead bodies – were very different destinations. A discourse of national martyrdom, with the concentration camp as symbolical depository of national suffering, which excludes deported workers but includes the victims of genocide, creates, consciously or unconsciously, a regrettable confusion and colludes in the oblivion of the singular treatment of Jews by the Nazis, which is the subject of the next chapter.

The 'Byzantine quarrel' became an unending story.[87] The federation of labour conscripts (FNDT) could bring a number of communist deputies to submit new proposals to recognise the title, at least, of 'victims of Nazi deportation'. The campaign by the federation resorted to some of the mimicry of the first post-war years, reiterating fabulous statistics of martyrdom and claiming that labour deportation was 'a crime against humanity', which, according to the terms of international law, not even the deportation to concentration camps of political opponents and resisters (as opposed to genocide) had been.[88] The

---

[86] *Déportation et Liberté* (Apr.–Sep. 1956).

[87] Sad examples in *Le Déporté (UNADIF)* (Dec. 1976) and *Pourquoi nous sommes des victimes de la déportation du travail*, brochure (Jan. 1961), published by the FNDT-Seine in *dossier déportés du travail*, SerDoc FNDIRP.

[88] See, for example, *Le Proscrit* 1 (Dec. 1992) and André Leroy in *L'Humanité* (21 Oct. 1980).

militancy of the FNDIR also attained its goal of dividing its rival.[89] The campaign 'for the defence of the title' had a wide appeal in FNDIRP circles too, and until 1967 only the tactical mastery of the communists at the head of the organisation could avoid hostile motions against the FNDT.[90] The fact that Marie-Claude Vaillant Couturier, vice president of the FNDIRP and communist deputy, was amongst the signatories of the proposal for the title of 'victims of labour deportation' of 1 December 1967 stirred something of a *fronde* in its ranks and finally forced the organisation to denounce her initiative and adopt a more prudently hostile position. The UNADIF and its allies now embarked on a judicial collision course. After a long legal saga with judgements in 1976, 1978 and 1979, on 10 February 1992 the highest court, the Cour de Cassation, finally prohibited the FNDT from using the word 'deportee' in its name.[91] The federation's journal changed its name to *Le Proscrit*, with the double meaning of 'the exile' and 'the outlaw'.[92] Monuments to the labour deportation, including the memorial in the Père Lachaise cemetery, became the target of claims to remove inscriptions mentioning the 'D'-word. The federation itself made matters noticeably worse, adopting the name of 'National Federation of Victims and Survivors of the Nazi Camps of Forced Labour'. Historically speaking, 'labour deportees' covered the experience of the victims of wartime labour conscription much better. It created much less confusion, and was less intent on doing so, than the reference to 'Nazi camps'. Yet whilst the battles were being fought over the post-war icon of 'Deportation', this icon had itself lost most of its appeal, and had been replaced by a memory of Nazi persecution in which heroism had been reduced to a footnote. From the late 1980s onwards the Réseau du Souvenir would engage in a much more delicate commemorative battle, in an attempt to reconquer the commemorative hegemony it once had over a new challenger: the memory of the genocide.

The reactions of society in France and Belgium to the trauma of Nazi persecution, as described above, were broadly similar. In both societies

[89] See, for example, the vitriolic anonymous letter by a Buchenwald survivor (Feb. 1968), in *dossier déportés du travail*, SerDoc FNDIRP.

[90] The manipulation by the PCF of its delegates in the FNDIRP is laid bare in a letter by Marcel Paul to Marie-Claire Vallant Couturier (Paris, 4 Feb. 1970), and the *Note sur les problèmes posés par la revendication de la FNDT, du titre de 'victimes de la déportation du Travail'* (27 Mar. 1968), both in *dossier déportés du travail*, SerDoc FNDIRP.

[91] 'Arrêt No. 334P'; see *Le Monde* (4 and 12 Feb. 1992).

[92] *Le Proscrit. Organe de la Fédération Nationale des Victimes et Rescapés des Camps Nazis du Travail Forcé. Le plus fort tirage des journeaux de victimes civiles de guerre* 1 (Dec. 1992); 2 (Feb. 1993).

the memories of persecution were central to the experience of the war years. This was so in its immediacy, at the time of the repatriation, when the return of the 'national martyrs' was celebrated as a supreme moment of both national martyrdom and patriotic triumph. Representation of the extraordinary and extra-territorial suffering in the concentration camps was symbolic for national remembrance as a whole, and the survivors of the camps performed to perfection the role of the national *milieu de mémoire*. The discourse of national martyrdom personified by a group that had suffered exceptional afflictions initially had a strong unifying appeal. The anti-fascist identification of the Nation propagated by a broad left wing, but particularly promoted by the communist parties, implied an innovation in traditional concepts of patriotism, through the integration of previously excluded groups: communists, Jews, immigrants. Yet the discourse and rituals of this memory were embedded in a post-1918 tradition. Victims of persecution emulated the model of a veterans' movement with symbols drawn from a military context, such as banners and the laying of wreaths at the memorial to the unknown soldier. They also emulated the vocabulary and legal framework that was elaborated after 1918: the terminology of 'political prisoner' in Belgium; the sacrosanct ninety days of the veterans, and through it the reference to the notion of effective combat, in France. This reappropriation of patriotic symbols stirred protest from the defenders of traditional patriotism, who resented the amalgamation of combatants in a traditional sense with new groups of anti-fascist martyrs. However divisive this conflict, particularly in France, organisations of victims of Nazi persecution would continue to perform their role as witnesses to the national past, with more authority, respect and recognised legitimacy than organisations of former resisters.

The reaction of Dutch society to the legacy of Nazi persecution was fundamentally different. First of all, the Netherlands had remained neutral during World War I. Unlike Belgium and France there was no pre-existing memory of the previous war to impose itself as a ready-made interpretation of the most recent war. The paradigm of the combatant and the social reality of veterans' movements, which were so pervasive in Belgian and French society, could not serve as a reference, nor as a device by which to assimilate the disruptive memory of the Nazi occupation with the heroic memory of the Great War. Secondly, as described in chapter 5, extraordinary and extra-territorial suffering in German camps did not reach public attention as it did in Belgium and France, nor was the return of the survivors anxiously awaited. The peculiar chronology of the military operations that liberated Western

Europe set Dutch society apart from its southern neighbours. The failure of the assault on the Rhine at Arnhem in October 1944 condemned the greater part of Dutch territory to nine more months of occupation, until the German surrender in May 1945. The harsh final winter – the 'hunger winter' – caused the whole population to suffer. Whereas the previous years of occupation had been characterised by suffering in specific groups – communists, deported workers, Jews, etc., now famine, large-scale material destruction, massive migrations of civilians to escape hunger, flooding and Allied bombing brought indiscriminate suffering to all. At the time of the liberation, nine months later than in France and Belgium, one and a half million Dutch citizens were displaced. This greatly reduced the availability of public opinion to identify with specific groups of martyrs, the *milieux de mémoire* that had represented the national experience in Belgium and France. Most concentration camps were liberated earlier than the Dutch heartland, and displaced persons repatriated from Germany were greatly outnumbered by domestic refugees. Dutch DPs in Germany saw their French and Belgian companions leave for home weeks before the first Dutch delegation appeared. The atmosphere of indifference towards repatriates is illustrated, amongst many other reactions recorded by the Dutch historian Dienke Hondius, by the welcome one Jewish survivor received: 'Well, quite a lot of your kind came back. Just be happy you were not here. How we suffered from hunger!'[93] I mentioned in chapter 5 how this homecoming, contrasting so sharply with what most repatriates had seen earlier as they travelled through France and Belgium, determined their own experience of abandonment and neglect by the home front.

Both differences mentioned above helped to shape the peculiar Dutch policy of 'anti-veteranism', described in chapter 3. The rejection of veterans' movements for former resistance fighters applied even more strongly to victims of persecution. With regard to the absolutely primordial role played by associations of victims of Nazi persecution in France and Belgium, organised on the model of veterans' movements, the ostracism against such organisations in the Netherlands constituted a third fundamental difference. Finally, the absence of the Communist Party in the post-war Dutch governments, combined with the moderate centre position of the Labour Party, helps to explain the absence of inclusive policies inspired on the anti-fascist paradigm in the post-war reception of victims of Nazi persecution.

The experience of neglect and the ensuing repatriation controversy, as

---

[93] Rita Koopman, quoted by Hondius, *Terugkeer*, p. 94.

in the case of the labour conscripts, immediately motivated associational militancy amongst repatriated concentration camp survivors, but unlike the former group, this activism had a much wider appeal. In chapter 5 I mentioned how moral indignation over the delay in the repatriation of Dutch DPs focused entirely on KZ survivors, and in chapter 9 I described how the National Resistance Council (the GAC) claimed absolute priority for 'political prisoners' over all other categories of repatriates. Particularly in the liberated southern part of the Netherlands, indignation amongst former resisters over the incompetence or unwillingness to hasten the repatriation of their arrested comrades in German camps as much as possible ran high in the spring of 1945. The militancy in the ranks of the Community of Former Illegal Workers (the GOIWN) and the Dutch Internal Forces, supported by their chief Prince Bernhard, had contributed to the dismissal of repatriation commissioner Ferwerda. Reports indeed reveal the insensitivity, or at least the incapacity, of officials too overwhelmed by acute problems of local relief to understand the tragic conditions of KZ survivors, and the pressing urgency of their repatriation.[94] The numerous protests all originated in resistance organisations, which protested on behalf of their comrades who had been victims of the repression of resistance activities and invoked the nation's 'debt of honour' towards its defenders.[95] The first local associations of 'political prisoners' were branches of resistance organisations, submitting joint protests against the organisation of relief or claims for priority employment, or even using the letterhead of resistance organisations in their own correspondence.[96] Many of these and subsequent petitions cited the Belgian example of governmental generosity, yet references to the anti-fascist discourse prevalent in Belgium and France were rare, and they did not emanate from resistance organisations.[97] Indignation over the deficiencies in the repatriation and reception of KZ survivors temporarily provided a common ground for patriots and communists to set up local associations of

---

[94] See, for example, *Rapport NBS Apeldoorn. Bureau Informatie en Opsporing Nederlanders vermist in Duitsland* (3 July 1945), RIOD, DOC II, 673A; the unsettling report on the expedition to Ravensbrück (24 Aug. 1945); and the report by the *Missie Boon* (15 Sep. 1945), in ARA, cab. PM, box 132. See also *Rapport van de Commissie van onderzoek inzake het verstrekken van pakketten* (see ch. 11, n. 11); *Missie tot opsporing van vermiste personen uit de bezettingstijd. Eindverslag* (The Hague, 1952), ARA, cab. PM, box 131.

[95] See, for example, GOIWN-Gorssel to prime minister (30 June 1945), ARA, cab. PM, box 126.

[96] See, for example, letter, ExPoGe to prime minister (29 Apr. 1946), ibid., and letter, ExPoGe Noord-Brabant to prime minister (4 Apr. 1946), ARA, cab. PM, box 97.

[97] See for example *Wij klagen aan. Repatriërenden zonder Vaderland*, the accusatory pamphlet distributed by the International Socialist Solidarity Action (Amsterdam, June 1945), where Jewish victims figured prominently: RIOD, DOC II, 673A.

'former political prisoners' – the Belgian example provided not only an enviable model, but also the vocabulary. In the Dutch situation, however, the associations vehemently declared their aim to unite only resisters, that is, prisoners arrested because of their political action. In the last months of 1945 the local associations joined forces to form the National Union of Former Political Prisoners, known by the acronym ExPoGe, or NVEPG.

The first creations of 'Unions of Former Prisoners' in June 1945, that is, in the middle of the repatriation controversy, immediately stirred up protest. The president of the patriotic and royalist Oranje-Committee of the province of Limburg published a letter in the local newspaper under the heading 'No dividing line. What matters are the good Dutchmen':

In response to your advertisements in the papers, I allow myself, as an UNTAINTED DUTCHMAN but NO FORMER PRISONER, the following observation. Why create division again? Is the naked fact of having been CAUGHT, NOW, on the eve of the Reconstruction, really a sufficient reason? . . . I was not caught, and this although I did nothing for, but quite a few things against the enemy. Can I, only because I was not caught, not co-operate with you? Tell me honestly: what could one, once caught, still do for his country and his people? There are also many untainted Dutch, who had the good fortune not to get caught and others who, coûte que coûte, did not let themselves be caught. Moreover, was this capture also often not a matter of coincidence, or . . . imprudence maybe? That you want to entertain and strengthen the friendships that were welded under such a difficult circumstances I naturally understand and applaud, but that is not the only aim of your National Union of Former Prisoners, because . . . you claim the right, amongst others, to be represented in court, in purge committees etc. If you claim these rights as good Dutchmen, then I agree, on condition that the candidates respond to the requirements of capacity and adequacy! Or do you claim these rights because you were caught? Then I say: no! That is no criterion! [An excursus on the hard life of draft-evaders, living in hiding follows.] Can you imagine what it means, during five long months, NOT to get caught?[98]

The indignant letter-writer was certainly not an isolated case. In November 1945, the pro-government GAC, the official voice of the resistance establishment (see chapter 3), motivated its officially hostile position regarding the embryonic association for resister-victims of repression in comparable terms, invoking its general condemnation of all veterans' movements:

After some time they ended up, as for example in Belgium after the previous world war, whereby veterans' formations emerged, which after only a short while became completely useless in social terms because the associations slowly degenerated into a bunch of quarrelmongers, who knew nothing else and had nothing better to do than, for example, to claim all sorts of rights for themselves,

[98] P. J. J. Jansen, president, Oranje-Committee, in *Limburgs Dagblad* (21 June 1945).

not on the ground of what they were, but on the grounds of what they had been. We see the same danger in associations of political prisoners.[99]

This did not imply that the GAC did not care about the victims in its own ranks and the widows or orphans of their martyrs. In its discussions on the post-war role of the resistance movements, both during the occupation and afterwards, this task stood out above all divisions as a debt of honour.[100] The plan for one single charitable foundation for all resistance movements grew in the course of 1943 in LO circles. The LO's wartime activity was the organisation of support for people in hiding and for the families of arrested or deceased resisters. The plans for a post-war foundation for resistance victims was no more than a normal extension of its activities. The organisation soon involved representatives of other resistance movements in its plans. After the liberation, now officially endorsed by the GAC, the 'Foundation 1940–1945' tried to centralise the proliferation of assemblies and social actions in favour of resistance victims, with the official support of Queen Wilhelmina and Prime Minister Schermerhorn.

The founding statute of the foundation defined its task as 'the care for the moral, spiritual and material needs of persons or groups of persons who during the occupation contributed to the internal resistance by deed or attitude, their families or next of kin'.[101] This definition marked the narrow national and resistance-oriented position of the foundation: victims of German repression who did not commit acts of resistance were excluded – hostages, victims of retaliation, people arrested because of their pre-war anti-fascist activities, racial deportees, Dutch resisters active outside the national boundaries. The foundation also harboured a particular concept of the way the assistance to resistance victims had to be organised. The founders abhorred the idea that the patriotic martyrs would have to stand in line like beggars for aid at the office windows of the government social assistance. The work of the foundation had to be inspired by the confidence of resisters in their fellow resisters, or the comrades of the deceased father or husband. In practice this meant that the volunteers of the foundation visited the indigent families, and personally investigated their financial needs; but also offered social assistance, good advice, friendship. At the same time, the personal contacts allowed for social control. *Concubinage* was considered shameful for a widow of a national resistance hero and a new marriage in any

[99] Letter, Sandberg to Plaatselijke Adviesraad der Illegaliteit te Dordrecht (13 Nov. 1945), RIOD, GAC archive, 184, 4D.
[100] See Florine Boucher, Els Kalkman and Dick Schaap, *Woord Gehouden. Veertig jaar Stichting 1940–1945* (The Hague, 1985).
[101] Ibid., pp. 18 and 22.

case implied the suspension of all benefits.[102] The charity of the foundation was also characterised by an acute class awareness: the situation of
the victims had to be equal to the one they had held before the war, not
equal as regards the fate of their fellow victims. The aim was to assure
that the victims could 'keep their standing'.[103] This very unequal
distribution of available funds, calculating the amount of aid on the
basis of pre-war incomes, was a moral imperative. It was deemed
unacceptable that a director-general's wife should have to live on the
budget of a welfare mother, nor would the widow of a docker be allowed
to move to a better neighbourhood thanks to the pension of her late
husband-resister.[104] The foundation was best known to the public
through the collections held throughout the country on liberation day.
The posters of the foundation were omnipresent with the message that
the Dutch people had a debt of honour towards the victims of the
resistance who had sacrificed their life for their freedom. Yet the most
important part of its funding originated in sponsorship by major Dutch
private companies.

No matter how successful the fund-raising in the first post-war years,
the foundation was very well aware it would never be able to assure the
payments of pensions for many more decades. From the beginning, the
foundation advocated a law recognising the legitimate claims of
the resistance victims, but such a law had to follow the foundation's two
principles: no bureaucracy, and pensions according to standing. Socialist ministers in the cabinet opposed the transfer of government money
to a private charitable foundation and preferred a public structure for
resistance victims.[105] The Dutch Red Cross filed an alternative proposal, inspired by the Belgian, French and Danish examples, organising
a state pension for resistance fighters who had suffered a minimum of
three months of detention, adding, 'It remains to be seen whether this
also comprises Dutchmen arrested as Jews. The enumeration [of
resistance acts] could be extended to stateless individuals who fought
for the Dutch cause during the occupation and were arrested as
such.'[106] Beel, a Catholic, minister of the interior in the first post-war
cabinet and prime minister from July 1946 to September 1947, overruled these objections and alternatives and submitted the more or less

---

[102] Ibid., p. 171, and *Adres aan de leden der Eerste Kamer en Tweede Kamer der Staten-
Generaal door de Landelijke Raad van Verenigd Verzet 1940–1945* (Nov. 1952), ARA,
cab. PM, box 128.
[103] Boucher, Kalkman and Schaap, *Woord Gehouden*, p. 54.
[104] Ibid., pp. 69–71.
[105] *Notulen Ministerraad* (17 Jan. 1946), ARA.
[106] Afwikkelingsbureau concentratiekampen van het Nederlandse Rode Kruis to prime
minister (29 Jan. 1946), ARA, cab. PM, box 97.

unaltered proposal of the foundation to parliament in the summer of 1947.[107] Discussions in the second parliamentary chamber made it abundantly clear that the law was concerned only with deliberate and active participation in the internal resistance, the heroes, and not the victims of Nazi repression. Victims of mass executions in retaliation for resistance actions, hostages or people arrested because of their pre-war action were excluded. Several members pleaded for the inclusion of other victims of Nazi terror, such as the inhabitants of the villages of Putten and Woeste Hoeve, victims of German mass retaliation against civilian populations. Others argued that people arrested in 1940 or 1941 were 'potential resisters',[108] and that it was unfair to exclude them, since they did not get the chance to engage in resistance activity because of their deportation, an argument echoing the one developed by the FNDIRP in France. In the same vein was the example of a Calvinist minister arrested and shot after the discovery of weapons in his church, of whose existence he was ignorant.[109] Unlike the French and Belgian parliamentary debates, the exclusion of Jewish victims was not even mentioned, despite the exceptional number of Jews deported from the Netherlands.

The Foundation 1940–1945 was responsible for the examination of each demand – as much its resistance merits as the medical report on the causal relationship between resistance and invalidity/death of the demander – and decided independently on the level of the pension. At the same time the foundation was in charge of payments to the claimants. As such, the Foundation 1940–1945 was a special institution. It was not an association of resistance victims, but an association for them, in which their role was one of passive beneficiaries. It was simultaneously a private organisation and the executor of governmental legislation, at once both judge and advocate in the distribution of remittances. This position would inevitably lead to criticism from the more militant associations of ex-resisters. The LO, the confessional underground relief organisation in which the foundation originated, continued to furnish about 90 per cent of the volunteers.[110] In 1948 these volunteers tried to oust the representative of the former communist underground newspaper *De Waarheid* and in 1950 they attained

---

[107] *Gedrukte stukken Tweede Kamer* 449 (1946–7); *Gedrukte stukken Eerste Kamer* 160 and 160a (1946–7); *Handelingen Tweede Kamer* (8–9 July 1947), pp. 1951–8 and 1982–2000; *Handelingen Eerste Kamer* (31 July 1947 and 21 Aug. 1947); *Staatsblad* H313 (22 Aug. 1947).

[108] *Handelingen der Staten-Generaal. Bijlagen* 449 (1946–7), pp. 9 and 15.

[109] Ibid., p. 15.

[110] Boucher, Kalkman and Schaap, *Woord Gehouden*, p. 91.

their goal of a communist-free organisation (this situation remained unchanged until 1980).[111] The predominant influence of the LO, Calvinist and Catholic in various regions, the financial weight of the industrial and commercial elites, the paternalist and patronising structure of the assistance, the protection of the social *status quo* of the victims and the official role in the distribution of government pensions – all converged to turn the Foundation 1940–1945 into a respected national institution of charity. The victims of the resistance were taken in charge. Clearly, with an institution invested with national dignity and legal authority as their patron, the martyrs of the resistance would not become a focus for resister discontent, let alone allow the political exploitation of their social claims.

The procedures for official recognition as a 'political prisoner' in Belgium or 'deportee' in France had contributed to the establishment of their national associations as indispensable helpers in dealing with applications. The Dutch organisation of former political prisoners was effectively side-tracked through the construction of publicly funded assistance channelled through a private charity. The history of ExPoGe ran parallel with the history of the federations of resistance veterans. As long as the organisation admitted communist members into its ranks, it had a poor press in government circles. In 1948, a first motion to exclude the communists from the organisation failed.[112] The mythical unity of the common experience in the camps retained its appeal, even in the very anti-communist Netherlands. At the national congress held in Utrecht on 21 May 1949, the declaration by the secretary-general of the Dutch Communist Party Paul De Groot that the party would choose the Soviet side, if it was victim of an attack, was the occasion to vote for the exclusion of all communists, albeit with only a small margin of fifty-two to forty-one votes.[113] The local section in Amsterdam, in which the communists were strongly represented, decided to set up a new organisation, which was soon joined by local associations from Enschede, Hilversum, Apeldoorn and Arnhem.[114] At the founding congress on liberation day 1950 the organisation adopted the new name of 'United Resistance of the Netherlands 1940–1945'.[115] Prefiguring

---

[111] Ibid., pp. 92–3.
[112] See *Rapport van de Binnenlandse Veiligheidsdienst over het eerste landelijke Congres Verenigd Verzet 1940–1945* (20 June 1950), ARA, cab. PM, box 128.
[113] *De Volkskrant* (23 May 1949).
[114] See *Rapport Binnenlandse Veiligheidsdienst* (20 June 1950), ARA, cab. MP, box 128; and *Het Parool, Het Vrije Volk, Het Algemeen Handelsblad* (27 May 1949), RIOD, KB II, box 72.
[115] See *Rapport Binnenlandse Veiligheidsdienst* (20 June 1950), ARA, cab. MP, box 128. See also *Voormalig Verzet Nederland* (15 and 29 Oct. 1949); *Het Vrije Volk* (26 Oct. 1949); *De Waarheid* (25 Oct. 1949): all in RIOD, KB II, box 72.

the transformation at the international level (see chapter 14), it was a new type of wholesale anti-fascist front organisation, uniting all anti-fascists, from the veterans of the International Brigades of the Spanish Civil War to the – very explicitly mentioned – victims of anti-Semitism, victims of arbitrary arrest and all sorts of resistance veterans. Right from its founding congress onwards, the organisation was banned from public demonstrations, and the target of the closest secret police scrutiny. 'United Resistance' successfully organised demonstrations commemorating the strike of February 1941 and in support of the communist hero Hannie Schaft, one of the ninety heroes decorated with the Resistance Cross, despite interdictions, police cordons etc.[116] Or perhaps, as one police report suggested, the success of its commemorations could rather be explained by the police measures.[117] In 1952, communist commemoration of the February strike on a Sunday was forbidden: the official commemoration at 9:00 that morning attracted very little public attention, whilst the communist demonstration, forced to change to 5:00 p.m. on Monday, was an overwhelming success, drawing, according to the sources, between 7,000 and 20,000 attendants, mostly workers leaving their factories at that moment.

The success of 'communist agitation' in implementing the commemoration of the war contributed greatly to improving the stance of the now solidly anti-communist ExPoGe with the government. ExPoGe and United Resistance competed in defending the victims of Nazi persecution against the parsimony of the Foundation 1940–1945.[118] United Resistance, whose representatives had been ousted from the foundation's board of management in 1950, embarked on a campaign to extend the assistance to non-resistant victims of persecution, pleading for 'equal treatment for all victims of persecution during the German occupation on behalf of their attitude, their political conviction, their origins or their resistance'.[119] This plea was dismissed out of hand by the foundation, who claimed that its entire action, and the law of 1947, was the fulfilment of the formal debt of the Dutch Nation towards the

---

[116] *Rapport Binnenlandse Veiligheidsdienst n.a.v. februari-staking herdenking* (24 Mar. 1952), and the reports on the less successful manifestation of 1953 (22 Jan., 9 Feb. and 26 Feb. 1953), in ACPM, 351.855.23. See also the report *Verenigd Verzet* (30 July 1952), in ARA, cab. PM, box 128.

[117] *Rapport* (24 Mar. 1952), ACPM, 351.855.23.

[118] *Adres aan de leden der Eerste Kamer en Tweede Kamer der Staten-Generaal door de Landelijke Raad van Verenigd Verzet 1940–1945* (Nov. 1952). See also the earlier addresses (3 Aug. and Feb. 1951), ARA, cab. PM, box 128, and *Handelingen Tweede Kamer* (18 May 1951), p. 1720.

[119] *Adres* (3 Aug. 1951).

sacrifices of the resistance and could never be concerned with other types of victim.[120]

The militancy of ExPoGe was more successful. The association directly challenged the foundation on its own field of social aid to resistance victims, through successfully competing collections and charity events, and relentlessly criticised the old-fashioned charity that characterised the official institution.[121] Prime Minister Drees, a socialist, sympathised with the dynamic militancy of ExPoGe, all the more since the socialist businessman Karel Van Staal, the central animator of ExPoGe, was a close friend. He intervened personally to broker a deal between ExPoGe and the foundation, through the participation of the former in the direction of the latter, to complete mutual satisfaction. In 1952, carried on the same wave of governmental benevolence for its anti-communist zeal in the face of the agitation of United Resistance, the minister of the interior created the 'Neher Commission' to investigate whether the general feeling of official neglect experienced by resistance survivors of the camps, when they compared their own situation with that in Belgium and France, did not constitute a sufficient reason to grant them an exception to the rule of non-decoration – the stalemate of 1948 described in chapter 3.[122] The commission arrived at a positive conclusion and added that the distribution of the distinction had to take into account whether or not the post-war behaviour of the applicants could be considered patriotically worthy of the distinction. In an accompanying confidential note to the prime minister, it was expressly mentioned that this condition of 'national loyalty' was designed to exclude all communist applicants and avoid the political exploitation made by the latter of, for instance, the posthumous Resistance Cross of Hannie Schaft. The council of ministers finally decided on 11 August 1952 that granting one exception would let things get out of hand, and that there would be no way of stopping any other claimants for medals afterwards.[123]

---

[120] Letter, Foundation 1940–1945 to prime minister (25 Apr. 1951), ARA, cab. PM, box 128.

[121] See the files *Landelijke Vereniging Ex-Politieke Gevangenen* and *Verhouding Expogé/ Stichting 1940–1945*, ARA, cab. PM, box 128.

[122] *Memorandum C. L. W. Fock aan MP* (7 Dec. 1951); *Advies van de Commissie . . . herinneringskruis voor politieke gevangenen* (12 July 1952); *Nota voor de Minsterraad* (22 July 1952); *Nota voor de MP door J. M. Kielstra* (5 Feb. 1965): all in ACPM, 354.075.31–911.5.

[123] See ACPM 355.358.061.2, 355.358.061.21, and 355.358.069, esp. the Fock memorandum (19 July 1954).

13   Patriotic memories and the genocide

The three national memories organised around the paradigm of national martyrdom, described in the previous chapter, were only a partial representation of the plural persecutions distinguished in chapter 11. The way in which wartime persecutions were represented in the post-war years indeed functioned as a metaphor, and more particularly a *pars pro toto*. The central image was that of the hero-victim of the repression of the Resistance combat, numerically only a modest part of all the victims of Nazi persecution. In a traditional patriotic memory, the metaphor excluded all other victims. In an 'anti-fascist' memory, the metaphor was inclusive by assimilation: all victims of fascism were *per se* anti-fascists and thus somehow, if not heroes, at the very least martyrs in a noble cause. In the Netherlands, the commemoration of persecution was essentially traditional and patriotic, and the anti-fascist discourse remained marginal and oppositional. In France and Belgium, the commemoration was largely inspired by the anti-fascist discourse, but amended by traditional patriotism. Contrary to the Netherlands, the memory of persecution was inclusive of all victims, but symbolic features distinguished the heroes from the rest: the 'title' and medal in Belgium, the separate law for 'deportees of the resistance' in France. Whether by exclusion or assimilation, these memories did not represent the distinct experience of one particular group – one group amongst many, but numerically by far the most important: the Jewish victims of the genocide perpetrated by the Nazis. The previous chapter pointed repeatedly to the marginal presence in France and Belgium, and the almost complete absence in the Netherlands, of references to Jewish victims in post-war debates on recognition for the victims of Nazi persecution. This marginality or oblivion is primarily striking because of its sharp contrast with perceptions in the final decade of the twentieth century, a contrast that supposes a radical reversal of memories in the course of the last five and a half decades that this chapter must address.

The 'reversal' of memories of Nazi persecution over these decades since the end of the Second World War – from the hegemony of the resistance fighters to a predominant attention for the Jewish victims in the remembrance of the occupation years – has been observed by several authors in different European countries.[1] Any researcher who investigates public opinion as regards the genocide and the return of survivors of the Nazi persecution in April–July 1945 discovers a picture that contrasts with expectations, expectations conditioned by the overwhelming impact of genocide on the memory of Nazi crimes today. Repatriation was indeed a major event that influenced the perception of the Second World War in occupied societies. Public opinion was shocked and sometimes obsessed by the images of the return, the arrival of the repatriation convoys in the railway stations and the welcome parades organised in honour of the survivors. But the experience of the Jews and the discovery of the systematic killing of Jewish 'deportees' made far less impression than the 'concentration', bad treatment and underfeeding of the other deportees, which resulted in relatively high death rates and the often shocking physical condition of the returning survivors. A large proportion of Jews deported from Western Europe had transited through the concentration camps on their way to extermination and a small number of them survived the liberation. This fact contributed to their assimilation into the undifferentiated mass of 'deportees'. It seems to the contemporary observer that the awareness, the *prise de conscience*, of the specificity of the Jewish experience in the universe of Nazi persecution had not permeated public opinion and that in reactions towards the survivors of genocide open hostility often prevailed.

The simple observation of the 'reversal of memories' does lead most authors to much broader interpretations, whereby two competing commemorative discourses are confronted. The marginal attention, the failure to perceive or even – worded more strongly – the refusal to acknowledge the specificity of the treatment of Jews in the Nazi policies of persecution in the first two decades after the war nurtures the retrospective indignation of those writers who put genocide at the heart of the history of the Nazi period. The rediscovery of a period much closer to the atrocities, when governments, media and public opinion seemed untouched by the unprecedented tragedy of European Jews, is seen as an extension of the injustice and discrimination Jews suffered during the war and as a form of ongoing anti-Semitism. In this

---

[1] For full reference, see Pieter Lagrou, 'Victims of Genocide and National Memory. Belgium, France and the Netherlands 1945–1965', *Past & Present* 154 (1997), pp. 181–222. For France, see especially Annette Wieviorka, *Déportation*, and, for the Netherlands, see Dienke Hondius, 'A Cold Reception. Holocaust Survivors in the Netherlands and Their Return', *Patterns of Prejudice* 28 (1994), pp. 47–65.

perspective, the place occupied by the Jewish experience in the respective national memories is a matter of the national conscience and a denial of justice which must be remedied in retrospect. The unmasking of the 'de-Judifying' of the victims of genocide in post-war perceptions leads some commentators to an overall indictment of the prevailing ideologies of the post-war years. The 'mythical amalgamation' of very different categories of victims would have been the result of a *gauchisse-ment*, a 'fabricated universality' or a very outdated form of 'Polish' anti-fascism.[2] Some British historians do not hesitate to blame the perception during the same period in their country – which by all accounts was rather peripheral to the continental genocide – on the 'exclusive national framework', 'assimilationism' and 'universalism'. All three terms are identified as devices for the imposition of a mono-cultural society: 'exclusivism' through the exclusion of people from other ethnic, cultural or religious backgrounds, 'assimilationism' through the absorption of these people into the mono-cultural society, eradicating their distinct identities, and 'universalism' through the axiomatic proclamation of the global validity of strictly West European, Enlightenment values. For one commentator the failed perception of the particular Jewish suffering even calls into question 'the liberal imagination', which supposedly lies at the source of the enumerated ills.[3] In a rather perplexing combination, both universalism and anti-Semitism, assimilationism and exclusivism stand accused of 'de-Judification'.

The 'reversal of memories' that has taken place in more recent decades is, on the other hand, a major source of frustration for the last surviving guardians of patriotic memories of Nazi persecution, such as the Réseau du Souvenir, who resent their marginalisation in the contemporary interest in the Nazi period and cultivate a certain nostalgia for their post-war hegemony. It is also of concern to some historians, who are alarmed by the one-sidedness of a historical consciousness of the Nazi period that is induced by a commemorative activism which isolates genocide from its context of 'ordinary' persecution.[4] They claim that a 'Judeo-centric memory' is, from a historian's point of view, hardly preferable to a patriotic memory.

---

[2] Maxime Steinberg, 'Les Dérives Plurielles de la mémoire d'Auschwitz', *Centrale. Périodique Trimestriel de la Vie Communautaire Juive* 259 (1993), pp. 6–9, and 260 (1993), pp. 11–14.

[3] Tony Kushner, *The Holocaust and the Liberal Imagination. A Social and Cultural History* (Oxford, 1994).

[4] See Jean-Michel Chaumont, 'Connaissance ou reconnaissance? Les Enjeux du débat sur la singularité de la Shoah', *Le Débat* 82 (1994), pp. 69–89; Alain Finkielkraut, *La Mémoire Vaine. Du crime contre l'humanité* (Paris, 1989), particularly pp. 35–47, and Conan and Rousso, *Vichy.*

This book, focusing exclusively on the first two decades after the war, during which the hegemony of memories of national martyrdom remained largely intact, is not concerned with the issues of contemporary commemorative rivalries. At the most, we can survey some of the factors which explain the failure to perceive the singular experience of the tens of thousands of Jews deported from the national territory of Belgium, France and the Netherlands. This research cannot claim to study the perception of the 'Holocaust' or the 'Shoah', the continental tragedy taking place mainly in Central and Eastern Europe in which one-third of world Jewry and two-thirds of European Jewry were murdered, and a centuries-old local Jewish culture destroyed. To attempt such a study for the two decades before 1965 would evince an anachronistic state of mind, since the very dimensions of the continental tragedy, as manifested in contemporary terminology, were very slow to emerge, even amongst professional historians.[5] As it is, the three countries we are concerned with here failed to assess even the tragedy of their own Jewish population, which made up only a numerically marginal part of the continental tragedy. Neither does this book address the issue of Jewish memory, that is, how a community that scarcely escaped total annihilation in Europe struggles to build a future after a catastrophe that left only memory of millions, that community that only persists in memory. It cannot pretend to place the genocide in Jewish history and culture, or to search for meaning in the Jewish – or any other – tradition. It only assesses externally and summarily how and whether national societies acknowledged the tragedy that befell their Jewish fellow citizens. This is not a statement of insensitivity, but of impotence in the face of the legacy of genocide.

If we search for what accounts for the place of Jewish victims in post-war national memories – the exclusion of their distinct experience of a persecution designed to annihilate their 'race' in its entirety, or its assimilation with other forms and experiences of persecution – cannot dismiss out of hand the preliminary question of anti-Semitism. First of all, did anti-Semitism occur after 1945? If this question obtains a positive answer, it would be a powerful confirmation of the very feeble impact of the discovery of the genocide. It would imply that in the eyes of contemporaries anti-Semitism was not even discredited by its most recent and most horrible excesses. A second and quite different question is whether the marginality of the Jewish experience in national memory is the result of anti-Semitism and of anti-Semitism alone. The two

---

[5] See Raul Hilberg, 'Opening Remarks. The Discovery of the Holocaust', in Peter Hayes (ed.), *Lessons and Legacies. The Meaning of the Holocaust in a Changing World* (Evanston, IL, 1991), pp. 11–19.

questions are in fact mirror images of each other: whereas the first question asks whether the place of anti-Semitism in post-war society was a result of the genocide, the second question asks whether the place of genocide in post-war society was a result of anti-Semitism.

In the eyes of most authors the first question seems to ask the unthinkable. How could one continue to hold anti-Semitic opinions after witnessing the horrible outcome of Nazi anti-Semitism? Yet to suppose that anti-Semitism all of a sudden evaporated in the light of the evidence of Nazi crimes would be to underestimate the inveterate nature of anti-Semitism in Western European societies.[6] After all, both blatant and latent anti-Semitism had been necessary preconditions for the massive deportations from the occupied societies, which the occupier would not have been able to carry out without local accomplices and impassive bystanders.

First of all, there are manifestations of continuing anti-Semitism. The same report by the Gendarmerie Nationale of 13 June 1945, quoted in the previous chapter, which described all 'deportees' as 'the best of the Nation', heroes of the 'clandestine struggle', returning with undiminished abnegation and courage, some pages later describes without comment an incident in the fourth arrondissement in Paris on 19 April: '250 to 300 people demonstrated, shouting "France for the French!" A fight broke out with the Jews of the neighbourhood. The demonstration was sparked off by the expulsion of someone occupying the apartment of a Jew who returned to Paris.'[7] On several occasions returning survivors were registered as 'Jews' on official repatriation documents, both upon their departure from Germany and on their homecoming.[8] Contrary to what critics of the 'de-Judification' of the survivors claim today, these repatriates very much resented being once again singled out as Jews, after they had barely survived racial persecution.[9]

The most shocking aberrations by repatriation officials were recorded by Dienke Hondius in the Netherlands. Stateless Jews who had

---

[6] See Dienke Hondius, *Terugkeer*, and 'A Cold Reception'; Matard-Bonucci and Lynch, *La Libération des camps*, p. 169. See also Richard C. Vinen, 'The End of an Ideology? Right-Wing Antisemitism in France, 1944–1970', *Historical Journal* 37 (1994), pp. 368–73.

[7] *Direction de la Gendarmerie. Synthèse pour la période du 15 avril au 15 mai 1945* (13 June 1945), AN 72 AJ 384.

[8] See, for example, the oral evidence of Jo Van Dam in Amsterdam to Hondius in *Terugkeer*, p. 89, and Fanny Segal in Paris to Edouard Lynch in Matard-Bonucci and Lynch, *La Libération des camps*, p. 122. Similar incidents occurred in Germany, where German civilians requisitioned by the Allies for the distribution of food-rationing cards marked the cards of Jewish survivors with the rubber stamp *Jude* left over from the Nazi administration: Jacobmeyer, *Zwangsarbeiter*, p. 44.

[9] See Annette Wieviorka, *Déportation*, p. 67, and *Rapport sur l'activité du Commissariat Belge*, p. 8.

emigrated from Nazi Germany to the Netherlands in the 1930s and who were deported during the occupation were arrested upon their return from Bergen-Belsen and imprisoned together with collaborationists as 'former enemy DPs'.[10] These repeated incidents caused indignant protest, but they indicate how weak the impact of the discovery of the genocide had been in wider circles, including those involved in administering the repatriation. In France, the Gendarmerie Nationale registered anti-Semitic graffiti appearing in the first six months of 1945, like the scrawl discovered in Courbevoie on 19 February: 'Down with the war, down with the denouncers, the firing squad for all Jews.'[11] The repatriation officials in Toulouse observed that 'the intrigues' of repatriated Jews risked 'provoking or fostering a new crisis of anti-Semitism' and reported its efforts to halt the militancy of this group, 'excessive both because of their small number and because of the fact that they are foreigners'.[12] Forced 'assimilationism' occurred when Christian churches – not the State – hid, educated and baptised Jewish children and refused to return the children to their Jewish relatives or Zionist organisations.[13]

Secondly, anti-Semitism seemed in part to be strengthened by the genocide, taking up new themes, such as the lack of Jewish resistance or Jewish treason; and a general tendency developed of thinking that, if the Jews attracted such unprecedented persecution, they must be guilty of something. Traditional Christian anti-Semitism felt the need to reappropriate a theme of which it had been dispossessed by the Nazis. In the spring months of 1945, a Dutch author living in liberated Belgium, when the majority of the Netherlands was still occupied, took stock of the years of the German occupation in both countries and of the challenges ahead. The book was published in May 1945 by a publisher situated close to the border, and was immediately distributed in the Netherlands. In his chapter on the persecution of Jews by the Nazis, the author felt compelled to warn his readers not to credit Hitler for his accomplishments:

[10] Hondius, *Terugkeer*, pp. 79–85. Steven Hess, one of these repatriates interned as a child, testifies on this experience in *The Netherlands and Nazi Genocide. Papers of the 21st Annual Scholars' Conference* (Lewiston, Queenston and Lampeter, 1991), p. 64.

[11] 'A bas la guerre, à bas les dénonciateurs, les juifs au poteau': *Synthèse pour la période du 15 février au 15 mars 1945* (Paris, 12 Apr. 1945), AN 72 AJ 384. The subsequent report, *Synthèse pour la période du 15 mars au 15 avril 1945* (22 May 1945), mentioned 'Quelques graffitis prennent à part Juifs et communistes', ibid.

[12] *Extrait du rapport de la Direction Régionale de Toulouse* (12 Feb. 1945), AN F9 3172.

[13] For the Netherlands, see Elma Verhey, *Om het joodse kind* (Amsterdam, 1991). For France, especially the *affaire Finally*, see Rousso, *Le Syndrome de Vichy*, pp. 66–7; Vinen, 'End of an Ideology', pp. 372–3; and Annette Wieviorka, *Déportation*, pp. 368–90.

Even if we accept that the power and influence of Jewry in our modern society are not imaginary, yes, if we even willingly admit that the righteous resistance and fair measures against numerous Jewish practices positively benefit Christian society, then it still remains no less true that no Christian of conviction can approve the phenomena that present themselves nowadays under the universal as well as meaningless name of anti-Semitism. If today we find a certain category of Christians (and this is not unimportant) who sympathise with this persecution, we should not in the first place forget that, if we Christians had in general shown more courage and conviction and faith, Jewish and liberal influences would never have permeated society to the degree they did. The Jews were guilty of the murder of the Son of God, but Pontius Pilate was no less guilty when he nailed an innocent to the cross out of cowardice . . . Of course, the Jewish problem is a burning question, but those who wish its solution from the perspective of hatred and often of angry envy have rejected Christian love and with it their Christianity . . . Christian love requires a different struggle, a different anti-Semitism. The mass murder of the Jewish people is the clearest proof that national-socialism is not anti-Semitic, but anti-Christian. Of course the Christian world will have to fight its war against Jewish hegemony, but in a struggle according to its own principles and not according to the whispering of some evil spirit . . . The freedom we yearn for must not lead to licentiousness and anarchism, because they are the trump cards through which the liberal–Jewish hegemony can establish itself.[14]

An early awareness of 'the mass murder of the Jewish people' was not at all incompatible with a continuing, traditional, anti-Semitic discourse. The first question is hereby positively answered. The discovery of the genocide did not rule out all anti-Semitic sentiment in the societies from which tens of thousands of Jews had been deported.

Even if anti-Semitism was more widespread in 1945 and thereafter than a contemporary observer would expect, and was underestimated rather than overestimated in most literature on the subject, it cannot account for the marginality of the memory of the genocide in society as a whole. Anti-Semitic attitudes are often concealed in the arguments of protagonists in the commemorative debate. The previous chapter repeatedly mentioned that patriotic exclusivism in France and Belgium was explicitly accused of hiding an anti-Semitic bias. Some of the arguments developed by patriots who refused to be assimilated with the Jewish victims indeed expressed anti-Semitic resentment and contempt. Yet, in the light of the integrated picture this book tries to draw of post-war national memories, anti-Semitism cannot be the only explanation. In the same way as the memories of resistance, labour conscription and national martyrdom can only be understood in relation to one another, the memory of the genocide finds its place, or

[14] Leo Hendrickx, *Gekneveld en Bevrijd* (Maaseik, 1945), pp. 140–1.

rather fails to find its place, in a much larger whole. The second question, whether anti-Semitism explains the marginality of the memory of genocide, cannot be answered positively, since the explanation is much more complex.

In retrospect, for reasons of historical analysis the Nazi persecution of the Jews can, rightly or wrongly, be distinguished and isolated from the experience of other groups, as well as compared and amalgamated with them, yet it is beyond dispute that the victims and survivors of the genocide were physically intermingled with victims and survivors of other forms of persecution and that it was this mixture which conditioned contemporary perceptions. The fact that genocide was not perceived in its specificity does not in itself provide an explanation, nor does the self-understanding by survivors of their experience as expressed in eyewitness accounts explain the receptiveness of post-war society for such accounts. In order to understand the marginality of the memory of genocide, an investigation is required into what has hidden it from view, as well as an analysis of the more urgent and obtrusive memories that mobilised post-war societies. This chapter on the Jewish victims therefore logically finds its place at the very end of our long development on displaced persons from the occupied countries of Western Europe to Germany.

Repatriation planners were concerned with volumes of potential repatriates, as were the policies of reintegration. Workers and, for France, PoWs were their main preoccupation. From the massed number of repatriates, one group stood out as particular heroes and martyrs, the concentration camp survivors. Numerically, they were even fewer than repatriated collaborationists: but they gradually came to embody national martyrdom, over time even to some extent in the Netherlands. Even if their symbolic weight bore no relation to their share in the total population of repatriates, the memory they incarnated mirrored the social composition of their own group. Associations of concentration camp survivors, the central protagonists of the memory of Nazi atrocities in the first decades after the war, were necessarily a distorted representation of the victims of Nazi persecution. They included inmates of national prisons, hostages or victims of torture who had never left the national territory for German camps; but they did not incorporate the tens of thousands of victims who disappeared in deportation. Most importantly, there were by definition, strictly speaking, no survivors of the genocide. The only Jews who escaped the immediate annihilation upon arrival that characterised the genocide, and who had a chance of survival, were those who were selected and registered to enter the concentration camp, or ended up in concentration camps on their way to the centres of mass death. They were a very small minority in the category of survivors, repatriation convoys and associations. In the mechanisms of a social memory the dead had no role to play. Only after a historical memory had emerged – that is, a memory integrating the dead – were the calculations different.

Chapter 11 enunciated all the reservations that apply to the comparative statistics of Nazi persecution. When dealing with its repercussions on collective representations, the comparison of the absolute figures of Jewish victims with the post-war figures of whoever was considered a Nazi victim is revealing, precisely because of the phenomenological value of the latter figures. If those victims of Nazi persecution who survived the war are counted, Jewish repatriates are outnumbered by non-Jewish repatriates by one to twenty. As far as the departures are concerned, there were five Jewish to one 'non-Jewish' 'deportee' in the Netherlands. In Belgium, the figures show five Jewish deportees to eight 'political prisoners', the mass of Nazi victims entitled to national recognition (allowing for possible overlapping). In France, Jewish deportees and 'political deportees and internees' and 'deportees and internees of the resistance', a comparable conglomerate, stand almost one to one (again, allowing for possible overlapping). These figures show the tragic proof of two very different realities: the genocide on the one hand and the concentration camp system (for the Netherlands) and Nazi persecution in general (Belgium and France) on the other.

Crude and disconcerting statistics such as these should not, however, lead to mechanical interpretations of a memory conditioned by volumes and categories. Probably the most important conclusion of the previous chapter is the importance of the identification of victims, that is, both their identification by the societies to which they returned and their individual identification with a cause, an ideology, a narrative of their own experience. The conflict between the exclusive definition of national martyrdom by traditional patriots, insisting on the distinction between authenticated resisters and the others, and the inclusive definition of anti-fascism, was finally a conflict between a categorisation from the perspective of the persecutor and a free-floating categorisation whereby the victim could choose his or her identification. Anti-fascism might indeed have 'imposed' an overarching interpretation and glossed over the tragic distinctiveness of the Jewish experiences, but it remained a large and welcoming family which anybody could join at any time and become part of. There may have been an ideological hegemony assimilating various experiences to some holistic martyrdom, but this was at the same time what many of the Jewish victims who actively adhered to

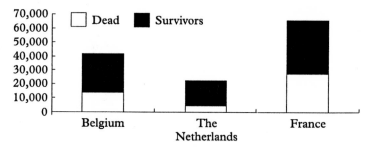

13.1 Figures and death rates of 'political' 'deportees' and 'prisoners'

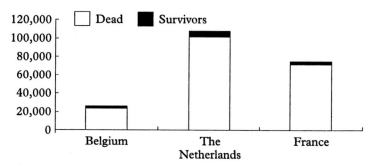

13.2 Figures and death rates of Jewish 'deportees'

the anti-fascist paradigm needed at that moment.[15] Anti-fascism as a 'universalising' device offered a generous and heroic interpretation. For individuals who had barely survived inconceivable suffering, the identification with anti-fascism was a means of overcoming the appallingly arbitrary affliction that had hit them, a way to take possession of their own destiny, a retrospective revenge on an inhuman enemy. Many of the victims of anti-Semitic persecution rejected their identification by their persecutor as 'Jew' and, even if they did not, the combative identification as anti-fascist often mattered more in its immediacy than deeper cultural or religious identifications. A senseless experience gained a new meaning, and individuals traumatised and humiliated by a cruel enemy regained dignity and sense of self.

The moral indignation of authors like Tony Kushner, Maxime Steinberg and even Annette Wieviorka over 'anti-fascist assimilationism' therefore seems ill directed when seen in the perspective of the com-

---

[15] See Charles Van West, interviewed by Jean-Michel Chaumont, 'Ce n'était pas encore une nécessité, mais maintenant c'est devenu une obsession', *Bulletin Trimestriel de la Fondation Auschwitz* 32–3 (1992), pp. 49–79.

memorative battle between exclusivist nostalgic patriots harbouring anti-Semitic resentment and the innovative, inclusive, generous discourse of anti-fascism. When judged with today's measures of multiculturalism (and today's anti-communist sensibilities?), anti-fascism may look intolerant. When compared with the xenophobic hyper-patriotism of the anti-anti-fascists, the defence of the inclusion of Jewish victims by anti-fascist organisations does deserve a re-evaluation that is free from anachronistic moral indignation. To point at the fact that this commemorative activism was politically instrumental is a tautology. What matters in any commemoration is the degree of contortion imposed by the commemorators on the commemorated. For the commemoration of Nazi persecution in the years immediately following the end of it, this was an issue of social justice rather than of historical veracity. As long as the object of the commemorative battle was the admission of victims of Nazi persecution into the national community of patriotic martyrs, moral indignation addressed towards anti-fascists seems literally misplaced – that is, it would be much more à propos addressed to their opponents. When, from 1948 onwards, the matter became the identification with the great causes of post-war international politics, there was no longer any social justice at stake and anti-fascism appeared under a different light. Boundless instrumentalising of memories, propaganda and contortions of sorts in the area of international politics are the subject of the next chapter.

14   Remembering the war and legitimising the post-war international order

In strong contrast to the endless controversies over the resistance contribution to post-war domestic politics – restoration or renewal – is the apparent consensus over its contribution to international politics. According to this consensus, European integration is the most enduring ideological heritage that can be credited to the resistance movements. United in their revolt against war, oppression and nationalism, these movements were very early protagonists in the global conflict, in total unanimity after the defeat of Nazism, on the need to build a new Europe based on co-operation between the peoples that had suffered so cruelly in this internecine struggle. The plans elaborated during the war by the underground movement were gradually implemented after the war, and gave birth to the Treaties of Rome and Maastricht. This consensus was of course primarily promoted by pro-European militants, for whom the resistance heroes were a very convenient, noble and consensual set of founding fathers.[1] After all, any new nation-building requires some sort of historical legitimisation, and in this respect European federalists are no different from pan-Hellenic enthusiasts 2,500 years earlier, from the heralds of the nineteenth-century nation-states or the apologists of the colonial order. Under this premise, the resistance offered a better common ground than other pretenders – medieval Europe united by one language, one education system and one religion, just as that same religion was losing most of its unifying potential in a European homeland of secularisation, or the Europes of the Renaissance or the Enlightenment, eras of less than edifying dynastic warfare.

More surprisingly, the same consensus applies to most textbooks on the history of European integration and European post-war history in general. Derek W. Urwin's *Western Europe Since 1945*, probably the most

---

[1] For recent examples of Europeanist rhetoric, see *Europe. Dream–Adventure–Reality* (Brussels, 1987); Henri Rieben, *Des guerres européennes à l'Union de l'Europe* (Lausanne, 1987); Henri Brugmans, *L'Idée Européenne, 1920–1970* (Bruges, 1970). For a complete reference, see Pieter Lagrou, 'La Résistance et les conceptions de l'Europe, 1945–1965', in Antoine Fleury and Robert Frank (eds.), *Le Rôle des guerres dans la mémoire des européens* (Bern, 1997), pp. 137–81.

262

popular textbook for students of European post-war history in the last quarter-century, asserts that: 'Above all, the resistance can claim some credit for the establishment of the EEC in 1957.'[2] The same theme recurs as an obligatory introduction in many other textbooks, especially in Germany and Italy. The Europeanism of the anti-fascist resistance here compensates for feelings of national guilt. On the one hand it proves that there were German and Italian anti-fascists who were strongly in favour of another Europe and on the other hand it proves that the resistance fighters in the occupied countries were not anti-German or anti-Italian, but anti-fascist and hence also partisans of a genuine union with Germany and Italy.[3] The most important of these publications, at the least in volume, is Walter Lipgens's oeuvre, including an impressive published documentation.

At first sight, this unanimity is surprising. Lessons drawn from the First World War cannot be applied unaltered to the Second. The former was indeed primarily perceived as the outcome of aggressive nationalism in the European nation-states, and it did engender an anti-nationalist and anti-militarist pacifism, particularly in France. The latter, however, was first of all an ideological conflict and it was moreover much less a European than a worldwide conflict, both in the alliances it opposed and in its consequences. Nor does the mythical and ecumenical idea of 'The Resistance', united in the same battle and inspired by the same ideals, stand up to historical proof. How could the various resistance movements, internally divided and even violently opposed, so easily reach a consensus over the future of the entire continent? What about the main divide that ran across the resistance ranks in all European countries, opposing communists and anti-communists? Methodologically, the constitution of an anthology of excerpts from a corpus without any political, ideological or organisational coherence is highly problematic. Underground publications of whatever sort are a very heterogeneous assortment, and one could fill volumes of contradicting statements on topics as crucial as parliamentary democracy or the Western Allies, to mention only two topics of immediate relevance to the Resistance. Consensus on

---

[2] Urwin, *Western Europe Since 1945. A Political History* (Harlow, 1968 [later edns., 1972, 1981, 1989]). See also Dusan Sidjanski, *L'Avenir Fédéraliste de l'Europe. La Communauté Européenne, des origines au Traité de Maastricht* (Geneva, 1992); Werner Weidenfeld (ed.), *Die Identität Europas. Fragen, Positionen, Perspektiven* (Munich and Vienna, 1987).

[3] See Walter Lipgens, *Europa-Föderationspläne der Widerstandsbewegungen 1940–1945. Eine Dokumentation* (Munich, 1968); Lipgens, *A History of European Integration*, vol. I, *1945–1947* (Oxford, 1982); Lipgens, *Documents on the History of European Integration*, vol. I, *Continental Plans on European Union, 1939–1945* (Florence, 1985). For Italy, see Lucio Levi (ed.), *Altiero Spinelli and Federalism in Europe and in the World* (Milan, 1990); Gaetano Arfe (ed.), *L'idea d'Europa nel movimento di liberazione, 1940–1945* (Rome, 1986).

the future international order of Europe would therefore be most improbable.

On the other hand, if there was one theme on which European resistance movements did agree, it was their hostility to the German occupier. In spite of the lofty efforts of historical exegesis which seek to demonstrate the brotherly nature of the European resistance, resistance fighters and Nazi victims above all shared one common claim for the post-war future of Europe: the merciless punishment of Germany and its accomplices. In the pro-European narrative of the experience of the war, no trace can be found of the disconcerting anti-German hatred that so thoroughly pervades the sources of the time.[4] Documentation attesting to the latter could easily fill the volumes on pro-European positions five times over. To pretend, with the late Walter Lipgens, that 'hardly ever in the non-communist resistance did any underground newspaper or leaflet favour a return to the pre-war system of national states', or that 'One of the basic themes of the resistance, expressed in many documents, was the repudiation of the principle of intellectual totalitarianism, state worship and nationalism', requires a considerable and systematic disregard for the insulting anti-German vocabulary in the sources he quotes, and even the very titles of the major publications, like *France d'Abord, Vrij Nederland, La Libre Belgique* etc.[5] It requires, moreover, the careful omission of the explicitly anti-European discourse of many resistance movements in their reaction against the pro-European discourse of the Nazi New Order, an ideological project rarely mentioned as a conceptual precursor of post-war European integration.[6] To describe the first decades of European integration as the simple feat of economical progress and the furthering of friendship amongst the people of Europe is to omit the central dimension of the construction of Europe at that time, particularly for resistance veterans and former Nazi victims: the German problem.

The historiography of European federalism as the intellectual child of the resistance is based on an accumulation of omissions: the political, ideological and organisational fragmentation of the European resistance which impedes conclusions drawn from a putative unity, the reminiscence of Nazi Europeanism and the rampant anti-German sentiment created by the war, and more. It fosters, moreover, an anachronistic vision of Europe itself. Assimilating the Europe envisaged in some resistance movement tracts to the Europe integrated in the course of the

---

[4] See, for example, the quotes in Annette Wieviorka, *Déportation*, pp. 320–8.
[5] Lipgens, *History of European Integration*, vol. I, pp. 46 and 47.
[6] See, for example, Dominique Veillon, *La Collaboration. Textes et débats* (Paris, 1984), pp. 361–90.

1950s–1980s in the EEC or NATO requires the omission of the central context that dominated these initiatives: the Cold War, and that entire part of Europe that has been rediscovered only after it ended.[7] The apparent consensus over the mythical vision of 'The Resistance' giving birth to 'Europe' cannot be explained through the history of the Second World War, but through what followed it – the redesigning of the recent past in the light of the urgent challenges of the day: in chronological order, the German problem, the Cold War, and European integration as an answer to both. This history of the politics of memory in the international arena demonstrates a high degree of integration of the political activism of Cold War militants, that of veterans and victims of the last war and even of professional historians.

The first two years following the end of the war were a period of transition, both for the resistance movements and for political life in the liberated countries. The resistance movements had ambitious plans for the post-war period, and they saw themselves as the legitimate representatives of a sovereign public opinion until the restoration of procedural democracy through regular elections. The National Resistance Councils in France (the CNR) and the Netherlands (the GAC) did not see themselves as veterans' leagues, but as the heralds of political renewal, invested by their wartime activities with a natural authority. As described in chapters 2 and 3, the international context was a central point of reference during this period. Contemporary observers interpreted the events of 1944 and 1945 as the failure of the mirage of a new European order inspired by the resistance. Most spectacularly, resistance movements had been eliminated by conservative governments with the help of the British in Greece and Belgium, and in Poland the Warsaw uprising had been massacred under the eyes of a temporising Red Army. Less spectacularly, the influence of resistance movements had been effectively contained in Italy and France, and in the Netherlands they even explicitly distanced themselves from what they considered to be the political adventurism of their southern neighbours. Even before the war was over, it was clear to everyone that the New Europe would be dictated by the three victors of the European conflict.

In the margins of this ineluctable course of events, international gatherings of resistance movements were first of all destined to keep up the appearances of the deceased Europe of the Resistance, a Europe of occupied countries, defeated by Nazi Germany, liberated by either one or two of the Big Three and trying to formulate their claims for a contribution to the post-war order by asserting Resistance merits. The

[7] See, for example, the fiercely anti-communist Tadeusz Wyrwa, *L'Idée Européenne dans la résistance à travers la presse clandestine en France et en Pologne, 1939–1945* (Paris, 1987).

most resounding initiative was the international rally organised by the French Conseil National de la Résistance in Paris from 10 to 14 July 1946, uniting delegations from Belgium, Denmark, Greece, Luxembourg, the Netherlands, Norway, Poland, Republican Spain, Czechoslovakia and Yugoslavia.[8] The official splendour of the reception made it clear that this was not a meeting of veterans but a diplomatic gathering at the highest level, deserving the *honneurs d'Etat*: dinner at the Quay d'Orsay, a visit to the Louvre and the memorials to the Paris insurrection, champagne in Versailles park and, as apotheosis, the honorary grandstand at the 14 July military parade. To counterbalance the international prestige and military power of the Big Three, France explicitly posed as the homeland of the European Resistance.[9] The conclusions of the rally did not plead for European integration, nor did they invoke any grand plans drafted during the occupation – they asserted the national claims of the liberated countries: participation in the policy of occupying Germany, reparation payments and representation at the Nuremberg trials. Similar initiatives in Prague, Warsaw, Brussels and The Hague arrived at similar results.[10] 'Resistance' was the language of the small countries facing the Big Three.

Quite distinct from this political retrieval at the highest level were the many spontaneous initiatives that sprang up in these chaotic months. The overwhelming 'association-mania' described in chapters 2 and 3, leading to the creation of resistance sports clubs, cultural clubs or clubs of resistance veteran-electricians, railway personnel or postmen-resisters, inevitably spilled over into the international arena. The Paris-based 'Centre for Exchange and Information Amongst European Resisters' offered reciprocal tourist exchanges between French and foreign resistance veterans and their children, and promoted the circulation of information on the resistance in other countries.[11] More ambitiously, the centre even projected a new 'resistentialist' economic order as an alternative to the monetary and political constraints of post-war Europe. A first experiment organised the exchange of watches produced by French resisters in the Franche-Comté against sugar produced by Czech resisters, at the rate of 20 tons of sugar for 500 watches. Utopian projects like these were favoured by the generalised confusion of an international landscape crowded with all sorts of resistance organisations, in which it was difficult for any organisation to categorise foreign

---

[8] *Programme des journées de conférences européennes de la Résistance* (Paris, 10–14 July 1946), in RIOD, GAC archives, 184, 14B.

[9] Letter, CNR to GAC (27 July 1946), RIOD, GAC archives, 184, 1D.

[10] See correspondence (1945–7) in RIOD, GAC archives, 184, 14B and 14C.

[11] Letter to GAC (9 Sep. 1946), RIOD, GAC archives, 184, 14B.

counterparts; this contrasted strongly with the highly structured inter-national landscape of the subsequent Cold War period.

The Dutch Grote Adviescommissie der Illegaliteit, for example, was bewildered to be contacted, in the course of the summer of 1945 alone, by three different Belgian resistance organisations, each claiming to represent the entire Belgian resistance, in order to form a Benelux federation of resistance organisations.[12] The Southern conservative veterans' league (the GOIWN) simply rejected international co-opera-tion on nationalist grounds, answering one of the Belgian invitations as follows: 'We do not wish for an International Union such as you propose. The resisters resisted for their Fatherland. Love for one's country, that is the core value of the constitution on which our "Com-munity" is based. Since the origins and the aim of the resistance are national, we do not understand the need for a supra-national forma-tion.'[13] The GAC was averse to any form of what it defined as 'veteranism' at a national level, and its objections applied all the more intensely at the international level.[14] Its very hesitant participation in post-war international resistance gatherings was ordered by the minister of foreign affairs, who attached the highest importance to the image of the Netherlands abroad as a nation which had played a prominent role in the resistance.

The most striking characteristic of this first period of ill-coordinated initiatives, abundant enthusiasm and nationalist reticence was precisely that it all took place in a spontaneous confusion, offering changing and surprising alliances. The French and the Dutch were very often antago-nists, allying themselves with Poles, Belgians, Czechs or Norwegians according to the issue of the day. Europe had not yet assumed the ossified contours of its Cold War shape. That is not to say that unlimited pan-European feelings flowed freely across all national boundaries and continental divides. On the contrary, international resistance gatherings were designed to underline national claims, particularly formulated against the former German enemy, whose destiny was now presided over by the Big Three. International contacts would soon lose their fluidity, and, it has to be admitted, their exclusively nationalist character.

From 1947 onwards the Cold War brought change to some of the basic features of the politics of memory in Belgium, France and the Netherlands. The communist ministers left the government in the former two countries, in March and May respectively. In the Netherlands

---

[12] See ibid.

[13] Letters from GIOWN-Eindhoven (15 Oct. 1945) and GOIWN-Groningen (21 Mar. 1946) to GAC, ibid.

[14] Plenary assembly, GAC (27 June 1945), RIOD, GAC archives, 184, 1C.

the Communist Party had never entered a coalition government, as had happened with the Socialist Party before the outbreak of the Second World War (they entered a government of national unity shortly before the invasion), but the traditional state anti-communism became invigorated. Only two years lay between the end of the last war and the start of the new 'war', which was fought in terms of propaganda and domestic politics. Inevitably both camps developed a discourse concerning the memory of the Second World War, which was shaped in order to establish direct continuity between yesterday's struggle and tomorrow's and, particularly, between yesterday's enemy and today's.

Beyond the political battles of the day and the reappropriation of symbols was a sharp confrontation between two general interpretations of the last global conflict. The anti-fascist discourse denounced the aggressive fascism that had caused this war as the ultimate stage of capitalism. The elimination of fascism therefore required the transformation of society and the socio-economic structures that had made the parasitic growth of fascism possible. During the occupation, the anti-fascist interpretation was widespread in left-wing resistance circles, who insistently claimed that their struggle was one of social no less than of national liberation. After the division of Germany, however, this identification became much more specific. On the one hand, capitalist Germany, where the 'fascist trusts' which had 'supported Hitler' were still intact, including IG Farben and Krupp, where the Wehrmacht was renamed the Bundeswehr and rearmed to take up its war against the Soviet Union once more, was the heir of the Third Reich. The Western occupation policy, emphasising German reconstruction, leaving former Nazis in managerial positions in industry and administration because of their expertise and their anti-communist zeal, attained the very opposite of what an anti-fascist policy required. Military revanchists, captains of industry, neo-Nazis, SS veterans' leagues and anti-Semites were left in peace. On the other hand lay the perspective that the German Democratic Republic was the new Germany, truly de-Nazified. The social structures that had allowed Nazism to succeed had been overturned, and the Nazified population re-educated. If there was a risk of German revenge, of militarism, arms race and aggression, this danger could come only from the West, since the transformed East was inspired by a sincere desire for peace. A European alliance with the Federal Republic of Germany was high treason, a betrayal of the anti-fascist struggle.

The anti-communists went one step further, and bluntly assimilated Nazism with communism through the concept of totalitarianism. Yesterday's enemy and today's enemy were fundamentally two faces of the same regime, first brown totalitarianism and next red totalitarianism. The struggle for the Free World or Christianity continued, without any real change. In this view, the resistance struggle had ultimately been a fight for civil liberties and human rights against a regime of terror. From the 1950s onwards, a 'totalitarianism school' developed, producing more or less sophisticated academic models to compare Nazism and communism, the most influential of which came from Hannah Arendt.[15] The 'totalitarian' state strove for total control of all spheres of public life – education, culture, press, social organisations etc. – through propaganda, and through generalised terror and persecution. In this perspective, the integration of Western Europe and the Atlantic alliance, both of which included Western Germany as an indispensable ally, was an essential military and economic requirement for the durable success of the anti-totalitarian struggle which started against Hitler and continued against Stalin.[16] The supreme symbol of totalitarianism, the central cog in the wheels of the totalitarian state, was the concentration camp. In this way, the memory of Nazi persecution became the battle horse of anti-communism.

The continuity was not only one of discourse. The existence of a Gulag system initiated a diplomatic conflict that resulted from the administration of the DPs left behind on German territory after the defeat of the Third Reich, and the repatriation of Western citizens left behind in the Soviet occupation zone. In strict application of the Yalta agreements the Allies mutually exchanged displaced citizens. Anti-communist activists spread rumours from the very first weeks of the repatriation that Western survivors of Nazi camps were transferred directly to Soviet camps. Repatriation authorities soon proved that these allegations were false. More importantly, for the sake of good understanding with their Soviet partner, Soviet DPs were forcibly repatriated to the Soviet Union by Americans, British and French alike, in spite of their protests, acts of insurgency and collective suicides. Only in 1947 did forced repatriations cease and Soviet DPs gain recognition as political refugees. The ensuing conflict with the Soviet authorities led in 1949 to the first official pronouncement by the US Department of State of the syllogism: Gulag = Concentration Camp => Communism =

---

[15] Hannah Arendt, *The Origins of Totalitarianism* (New York, 1951). For the origins of the concept, see Abbott Gleason, *Totalitarianism. The Inner History of the Cold War* (New York and Oxford, 1995); Walter Schlangen, *Die Totalitarismus-Theorie. Entwicklung und Probleme* (Stuttgart, 1976).

[16] See, for example, the first major textbooks pleading for European integration: R. G. Hawtrey, *Western European Union. Implications for the United Kingdom*, Royal Institute of International Affairs (London, 1949), and Maurice Allais, *L'Europe Unie, route de la prospérité (Grand Prix de la Communauté Atlantique)* (Paris, 1960).

Nazism.[17] Anti-communists could henceforward use the concentration camp as a metaphor for the entire Soviet bloc. After a visit behind the 'Iron Curtain', one of the most active anti-communist propagandists, Hubert Halin (see below, pp. 282–4), reported: 'The only danger that exists in Germany is the danger of totalitarianism, and the wind of totalitarianism blows from the East and not from elsewhere. The barbed wire near Helmstedt, at the demarcation line, surrounds a gigantic concentration camp, where entire nations are imprisoned, who yearn to live in freedom.'[18]

In this confrontation, Nazi camp survivors were mobilised as 'experts'. Their life experience in the camps during the Second World War charged them with the moral duty to prevent or resist its repetition in the Soviet Union. At the end of the 1940s, the appeal was launched to create committees of investigation to prove the existence of concentration camps in the Soviet Union. The issue was first raised by the US government in the United Nations in 1949. An American Federation of Former Totalitarianism Prisoners and substantial US funding soon created followers in France, drawing on the appeal of David Rousset,[19] in the Netherlands, animated by the anti-communist businessman Van Staal,[20] and in Belgium.

In November 1949 David Rousset, whose *L'Univers Concentration-naire* and *Les Jours de notre mort* were amongst the most successful and influential accounts of life in Nazi camps, launched an appeal addressed to former 'deportees' and their organisations to constitute a 'Commission of Investigation Against the Concentration System' in the Soviet Union. In 1950 Rousset's commission became an international commission, based in Brussels. In France, Rousset was attacked as a slanderer and a liar by communist KZ survivors, wearing their striped prison suits as they distributed 200,000 anti-Rousset pamphlets. The journal of the FNDIRP denounced Rousset as an *agent provocateur* and a prime anti-communist.[21] The investigation in the Soviet Union never took place, since the commission could not obtain permission to enter the Soviet territory. An 'International Court' organised by the commission in May 1951 'condemned' the Soviet Union on the basis of much publicised

---

[17] *Department of State Bulletin* (27 Feb. 1949), quoted by Cathal J. Nolan, 'Americans in the Gulag. Detention of US Citizens by Russia and the Onset of the Cold War 1944–1949', *Journal of Contemporary History* 25 (1990), pp. 523–45.

[18] *La Voix Internationale de la Résistance* (Jan.–Feb. 1960).

[19] Emile Copfermann, *David Rousset. Une vie dans le siècle* (Paris, 1991), pp. 113–42.

[20] See complete records in ACPM, file 355.358:343.819.5 (1954–65), *concentratie kampen*.

[21] *Le Patriote Résistant* 88 and 89 (12 and 31 Dec. 1949).

documentary evidence and eyewitness accounts. To counter the accusations that the commission was a purely anti-Soviet venture, later investigations tackled Greece, China, Tunisia and even, in 1957, Algeria. In 1959 the commission ceased all its activities due to a lack of funding. Van Staal, the dynamic president of the Dutch Battle Committee Against the Concentration Regime declared in October 1959 that its liquidation had become inevitable, 'now that the political situation has changed since Khrushchev's visit to Washington and the US stopped its subsidies'.[22]

The impact on the associations of survivors of the camps was devastating. As described in the previous chapter, the Belgian confederation (CNPPA/NCPGR) barely survived a schism and succumbed a year later. The communists were excluded from the Dutch organisation ExPoGe in 1949 and had to take refuge in an anti-fascist front organisation, United Resistance 1940–1945. Though the anti-Soviet campaign was not the direct cause of their exclusion, it constituted an enduring propaganda theme in the polemics between United Resistance and ExPoGe. The most important effect was the defection by non-communist members of the FNDIRP, headed by Riquet, to join the rival nationalist FNDIR under the flag of the UNADIF. Exclusive associations of resister-survivors, fiercely nationalist and anti-communist, took the fore in this campaign, to the detriment of inclusive organisations which were open to Jewish survivors but stigmatised for their communist adherence. In all three countries, the Cold War divide supplanted the earlier division between inclusive anti-fascist and exclusive patriotic organisations of Nazi victims.

This anti-communist offensive provoked an obvious communist reply, aimed at proving that the concentration camp, which was used as a central charge against communism, was historically nonsense. On the contrary, the Nazi camps had been the destination of millions of anti-fascist militants all over Europe, and as such they needed to be commemorated as examples of what anti-communism leads to and of what a re-militarised Germany that had not been purged of twelve years of Nazification would be capable of doing. To centralise this campaign the Warsaw-based Fédération Internationale des Anciens Prisonniers Politiques (FIAPP) was transformed into the Fédération Internationale des Résistants (FIR), open not only to resisters, but also to all members

---

[22] Van Staal in *Aantreden* (the journal of ExPoGe) 36 (Nov. 1959). A clipping of this article, forwarded by Verenigd Verzet 1940–1945, transited through the Vienna office of the FIR to the FNDIRP in Paris, with the observation: 'Il est intéressant de constater que pour certains la détente ne paye pas.' See *dossier activités FIR, 1951–1979* in SerDoc FNDIRP.

of the previous organisation, victims of fascism, ergo anti-fascists, ergo resisters. Its headquarters were moved from Warsaw to Vienna, in the eyes of its detractors a manoeuvre to mask Moscow's hold on the organisation, even if the address was situated in the Soviet zone of the city.

The FIR launched a vast campaign 'to expose the immense danger threatening all patriots whose country is threatened by German militarism, . . . to unmask the annexationist and militarist policy of the Adenauer regime and its methods of fascist terror, and to annihilate the arguments put forward by the partisans of the "European Army"'. As a means to this end, the organisation appealed to its national branches 'to undertake the conversion into sites of remembrance, of reminders of Nazi barbarity and the heroic sacrifices of the Resistance, of the concentration camps, prisons, execution sites, battlefields of the Resistance etc.; to set up memorials on these sites and to organise regular pilgrimages, commemorative demonstrations, calling upon the population to participate *en masse*'.[23] Its central office was well organised, and the organisation had a tight network of national activists. The programme quoted above was implemented systematically, particularly after the second congress of the FIR in 1954, through the creation of International Camp Committees, the activities of national *amicales* of camps dominated by communist militants and through the conversion into sites of remembrance of former concentration camps in the GDR – Buchenwald, Sachsenhausen, Ravensbrück – and in Poland – Auschwitz. The tenth anniversary of the liberation of the camps was the first target for this campaign.[24] The events of 1956 – the twentieth congress of the Soviet Communist Party in Moscow and the repression of the October Spring in Poland and Hungary – stirred the communist management of the FIR to redouble its efforts. To respond to anti-communist attacks and the massive defections in their own ranks, they chose the ideological and commemorative offensive as their best defence.

The international committees affiliated to the FIR were the committees of Auschwitz, Buchenwald, Dachau, Mauthausen, Ravensbrück and Sachsenhausen. The Buchenwald committee was the most prestigious amongst them, thanks to the activities of the international communist committee in the camp during the war, of which it claimed to be the direct descendant. The committee cultivated the legend of the

[23] *Réunion du bureau de la FIR* (Berlin, 15–17 Sep. 1953), in *dossier FIR*, SerDoc FNDIRP.

[24] Letter, FIR secretary to national associations (Vienna, 24 Sep. 1954); see also *FIR. Compte rendu de la réunion du bureau* (Rome, 26–28 Oct. 1956): both ibid.

liberation of the camp by the committee of inmates, partially to minimise the role of the American troops who in fact liberated it. The committee published a whole series of brochures and commemorative books, and could count on the total support of the East German government.[25] Buchenwald, near Weimar, was also the first focal point of the FIR campaign.

The commemoration of the tenth anniversary of the camp's liberation was officially celebrated in the presence of delegates from the East German party with the announcement of the inauguration of a monument in 1958. Foreign delegations were invited at the expense of the GDR government,[26] and funds for the monument were collected entirely in East Germany.[27] The inauguration of the memorial by Walter Ulbricht, secretary of the central committee of the East German Communist Party, was seen as provocation by the non-communist members of the national delegations of Buchenwald committees from Western Europe. They reported that Ulbricht had dedicated five minutes to the memory of the war dead in Buchenwald and half an hour to a diatribe against NATO and the Federal Republic.[28] In 1960, at the fifteenth anniversary of the liberation of the camp, Erich Honecker stressed the 'anti-fascist' meaning of the memorial: 'We can now announce to our foreign friends that the oath of Buchenwald has been realised in the German Democratic Republic. Fascism has been eradicated root and branch by us here, so that it will never raise its head again in the GDR, the first Nation of Peace.'[29] The central message propagated by the camp site exhibition was subsequently detailed by the Statut der Nationalen Mahn- und Gedenkstätten of 28 August 1961, which also served as a guideline for the memorials in Ravensbrück and Sachsenhausen. The narrative had to express the role of the German working class in the combat against fascism, the central role of the Communist Party in organising the Resistance, the resurrection of

[25] See Hermann Langbein, 'Internationale Organisationen der Überlebenden der nationalsozialistischen Konzentrationslager ab 1954 bis heute – vor allem Auschwitz betreffend', unpublished paper, presented at conference sponsored by the 'Fondation Auschwitz', Brussels, 23–27 Nov. 1992.

[26] *Hier cauchemar, aujourd'hui espoir. Bulletin intérieur d'information et de liaison de l'amicale des déportés politiques de Mauthausen* (Paris) 38 (June 1954).

[27] *Compte rendu du bureau de la FIR* (Rome, 26–28 Oct. 1956); *Rapport sur l'activité du Commissariat Belge; dossier FIR*, SerDoc FNDIRP.

[28] Report, secret service (DEU/ME) concerning the monument at Auschwitz to prime minister (6 Mar. 1962), ACPM, Con.

[29] Quoted in Peter Sonnet, 'Gedenkstätten für Opfer des Nationalsozialismus in der DDR', in Ulrike Puvogel (ed.), *Gedenkstätten für Opfer des Nationalsozialismus. Eine Dokumentation*, Schriftenreihe der Bundeszentrale für politische Bildung 245 (Bonn, 1987), p. 798.

fascism and militarism in the Federal Republic, and the historical role of the GDR.[30]

The FIR control of national *amicales* was not always guaranteed. In France, most *amicales* were affiliated to the FNDIRP and housed in the same building, but they were not subordinated to the political line of the FIR in the same way as the FNDIRP itself. The *amicales* of Buchenwald and Mauthausen were well integrated into the FNDIRP, and their international committees into the FIR. Communist members most often dominated national *amicales* of Ravensbrück women's camp. Amongst the Belgian *amicales*, only Buchenwald, Dachau and Neuengamme belonged to the FIR.[31] The Western Sachsenhausen committees were a notable exception in escaping communist control.

The International Auschwitz Committee was founded in Vienna in May 1954, on the initiative of the FIR.[32] Hermann Langbein, a member of the Austrian Communist Party, was appointed to head the committee as secretary-general. The committee immediately undertook the preparation of the tenth anniversary of the camp's liberation, gathering charges and depositions against the Nazis responsible for the crimes that took place in Auschwitz. The Conference on Jewish Material Claims Against Germany had sued IG Farben on behalf of the victims of genocide; the International Auschwitz Committee followed its lead and sued IG Farben on behalf of the non-Jewish victims. The committee also sought to involve national *amicales* of all European countries in its activities. When Langbein left the party in 1956, protesting against the repression of the Hungarian uprising, the communists in the committee tried to oust him from its board. In June 1960, after three years of conflict, they succeeded in obtaining the majority at a general assembly

---

[30] In addition to Sonnet, 'Gedenkstätten', see also Eve Rosenhaft, 'The Uses of Remembrance. The Legacy of the Communist Resistance in the German Democratic Republic', in Francis R. Nicosia and Lawrence D. Stokes (eds.), *Germans Against Nazism. Nonconformity, Opposition and Resistance in the Third Reich* (New York and Oxford, 1990), pp. 369–88; Claudia Koonz, 'Between Memory and Oblivion. Concentration Camps in German Memory', in John R. Gillis (ed.), *Commemorations. The Politics of National Identity* (Princeton, 1994), pp. 258–80; *Zur Neuorientierung der Gedenkstätte Buchenwald. Die Empfehlungen der vom Minister für Wissenschaften und Kunst des Landes Thüringen berufenen Historikerkommission* (Weimar-Buchenwald, 1992); Monika Zorn (ed.), *Hitlers zweimal getötete Opfer. Westdeutsche Endlösung des Antifaschismus auf dem Gebiet der DDR*, Unerwünschte Bücher zum Faschismus 6 (Freiburg, 1994); and Sarah Farmer, 'Symbols That Face Two Ways. Commemorating the Victims of Nazism and Stalinism at Buchenwald and Sachsenhausen', *Representations* 49 (1995), pp. 97–119.

[31] *La Voix Internationale de la Résistance* 32 (Oct. 1960).

[32] Hermann Langbein, 'Entschädigung für KZ-Häftlinge? Ein Erfahrungsbericht', in Ludolf Herbst and Constantin Goschler (eds.), *Wiedergutmachung in der Bundesrepublik Deutschland. Sondernummer Schriftenreihe der Vierteljahrshefte für Zeitgeschichte* (Munich, 1989), pp. 327–40, and Langbein, 'Internationale Organisationen'.

held in Warsaw, replacing the existing bureau with a directorate dominated by communists. Langbein's place was taken by a Polish secretary-
general.[33] The headquarters were moved from Vienna to Warsaw.
Financially, the Committee had depended from its creation on the
Zwiazek Bojownikov Wolnosc i Demokracje, the Polish organisation of
Nazi victims, which was tightly supervised by the Polish government.[34]
Like its East German counterparts, the International Auschwitz Committee undertook the construction of an international monument, this
time funded through an international subscription. Most European
governments – the Belgian and French in particular – and even the
People's Republic of China contributed. (For the Dutch contribution,
see below, pp. 287–9.) Much as the memorials on the camp sites in the
GDR had to prove the political virginity of the New Germany, the
Auschwitz memorial, inaugurated in April 1967, was designed as a
monument to the international anti-fascist and national Polish martyrdom. The genocide of the Jews, responsible for the great majority of
casualties on the site of Auschwitz, was not explicitly represented. The
passive attitude of the committee in the face of the anti-Semitic incidents in Poland during the Six Days' War two months later, and the
anti-Semitic purge of the Polish party apparatus one year later, created
an irreversible rupture with most Western European *amicales* and the
departure of its French president Robert Waits.[35]

Control *in situ* was at least guaranteed for camps in the GDR
and Poland, but this was not the case for camp sites in the FRG and
Austria. Two of these had a central symbolic value: Dachau and
Mauthausen. In Mauthausen, near Vienna, the Austrian government
imposed its conditions on the commemorations by the International
Committee.[36] Before the commemoration of the tenth anniversary of
the liberation of the camp, the Austrian minister for the interior Helmer
charged the international committee not to turn the celebration into a
political demonstration, as had happened during three pilgrimages in
the course of 1954.[37] The collaboration between the international
committee and the Austrian government over the organisation of the
museum and the memorial similarly asserted the apolitical character of
the commemoration.

The camp barracks in Dachau, near Munich, were used until the

---

[33] Luc Sommerhausen in *La Voix Internationale de la Résistance* 33–4 (Nov.–Dec. 1960).
[34] On this organisation, see Lucy Dawidowicz, *The Holocaust and the Historians* (Cambridge, MA, 1981).
[35] Langbein, 'Internationale Organisationen'; *La Voix Internationale de la Résistance* (July
1968).
[36] *Hier cauchemar, aujourd'hui espoir* 38 (June 1954).
[37] *Hier cauchemar, aujourd'hui espoir* 39 (Nov. 1954).

early 1950s as a refugee camp for displaced persons.[38] The outward
appearance of the site had been wholly transformed: the barracks were
divided into individual homes with gardens, there were small shops, a
cinema, a school, churches. An international committee of former
prisoners of the Nazi period was founded on the tenth anniversary of the
liberation of the camp, campaigning to preserve the remains of the
former KZ and build a monument and a museum, recalling the former
function of the site. Dachau town council had indeed decided in the
same year to destroy the crematorium of the former KZ, to efface 'this
shame upon our region'.[39] The international committee could *in ex-
tremis* preserve the construction. The international memorial was inaugurated as part of the ceremony of the twentieth anniversary of the
camp's liberation in 1965, and completed in 1968. During the ten years
that passed between the foundation of the International Committee and
the inauguration of the monument, Dachau was the central stake in a
commemorative battle between communists and anti-communists.[40]
National committees affiliated to the FIR were matched by anti-
communist committees, and both competed to control the site. In the
Netherlands, for example, a communist Dachau committee was created
in July 1960, following the lead of the very active Auschwitz committee
created a few years earlier.[41] Alerted by his secret services, Prime
Minister Drees urged non-communist former Dachau inmates to gather
in an anti-communist Dachau committee in 1961, actively supported by
the cabinet and sponsored by major Dutch private companies. A commemorative meeting of Bavarian youth and survivors of the camp,
organised in June 1961, courted disaster. Both Dutch committees were
involved in a scuffle to assert their representativeness, whilst the
Bavarian *Lagergemeinschaft* staged a political demonstration along the
lines set out by the FIR, much to the resentment of anti-communist
delegates. Non-communist survivors who had previously belonged to
the international committee, such as the Belgians Albert Guérin and
Arthur Haulot or the French Dr Marsault, now pulled out of the FIR-
related committee and set up a new anti-communist international

---

[38] Harold Marcuse, 'Das ehemalige Konzentrationslager Dachau. Der mühevolle Weg zur
Gedenkstätte 1945–1968', *Dachauer Hefte* 6 (1990), pp. 182–205.

[39] Barbara Distel, 'Orte der Erinnerung an die Opfer im Lande der Täter – Gedanken zur
Arbeit an der Gedenkstätte des ehemaligen Konzentrationslagers Dachau', unpub-
lished paper, presented at conference sponsored by the 'Fondation Auschwitz',
Brussels, 23–27 Nov. 1992.

[40] Complete records of meetings 2 (2 Mar. 1962) to 13 (7 Apr. 1965) plus abundant
correspondence in ACPM, Con.

[41] Letter, Boulaert to prime minister (1 Nov. 1960); *Memorandum Fock voor PM* (3 Nov.
1960); *Nota voor Minister-President* (15 Feb. 1962); *Financieel rapport* (31 July 1961): all
in ACPM, Con.

committee. It organised all its commemorations separately with the closest support of the Bavarian government, which granted it a subsidy of 100,000 DM.[42]

The transformation of the former concentration camp into a site of anti-communist remembrance included the construction of three temples of religious worship: a Catholic church in 1961, baptised 'The Church of the Sorrows of Christ', followed a few years later by the construction of a Protestant church and a synagogue.[43] The construction of the Protestant church – Bavaria is a Catholic state – had been the initiative of the Dutch committee, but it was quickly usurped by the German Protestants who, much to the resentment of the Dutch, baptised it 'The Church of the Sins of Christ'.[44] In Bergen-Belsen, another symbol of Nazi atrocities – because it was the first concentration camp to be liberated by the Western Allies through which their domestic opinion discovered the images of horror – the first stone of the Catholic church, 'The Church of the Precious Blood', was laid on 17 June 1960, the 'Day of German Unity', in a double provocation to the communist survivors of the camp.[45]

The link that the FIR wanted to establish between the memory of the war and international politics was most explicit. The editorials in *Résistance Unie* proposed a hard-line political and ideological programme. In 1955, the year of the tenth anniversary of the liberation of the camps – but also the year of the Federal Republic's entry into NATO – FIR's secretary-general, André Leroy, wrote:

This is a strange way to honour the memory of all those who died to defend the cause of liberty and national independence against the Hitlerian invader. It did not take even ten years to rehabilitate and rearm the most criminal enemy, under whose cruel yoke our people bent. If the millions of dead – tortured, gassed, executed, hanged by Nazism – could speak up, their verdict would be terrible for those who are themselves today accomplices of their sadistic murderers . . . Would Hitler's generals hesitate to use the arms of massive destruction put at their disposal, the very same individuals who did not hesitate a single instant to gas millions of human beings in Auschwitz?[46]

One year later, condemning the Common Coal and Steel Market, he denounced the very idea of Europe in the name of the memory of the war: 'Behind the idea of Europe looms the shadow of Nazism, of militarism and pan-Germanism.'[47]

[42] *La Voix Internationale de la Résistance* (Aug.–Sep. 1960).
[43] Ibid.
[44] Letter, C. C. Steensma to Dutch Dachau Committee (1 Mar. 1964), ACPM, Con.
[45] *La Voix Internationale de la Résistance* (Mar. 1960).
[46] *Résistance Unie* (Mar.–Apr. 1955).
[47] *Résistance Unie* (Jan. 1956).

At the end of the 1950s, the FIR coupled its commemorative activism with a historiographical venture: the *Cahiers Internationaux de la Résistance*. Six issues appeared between 1959 and 1961, accompanied by international historical conferences.[48] The *Cahiers* offer a varied sample of the 'anti-fascist' school, with particular attention to the teaching of the history of the Resistance. On the one hand, contributions by East European historians elaborated a dogmatic historiographical programme, with titles such as 'The Circle of Friends of Himmler. The Subordination of the Nazi Party and the Fascist State Apparatus to the German Financial Oligarchy' or 'Prisoners of the Concentration Camps. Work-Slaves for the German Capitalist Monopoly'.[49] On the other hand, the *Cahiers* also offered some justified criticism of the dominating historiographical production of the time, reducing the resistance to 'some sort of counterespionage service'.[50] The concept of a social and ideological 'civil war', resurfacing in contemporary Italian historiography, was already explored in the journal. It is interesting to observe in this context that these pro-communist historians do not claim the monopoly of the resistance merit for the communist parties, but on the contrary defend the vision of a massive and popular resistance. In this context, one finds a very different 'Europeanism' than that defended by the anti-communists. Through particular attention to the role of foreigners in the resistance movements of different countries, the international character of the resistance is documented, a universal anti-fascism, a combat without frontiers in the name of a selfless ideological conviction.

The creation of the FIR stirred two reactions. The first initiative was French. When the anti-communists, headed by Michel Riquet, left the FNDIRP to join the FNDIR under the banner of the UNADIF, conflicts over the FIR's predecessor FIAPP had been one of the sources of discord. With the Fédération Internationale Libre des Déportés et Internés de la Résistance (FILDIR), the UNADIF wanted to provide a counterweight to the international action of its rival. The second initiative, or rather series of initiatives, was Belgian. Under the aegis of the national Comité d'Action de la Résistance, Hubert Halin, a pro-Atlantic propagandist, developed political activity through a network of half a dozen organisations uniting anti-communist personalities, former resisters or KZ inmates.

FILDIR started its activities in 1952, animated by UNADIF

---

[48] *Cahiers Internationaux de la Résistance* 1 (Nov. 1959), 2 (Mar. 1960), 3 (July 1960), 4 (Nov. 1960), 5 (Mar. 1961), 6 (July 1961).

[49] *Cahiers Internationaux de la Résistance* 1 (Nov. 1959), pp. 31–6, and 4 (Nov. 1960).

[50] *Cahiers Internationaux de la Résistance* 3 (July 1960).

executives.[51] The climate of the day favoured its creation: in many
Western European countries young schismatic anti-communist organisations, formerly affiliated to FIAPP through the inclusive national
organisation, were looking for foreign allies. FILDIR emulated the
model it wanted to combat, the FIR: a federation of national organisations with annual congresses, where duly mandated delegations voted
on the activities of the international bureau. The central office was
established in Paris, hosted by Les Amis de la Liberté, an anti-communist organisation which provided most of the finance for the federation
in the first years of its existence.[52] As its name indicated, FILDIR
defended 'the Free West'. In the words of its president during the
founding congress in Rome, this implied that 'the world is engaged in a
battle that is above all an ideological conflict. Two concepts of life clash
– one that sees man as the exclusive and blind servant of a statist society,
the other that pretends to see man as the reasonable animal of Christian
tradition.'[53] The discourse was followed by a papal benediction for all
participants.

The ambition of FILDIR was to be a major international organisation. Its 'adviser' status at the United Nations assembly and the Council
of Europe gave it some much publicised prestige, even if this was of little
use for its activities. The columns of its periodical, *Déportation et Liberté*,
were filled with declarations of human rights, ceremonial speeches at the
United Nations and the Council, which make it barely readable. The
discourse on human rights as the main accomplishment of the international resistance movement was integrated into a pro-European discourse: only the integration of 'Free Europe' could defend the influence
of the values of the Old Continent. In 1953, for example, Paul-Henri
Spaak gave a symbolic speech entitled: 'From the Europe of Dachau to
the Europe of Strasbourg'.[54]

From 1953 onwards, 'the battle for a unified Germany, for German–
French friendship and the admission of Germany to the community of
free nations' became the central objective of FILDIR.[55] During the
second half of the 1950s, the organisation was involved in negotiations
with the Federal Republic government, and then with the Bundestag, on
reparation payments to victims of Nazism. *Wiedergutmachung* was a
legacy transferred by the Western Allies to the FRG at the new state's
founding moment. In 1952 and 1956 two major agreements on

---

[51] *Déportation et Liberté. Bulletin Trimestriel de la Fédération Internationale Libre des Déportés et Internés de la Résistance* 1 (Jan. 1953).
[52] *Déportation et Liberté* 2 (Apr.–June 1953) and 10–11 (Apr.–Sep. 1956).
[53] *Déportation et Liberté* 1 (Jan. 1953).
[54] *Déportation et Liberté* 2 (Apr.–June 1953).   [55] Ibid.

reparation payments to the victims of the genocide had been concluded with the State of Israel.[56] The rejection of the European Defence Community in the neighbouring countries by a public opinion that remained hostile to the former German enemy and the desire to establish good relationships with their governments – with whom the Federal Republic government was then negotiating the agreements that led to the Treaty of Rome – motivated West Germany to extend this *Wiedergutmachung* to Nazi victims who were citizens of these countries. On behalf of the FRG, this was a voluntary expiatory sacrifice, a gesture demonstrating German good-will. Neither international law, German law nor even the London agreements stipulated such an obligation. The West German government therefore intended to organise this *Wiedergutmachung* on its own conditions.

These conditions were threefold. First, the agreements should exclude the communists, that is, both the citizens of communist countries, for whom, according to Bonn, the Democratic Republic had to take its share of responsibility, and the German and Western communists. Secondly, resistance fighters were not seen as Nazi victims. West German law recognised as such only individuals who had been persecuted for their race, religion or opinion and not for the consciously assumed risks of resisting the occupation. Moreover, the claim of resistance fighters to be assimilated with soldiers of the regular army, both during and after the war, invalidated all legal claims for reparation payments, since they should in consequence, and despite the particular conditions of their detention, be considered PoWs for whom international law never foresaw reparation. German public opinion resented indemnification for 'terrorists' responsible for what it considered the cowardly murders of German soldiers outside regular combat. The third condition concerned the way reparation payments should be made: no financial transfers to national governments, only direct indemnification to individual victims. National governments had indeed announced their intention to use German payments to recover the sums paid out by them to victims since the liberation. In that case, the West German government's efforts would simply have provided a net financial benefit for the governments in question, without any benefit for the victims, nor, consequently, for the image of the Federal Republic.

In this last perspective, FILDIR was a perfect negotiating partner.[57] As a Western European federation, claiming to represent all Nazi

---

[56] See Herbst and Goschler, *Wiedergutmachung*.

[57] See systematic reporting in *Déportation et Liberté* and Roland Teyssandier's *Rapport moral et d'activité* (Montpellier, 18–21 May 1962), in *dossier organisations françaises*, SerDoc FNDIRP.

victims and presenting itself as a major international organisation, it
enabled the German government to bypass the national governments.
The exclusion of the communists fitted FILDIR well, and the West
German government seemed ready to negotiate over the exclusion of
resistance fighters, which was unacceptable for FILDIR. FILDIR
indeed consisted mainly of organisations of resistance victims who had
defended the opposite policy at the national level: reparation payments
to resistance fighters excluding all others. FILDIR launched the idea of
an independent international foundation distributing funds according to
the individual needs of the victims, and seeking out victims who would
have been omitted by their national legislation. Here was a noble and
genuinely European idea, albeit much too ambitious for an organisation
whose representativeness was highly problematic. FILDIR was indeed
composed of national anti-communist organisations, the result of the
Cold War conflicts of the late 1940s, an organisational base that proved
insecure in the second half of the 1950s. Its Belgian component was an
anti-communist secession from the unitary Confédération Nationale,
which never succeeded in really establishing itself. From 1955 onwards,
the organisation was put into abeyance and in June 1957 most secessio-
nists returned to the Confédération. This poor Belgian representation
damaged the prestige and international representativeness of FILDIR.[58]
Much more serious was the subsequent disavowal by the French
organisation UNADIF, of which FILDIR was in reality only the international branch. In the course of the years 1958-9, when the negotiations on the German reparation payments entered a decisive stage, the
French government, which had always disliked the idea of an independent international foundation beyond its control, intervened with the
executives of UNADIF to halt the plans of FILDIR and continue the
negotiations on a bilateral French–German basis in order to obtain
the distribution of the German payments through the Ministry of
Veterans and War Victims.[59] Suddenly deserted by UNADIF, the
French president of FILDIR then seceded from UNADIF, together
with a few departmental associations in the north of France, financed
from the FILDIR budget, to retain a French presence at the international federation.[60] UNADIF itself defected to the initiatives of the
Belgian Halin, who was much more inclined to promote governmental
bargaining.

Excluded from the negotiations on the *Wiedergutmachung*, FILDIR
soon collapsed. The organisation and financing of the federation passed

[58] *Déportation et Liberté* 17–18 (Jan.–Mar. 1958).
[59] See *Déportation et Liberté* 20 (Oct.–Dec. 1958), and 21–2 (Jan.–Mar. 1959).
[60] *Déportation et Liberté* 24–5 (Oct.–Mar. 1960); *Le Déporté* 138–9 (Jan.–Feb. 1960).

into the hands of the German association, which discovered irregular
withdrawals from the federation's bank account by the French secretary
and a stock of 600 kilos of undistributed journals.[61] Thanks to substantial financial support from NATO, the Germans now tried to make a
new start, including associating two Israeli associations to FILDIR. A
congress in Israel in 1962 or 1963 should have signalled the rebirth of
FILDIR. After the Israeli refusal, in the wake of the Eichmann trial, to
welcome the German delegation, who carried the entire organisation
and occupied the presidency of the new FILDIR, the latter pulled out
and FILDIR ceased to exist.

The second centre of anti-communist activity was constituted around
the personality of Hubert Halin. During the occupation Halin, former
leader of the Belgian Socialist Party youth branch, had been involved in
Groupe G, a network of mostly white-collar specialists in sabotage.
After the war, he became frenetically active as a professional resistance
activist and secret services agent, and spent a substantial part of his time
in the cabinet staff of the prime minister or the minister of justice.[62]
Halin excelled on the international scene as an inexhaustible and
articulate anti-communist militant, with an exuberant organising
energy. By his own efforts he filled the columns of *La Voix Internationale
de la Résistance*, a periodical of which he was at once founder, editor and
the only journalist until his death in March 1974, which also brought
the journal to an end. He was similarly the central pivot of the half-
dozen organisations he created between 1953 and 1961. Halin used the
same recipe for each of his ventures: rather than complicate matters
with federations of national organisations, with mandated delegates and
democratic procedures, the paralysing effects of which had been illustrated by the misadventures of FILDIR, Halin brought together a few
individuals with shared opinions, former resistance fighters or victims of
persecution, whom he would regularly invite for gatherings where
declarations, carefully prepared beforehand, were accepted by acclama-
tion without any discussion or vote. Halin's two main lines of action
were the UIRD – Union Internationale de la Résistance et de la
Déportation (and not 'des résistants et des déportés') – founded in
Turin in 1961, with its successive precursors since 1953, the Comité
d'Action Interallié de la Résistance, the Commission Internationale de
Liaison et de Coordination de la Résistance and the Comité Technique
International pour les Réparations Allemandes, all outwardly politically
neutral and serving as a cover for dealings on the *Wiedergutmachung* with
the West German government and the Bundestag; and the Union de la

---

[61] See *Déportation et Liberté* 30 (Apr.–June 1962).
[62] See Lagrou, 'Welk vaderland voor de vaderlandslievende verenigingen?'

Résistance pour une Europe Unie (URPE), a platform of open political proselytism. The separation between these phantom organisations was purely formal: they consisted of the same individuals, and the gatherings, called 'European Conference' or 'Grand Congress', were most often combined: the resolutions of the UIRD were read before the coffee break and those of the URPE afterwards.

The diverse propaganda activities led, gathered or supported by Halin can be summarised as a campaign on three different levels. The first level is anti-FIR. *La Voix Internationale de la Résistance* was conceived as a systematic response to *Résistance Unie*. Every single issue answers the articles of the previous issue of the journal of the FIR, challenges the accusations, denounces the manoeuvres of 'Moscow' behind every single initiative of the FIR or the national organisations affiliated to it. On the second level, in the polemic with the FIR and *Résistance Unie*, one theme monopolises almost all the attention: the 'question of the two Germanies'. Halin and his court of unions, commissions and committees were regular guests of the Federal Republic government for conferences with gala dinners or boat trips on the Rhine, offered by Adenauer or other heavyweight political personalities. Every one of these 'Congresses', 'International Encounters' and 'Study Tours' led to a series of articles in *La Voix Internationale de la Résistance* offering an apologia for the Federal Republic and proving that the Democratic Republic was the direct inheritor of the Third Reich. The accusations of the FIR that Halin's activities were financed by the Aussenamt and Presseamt in Bonn are probably not so far-fetched.[63] As a confidant of Bonn, and disposing of a highly flexible network of organisations, Halin naturally played a role in the dealings over the *Wiedergutmachung*, once the idea of the international foundation had been dropped and FILDIR dismissed.[64] In the course of 1959, during gatherings in Munich, The Hague and Bonn, Halin borrowed the name of three of his organisations to serve as a cover for the bilateral agreements that were *de facto* simultaneously concluded with the governments of eleven Western European countries. In return, Halin boasted that he had personally obtained the inclusion of resistance fighters in reparation payments to the victims of Nazi persecution.

The pro-European propaganda, the third level of Halin's campaign,

---

[63] Clipping, 'Aus der Praxis der URPE-Funktionäre', *Die Tat*, n.d., *dossier organisations internationales*, SerDoc FNDIRP.

[64] Joint edition, *La Voix Internationale de la Résistance* and *Risorgimento, periodico della resistenza* (Turin, 6–8 July 1961); Roland Teyssandier's *Rapport moral et d'activité* (Montpellier, 18–21 May 1962) in *dossier organisations françaises*, and *Union der Widerstandskämpfer für ein vereinigtes Europa, Deutsche Sektion* (The Hague, 1 Sep. 1959), in *dossier organisations internationales*: both in SerDoc FNDIRP.

was only an extension of his endeavours towards reconciliation with Germany. According to his funeral oration Halin had 'the grand design of a united Europe, a Europe wholly enlightened by a fraternal encounter with the Germany of the great philosophers and genius composers, a Germany that had finally found its way, in which he trusted, in which he believed'.[65] His Union de la Résistance pour une Europe Unie, the first of all the organisations that he founded, combined 'antitotalitarian' action with warnings that a divided Europe was 'threatened by the dawning of Africa and the rebirth of Asia'[66] and pleas for direct election to the European parliament.

The efforts to create a commemorative discourse sustaining this proEuropean and anti-communist rhetoric never equalled the impact of the parallel FIR commemorative dynamic. On 8 May 1960, on the occasion of the fifteenth anniversary of the end of the European war, Halin tried to create 'the first sanctuary of the European resistance' in Oostakker, a small Flemish village, on the burial site of eighty-one Belgian resistance fighters murdered by the occupier. During the ceremony, the French deposited a little bit of soil taken from Mont Valérien, the Dutch, the Austrians and the Germans earth from the concentration camps situated on their territory, joined by similar samples carried by the Luxembourgeois, Danes, Norwegians, Greek and Italians. Halin concluded: 'When the earth from ten European countries was mixed into the soil of Oostakker, . . . we felt more than ever that Europe would only preserve its greatness and influence by fraternally uniting all its citizens in faithfulness to the ideal of Liberty for which so many men and women in so many countries have died.'[67] Yet the site had never occupied an important place in the national commemorations in Belgium and its 'Europeanisation' made little difference to it.

The historiographical activism that accompanied the anti-communist propaganda for a united Europe had a much more lasting influence. First of all there was the 'home' production, very close to open propaganda, including Halin's own L'Europe Unie, objectif majeur de la Résistance.[68] Next, La Voix Internationale de la Résistance and Déportation et Liberté frequently used references to the non-communist academic historiography to legitimise their action. They drew on international initiatives developing from 1958 onwards, with international conferences bringing together historians from the Institut für Zeitgeschichte in

---

[65] Posthumous La Voix Internationale de la Résistance (July 1974).
[66] La Voix Internationale de la Résistance (Apr. 1960).   [67] Ibid.
[68] Prefaced by Paul-Henri Spaak (Brussels and Paris, n.d.). Halin is the only source for the relevant chapter in Dusan Sidjanski, L'Avenir Fédéraliste de l'Europe. See also, dedicated to Halin, Henri Bernard, Esprit de la résistance et conscience européenne/Geest van het verzet en Europees bewustzijn (Brussels, 1980).

Munich, Yad Vashem in Tel Aviv, the Rijksinstituut voor Oorlogsdocumentatie in Amsterdam and the Commission d'Histoire de la Seconde
Guerre Mondiale in Paris. The conferences were dominated by the tenor
of national resistance historiography, such as Haestrup for Denmark, De
Jong for the Netherlands and most prominently of all Henri Michel for
France. However, Michel in particular was very prudent in his publications at the time, observing the 'factual unity' of the European resistance,
through a common struggle against the same Nazi enemy – both German
and collaborationist – with the same arms and the same methods of
combat.[69] The explicit reservations made by Michel concerning the
political programmes for Europe's post-war future were carefully omitted
by the anti-communist publicists, for whom *la Pensée de la Résistance*
became a key reference, more for the utility of the expression than for its
content.[70] Finally, in 1968, Walter Lipgens produced the dreamed-of
reference work, *Europa-Föderationspläne der Widerstandsbewegungen,
1940–1945*, a collection of excerpts from the underground press and
resistance movement programmes, creating an impression of brotherly
unanimity amongst all resisters. From then onwards, explicit anti-
communism disappears and the way is laid open for the integration of
the thesis of 'The Resistance', giving birth to 'The Idea of Europe' in
textbooks on the history of European integration.

Despite their antagonism, the anti-fascist and anti-totalitarian memories
shared one major feature: they systematically obscured the specificity of
the genocide. The anti-fascist discourse assimilated all victims of
fascism with anti-fascists. The genocide was not recognised as distinct
from the overall anti-fascist martyrdom. Nevertheless, this discourse
was inclusive of all victims. The anti-totalitarian discourse was more
exclusive; its freedom fighters were mostly recruited from nationalist
resistance circles, who did not admit victims of the genocide to their
clubs. Above all, not only did it obscure the genocide, but genocide was
strictly incompatible with its aim. An assimilation between Nazi persecution and the Gulag essentially required the omission of genocide.

In the post-war years Europe's occupied countries were in desperate
need of patriotic memories. Defeat and occupation, and even liberation
by Allied foreign armies, constituted an unprecedented trauma for the
national identities of France, Belgium and the Netherlands: a 'national
memory' glorifying the resistance was a precondition for post-war

[69] See *Déportation et Liberté* 19 (July–Sep. 1958), and 'Histoire de la Resistance ou
diversion anticommuniste?', *Le Drapeau Rouge* (19 Sep. 1958).
[70] See Henri Michel and B. Mirkine-Guetzevitch, *Les Idées Politiques et sociale de la
résistance* (Paris, 1954).

recovery. The search for heroism comprised a patriotic commemoration of persecution and the concentration camp became the symbolic depository of national martyrdom. Yet the patriotic commemoration of the camps denied the heterogeneity of Nazi persecution, commemorating the heroic few at the expense of the majority of victims, particularly the Jews. The patriotic remembrance of the *univers concentrationnaire* was a mythical amalgamation of very different realities, blurring the singular character of genocide. A commemoration of the genocide as such had threatening implications which made it incompatible with the reconstruction of national self-esteem. National reaffirmation was, however, perfectly compatible with European integration. National and European myths completed and re-enforced each other seamlessly, in the anti-communist and anti-fascist narratives respectively.

Guilt and shame were certainly equally responsible for the inexpressibility of genocide in post-war commemoration. Yet the failure of post-war memories to recognise the otherness of genocide formed only part of national memories of the occupation as a whole. The absence of such a commemoration was caused by the limited capacity of traumatised post-war societies to commemorate something singular, which lay outside the ordinary and recognisable context of persecution. Societies absorbed by their own crises of national confidence granted a very low priority to the commemoration of a tragedy that was, because of its extraordinary and extra-territorial character, peripheral to their national existence. The construction of a national epic had a pressing urgency about it. Since the commemoration of genocide could not be instrumentalised and was not constructive for patriotic memories, it had the lowest possible urgency. De-Judification – assimilationism in the case of inclusive anti-fascist memories, exclusion and sometimes anti-Semitism in exclusive anti-communist and patriotic memories – was a consequence of this, and not its primary motivation. Besides, it is revealing that the requirements for patriotic memories in recovering nations are very similar to the requirements for a patriotic memory in an emerging nation. As the research of Idith Zertal and Tom Segev illustrates, the memory of genocide was incompatible with national affirmation and also threatened the national identity of victorious Israel.[71]

From the late 1940s onwards, this construction of patriotic memories was redoubled by the construction of Cold War memories. The anti-communists chose the concentration camp as the symbolic target of their campaigns. The equation of the Gulag with Nazi camp and the

---

[71] Idith Zertal, 'Du bon usage du souvenir. Les Israeliens et la Shoah', *Le Débat* 58 (1990), pp. 92–103; Tom Segev, *The Seventh Million. The Israelis and the Holocaust* (New York, 1993).

accompanying assimilation of Communism with Nazism in the totalitarianism doctrine both presupposed active oblivion of the genocide. The communist reply to this turned the Nazi camps into the symbols of anti-fascist martyrdom. Buchenwald and Sachsenhausen became symbols of a truly de-Nazified, popular democratic Germany, whereas Auschwitz became the monument to international communist and national Polish martyrdom. Genocide did not meet the requirements of ideological mobilisation on either side: yet the commemorative dynamic launched around the sites of the Nazi camps by pro-communist organisations, which created organisations, monuments, pilgrimages and rituals, would go on to contribute to the 'discovery' of the genocide in the national remembrance in the Netherlands, France and Belgium during the 1960s and 1970s.

Commemoration of the persecution during the Second World War as a strategy for mobilising public opinion would prove self-defeating. The culmination of the Cold War commemoration on the occasion of the twentieth anniversary of the liberation in 1965 signalled at the same time the end of the hegemony of anti-communist and anti-fascist memories. In the course of the 1960s the genocide emerged as a central challenge to commemorators and historians alike, that is, a process of acknowledging the systematic attempt to murder the Jewish population of Europe as an experience distinct from the amalgamations of 'freedom fighters' and 'anti-fascists'.

The Dutch example is illuminating in this respect. Until 1966, the stern policy of national consensus and state anti-communism had stifled the official refusal to participate in any commemorative initiative concerning Auschwitz.[72] The secret services monitored the Dutch Auschwitz Committee closely, and warned the government that the creation of this committee in 1956 was inspired by the 'pro-communist' FIR and that it was entirely manipulated by Dutch communists, even though it admitted that 'the overwhelming majority of ordinary members are not communists and belong to the Jewish part of the population'.[73] The Catholic prime ministers De Quay and Marrijnen systematically instructed the members of their cabinet not to accept the annual invitations to commemoration ceremonies of the liberation of Auschwitz, and the Dutch government refused any subsidy for the construction of the international monument in Auschwitz. Although the

---

[72] See the correspondence on this matter in ACPM, Con. See also Maarten Bijl, *Nooit meer Auschwitz! Het Nederlandse Auschwitz Comité, 1956–1996* (Bussum, 1997).

[73] *Binnenlandse Veiligheidsdienst*, report 784.128 (24 May 1965); see also reports (10 May 1962), (10 Sep. 1964), (21 Jan. 1965), (22 Dec. 1965), (18 and 28 Jan. 1966) and (18 Feb. 1966), all in ACPM, Con.

official motivation for this refusal was the standing policy not to subsidise any monument abroad, internal documents, most of which were drafted by the secret service, argued that, Auschwitz being situated in Poland, any subsidy for the monument would mean Dutch governmental finance for communist propaganda against its own foreign policy.

This line of conduct by the government of the Western European country that had the largest number of Jewish dead to mourn in Auschwitz became increasingly embarrassing. Only Denmark, from where no Jewish citizens were deported to Auschwitz, and the Greek dictatorship had joined the Dutch refusal, whilst France, Norway and Belgium had made generous contributions. The campaign for a Dutch contribution to the Auschwitz monument gathered increasing support. Intellectuals, university rectors and non-communist politicians signed up to a patronage committee and the socialist former prime minister Drees even called for a Dutch effort on public television. Secret services reports also registered increasing support from the official representatives of the Dutch Jewish community. Until 1962 only the rabbi of the liberal Jewish community of Amsterdam had agreed to support the Auschwitz Committee but in 1962 – that is, after the Eichmann trial in Jerusalem – the four main rabbis of the Netherlands joined the committee and Jewish organisations took part in distributing invitations for the commemorative events organised by the committee.[74] Even the consul of Israel participated in the commemorations, assisted only by his Polish and Soviet colleagues, and the ambassador pressed the government to give more weight to the martyrdom of its Jewish citizens than to its anti-communist reflexes.[75] In articles in the press, the repeated official refusal was criticised as 'heartless'.[76]

Meanwhile the public notoriety of Auschwitz as a particular site of Jewish suffering received an enormous impetus with the great Auschwitz case in Frankfurt in 1964, whilst public awareness of the Dutch part in the genocide first broke through with the contemporary transmission by public television of the documentary series, 'The Occupation', starring the national war historian Lou De Jong. The first comprehensive history of the persecution and mass murder of Dutch Jews by J. Presser appeared in April 1965. Presser initially worried whether the

[74] *Binnenlandse Veiligheidsdienst*, report 784.128 (24 May 1965), ibid.
[75] *Nota voor de MP* (14 Sep. 1961) and *Nota voor minister-president* (15 Feb. 1962), both ibid.
[76] *Het Vrije Volk* (28 Jan. 1963). Earlier criticism is in *De Waarheid* (23 June 1961) and later in *De Tijd/Maasbode* (1 May 1965).

10,000 printed copies would find buyers in the first two years after its publication, as his publisher expected. The copies were sold out in two days and before the end of the year more than 100,000 copies had been printed, including a pocket edition. Presser, overwhelmed by the completely unexpected public reaction, described it as 'an explosion' and 'a crushing experience'.[77] Only a year after the twentieth anniversary of the liberation of Auschwitz the Dutch government finally decided to contribute to the monument. The new Catholic prime minister, Cals, abandoned the refusal of his predecessors; he argued that 'The government is fully aware that Auschwitz is not the only place where an extermination camp was established, but the name of Auschwitz – and as such it occupies a very particular place – has grown into a symbol of the mass destruction of the opponents of the Nazi regime in the years 1933–45.'[78] The declaration did not specifically mention the Jews and continued the assimilation of victim-opponents, particularly by chronologically extending Auschwitz's symbolism to the beginning of the Nazi regime – that is, long before the invasion of Poland in 1939, where Auschwitz is located, and long before the opening of the camp and the implementation of the genocide in 1942. The Auschwitz Committee continued its campaign in the following years, this time against official neglect of Jewish survivors by the Dutch state, as opposed to its treatment of resistance victims, who benefited from a special pension from 1947. A television documentary in February 1968 prompted interventions in parliament, which finally in 1972 achieved belated recognition by the Dutch state of its financial responsibility for the survivors of the genocide.

The conclusions from the Dutch example cannot easily be generalised. The dimensions of the Jewish tragedy in the Netherlands were immeasurably greater and the ostracism against victims of the genocide during the first two post-war decades more absolute, but the acknowledgement of national responsibilities in the genocide in the national remembrance of the war years probably took place earlier than in France and Belgium. One possible explanation could be the early official acceptance of the anti-fascist paradigm in the latter two countries. Jewish victims there were, after all, not excluded from patriotic commemoration and from legal recognition, as had been the case in the Netherlands. Jewish survivors were welcome in the French FNDIRP and the Belgian CNPPA. The peaceful coexistence of Jewish remembrance and pro-communist commemorative activism would come to an

---

[77] Presser, 'Een boek ziet het licht', *Nederlands Auschwitz Comité* (Jan. 1966).
[78] *Rijksvoorlichtingsdienst* (14 Sep. 1966), ACPM, Con.

abrupt end only with the Six Days' War in 1967 and the anti-Semitic purges in Poland of 1968. From then on, survivors were divided by the inescapable choice between their communist and their Jewish allegiances. Auschwitz as a joint symbol of international Jewish and national Polish martyrdom became politically incompatible. Accusations from the communist side that anti-Semitism was a West German monopoly would be replaced with anti-communist accusations of anti-Semitic campaigns orchestrated from Cairo and Moscow. Henry Rousso points to the changing perceptions in France of the state of Israel, and the repercussions of De Gaulle's pro-Arab declarations, stirring comparisons of anti-Zionist policies and Vichy's anti-Semitism. Yet he situates the emergence of a proper acknowledgement of the genocide only in the second half of the 1970s, with the 'affairs' involving Vichy officials implied in the deportation of Jews, the polemical transmission of the American television drama 'Holocaust' in 1979 and the emergence of 'negationist' militants on the fringe of the French historical profession denying the very existence of genocide.[79] In contrast to France and the Netherlands, Belgium has had scarcely any public debate on national responsibility for the genocide. This absence of moral scrutiny is caused mainly by the current dismemberment of Belgium. No new nation is eager to inherit the moral debts of its predecessor, and the legacy of the genocide is one of the very few Belgian competencies none of the regions claims. This absence of a public debate seems furthermore to suggest that references to the particular experience of the Jews only really permeated the public discourse when they became instrumental in combating the openly xenophobic extreme right as it entered parliament in the 1980s. The 'reversal of memories', referred to at the start of chapter 13, was in any case a very gradual process, allowing for different chronologies in different countries, whereby the emergence of a commemoration of the genocide did not signal the immediate and complete decay of patriotic and Cold War memories.

The memory of Nazi persecution, for patriots and Cold War activists alike, required the opposite profile to be *commémorable*, worthy of commemoration. When heroism, choice and ideology are the criteria, the victims of genocide do not stand out. Persecuted for something they did not choose, for the simple reason of being born Jewish, they are placed at the bottom of the hierarchy of martyrs. In a properly historical memory the hero-victims, the examples of martyrs of national liberation or political opposition, are legion in human history. They were commemorated because they could be integrated in a national epic and an

[79] Rousso, *Le Syndrome de Vichy*, pp. 147–82.

ideological discourse. The victims of genocide were not commemorated, because they could not be integrated in a national epic, because their memory was inert in the chemistry of post-war commemoration. It is precisely this singular character that has taken more time to be recognised, but it has also proved less ephemeral in the longer run.

Conclusion

The juxtaposition of three national case studies, with their inevitable and apparent differences, could easily lead to the conclusion that, even within Western Europe, national distinctiveness was, in the final analysis, primordial in shaping memories of the Second World War. This would contradict the hypothesis at the start of this book, that the fundamental differences in the Western European experience of the war were not national frontiers but particular experiences at the heart of this particular war: resistance, labour conscription, persecution. It is a rudimentary conclusion of this study that 'national' memories did exist in post-war years. How to deal with the memory of the war was a central challenge to the reconstruction of the State and to the continuing existence of the Nation, after their spectacular failures of the years 1939–45. The state became a central agent of a collective memory that was at the same time self-justification and recovery of national honour. This was a matter of survival. The state was the source and the destination of these memories.

In February 1945, in the midst of the last, cold 'hunger winter' of the German occupation of the Netherlands, an anonymous plan was presented to the National Resistance Council (the GAC) for the commemoration of the Dutch resistance. The idea was to erect a national monument at the very heart of Amsterdam, facing the royal palace in the Dam-square. The initiators justified their proposal by pointing to the lack of a monument symbolising and enhancing national unity, such as the tomb of the unknown soldier in Paris, or the Lenin mausoleum in Moscow, observing that 'the history of our nation in earlier centuries was apparently not heroic or eventful enough to provide sufficient impetus for such a creation'. It was the Nazi occupation and the heroic resistance to it which finally provided sufficient substance for a national monument. The creation of the monument would stimulate national cohesion at a time when the nation had greatest need of it, and avoid 'the sordid performance offered to world opinion in Belgium and Greece'.[1]

---

[1] *Memorandum* (28 Feb. 1945), RIOD, GAC archive, 184, 1B.

Although the GAC judged the initiative premature, and its elaboration too perilous as long as the German troops still remained in the
Netherlands, the memorial was eventually built and inaugurated on
Liberation Day, 4 May 1956. It corresponded fairly closely to the design
proposed in February 1945.[2] The fundamental concept was the collective nature of the monument, a memorial to the resistance, but at the
same time to the entire Dutch nation. To strengthen the personal
involvement of all citizens with their national monument, it had been
partially funded through public subscription, organised as a manifestation of popular capitalism. Donors obtained property certificates of the
public land on which the monument was to be built, at a rate of half a
guilder per square centimetre. Its form expresses the culmination of the
monuments policy described in chapter 3, with a combination of
abstract elements – primarily a central pillar 22 metres high, a series of
symbolic doves, lions and dogs (the last symbolising the occupier) – and
a modicum of social realism, with two male figures symbolising the
resistance and a mother and child symbolising victory. The consensual
nature of the monument was strengthened by its lack of recognisable
elements. Instead of named martyrs, the monument contained urns
with soil from sites where the blood of anonymous Dutch martyrs from
all provinces of the country and its colonies had been spilt. The heavy-
handed symbolism of the poem by Roland Holst was also unlikely to stir
controversy: when *Elseviers' Weekblad*, a major Dutch weekly, asked
ninety-eight bystanders to comment on the poem, eighty-four of them
could not even figure out whether it was supposed to be read from left to
right or from top to bottom.

In its anonymous asceticism, the monument epitomises Dutch collective memories of the Second World War. The occupation had been
experienced as a collective affliction for the whole of society, an external
aggression and a moral outrage to a country that saw itself as the model
pupil in the school of nations. In the austere reconstruction ethic that
dominated Dutch society in the first two post-war decades, the war was
presented as an ordeal that had strengthened social cohesion and
national identity. This anonymous and genuinely 'national' memory was
harsh towards those who had suffered more and suffered differently.
Milieux de mémoire were disruptive for the consensual commemoration;
resistance veterans, labour conscripts, survivors of concentration camps

[2] *Nota voor de Centrale commissie voor oorlogs- en vredesgedenktekens* (Aug. 1946), ACPM,
351.853, *monumenten*. See also Mariette Van Staveren, 'Moraliteit, sekse en de Natie.
Een geschiedenis van het Monument op de Dam en de oorlogsherinnering,
1945–1969', in *Sekse en Oorlog. Jaarboek voor vrouwengeschiedenis* 15 (Amsterdam,
1995), pp. 94–116, and Ramaker and Van Bohemen, *Sta een ogenblik stil*, pp. 79–83.

11 The Dutch national monument, Damplein Amsterdam. Photo, Dick Van Galen Last, Amsterdam.

and Jewish survivors of the genocide in particular suffered from a lack of recognition of their particular fate, from a lack of support, in the face of both their material indigence and their need for consolation and integration into the national narrative. This kind of 'national memory' faded as soon as the generalised austerity dominating Dutch public life faded, that is, with the arrival of wealth and welfare in the course of the 1960s. Finally there was room for particular measures for particular groups. A society obsessed with reconstruction and with ending economic backwardness relative to its neighbours could begin to pay attention to 'damaged groups', as the patriots and anti-fascists of the 1940s and 1950s were redefined in the welfare era. Dutch victims of persecution achieved a law in 1972; resistance veterans a medal in 1980; labour conscripts an association at the very end of the 1980s.

The Dam monument, symbol of the austere war memory of the reconstruction years, also became the symbol of the acute difficulties of the Dutch transition into a less disciplined and more leisured society. In the summer of 1960 the first protests were heard against the growing custom of Amsterdam youth of sitting on the steps of the monument, to picnic or even make love. On hot days, the monument drew such crowds that it had become impossible to read Roland Holst's poem through the many dangling legs. Indignation over this lack of respect for the national monument increased in the course of the 1960s, with the length of the picnickers' hair. By 1969, youngsters not only spent their day on the steps of the monument, but even brought their sleeping bags to spend the night. The 'Dam sleepers' or 'Dam rascals' became the symbol of Provo, the provocative Amsterdam hippie movement, and associated in the conservative press with drugs, lice and venereal disease, in short, with a degeneration of permissiveness that embodied the absolute opposite of the disciplined asceticism of the war memory that the monument stood for. A national controversy developed and public belief that a majority of young tourists sleeping on the war memorial were German nationals could only increase hostility. On 24 August 1970, young Dutch marines 'cleansed' the Dam monument of its unpatriotic occupants, in what passed subsequently as the 'Dam riots'. A period of national consensus had definitively come to an end.

The French memory of the Second World War in the first two decades after the liberation is often presented as a memory centred around the Resistance as a means to the *honneur inventé* and dominated by Gaullists and communists, the most legitimate claimants of resistance merit. My findings only very partially confirm this representation. After all, if indeed French memory was wholly dominated by Gaullists and communists, it would mostly be an opposition memory. De Gaulle left power in January 1946, and the Communist Party in May 1947. In the meantime, the governments of the Fourth Republic had not been dispossessed of the remembrance of the war. De Gaulle returned to power twelve years later, and then indeed staged grandiose commemorations, representing in part a return to resistance rhetoric, such as the transfer of the remains of Jean Moulin to the Pantheon, launching a hitherto secondary figure in the national memory to the first ranks of prominence.

There is, in France much more than in the Netherlands or Belgium, an archetypal memory of the resistance as embodied in the *maquis-fighter*, as an omnipresent character in popular culture. The issues of *Photoromans de la Résistance*, portraying the heroism and romance of shepherds and village doctors in a rural, mountainous setting fighting only German soldiers, published monthly from November 1969 through December 1975, are probably the most telling memorial of this type of memory.[3] Yet this memory of the resistance, which concealed the more traumatic and humiliating memory of Vichy from view, was never nearly as dominant as it was in the Netherlands, not even during De Gaulle's reign. To some extent the place of the resistance in the social memory of the nation was, like that of De Gaulle and the communists, somewhat unsure. The place of the resistance veterans in the arena of the French *milieux de mémoire* was much more in retreat than speeches, *photoromans* and historiography might give reason to believe, crushed between the *anciens combattants* of the Great War and the *déportés* of the last war. Indeed, both numerically and in symbolic strength, resistance veterans were the lesser quantity.

Déportation, much more than *Résistance*, has been the keyword in my analysis of French memories of the Second World War. At first sight, this is an unexpected finding. One would rather anticipate the Dutch collective memories of the war to be embodied in a group and a concept symbolising martyrdom and suffering, since this country described itself first and foremost as a victim of outrageous aggression by an immeasurably stronger enemy. Yet, compared to France, deportation was purely marginal in Dutch post-war memories and the entire nation rallied behind the resistance as an abstract reference. France, Germany's rival and victor of the previous conflict, twenty-two years earlier, was imbued with notions of combat and military *grandeur*. The experience of the Second World War was indeed to a large extent read backwards, assimilated into the First World War, imposing the paradigm of the 'combatant' even on those groups to whom it was least suited. Yet at the

---

[3] *Photoromans de la Résistance* 1 (Nov. 1969), followed by *Résistance* (Dec. 1972–Dec. 1975), Bibliothèque Nationale, Fol. Jo. 15518.

same time the experience of the First World War had also left deep marks in the associational life of French society, an entire frame of reference of rituals, organisations, veterans' discourse, and a set of mechanisms by which the nation could show its recognition and solicitude for populations hit by war. The inability of Dutch society to do just that was partly a result of its lack of experience with the ordeals of war and its aftermath. The dispersed and infinitely fragmented experience of resistance could not match the mud-soaked solidarity of the *poilus* in the trenches. Resistance organisations did not long survive the liberation; and the type of veterans' movements that surfaced in the early 1950s were of an entirely different kind, and did not inspire national respect in the way that the veterans' organisations of the Great War had done.

Major organisations of 'authentic' veterans who had had experiences offering a lived-through solidarity that could turn them into real *milieux de mémoire* were formed by the victims of Nazi persecution and labour conscription. Old-fashioned notions of a patriotism of heroes and combatants and its nostalgic defenders clashed with innovative interpretations of belonging to the nation, seen as a community of the suffering. It was not only those who fought more or better than the others who had a special message and a special authority for post-war generations – so did those who had suffered more, who had a special responsibility in recalling the horrors of past times and past regimes. As the resistance aura dwindled and became devalued, the aura of deportation was increasingly sanctified as an acme of national martyrdom. What had initially been a generous device for a massive conversion of victims of a humiliated nation into heroes of a reborn one became a coveted title of honour, leading to the saddest of *batailles de mémoire* whereby victims competed in claiming the horror of their experiences – the victims of labour conscription appropriating the experience of the victims of the Nazi concentration camps, and the victims of Nazi concentration camps appropriating that of the victims of genocide. Yet, the term *Déportation* could become a battleground only because it epitomised the experience of French society better than any other phrase and certainly better than *Résistance*.

Mont Valérien and the Mémorial de la Déportation symbolise the double character of French memory of the Second World War in the first two post-war decades. Mont Valérien is peripheral, in an isolated setting, characterised by an attempt to assimilate the Second World War into a purely military conflict. Its heroic elitism failed to embody a national consensus in its fifteen, sixteen or seventeen symbolic graves. Victims of genocide and of labour conscription resented their exclusion, whilst the explicit inclusion of references to a global empire in decay harmed its future. The Mémorial de la Déportation, at the tip of the Ile de la Cité, lies in the very heart of Paris. The thousands of faceless names, symbolising a community of the suffering, are much more of a rallying symbol than the sixteen heroes of Mont Valérien. Behind the eternal commemorative rivalries which set French collective memories apart from Dutch, where 'damaged groups' were ignored until the end of the 1960s, both countries have symbols behind which, after all, an entire nation can rally. Even if there is disagreement on who belongs to the categories of resistance heroes and Nazi victims, at the least there is agreement on the categories themselves.

Belgian collective memories of the Second World War ran parallel to French memories; but in Belgium they lost their consensual appeal in the course of the first two post-war decades.[4] As in France, Belgian patriotism was moulded by the experience of the First World War. Yet for the Flemish national movement the First World War was an even stronger formative experience. The Yser Tower, built on the battlefields of the Flemish lowlands near the coast and the French border, had become the symbol of the emancipation of Dutch-speaking rank-and-file soldiers fighting in an army commanded by French-speaking officers. It was a Flemish and very explicitly Catholic monument rallying, in the first instance, a broad spectrum of Flemish militants. In the course of the 1930s, the annual pilgrimage grew into a demonstration monopolised by the radical fascist wing of the Flemish nationalist movement. During the occupation the pilgrimage became a setting for pro-collaborationist demonstrations and the tower was adorned with swastikas. In revenge, it was dynamited in 1946 in an attack associated by Flemish opinion with the resistance. A Committee for Action and Vigilance, animated by the CNPPA, the national confederation of survivors of the camps, tried in the post-war years to participate in the annual pilgrimage and, by uniting the two *générations du feu*, to claim back the memory of the First World War from the radical Flemish nationalists. A first attempt in 1949 was a failure. The pilgrimage was a public rally of former collaborators, and the participating survivors of the concentration camps, who had asked to be allowed to sing the Belgian national anthem in addition to the Flemish anthem, were forbidden to do so. By 1953, in the presence of several cabinet members, the pilgrimage had turned into an open demonstration for an amnesty for all former collaborationists and war criminals, including a public tribute to the Flemish SS troops on the eastern front.

The Committee of Former Victims of Nazi Terror organised a

---

[4] See Lagrou, 'Welk vaderland voor de vaderlandslievende verenigingen?'

counterdemonstration uniting two commemorations on the same day, in the morning at the Yser Tower and in the afternoon in Breendonk, the former torture camp which had become the national monument to the Second World War, thus uniting the victims of both wars in one tribute. The committee, of which many Flemish Catholics were members, was motivated by a concern not to alienate the Flemish movement from the cause of anti-fascism and was alarmed by the increasingly firm hold of former collaborationists on the movement. The commemoration, staged as a display of tolerance and respect for the victims, drew a violent counterdemonstration of radical Flemish students who tried to prevent the former KZ inmates gaining access to the Yser Tower. Breendonk and the Yser, the memory of the victims of Nazism and the soldiers of the war in the trenches, would never again be united in a single commemoration. Only in this second half of the 1990s, after the ominous electoral breakthrough of the xenophobic and radical Flemish Vlaams Blok, has there been a reaction to the exploitation of the monument by fascist nostalgics, and an effort to include a reference to the horrors of the Second World War in this high mass of Flemish nationalism.

The identification of Flemish Catholic opinion with the legacy of collaboration occurred during the 1950s. By appropriating the legacy of resistance and persecution from August 1945 until March 1947, presenting itself as 'the government of the resistance' against the Catholic opposition and its defence of the king, the anti-royalist coalition had created some rancour in Flemish Catholic circles. But, as described in chapter 2, there was also a desire to reappropriate the Resistance aura once they returned to power. The political use of the commemoration of the resistance as an opposition strategy was much less acceptable to Catholic opinion. In November 1948 and September 1952, demonstrations of protest against the liberation of former collaborationists had twice led to the dismissal of a Catholic minister of justice. Catholic frustration dated, paradoxically enough, from the period when the Catholic Party had an absolute majority and governed the country alone, between June 1950 and April 1954. Particularly in Flanders, where the Catholics had an overwhelming majority and where royalist opinion had scored 72 per cent in the referendum over the return of Leopold III, resentment accumulated over the discovery that even with an absolute majority the party could not govern the country against the opposition.

After the Catholic electoral defeat of 1954, the new anti-Catholic coalition once again presented itself as 'the government of the resistance' and staged grandiose commemorations such as the inauguration of 'the

12 Poster, 'Yser-front of Belgium, Diksmuide-Breendonk' (25 October 1953).
Two generations, two sites of memory, two nations. CEGES/SOMA, Brussels.

monument to the thirteen colonels of the Armée Secrète' in November 1957. Agitation against the massive liberation of former collaborationists suddenly stopped, thanks in part to the activities of Hubert Halin, organisational mastermind of resistance activism as an opposition strategy and now personal counsellor to Prime Minister Van Acker. The conservative Catholic paper *La Libre Belgique* protested against the sudden approval by resistance activists of measures for which a Catholic minister had been dismissed two years earlier, denouncing the 'professional manipulators of patriotism'. On the rebound, the Catholic Party in Flanders steadily identified more with the cause of collaboration as an opposition strategy, and, faced with the electoral competition of a new Flemish nationalist party, pleaded for an amnesty for wartime offenders. By 1958, the memory of the war had become a central stratagem in the Belgian ethnic conflicts, leaving the Flemish victims of Nazi terror in particular disinherited and bewildered.

So much for 'national' memories, which resulted from the post-war effort for the reconstruction (and deconstruction) of national identities. Yet at all stages, this book has shown the real difficulty of this undertaking, the artificiality of the effort to extract homogeneously national memories from the continental upheaval of the Second World War and its disruptive, fragmented impact on the population. Experiences were not shared along national lines but according to the individual's fate in the turmoil of war. Resistance fighters, labour conscripts and victims of Nazi persecution each generated strong memories of their own, rooted in the particularity of their experiences, and largely regardless of national origins. In contrast, Nazi occupation policies often de-nationalised their life course. Each group had to integrate its own experience in a national memory that was itself composed of the various contradictory – often incompatible – experiences of other groups of the population. No experience, no memory stood alone, nor could their articulation be understood in isolation from the rest. The inescapable referential character of group memories is one of the most striking conclusions of this social comparative study. Resistance fighters, labour conscripts and victims of persecution defined their own experiences against each other, and referred to other groups, such as prisoners of war and, above all, to the model of the previous generation of soldiers of the Great War. Feelings of superiority and inferiority, feelings of guilt, assimilation of other narratives, identification with other paradigms and outright mimicry moulded their memories and imposed new interpretations of their wartime experience. Patriotism and anti-fascism were the two dominant narratives that restructured memories of war. This reinterpretation in conformity with the dominant narrative of wartime events took place over time. This frequently glossed over some of the most characteristic features of the wartime experiences of some groups, most prominently in the case of labour conscripts and victims of genocide.

If, on one level, the Nation-State was the source and goal of commemorative policies, on another level these policies were merely the result of a complex negotiation, of an intense and conflicting debate between various groups. Organisations of resistance veterans, and even more so of former labour conscripts and victims of Nazi terror, were very forceful agents of memory, at least in Belgium and France. These memories were partly for internal use, providing a narrative of their own particular experience, providing solidarity and consolation. Yet in their search, and their desperate need, for social recognition, for a memory acknowledged by society as a whole, they invested much of their energy in the project to inscribe their particular experiences in the national narrative, be it through laws, monuments, rituals such as participation in 11 November commemorations, or symbols such as the *carte du combattant* or medals. In this book I have concentrated only on national organisations, a factor which undervalues the astounding vitality of all sorts of 'veterans' organisations at the local or professional level. The astonishing volume and sheer variety of their press, the long lists of participating organisations in commemorative ventures of all kinds or merely the profusion of associations, federations and unions which carry *résistance* or *déportation* in their names, most often in some combination with *ancien combattant*, stand witness to this. What I have described elsewhere in this book as a generalised 'association-mania' is one expression of the management of the memory of the war at all levels of social life. All these organisations are the expression of a dense civil society as an intermediary between the State and the individual.[5]

The *milieux de mémoire* and the State did not strike the same deal in the three countries studied herein. Where civil society invaded the commemorative space, as happened prominently in France and Belgium, 'national' or governmental commemorative policies largely failed to provide national cohesion or a consensual script on the conduct of the nation in the recent war. Only in the Netherlands did such a 'national' memory succeed in establishing a hegemony for about two decades. The State succeeded in side-tracking all kinds of veterans' associations, in persisting in its rejection of separate laws of social assistance and of medals and in creating a homogeneous monuments policy. Not unlike Eastern European Academies of Science, the State

---

[5] For an elaboration of the concept of 'collective memory', on which this development is inspired, see Emmanuel Sivan and Jay Winter's contribution to Winter and Sivan, *War and Remembrance*.

Institute for War Documentation became the almost exclusive and in any case the dominant source of war historiography and Lou De Jong the personification of the history of the war both in writing and on television.[6] This situation originates in the distinctive war experience of the Dutch people and in the urgency of a national consensus in the barren post-war years, which tilted the balance of power towards the governments of national unity rather than the intermediaries. At the same time it also originates in the distinctive structure of Dutch civil society in the first half of the twentieth century. 'Pillarisation', whereby religious affiliation was the structuring principle of all forms of organised social life, from sports and the theatre to trade unions and health insurance, left no room for an alternative sociability, based on a different, and to the churches threatening, basis of a shared experience in the war. 'Pillarisation' was a highly crystallising and hierarchical organisation of society, a form of permanent tutelage by local and national elites, including in the interpretation and commemoration of the war. The 'bottom-up' legitimacy of veterans' movements in republican France was the antithesis of this. Belgium, in this context, stands between its neighbours. 'Pillarisation' in the Belgian context, based on political rather than religious affiliation (Belgium only had Catholics and anti-clericals), never came close to monopolising social life, and the strong tradition of veterans' movements places it much closer to its southern than to its northern neighbour.

A 'national' memory along Dutch lines served the State well, by removing the disruptive issues of legacy of the war from the public sphere. But within a 'national' memory, particular groups of citizens hit harder or marked deeper by the war experience struck a bad deal. No solidarity for them, no consolation, no integration of their particular experience in the national narrative. The disintegrated conflicting memories in France and Belgium succeeded much better in this and, by so doing, undermined the consensual national narrative. Here lies one very partial answer to the issue, briefly raised in the introduction, of the adequacy of collective memories of the Second World War in Western Europe. After all, the cacophony of commemorative rivalries in France and Belgium, even where it set victims of labour, concentration or extermination camps in macabre rivalries and opposition, carried more recognition for the diversity of the experiences of different groups of

---

[6] See Chris Vos, *Televisie en bezetting. Een onderzoek naar de documentaire verbeelding van de Tweede Wereldoorlog in Nederland* (Hilversum, 1995), and L. Beunders, 'Van Dr. L. De Jong tot Zeg maar Loe – de macht van de moderne media', in Madelon De Keizer (ed.), *'Een dure verplichting en een kostelijk voorrecht'. Dr L. De Jong en zijn Geschiedwerk* (Amsterdam, 1995), pp. 145–74.

citizens and, probably, more consolation than the austere consensus in the Netherlands. The plurality of voices coming from civil society, which invaded the public manifestations of remembrance in the former two countries, exploded public memories and offered space to some groups trying to come to terms with their own experience.

But where stands the individual in this story of collective remembrance, regardless of whether state or civil society gained the upper hand? After all, time and again this book has had to describe how any group could obtain recognition for its own experience only by conforming in some way to dominant narratives, by giving in to patriotic or anti-fascist rhetoric and by abandoning some of its wartime comrades, be it women workers, jobless 'volunteers' of the first war years, Jews or foreigners. They had to renounce part of their individual memories and experiences and speak a language that post-war society was ready to understand: stories of martyred workers or defiant anti-fascists, of heroism, martyrdom and patriotism. Survivors dreamt of 'the spirit of the camps' and of the everlasting solidarity of the common struggle. Much of it was lived through emotion, part of it was an ardent wish. Nazi occupation had atomised individuals, it had systematically disrupted solidarities, displaced, humiliated, dehumanised. The second *génération du feu* could not live up to the expectations raised by the first. The First World War had homogenised European societies through the horrors of mechanised warfare and mass death – but also through solidarity and a sense of *grandeur*, between the soldiers in the trenches, but also between them and the home front. The mutilated soldier, the orphan, the war widow – neighbours, relatives, schoolmates and distant acquaintances had all, after all, lived through the same war. They had shared experiences, or could, through the sheer scale of the impact of war, at least recognise these experiences and share some of the grief, some of the mourning.[7] The Second World War shattered these solidarities. Who, after 1945, had lived through the same war, had shared the same experience? Even within associations of survivors of concentration camps or of forced labour in Germany, members often acknowledged that they found a genuine solidarity only within the *amicale* of the same camp, or at occasional gatherings of workers in the same town, the same factories; and this was all the more true for resistance fighters.

Whether as a 'national memory' at the expense of the particular experiences of particular groups, or as a metaphorical memory privileging particular heroes and martyrs of particular *milieux de mémoire*,

---

[7] See Jay Winter, *Sites of Memory, Sites of Mourning. The Great War in European Cultural History* (Cambridge, 1995), and Winter, 'Forms of Kinship and Remembrance in the Aftermath of the Great War', in Winter and Sivan, *War and Remembrance*, pp. 40–60.

collective memories of the Second World War were framed in such a way
that they offered the individual only a particular memory that was often
outside his or her direct experience. The inevitable result was some form
of alienation between private memory and public discourse. The effect
of the inadequacy of collective ways of remembering the war was not
only that they did not suit the variety of individual experiences: they
were obtrusive to the point of invading private memories, of creating
silence instead of communication, since so many of these experiences
did not suit the patriotic or anti-fascist reading of the past. Public
remembrance, at the level of national monuments or discourse, or at the
level of the local association, often contradicted private memories to the
point of non-authenticity. How many former resistance fighters must
have felt at least some unease when leafing through *Les Photoromans de
la Résistance*? How did the call to 'remain united behind our flag, as we
were in the factory and in the camps' strike the labour conscripts of
Dieppe-Neuville or similar appeals to 'the army of political prisoners'
the Jewish survivor-members of the Belgian CNPPA? How many could
tell their true story, even to their own families: stories of horror without
heroes, ambiguous memories of homesick draft-evaders or adventurous
labour conscripts? Contrary to the collective mourning after 1918,
which helped individuals in the process of surviving and overcoming,
the heroicised remembrance after 1945 often rendered this process
more difficult. Whilst the choir leaders thundered martial hymns, many
in the back were humming private tunes, which no one heard or wanted
to hear.[8] Artists and memoir writers, film directors and even historians
preserved authenticity only in so far as their voices were out of tune with
the greater story.

Still, the conclusions of this book cannot be summarised in an overall
condemnation of post-war remembrance, echoing a simplistic opposition of 'memory' – partisan, instrumental, deforming, inauthentic – and
'history' – final, true and scientific knowledge of the past. Historians
would be ill advised to treat commemorative activists condescendingly.
We have in this study encountered too many instances where scholarly
histories were no more than erudite derivatives of political memories to
maintain such a pretentious distinction. Throughout these pages I have
rather tried to describe how difficult this search was, for meaning in the
aftermath of the Second World War. European – and other – societies
cannot claim today to have resolved this question. The Second World
War was a terrible challenge to democratic societies that had spent
much of their recent history in involving their citizens in politics,

[8] On this metaphor, see Winter and Sivan, 'Setting the Framework', in their *War and
Remembrance*, pp. 28, 30, 35.

guaranteeing their individuals' rights, in extending their legal protection, their social and economic welfare. It was a humiliating and traumatising experience, revealing the frailty of everything they had ever acquired. The horror of Nazism was moreover a devastating blow to the very ideas of progress and humanity, upon which the prevalent contemporary philosophical and political systems were based. Patriotism, anti-fascism, anti-communism were inadequate foci for a proper historical interpretation of the recent past. More relevant in its immediacy, they were often inadequate for consoling human suffering, imposing heroism as a yardstick to measure the experience of individuals afflicted by war and persecution. The post-war period was not a bright new dawn after the dark night of war, and ugly reflexes of anti-Semitism resurfaced, of moral and social contempt, of misogyny and national prejudice. Yet these post-war years were not unchanged either. It is precisely through the many conflicts on the boundaries of national community – a national community of combatants and patriots or a national community of suffering, including Jews and communists, immigrants and victims of all sorts – that the memory of the Second World War contributed to a profound transformation of concepts of national identity, citizenship and human rights in Western Europe. The point of reference by which to evaluate the impact of the Second World War is not today's standards of tolerance and inclusion, but those that preceded the end of the war by only a few years. The opinions of racists and xenophobes, fascists and authoritarians were not anathema to mainstream politics in the 1930s. That traditional patriotism resurfaced after 1945, including its xenophobic aspects, is not surprising. That it failed to impose its interpretation of the war is more telling. In this sense, the experience of the Second World War, the human consequences of occupation by a Nazi enemy aiming to implement its ideological designs in the defeated nations, deepened notions of democracy and citizenship in Western Europe. However slow and incomplete that process has been, the legacy of Second World War has been at the heart of it.

Bibliography

UNPUBLISHED SOURCES

I. BELGIUM

1.1 Public archives

1.1.1 Dienst voor de Oorlogsslachtoffers
Ministerie van Sociale Zaken, Volksgezondheid en Leefmilieu (Brussels)
Documentatiedienst: Series RAP 610
Directie Statuten: Dossiers Wetgeving en Procedures

1.2 Documentation centres

1.2.1 Centre d'Etudes et de Documentation Guerre et Sociétés Contemporaines/Studie- en Documentatiecentrum Oorlog en Hedendaagse Maatschappij (Brussels)
Periodicals collection
Series 11 R
Series S
Series BR (Brochures)
Series P: personal papers of André Alers, Léon Delsinne, Hubert Halin

1.3 Archives of associations

1.3.1 Confédération Nationale des Prisonniers Politiques et Ayants-Droits/ Nationale Confederatie van Politieke Gevangenen en Rechthebbenden (Brussels)
Archive, A. Régibeau
Series Comptes Rendus Conseil National
Series Repression de l'Incivisme
Box Comité National d'Action et de Vigilance
1.3.2 Nationaal Verbond voor Weggevoerden en Werkweigeraars/Fédération Nationale des Travailleurs Déportés et Réfractaires (Brussels)
Dossiers Statuts
1.3.3 Onafhankelijkheidsfront/Front de l'Indépendance (Brussels)
Individual records PM–PA

1.4 Interviews by author

Billion, Alfonse, 10 October 1987
De Coster, François, 20 December 1993

Delgoffe, Theo, 22 February 1987 and 24 January 1994
Dethier, 20 April 1989
Hahn, Frans, 24 January 1994
Hoste, Charles, 5 July 1988
Michotte, 20 November 1988
Potargent, Pierre, 15 February and 8 October 1987
Roeseler, Auguste, 18 and 29 November 1988
Rubens, 19 December 1986
Tilmans, Franz, 20 April 1989
Van Calster, 22 December 1986.

2. FRANCE

2.1 Public archives

2.1.1 Archives de l'Assemblée Nationale (Paris)
    Commission des Pensions Civiles et Militaires et des Victimes de la
    Guerre et de la Répression

2.1.2 Archives Nationales (Paris)
    Series F9: Commissariat aux Prisonniers, Déportés et Refugiés (Algiers)
    and Ministère aux Prisonniers, Déportés et Refugiés (Paris)
    Series 72/AJ: archives of the Commission d'Histoire de la Deuxième
    Guerre Mondiale: 384: Direction de la Gendarmerie, synthèses.
    Series F/60: Gouvernement Provisoire de la République Française: F60/
    10, 234, 240, 272 and 274.

2.2 Documentation centres

2.2.1 Institut d'Histoire du Temps Présent (Paris)
    Periodicals collection

2.3 Archives of associations

2.3.1 Fédération Nationale des Déportés et Internés Résistants et Patriotes
    (Paris)

3. THE NETHERLANDS

3.1 Public archives

3.1.1 Algemeen Rijksarchief (The Hague), Tweede Afdeling
    Notulen Ministerraad (microfiche)
    Archivalia van het Ministerie voor Algemene Oorlogvoering van het
    Koninkrijk, 1940–1946 en van het kabinet van de Minister-President,
    1946–58

3.1.2 Ministerie van Algemene Zaken, The Hague
    Archief van het kabinet van de Minister-President, 1945–69

3.1.3 Ministerie van Binnenlandse Zaken (The Hague)
    Archief Binnenlandse Veiligheidsdienst: CO 2148804 (resp. Bureau
    Nationale Veiligheid; Centrale Inlichtingsdienst; Centrale Veiligheidsdienst)
    inzagemap Bond Illegale Werkers
    inzagemap Stichting 1940–1945

inzagemap Voormalig Verzet Nederland
inzagemap Nationale Federatieve Raad van het Voormalig Verzet
inzagemap Gemeenschap Oud-Illegale Werkers Nederland
3.1.4 Ministerie van Justitie, The Hague
Residu-Archief van het voormalig bureau kabinet van de afdeling Politie,
1945–51
Depot 68
Depot 105

3.2 Documentation centres
3.2.1 Rijksinstituut voor Oorlogsdocumentatie, Amsterdam
Periodicals collection
Archive Gemeenschap Oud-Illegale Werkers Nederland: No. 197
Archive Grote Adviescommissie der Illegaliteit: No. 184
Series KB 2
Series DOC II

PUBLISHED SOURCES

I. OFFICIAL DOCUMENTS

1.1 Belgium
Belgische Staatsblad
Parlementaire Handelingen Kamer/Senaat
Parlementaire Documenten Kamer/Senaat

1.2 France
Annales Parlementaires: Assemblée Nationale Constituante; Assemblée Nationale;
Conseil de la République
Documents Parlementaires: Assemblée Nationale Constituante; Assemblée Nationale;
Conseil de la République

1.3 The Netherlands
Parlement en Kiezer. Jaarboekje samengesteld door F. K. van Iterson, bibliothecaris
van de Tweede Kamer der Staten Generaal
Verslag der Handelingen van de Tweede Kamer der Voorlopige Staten-Generaal
gedurende de zitting 1945–1946
Gedrukte Stukken Eerste Kamer en Tweede Kamer
Enquêtecommissie Regeringsbeleid 1940–1945. Deel 6, a–c. De vertegenwoordiging
van Nederland in het buitenland. Het beleid ten aanzien van Nederlanders, die
tengevolge van de oorlog hulp van node hadden (The Hague, 1952)

2. CONTEMPORARY JOURNALS AND NEWSPAPERS
Note: Group affiliations, if any, are given in parentheses after each title.

2.1 Belgium
Front (FI/OF)
Kracht/L'Effort (NCPRG/CNPPA)

La Voix des Belges (MNB)
Le Travailleur Déporté (FNTDR)
Pile ou Face (Groupe G)
Pygmalion (Armée Secrète)

2.2 France
Le Déporté (UNADIF/FNDIR)
Le Déporté du Travail (FNDT)
Le Patriote Résistant (FNDIRP)
Hier cauchemar, aujourd'hui espoir. Bulletin de l'amicale des déportés politiques de Mauthausen

2.3 The Netherlands
De Vrije Stem (GOIWN)
De Zwerver (LO–LKP)
Mededelingenblad van de Grote Adviescommissie der Illegaliteit
Voormalig Verzet Nederland (Nationale Raad van het Voormalig Verzet Nederland)

2.4 International
Cahiers Internationaux de la Résistance (FIR)
Déportation et Liberté (FILDIR)
La Voix Internationale de la Résistance (Halin)
Résistance Unie (FIR)

3. BOOKS AND ARTICLES

Abma, G., Kuiper, Y. and Rypkema, J. (eds.), *Tussen goed en fout. Nieuwe gezichtspunten in de geschiedschrijving 1940–1945* (Franeker, 1986).

Abzug, Robert, *Inside the Vicious Heart. Americans and the Liberation of the Concentration Camps* (New York and Oxford, 1985).

Allais, Maurice, *L'Europe Unie, route de la prospérité (Grand Prix de la Communauté Atlantique)* (Paris, 1960).

Andrieu, Claire, *Le Programme Commun de la Résistance. Des idées dans la guerre* (Paris, 1984).

Arendt, Hannah, *The Origins of Totalitarianism* (New York, 1951).

Arfe, Gaetano (ed.), *L'idea d'Europa nel movimento di liberazione, 1940–1945* (Rome, 1986).

Argwaan en Profijt. Nederland en West-Duitsland 1945–1981, Amsterdamse Historische Reeks 6 (Amsterdam, 1983).

Azéma, Jean-Pierre, *De Munich à la Libération, 1938–1944* (Paris, 1979).

Azéma, Jean-Pierre and Bedarida, François, 'L'Historisation de la Résistance', *Esprit* 198 (January 1994), pp. 19–35.

Azéma, Jean-Pierre and Bedarida, François (eds.), *La France des années noires* (Paris, 1993).

Le Régime de Vichy et les Français (Paris, 1992).

Balace, Francis and Dupont, Colette, 'Les Anciens et le roi. Facteurs de cohésion et de divergence, 1945–1950', *Cahiers du Centre de Recherches et d'Etudes Historiques de la Seconde Guerre Mondiale* 9 (1985), pp. 123–74.

Bank, Jan, *Opkomst en ondergang van de Nederlandse Volksbeweging* (Deventer, 1978).

Barcellini, Serge, 'Réflexion autour de deux journées nationales', *Bulletin Trimestriel de la Fondation Auschwitz* 38–9 (1993), pp. 25–43.

'Les Résistants dans l'oeil de l'administration ou l'histoire du statut de combattant volontaire de la Résistance', *Guerres Mondiales et Conflits Contemporains* 178 (1995), pp. 141–65.

Barcellini, Serge and Wieviorka, Annette, *Passant, souviens-toi! Les Lieux du souvenir de la Seconde Guerre Mondiale en France* (Paris, 1995).

Barnouw, David, de Keizer, Madelon and Van der Stroom, Gerrold (eds.), *1940–1945: onverwerkt verleden?* (Amsterdam, 1985).

Bastianetto, Mario, *Gli Stati Uniti d'Europa. Soluzione federale e vecchi stati sovrani* (Florence, 1973).

Baudhuin, Fernand, *L'Economie Belge sous l'occupation, 1940–1944* (Brussels, 1945).

Beerten, Wilfried, *Le Rêve Travailliste en Belgique. Histoire de l'Union Démocratique Belge, 1944–1947* (Brussels, 1990).

Bernard, Henri, *Esprit de la résistance et conscience européenne/Geest van het verzet en Europees bewustzijn* (Brussels, 1980).

Beschet, Paul, *Mission en Thuringe* (Paris, 1946).

Bethell, Nicholas, *The Last Secret. Forcible Repatriation to Russia, 1944–1947* (London, 1974).

Bijl, Maarten, *Nooit meer Auschwitz! Het Nederlandse Auschwitz Comité, 1956–1996* (Bussum, 1997).

Bloch, Marc, 'Pour une histoire comparée des sociétés européennes', *Revue de Synthèse Historique* 46 (1928), pp. 15–50.

Blom, Hans, *In de ban van goed en fout? Wetenschappelijke Geschiedschrijving over de Bezettingstijd in Nederland* (Bergen, 1983).

'The Persecution of the Jews in the Netherlands. A Comparative Western European Perspective', *European History Quarterly* 19 (1989), pp. 333–51.

Blom, Hans, 't Hart, A. C. and Schöffer, I. (eds.), *De Affaire Menten, 1945–1976* (The Hague, 1979).

Bogaarts, M. D., ' "Weg met de moffen". De uitwijzing van Duitse ongewenste vreemdelingen uit Nederland na 1945', in P. W. Klein and G. N. Van der Plaat (eds.), *Herrijzend Nederland. Opstellen over Nederland in de periode 1945–1950* (The Hague, 1981), pp. 159–76.

Bolchover, Richard, *British Jewry and the Holocaust* (Cambridge, 1993).

Bories-Sawala, Helga, *Franzosen im 'Reichseinsatz'. Deportation, Zwangarbeit, Alltag* (Frankfurt, 1996).

Boucher, Florine, Kalkman, Els and Schaap, Dick, *Woord Gehouden. Veertig jaar Stichting 1940–1945* (The Hague, 1985).

Bourdais, Henri, *La JOC sous l'occupation allemande* (Paris, 1995).

Bridgeman, Jon and Jones, Richard, *The End of the Holocaust. The Liberation of the Camps* (Portland, OR, 1990).

Brinckman, Bart, 'Een schakel tussen Arbeid en Leiding. Het Rijksarbeidsambt (1940–1944)', *Bijdragen van het Navorsings- en Studiecentrum voor de Geschiedenis van de Tweede Wereldoorlog* 12 (1989), pp. 85–161.

Brugmans, Henri, *L'Idée Européenne, 1920–1970* (Bruges, 1970).

Bruin, Kees, *Kroon op het Werk. Onderscheiden in het Koninkrijk der Nederlanden* (Amsterdam, 1989).

Bugeaud, Pierre, *Militant Prisonnier de guerre* (Paris, 1990).

Burrin, Philippe, *La France à l'heure Allemande, 1940–1944* (Paris, 1995).

Buton, Philippe and Guillon, Jean-Marie (eds.), *Les Pouvoirs en France à la libération* (Paris, 1994).

Calliau, Michel, alias Charette, *Histoire du MRPDG ou d'un vrai mouvement de résistance (1941–1945)* (Paris, 1987).

Cesarani, David (ed.), *The Final Solution. Origins and Implementation* (London and New York, 1994).

Champion, Lucien, *La Chronique des 53.000* (Brussels, 1973).

Chaumont, Jean-Michel, 'Ce n'était pas encore une nécessité, mais maintenant c'est devenu une obsession', *Bulletin Trimestriel de la Fondation Auschwitz* 32–3 (1992), pp. 49–79.

'Connaissance ou reconnaissance? Les Enjeux du débat sur la singularité de la Shoah', *Le Débat* 82 (1994), pp. 69–89.

Chénaux, Philippe, *Une Europe Vaticane? Entre le plan Marshall et les traités de Rome* (Brussels, 1990).

Chiti-Batelli, Andrea, *L'Italia e l'Europa* (Manduria, 1979).

Cholvy, G. and Bontahl, J. P. (eds.), *JOC–JOCF. Efficacité et postérité d'un mouvement d'action catholique de jeunesse, de 1927 à 1950* (Lyons, 1991).

Cochet, François, *Les Exclus de la victoire. Histoire des prisonniers de guerre, déportes et STO (1945–1985)* (Paris, 1992).

Coenen, Bert, 'De Bierkaai van de vergetelheid. Leuven, 1944–1995', unpublished MA thesis (Leuven, 1995).

Coine, Eugene, *Kajottersweerstand in Duitschland* (n.p., n.d. [1946]).

Conan, Eric and Rousso, Henry, *Vichy, un passé qui ne passe pas* (Paris, 1994).

Conway, Martin, 'Justice in Post-War Belgium. Popular Passions and Political Realities', *Cahiers d'Histoire du Temps Présent* 2 (1997), pp. 7–34.

Copfermann, Emile, *David Rousset. Une vie dans le siècle* (Paris, 1991).

Coudry, George, 'Le Rapatriement des ressortissants soviétiques de 1945 à 1947, avatars de la réciprocité', *Guerres Mondiales et Conflits Contemporains* 178 (1995), pp. 119–40.

Courtois, Stéphane and Rayski, Adam, *Qui savait quoi? L'Extermination des juifs, 1941–1945* (Paris, 1987).

Dawidowicz, Lucy, *The Holocaust and the Historians* (Cambridge, MA, 1981).

De Graaff, Bob and Wiebes, Cees, *Gladio der vrije jongens. Een particuliere geheime dienst in Koude Oorlogstijd* (The Hague, 1992).

De Jong, Louis, *Herinneringen* (The Hague, 1993–6), 2 vols.

Het Koninkrijk de Nederlanden in de Tweede Wereldoorlog (The Hague, 1969–91), 14 vols.

'Verzet en Illegaliteit 1940–1945', *Mededelingen der Koninklijke Nederlandse Academie van Wetenschappen, afd. Letterkunde* (nieuwe reeks) 39, 6 (1976), pp. 203–21.

De Jonghe, Albert, 'Aspecten van de wegvoering van koning Leopold III naar Duitsland (7 juni 1944)', *Bijdragen van het Navorsings- en Studiecentrum voor de Geschiedenis van de Tweede Wereldoorlog* 11 (1988), pp. 5–120.

Hitler en het politieke lot van België, 1940–1944 (Antwerp, 1982).

De Keizer, Madelon (ed.), *'Een dure verplichting en een kostelijk voorrecht'. Dr L. de Jong en zijn Geschiedwerk* (Amsterdam, 1995).

De Lajavie, Damascène, *Prêtre-ouvrier clandestin* (Paris, 1967).

De Liagre Böhl, Herman and Meershoek, Guus, *De bevrijding van Amsterdam. Een strijd om macht en moraal* (Amsterdam, 1989).

De Neve, Ed, *De Glorieuzen* (Enschede, 1946).

De Praetere, Hans and Dierickx, Jenny, *De Koude Oorlog in België* (Berchem, 1985).

D'Hoop, Jean-Marie, 'La Main-d'oeuvre française au service de l'Allemagne', *Revue d'Histoire de la Deuxième Guerre Mondiale* 81 (1971), pp. 73–88.

Dinnerstein, Leonard, *America and the Survivors of the Holocaust* (New York, 1982).

Distel, Barbara, 'Orte der Erinnerung an die Opfer im Lande der Täter – Gedanken zur Arbeit an der Gedenkstätte des ehemaligen Konzentrationslagers Dachau', unpublished paper, presented at conference sponsored by the 'Fondation Auschwitz', Brussels, 23–27 November 1992.

Dlugoborski, Waclaw (ed.), *Zweiter Weltkrieg und sozialer Wandel. Achsenmächte und besetzte Länder* (Göttingen, 1981).

Dumoulin, Michel (ed.), *La Belgique et les débuts de la construction européenne de la guerre aux traités de Rome* (Louvain-la-Neuve, 1987).

Durand, Yves, *La Captivité. Histoire des prisonniers de guerre français, 1939–1945* (Paris, 1980).

La France dans la 2e guerre mondiale, 1939–1945 (Paris, 1989).

Le Nouvel Ordre Européen Nazi, 1938–1945 (Brussels, 1990).

La Vie Quotidienne des prisonniers de guerre dans les stalags, les oflags et les commandos 1939–1945 (Paris, 1987).

Duynstee, F. and Bosmans, J., *Het kabinet Schermerhorn–Drees, 1945–1946* (Assen and Amsterdam, 1977).

Eck, Hélène, 'Les Françaises sous Vichy. Femmes du désastre, citoyennes par le désastre?', in Françoise Thébaud (ed.), *Histoire des Femmes. Le XXe siècle* (Paris, 1992), pp. 185–211.

Elliott, Mark, *Pawns of Yalta. Soviet Refugees and America's Role in Their Repatriation* (Urbana, 1982).

Endelman, Todd M., 'Jews, Aliens and Other Outsiders in British History', *Historical Journal* 37 (1994), pp. 959–69.

Engel, David, *Facing the Holocaust. The Polish Government in Exile and the Jews, 1943–1945* (Chapel Hill, 1993).

Europa padri e figli. Gli antesignani italiani dell'Europeismo (Roma, 1985).

Europe. Dream–Adventure–Reality (Brussels, 1987).

Evrard, Jacques, *La Déportation des travailleurs français dans le IIIe Reich* (Paris, 1971).

Faligot, Roger and Kauffer, Rémi, *Les Résistants. De la guerre de l'ombre aux allées du pouvoir, 1944–1989* (Paris, 1989).

Farmer, Sarah, *Oradour. Arrêt sur mémoire* (Paris, 1994).

'Symbols That Face Two Ways. Commemorating the Victims of Nazism and Stalinism at Buchenwald and Sachsenhausen', *Representations* 49 (1995), pp. 97–119.

Fein, Helen, *Accounting for Genocide. National Responses and Jewish Victimisation During the Holocaust* (New York and London, 1979).

Fein, Helen (ed.), *The Persisting Question. Sociological Perspectives and Social Contexts of Modern Antisemitism* (Berlin and New York, 1987).

Finkielkraut, Alain, *La Mémoire Vaine. Du crime contre l'humanité* (Paris, 1989).

Fishman, Sarah, *'We Will Wait'. Wives of French Prisoners of War, 1940–1945* (New Haven, 1991).

FNDIRP, *Le Choc. La Presse relève l'enfer des camps Nazis* (Paris, 1985).

Foot, Michael, *Resistance. An Analysis of European Resistance to Nazism, 1940–1945* (London, 1976).

Footitt, Hilary and Simmonds, John, *France 1943–1945* (Leicester, 1988).

Foulon, Charles-Louis, *Le Pouvoir en province à la libération. Les Commissaires de la République, 1943–1946*, Travaux et Recherches de Science Politique 32 (Paris, 1975).

Frénay, Henri, *Bilan d'un effort* (Paris, 1945).

La Nuit finira (Paris, 1973).

Galesloot, Hansje and Schrevel, Margreet (eds.), *In Fatsoen hersteld. Zedelijkheid en Wederopbouw na de oorlog* (Amsterdam, n.d. [1987]).

Gelin, Joseph, *Nuremberg (1943–1945). L'Expérience d'un prêtre-ouvrier* (Paris, 1946).

Gérard-Libois, Jules and Gotovitch, José, *Léopold III. De l'an '40 à l'effacement* (Brussels, 1991).

Gilissen, J., 'Etude statistique sur la répression de l'incivisme', *Revue de Droit Pénal et de Criminologie* (1950–1), pp. 513–628.

Gillis, John R. (ed.), *Commemorations. The Politics of National Identity* (Princeton, 1994).

Gleason, Abbott, *Totalitarianism. The Inner History of the Cold War* (New York and Oxford, 1995).

Goschler, Constantin, *Wiedergutmachung. Deutschland und die Verfolgten des Nationalsozialismus (1945–1954)* (Munich, 1992).

Gotovitch, José, *Du Rouge au tricolore. Résistance et Parti Communiste* (Brussels, 1992).

'Sous la régence. Résistance et pouvoir', *Courrier Hebdomadaire du CRISP* 999 (1983).

Gramsci, Antonio, *Sul fascismo. L'analisi del fenomeno fascista negli scritti più signicativi di Antonio Gramsci presentati da Enzo Santarelli* (Rome, 1974).

Grandmesnil, Georges, *Action Catholique et STO* (Paris, 1947).

Gratier de Saint-Louis, Michel, 'Histoire d'un retour. Les STO du Rhône', *Cahiers d'Histoire* 34 (1994), pp. 247–70.

Griffioen, Pim and Zeller, Ron, 'Jodenvervolging in Nederland en België tijdens de Tweede Wereldoorlog. Een vergelijkende analyse', in *Oorlogsdocumentatie '40–'45* 8 (Amsterdam, 1997), pp. 10–63.

Gross, J. T., *Polish Society Under German Occupation. The General Government 1939–1994* (Princeton, 1979).

Guldenboek van de Weerstand (Brussels, 1948).

Habermehl, Werner, *Sind die Deutschen faschistoid? Ergebnisse einer empirischen Untersuchung über die Verbreitung rechter und rechtsextremer Ideologien in der Bundesrepublik Deutschland* (Hamburg, 1979).

Halin, Hubert, *L'Europe Unie, objectif majeur de la résistance* (Brussels, n.d. [1967]).

Halls, W. D., *The Youth of Vichy France* (Oxford, 1981).

Ham, Bertie, *Arbeider in Moffenland* (Laren, 1945).

Harms, Ingrid, 'Russische vrouwen in Nederland. Portret van de verloren dochters van vader Stalin', *Vrij Nederland* (1 March 1986), pp. 2–36.

Haug, W. F., *Der hilflose Antifaschismus. Zur Kritik der Vorlesungsreihen über Wissenschaft und NS an deutschen Universitäten* (Cologne, 1977).

Haupt, Heinz-Gerhard, 'La Lente émergence d'une histoire comparée', in Jean Boutier and Dominique Julia (eds.), *Passés recomposés. Champs et chantiers de l'histoire* (Paris, 1995), pp. 196–207.

Hautecler, G., 'L'Origine et le nombre des prisonniers de guerre belges, 1940–1945', *Revue Internationale d'Histoire Militaire (Edition Belge)* (1970), pp. 949–61.

Hawtrey, R. G., *Western European Union. Implications for the United Kingdom*, Royal Institute of International Affairs (London, 1949).

Hayes, Peter (ed.), *Lessons and Legacies. The Meaning of the Holocaust in a Changing World* (Evanston, IL, 1991).

Hendrickx, Leo, *Gekneveld en Bevrijd* (Maaseik, 1945).

Henkes, Barbara, *Heimat in Holland. Duitse dienstmeisjes, 1920–1950* (Amsterdam, 1995).

Herbert, Ulrich, *Europa und der 'Reichseinsatz'. Ausländische Zivilarbeiter, Kriegs-gefangene und KZ-Häftlinge in Deutschland, 1938–1945* (Essen, 1991).

Fremdarbeiter. Politik und Praxis des 'Ausländer-Einsatzes' in der Kriegswirtschaft des Dritten Reiches (Berlin and Bonn, 1985).

Geschichte der Ausländer-Beschäftigung in Deutschland, 1880 bis 1980. Saisonar-beiter, Zwangsarbeiter, Gastarbeiter (Berlin and Bonn, 1986).

A History of Foreign Labor in Germany (Ann Arbor, 1990).

Hitler's Foreign Workers. Enforced Foreign Labour in Germany Under the Third Reich (Cambridge, 1997).

'Labour and Extermination. Economic Interest and the Primacy of *Wel-tanschauung* in National Socialism', *Past & Present* 138 (1990), pp. 145–95.

Herbst, Ludolf and Goschler, Constantin (eds.), *Wiedergutmachung in der Bundesrepublik Deutschland. Sondernummer Schriftenreihe der Vierteljahrshefte für Zeitgeschichte* (Munich, 1989).

Herremans, Maurice-Pierre, *Personnes Déplacées (rapatriés, disparus, refugiés)* (Ruisbroek, 1948).

Hilbrink, Coen, *De illegalen. Illegaliteit in Twente en het aangrenzende Salland, 1940–1945* (Oldenzaal, 1989).

In het belang van het Nederlandse Volk . . . Over de medewerking van de ambtelijke wereld aan de Duitse bezettingspolitiek, 1940–1945 (The Hague, 1995).

Hirschfeld, Gerhard, *Fremdherrschaft und Kollaboration. Die Niederlande unter deutscher Besatzung, 1940–1945* (Stuttgart, 1984).

Holla, H. B. S. and Van Riessen, H., 'Politiek en Verzet', in *Het Grote Gebod. Gedenkboek van het verzet in LO–LKP* (Bilthoven, 1951), vol. II, pp. 488–528.

Homze, Edward, *Foreign Labor in Nazi Germany* (Princeton, 1967).

Hondius, Dienke, 'A Cold Reception. Holocaust Survivors in the Netherlands and Their Return', *Patterns of Prejudice* 28 (1994), pp. 47–65.

Terugkeer. Anti-semitisme in Nederland rond de bevrijding (The Hague, 1990).

Hugaerts, Frans (ed.), *De KAJ, haard van verzet (1940–1945)* (Ghent, 1989).

Huyse, Luc and Dhont, Steven, *Onverwerkt verleden. Collaboratie en repressie in België, 1942–1952* (Leuven, 1991).

Huyse, Luc and Hoflack, Kris (eds.), *De Democratie heruitgevonden. Oud en nieuw in politiek België* (Leuven, 1995).

Jacobmeyer, Wolfgang, *Vom Zwangsarbeiter zum heimatlosen Ausländer. Die Displaced Persons in Westdeutschland, 1945–1951* (Göttingen, 1985).

Jacquemyns, G., *La Société Belge sous l'occupation allemande* (Brussels, 1950).

Janssen, W. J., *Tewerkstelling in Duitschland. Ervaringen tijdens mijn deportatie* (Eigenbergen, 1992).

Jocistes dans la tourmente. Histoire des jocistes (JOC–JOCF) de la région parisienne 1937–1947 (Paris, 1989).

Kedward, Roderick, *In Search of the Maquis. Rural Resistance in Southern France, 1942–1944* (Oxford, 1993).

Kershaw, Ian, 'Retour sur le totalitarisme. Le Nazisme et le stalinisme dans une perspective comparative', *Esprit* (January 1996), pp. 101–21.

Klarsfeld, Serge, *Mémorial de la déportation des juifs de France* (Paris, 1978).

Klarsfeld, Serge and Steinberg, Maxime, *Le Mémorial de la déportation des juifs de Belgique* (Brussels and New York, 1982).

Klein, Charles, *L'Aumônerie des barbelés, 1940–1947* (Cachan, 1967).

Le Diocèse des barbelés, 1940–1944 (Paris, 1973).

Kolko, Gabriel, *The Politics of War. The World and United States Foreign Policy, 1943–1945* (New York, 1990 [1968]).

Kossman, E. H., *The Low Countries, 1780–1940* (Oxford, 1978).

Kristel, Connie, '"De Moeizame Terugkeer". De repatriëring van de Nederlandse overlevenden uit de Duitse concentratiekampen', in *Oorlogsdocumentatie '40–'45* 1 (Amsterdam, 1989), pp. 77–100.

Kruls, H. J., *Generaal in Nederland. Memoires* (Bussum, 1975).

Kushner, Tony, *The Holocaust and the Liberal Imagination. A Social and Cultural History* (Oxford, 1994).

The Persistence of Prejudice. Anti-Semitism in British Society During the Second World War (Manchester and New York, 1989).

Lagrou, Pieter, 'Herdenken en Vergeten. De politieke verwerking van verzet en vervolging in Nederland/België na 1945', *Spiegel Historiael* 29, 3–4 (1994), pp. 109–22.

'Patriotten en Regenten. Het parochiale patriottisme van de na-oorlogse Nederlandse illegaliteit, 1945–1980', in *Oorlogsdocumentatie '40–'45* 6 (Amsterdam, 1995), pp. 10–47.

'La Résistance et les conceptions de l'Europe, 1945–1965', in Antoine Fleury and Robert Frank (eds.), *Le Rôle des guerres dans la mémoire des européens* (Bern, 1997), pp. 137–81.

'De terugkeer van de weggevoerde arbeiders in België en Nederland, 1945–1955. Mythen en taboes rond de verplichte tewerkstelling', in *Le Travail Obligatoire en Allemagne, 1942–1945* (Brussels, 1993), pp. 191–241.

'US Politics of Stabilization in Liberated Europe. The View from the American Embassy in Brussels, 1944–1946', *European History Quarterly* 25 (1995), pp. 209–46.

'Victims of Genocide and National Memory. Belgium, France and the Netherlands, 1945–1965', *Past & Present* 154 (1997), pp. 181–222.

'Welk vaderland voor de vaderlandslievende verenigingen? Oorlogsslachtoffers en verzetsveteranen en de nationale kwestie, 1945–1958', *Bijdragen tot de Eigentijdse Geschiedenis* 3 (December 1997), pp. 91–109.

Lane, Ann J., 'Putting Britain Right with Tito. The Displaced Persons Question in Anglo-Yugoslav Relations, 1946–1947', *European History Quarterly* 22 (1992), pp. 217–46.

Langbein, Hermann, 'Internationale Organisationen der Überlebenden der nationalsozialistischen Konzentrationslager ab 1954 bis heute – vor allem Auschwitz betreffend', unpublished paper, presented at conference sponsored by the 'Fondation Auschwitz', Brussels, 23–27 November 1992.

Laurens, A, 'Le STO dans le département de l'Ariège', *Revue d'Histoire de la Deuxième Guerre Mondiale* 95 (July 1974), pp. 51–74.

Lavabre, Marie-Claire, *Le Fil Rouge. Sociologie de la mémoire communiste* (Paris, 1994).

Levi, Lucio, *Federalismo e integrazione europea* (Palermo, 1978).

Levi, Lucio (ed.), *Altiero Spinelli and Federalism in Europe and in the World* (Milan, 1990).

Lewin, Christophe, *Le Retour des prisonniers de guerre français* (Paris, 1986).

Lipgens, Walter, *Die Anfänge der europäischen Einigungspolitik 1945–1950* (Stuttgart, 1977).

Documents on the History of European Integration, vol. I, *Continental Plans on European Union, 1939–1945* (Florence, 1985).

Europa–Föderationspläne der Widerstandsbewegungen 1940–1945. Eine Dokumentation (Munich, 1968).

A History of European Integration (Oxford, 1982).

Luykx, Theo, *Politieke Geschiedenis van België* (Antwerp, 1985).

Luyten, Dirk and Vantemsche, Guy (eds.), *Het Sociaal pact van 1944. Oorsprong, betekenis en gevolgen* (Brussels, 1995).

Madjarian, Grégoire, *Conflits, pouvoirs et société à la Libération* (Paris, 1980).

Maier, Charles, *In Search of Stability. Explorations in Historical Political Economy* (Cambridge, 1987).

Maier, Charles (ed.), *The Origins of the Cold War and Contemporary Europe* (New York and London, 1978).

Mantelli, Bruno, 'I lavoratori italiani transferiti in Germania dal 1938 al 1945. Un tema dimenticato', *Passato e Presente* 38 (1996), pp. 101–11.

Marcuse, Harold, 'Das ehemalige Konzentrationslager Dachau. Der mühevolle Weg zur Gedenkstätte 1945–1968', *Dachauer Hefte* 6 (1990), pp. 182–205.

Marrus, Michael R., *The Unwanted. European Refugees in the Twentieth Century* (Oxford, 1985).

Marwick, Arthur, *War and Social Change in the Twentieth Century* (London, 1974).

Marwick, Arthur (ed.), *Total War and Social Change* (London, 1988).

Matard-Bonucci, Marie-Anne and Lynch, Edouard (eds.), *La Libération des camps et le retour des déportés. L'Histoire en souffrance* (Brussels, 1995).

La Mémoire des Français. Quarante ans de commémorations de la Seconde Guerre Mondiale (Paris, 1986).

Michel, Henri and Mirkine-Guetzevitch, B., *Les Idées Politiques et sociales de la résistance* (Paris, 1954).

Miller, Judith, *One, by One, by One. Facing the Holocaust* (New York, 1990).

Milward, Alan, *The European Rescue of the Nation-State* (London, 1992).

The New Order and the French Economy (Oxford, 1970).

Molette, Charles, *'En haine de l'Evangile'. Victimes du décret de persécution nazi du 3 décembre 1943 contre l'apostolat catholique français à l'oeuvre parmi les travailleurs requis en Allemagne, 1943–1945* (Paris, 1993).

Moore, Bob, *Victims and Survivors. The Nazi Persecution of the Jews in the Netherlands 1940–1945* (London, 1997).

Muel-Dreyfus, Francine, *Vichy et l'éternel féminin* (Paris, 1996).

Namer, Gérard, *La Commémoration en France de 1945 à nos jours* (Paris, 1987).

Mémoire et société (Paris, 1987).

Neij, R. and Hueting, E. V., *Nederlands Volksherstel, 1944–1947* (Culemborg, 1988).

The Netherlands and Nazi Genocide. Papers of the 21st Annual Scholars' Conference (Lewiston, Queenston and Lampeter, 1991).

Nolan, Cathal J., 'Americans in the Gulag. Detention of US Citizens by Russia and the Onset of the Cold War, 1944–1949', *Journal of Contemporary History* 25 (1990), pp. 523–45.

Nora, Pierre, 'Gaullistes et communistes', in *Les Lieux de mémoire*, t. III, *Les Frances*, vol. I, *Conflits et partages* (Paris, 1992), pp. 360–71.

Novick, Peter, 'Pseudo-Memory and Dubious "Lessons". The Holocaust in American Culture', unpublished paper, presented at conference on 'Memory and the Second World War', Amsterdam, 1995.

Paape, Harry, Van der Stroom, Gerrold and Barnouw, David (eds.), *De Dagboeken van Anne Frank* (Amsterdam, 1990).

Péan, Pierre, *Une Jeunesse Française. François Mitterrand, 1934–1947* (Paris, 1994).

Pelissier, Jean, *Si la Gestapo avait su! Un prêtre à l'opéra de Munich et dans la haute couture* (Paris, 1945).

Perrin, Henri, *Journal d'un prêtre-ouvrier en Allemagne* (Paris, 1945).

Pertz, Erik, 'La Mise au travail des Courtraisiens en Allemagne (1940–1945)', *Cahiers d'Histoire de la Seconde Guerre Mondiale* 4 (1976), pp. 181–200.

Philippe, Béatrice, *Être juif dans la société française* (Paris, 1979).

Poliakov, Léon (ed.), *Histoire de l'anti-sémitisme*, vol. V, *1945–1993* (Paris, 1993).

Potargent, Pierre, *Déportation. La Mise au travail de la main-d'oeuvre Belge dans le pays et à l'étranger durant l'occupation* (Brussels, n.d. [1946]).

Poulantzas, Nicos, *Faschismus und Diktatur. Die Kommunistische Internationale und der Faschismus* (Munich, 1973).

Poulat, Emile, *Naissance des prêtres-ouvriers* (Paris, 1965).

Presser, Jacques, *Ondergang. De Vervolging en verdelging van het Nederlandse Jodendom, 1940–1945* (The Hague, 1965), 2 vols.

Prost, Antoine, *Les Anciens Combattants* (Paris, 1977).

'The Impact of War on French and German Political Cultures', *Historical Journal* 37 (1994), pp. 209–17.

Provoost, G., *De Vossen. 60 jaar Verbond van Vlaamse Oud-Strijders (1917–1979)* (Brussels, 1979).

Puvogel, Ulrike (ed.), *Gedenkstätten für Opfer des Nationalsozialismus. Eine Dokumentation*, Schriftenreihe der Bundeszentrale für politische Bildung 245 (Bonn, 1987).

Quereillhac, J. L., *J'étais STO* (Paris, 1958).

Ramaker, Wim and Van Bohemen, Ben, *Sta een ogenblik stil . . . Monumentenboek 1940–1945* (Kampen, 1980).

Ranson, Lucien, *De Gedeporteerden* (Kortrijk, 1983).

Rapport sur l'activité du Commissariat Belge au Rapatriement (Brussels, 1945).

Rieben, Henri, *Des guerres européennes à l'Union de l'Europe* (Lausanne, 1987).

Rings, Werner, *Leben mit dem Feind. Anpassung und Widerstand in Hitlers Europa, 1939–1945* (Brissago, 1979).

Romijn, Peter, *Snel, Streng en Rechtvaardig. Politiek beleid inzake de bestraffing en reclassering van 'foute' Nederlanders* (Amsterdam, 1989).

Rose, Clive, *Campaigns Against Western Defence. NATO's Adversaries and Critics* (London, 1985 [new edn., 1986]).

Rosenhaft, Eve, 'The Uses of Remembrance. The Legacy of the Communist Resistance in the German Democratic Republic', in Francis R. Nicosia and Lawrence D. Stokes (eds.), *Germans Against Nazism. Nonconformity, Opposition and Resistance in the Third Reich* (New York and Oxford, 1990), pp. 369–88.

Rossi, Pietro (ed.), *La storia comparata. Approcci e prospettive* (Milan, 1990).

Rousso, Henry, *Pétain et la fin de la collaboration. Simaringen, 1944–1945* (Brussels, 1984 [Paris, 1980]).

Le Syndrome de Vichy (Paris, 1987 [new edn., 1990]).

Sandberg, H. W., *Witboek over de geschiedenis van het georganiseerde verzet voor en na de bevrijding* (Amsterdam, 1950).

Schlangen, Walter, *Die Totalitarismus-Theorie. Entwicklung und Probleme* (Stuttgart, 1976).

Schram, D. H. and Geljon, C. (eds.), *Overal sporen. De verwerking van de Tweede Wereldoorlog in literatuur en kunst* (Amsterdam, 1990).

Schulten, C. M., *'Zeg mij aan wien ik toebehoor'. Het verzetskruis 1940–1945* (The Hague, 1993).

Segev, Tom, *The Seventh Million. The Israelis and the Holocaust* (New York, 1993).

Semelin, Jacques, *Sans armes face à Hitler. La Résistance Civile en Europe, 1939–1943* (Paris, 1989).

Shennan, Andrew, *Rethinking France. Plans for Renewal 1940–1946* (Oxford, 1989).

Sickenga, F. N., *Korte geschiedenis van de tuberculosebestrijding in Nederland, 1900–1960* (The Hague, 1980).

Sidjanski, Dusan, *L'Avenir Fédéraliste de l'Europe. La Communauté Européenne, des origines au Traité de Maastricht* (Geneva, 1992).

Sijes, B. A., *De arbeidsinzet. De gedwongen arbeid van Nederlanders in Duitsland, 1940–1945* (Amsterdam, 1990 [1966]).

Soucy, Robert, *French Fascism. The Second Wave, 1933–1939* (New Haven, 1996).

Spinelli, Altiero, *Il manifesto di Ventotene* (Bologna, 1991).

Steinberg, Maxime, 'Les Dérives Plurielles de la mémoire d'Auschwitz', *Centrale. Périodique Trimestriel de la Vie Communautaire Juive* 259 (1993), pp. 6–9; 260 (1993), pp. 11–14.

L'Etoile et le fusil (Brussels, 1983–6), 4 vols.

'Le Paradoxe Français dans la solution finale à l'Ouest', *Annales ESC* 3 (1993), pp. 583–94.

Les Yeux du témoin et le regard du borgne. L'Histoire face au révisionisme (Paris, 1990).

Storia del federalismo europeo (Cuneo, 1973).

Temmerman, Patrick and Boeckx, Bert, *Deportatie en Verzet. Een eerste globale statistische analyse op basis van erkenningsdossiers* (Brussels, 1995), 2 vols.

Termeer, Henk, *Het Geweten der Natie. De voormalige illegaliteit in het bevrijde Zuiden, september 1944–mei 1945* (Assen, 1994).

Thibaud, Paul, 'La République et ses héros. Le Gaullisme pendant et après la guerre', *Esprit* 198 (1994), pp. 64–83.

Trienekens, Gerard, *Tussen ons volk en de honger. De voedselvoorziening, 1940–1945* (Utrecht, 1985).

Voedsel en honger in Oorlogstijd 1940–1945. Misleiding, mythe en werkelijkheid (Utrecht, 1995).

Urwin, Derek, *Western Europe Since 1945. A Political History* (Harlow, 1968 [later edns., 1972, 1981, 1989]).

Van den Berg, M. A. P., 'De repatriantenkwestie na 1945. Terugkeer van Nederlanders uit de Sovjetunie', in M. L. Roholl, Emmanuel Waegemans et al. (eds). *De lage landen en de Sovjetunie. Beeldvorming en betrekkingen* (Amsterdam, 1989), pp. 11–27.

Van den Berghe, Gie, 'Het einde van de kampen en van een mythe', *Spiegel Historiael* 29, 3–4 (1994), pp. 156–60.

Getuigen. Belgische Bibliografie over de Nazi-kampen (Brussels, 1995), 2 vols.

Van den Berghe, Gie (ed.), *De Zot van Rekem* [of Louis Nauwelaers] (Antwerp, 1995).

Van den Wijngaert, Mark, de Bens, Els and Culot, J., 'De verplichte tewerkstelling in België (1940–1944)', *Bijdragen van het Navorsings- en Studiecentrum voor de Geschiedenis van de Tweede Wereldoorlog* 1 (1970), pp. 7–68.

Van der Zee, Nanda, *Om erger te voorkomen. De voorbereiding en uitvoering van de vernietiging van het Nederlandse jodendom tijdens de Tweede Wereldoorlog* (Amsterdam, 1997).

Van Doorslaer, Rudi and Verhoeyen, Etienne, *De moord op Lahaut. Het kommunisme als binnenlandse vijand* (Leuven, 1985).

Van Lingen, Joost and Slooff, Niek, *Van verzetsstrijder tot staatsgevaarlijk burger. Hoe progressieve illegale werkers na de oorlog de voet is dwarsgezet* (Baarn, 1987).

Van Ojen, G. J., *De Binnenlandse Strijdkrachten* (The Hague, 1972).

Van Oudenheusden, J. and Verboom, J., *Herstel- en vernieuwingsbeweging in het bevrijde zuiden. Eindhoven, 's Hertogenbosch en Waalwijk, 1944–1945* (Tilburg, 1977).

Van Staveren, Mariette, 'Moraliteit, sekse en de Natie. Een geschiedenis van het Monument op de Dam en de oorlogsherinnering, 1945–1969', in *Sekse en*

Oorlog. Jaarboek voor vrouwengeschiedenis 15 (Amsterdam, 1995), pp. 94–116.

Van Vree, Frank, *In de schaduw van Auschwitz. Herinneringen, beelden, geschiedenis* (Groningen, 1995).

Van Weezel, Max and Bleich, Anet, *Ga dan zelf naar Siberië! Linkse intellectuelen en de koude oorlog* (Amsterdam, 1978).

Veil, Simone, 'Réflexions d'un témoin', *Annales ESC* 3 (1993), pp. 691–701.

Veillon, Dominique, *La Collaboration. Textes et débats* (Paris, 1984).

Velaers, Jan and Van Goethem, Herman, *Leopold III. De Koning, het Land, de Oorlog* (Tielt, 1994).

Verhey, Elma, *Om het joodse kind* (Amsterdam, 1991).

Verhoeyen, Etienne, *België Bezet, 1940–1944. Een synthese* (Brussels, 1993); available in French as *La Belgique Occupée. De l'an '40 à la libération* (Brussels, 1994).

De Verplichte Tewerkstelling in Duitsland/Le Travail Obligatoire en Allemagne, 1942–1945 (Brussels, 1993).

Verrips, G., *Dwars, duivels en dromend. De geschiedenis van de CPN* (Amsterdam, 1995).

Vijftig jaar na de inval (Amsterdam, 1985).

Vinen, Richard, 'The End of an Ideology? Right-Wing Antisemitism in France, 1944–1970', *Historical Journal* 37 (1994), pp. 368–390.

Vittori, Jean-Pierre, *Eux, les STO* (Paris, 1982).

Volder, Karel, *Werken in Duitsland, 1940–1945* (Amsterdam, 1990).

Vos, Chris, *Televisie en bezetting. Een onderzoek naar de documentaire verbeelding van de Tweede Wereldoorlog in Nederland* (Hilversum, 1995).

Vos, Louis, 'La Jeunesse Ouvrière Chrétienne', in Emmanuel Gerard and Paul Wynants (eds.), *Histoire du Mouvement Ouvrier Chrétien en Belgique* (Leuven, 1994), vol. II, pp. 425–99.

Wagenaar, Marja, *De Rijksvoorlichtingsdienst. Geheimhouden, toedekken en openbaren* (The Hague, 1997).

Wahl, Alfred (ed.), *Mémoire de la Seconde Guerre Mondiale. Actes du Colloque de Metz, 6–8 Octobre 1983* (Metz, 1984).

Warner, Geoffrey, 'La Crise Politique Belge de novembre 1944. Un coup d'état manqué?', *Courrier Hebdomadaire du CRISP* 798 (1978), pp. 1–26.

Weidenfeld, Werner (ed.), *Die Identität Europas. Fragen, Positionen, Perspektiven* (Munich and Vienna, 1987).

Wielenga, Friso, *West-Duitsland. Partner uit noodzaak: Nederland en de Bondsrepubliek, 1949–1955* (Utrecht, 1989).

Wieviorka, Annette, '1992. Réflexions sur une commémoration', *Annales ESC* 3 (1993), pp. 703–14.

Déportation et génocide. Entre la mémoire et l'oubli (Paris, 1992).

Wieviorka, Olivier, 'Les Avatars du statut de résistant en France (1945–1992)', *Vingtième Siècle* 50 (1996), pp. 55–66.

Une certaine idée de la résistance. Défense de la France, 1940–1949 (Paris, 1995).

Nous entrerons dans la carrière. De la Résistance à l'exercise du pouvoir (Paris, 1994).

Winter, Jay, *Sites of Memory, Sites of Mourning. The Great War in European Cultural History* (Cambridge, 1995).

Winter, Jay and Sivan, Emmanuel (eds.), *War and Remembrance in the Twentieth Century* (Cambridge, 1999).

Wistrich, Robert S. (ed.), *Terms of Survival. The Jewish World Since 1945* (London and New York, 1995).

Wormser-Migot, Olga, *Le Retour des déportés. Quand les alliés ouvrirent les portes* (Brussels, 1985).

Wyman, Mark, *DP. Europe's Displaced Persons, 1945–1951* (Cranbury, NJ, 1989).

Wyrwa, Tadeusz, *L'Idée Européenne dans la résistance à travers la presse clandestine en France et en Pologne, 1939–1945* (Paris, 1987).

Young, James E. (ed.), *The Art of Memory. Holocaust Memorials in History* (Munich and New York, 1994).

Zertal, Idith, 'Du bon usage du souvenir. Les Israéliens et la Shoah', *Le Débat* 58 (1990), pp. 92–103.

Zorn, Monika (ed.), *Hitlers zweimal getötete Opfer. Westdeutsche Endlösung des Antifaschismus auf dem Gebiet der DDR*, Unerwünschte Bücher zum Faschismus 6 (Freiburg, 1994).

Zur Neuorientierung der Gedenkstätte Buchenwald. Die Empfehlungen der vom Minister für Wissenschaften und Kunst des Landes Thüringen berufenen Historikerkommission (Weimar-Buchenwald, 1992).

Index

The entries 'resistance', 'repatration', 'labour conscription', 'persecution' and 'resisters', 'repatratiates', 'labour conscripts', 'victims of persecution' and their equivalents ('DPs', 'STO', 'labour migration', *'Reichseinsatz'* , 'deportees', 'political prisonners', etc. are, for obvious reasons, not included in this index.

Studies in the Social and Cultural History of Modern Warfare

Titles in the series:

Printed in the United Kingdom
by Lightning Source UK Ltd.
120535UK00002B/196